The
Best of
THE OLD FARMER'S
ALMANAC

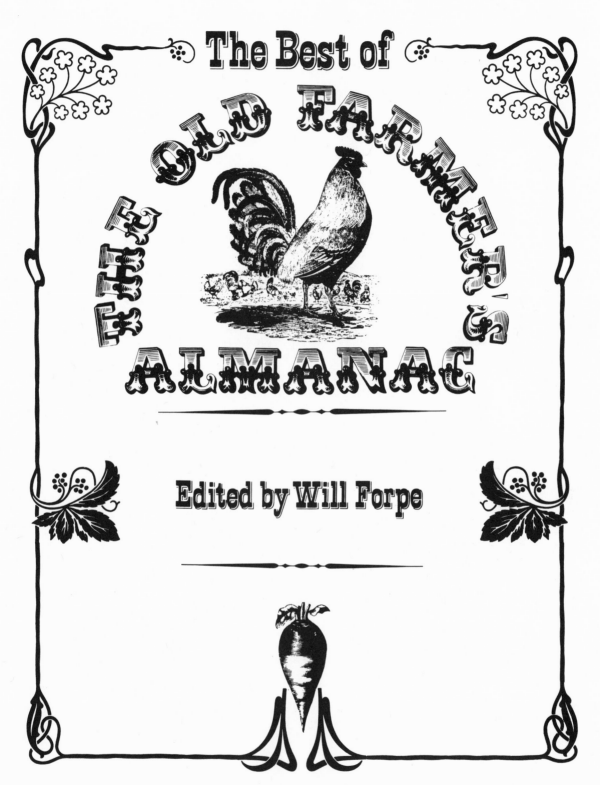

The Best of
THE OLD FARMER'S
ALMANAC

Edited by Will Forpe

A HARVEST/HBJ BOOK
HARCOURT BRACE JOVANOVICH
NEW YORK AND LONDON

Copyright © 1977 by Jonathan David Publishers, Inc.

Printed in the United States of America

Library of Congress Cataloging in Publication Data

Main entry under title:
The Best of the Old farmer's almanac.

(A Harvest/HBJ book)
Reprint of the ed. published by J. David Publishers,
Middle Village, N.Y.
I.   Forpe, Will.   II.   The (Old) farmer's almanack.
[AC5.B4227   1978]   973   78-6656
ISBN 0-15-611863-7

First Harvest/HBJ edition 1978
A B C D E F G H I J

Contents

INTRODUCTION

Although almanacs have been appearing for more than 2,000 years, the earliest about which bibliophile J.J.L. de Lalande could obtain definite information (as reported in *Bibliographie Astronomique*, **Paris, 1803**), is one of 12th century vintage.

Almanacs were important in the lives of practically all citizens of early America. Books being scarce, almanacs and Bibles were, for the most part, the only reading fare available.

In those days, an almanac was a slim pamphlet, published annually, that contained information on a variety of subjects. It included a calendar for the year to come; facts about the weather, the planets and the stars; information about holidays and feast days; recent historical and political events; advice on farming and industry; and guidance in the areas of good health, good manners and efficient homemaking. Many almanacs contained predictions based on astrology—often with dire consequences for those who took such prognostications seriously. Many early almanacs, in fact, had the word "prognostication" in their title, copying the forerunner of such publications issued in England in 1553 by the Stationers' Company, and called *Leonard Digges' Prognostication Everlasting of Right Good Effect.*

The first almanac published in the United States is believed to have been issued by the Bradford Press of Philadelphia, Pennsylvania, in 1687. *Poor Richard's Almanac*, which was created by Benjamin Franklin, began to appear in 1732. Franklin, using the pseudonym, Richard Saunders, continued to publish his almanac for 25 years—until 1757. It contained the usual information generally found in almanacs, but, in addition, had much advice to offer on such subjects as honesty, industry, thrift and patriotism. Some of Franklin's sayings and witticisms have become such an integral part of American culture that their origin is hardly remembered. They appear throughout the various editions of *The Old Farmer's Almanac*, and we have included many of them in this volume.

The Old Farmer's Almanac made its first appearance in 1793 and filled a void created by the discontinuance of Franklin's almanac. It is by far *the* almanac that has run the longest without interruption—and is almost as old as America itself. Although the title page of the most recent issues still list Robert B. Thomas as editor, Thomas died in 1846 at age 80, after issuing 54 successive editions of the *Almanac.*

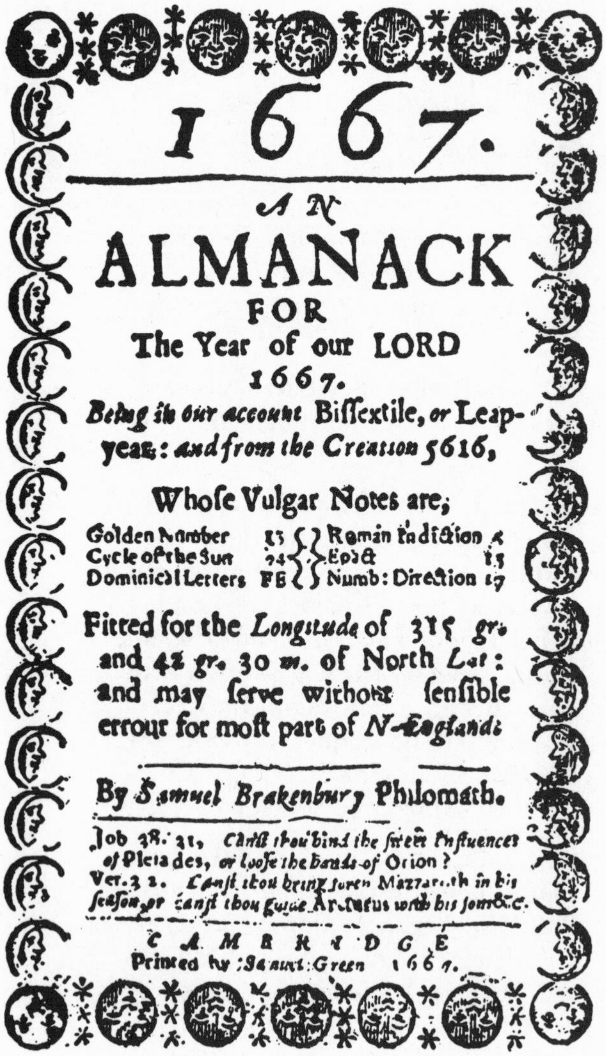

1667.

AN

ALMANACK

FOR

The Year of our LORD

1667.

Being in our account Bissextile, *or* Leap-year: *and from the Creation* 5616,

Whose Vulgar Notes are;

Golden Number 13 } Roman Indiction 5
Cycle of the Sun 24 } Epact 13
Dominical Letters FE } Numb: Direction 17

Fitted for the *Longitude* of 315 *gr.* and 42 *gr.* 30 *m.* of North *Lat*: and may serve without sensible errour for most part of *N-England*.

By *Samuel Brakenbury* Philomath.

Job 38. 31, *Canst thou bind the sweet Influences of Pleiades, or loose the bands of Orion?*
Ver. 32. *Canst thou bring forth Mazzaroth in his season, or canst thou guide Arcturus with his sons*&c.

CAMBRIDGE
Printed by Samuel Green 1667.

The title page of an almanac printed in 1667. Only two copies are known to exist: one in the library of the American Antiquarian Society in Worcester, Mass., and the other in a private collection.

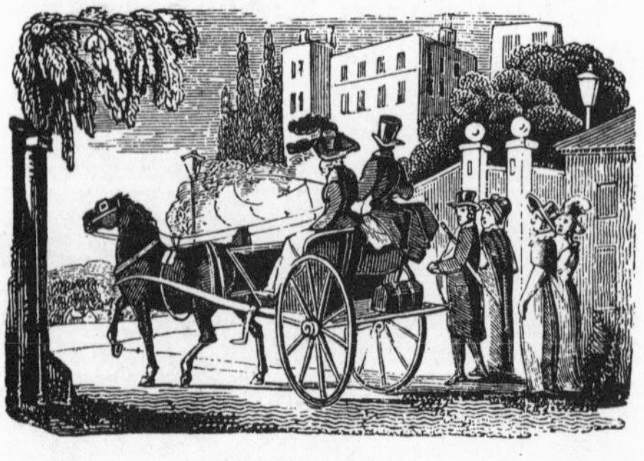

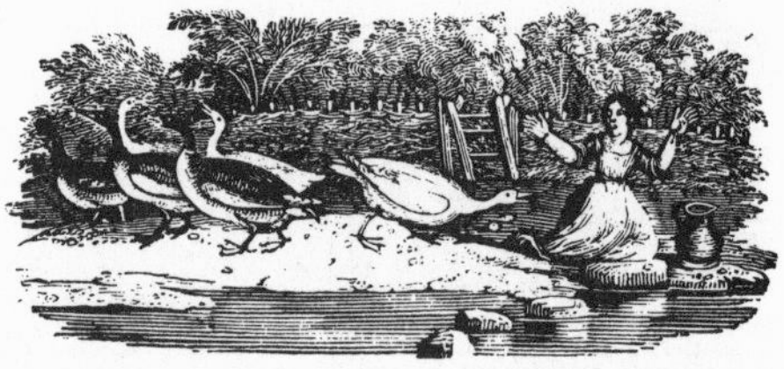

XII Mon. February hath xxviii days.

Man's rich with little, were his Judgment true,
Nature is frugal, and her Wants are few;
Those few Wants answer'd, bring sincere Delights,
But Fools create themselves new Appetites.
Fancy and Pride seek Things at vast Expence,
Which relish not to *Reason* nor to *Sense*
Like Cats in Airpumps, to subsist we strive:
On Joys too thin to keep the Soul alive.

M. D.	W. D.	*Remarkable Days, Aspects. Weather*	H w.	☽ pl	☉ *rises and sets.*			*Lunations, ☽ rises & sets*
1	7	⚹ ♃ ♀ plea	8	21	6	48	6	Last Quarter.
2	E	Sexagesima.	9	♐	6	47	6	☽ with ♃
3	2	sant, with	10	19	6	46	6	Sirius so. 8 41
4	3	△ ♄ ♀ wind	11	♑	6	44	6	☽ rise 3 42 mo
5	4	7* set 10 and	12	15	6	43	6	*A good Wife &*
6	5	perhaps some	12	28	6	42	6	♄ rise 9 7
7	6	rain ☌ ☽ ☿	1	♒	6	40	6	☉ in ♓
8	7		2	24	6	39	6	☿ rise 5 32
9	E	*Shrove* Sunday.	3	♓	6	38	6	New ☽ 9 day,
10	2	♃ rises 1 38	3h	18	6	37	6	at 3 morn.
11	3	*Shrove* Tuesday	4	♈	6	35	6	☽ with ♂ & ♀.
12	4	Ash-Wednesday.	5	12	6	34	6	☽ sets 8 56 af.
13	5	⚹ ♃ ☿ △ ♄ ♀	5h	23	6	33	6	*Health, is a*
14	6	Valentine.	6	♉	6	32	6	*Man's best*
15	7	☽ near 7*s	7	17	6	30	6	*Wealth.*
16	E	1 Sund in Lent	8	29	6	29	6	♂ sets 7 18
17	2	clouds with	9	♊	6	28	6	First Quarter.
18	3	wind and	10	25	6	26	6	Sirius so 7 43
19	4	Ember Week.	10	♋	6	25	6	7* set 12 0
20	5	□ ☉ ♃ rain	11	21	6	23	6	☽ sets 4 2 mo
21	6	or snow.	12	♌	6	22	6	♄ rises 8 11
22	7	then change-	1	18	6	20	6	*A quarrelsome*
23	E	2 Sund. in Lent.	2	♍	6	19	6	*Man has no good*
24	2	St. Matthias.	3	18	6	18	6	Full ● 24 day,
25	3	♃ rise 12 52	3h	♎	6	17	6	10 morn.
26	4	able even to the	4	18	6	15	6	☽ with ♄
27	5	⚹ ♄ ♃ very	5	♏	6	14	6	☽ rise 9 53 aft.
28	6	□ ♃ ♀ end.	6	17	6	13	6	*Neighbours.*

A page from *Poor Richard's Almanac*, which opens with the thought that man should emulate nature because nature is frugal; it doesn't demand much and is easily satisfied.

FOUNDER OF THE ALMANAC

ROBERT B. THOMAS, founder of *the Old Farmer's Almanac*, as pictured in the 1838 *Almanac*. Thomas was born on April 24, 1766 and died on May 19, 1846. He served as editor of the *Almanac* for 53 years.

A BIOGRAPHY OF ROBERT B. THOMAS

40

THE FOUNDER OF THE OLD FARMER'S ALMANAC.

In the early days of New England history the Almanac was second in importance only to the Bible and other religious works. With the exception of a small broadside or leaflet, the earliest printed work in what is now the United States was an almanac, published at Cambridge in the year 1639. Since that time numerous other almanacs in different parts of the country have made their annual appearance, but no one of them has reached a wide circulation that has continued for a century. The present issue of this almanac is the Centennial number, and it has been thought proper to give a short account of its founder.

Robert Bailey Thomas, the elder son of William and Azubah (Goodale) Thomas, was born at Grafton on April 24, 1766, at the house of his maternal grandfather. His father, William, a native of Marlborough, owned a farm in the present town of West Boylston, pleasantly situated between the Quinnepoxet and Stillwater streams, near their confluence, where they form the south branch of the Nashua River. At this house Robert and his younger brother, Aaron, were brought up, doing such chores as usually fall to the lot of farmers' boys in New England. In the winter they attended the district school, and at other seasons were taught by their father, who was considered to be quite a scholar for those days. The father was a great reader of books, and had a considerable library. Among these books Robert used to be turned loose, where he passed his leisure hours in browsing. Of all the works there found, none absorbed his attention so much as James Ferguson's Astronomy. At an early age he had made various calculations in regard to lunar and solar eclipses. In 1781 he lost his mother, who died of apoplexy, and in the next year his father was married again.

When Robert was twenty years of age he taught school at Sterling, "boarding round," as was the custom of that period in New England towns. During the next six years he kept no less than nine schools in the towns of Princeton, Sterling, and Boylston. While teaching at Princeton in 1792, he became acquainted with a family, of which, some years later, he married one of the daughters. Before this time, while working on the farm, he passed many of his spare hours in mending old and worn-out books for his father and others, and thus, self-taught, picked up a little knowledge of the bookbinder's trade. He used to buy school-books in sheets, and sell them as bound volumes to the storekeepers and schoolmasters in the neighborhood. The main object of his ambition, however, was to make an almanac and publish it himself, and he had tried to fit himself for this work, by devoting his leisure hours to the study of astronomy.

In the summer of 1792 he placed himself, for special instruction in the required studies, under the charge of Osgood Carleton, a teacher in Boston, and the author of an almanac. Proving himself an apt scholar, in the course of two or three months he made all the calculations, and prepared the "copy" of an almanac for the year 1793. He found publishers for the work, who made liberal terms with him in the way of a percentage on the sales. They were Belknap and Hall of Boston, and in connection with their names on the title-page of the pamphlet, it is

41

there stated that the almanac is sold "also by the *Author* and *M. Smith, Sterling*." This number was the first issue of the (OLD) FARMER'S ALMANACK, which has appeared each year since 1793. Its success from the beginning was marked, and until his death Mr. Thomas kept up the publication.

In the early part of the present century he was married to Hannah, daughter of Phineas and Hannah Beaman, a native of Princeton; but he continued to live at the old homestead, where he carried on the farm, working at the almanac in the winter, and looking after the crops at other times. During his life he was a resident of four different towns, and yet always living on the same farm. The last was West Boylston, incorporated January 30, 1808, where he held various offices, and was always a prominent citizen. He was the first Town Clerk, serving as such for one year, and several times Chairman of the Board of Selectmen. He represented the town in the Convention of 1820 for revising the State Constitution, and also in the General Court during the sessions of 1833 to 1837, inclusive. After a long life of honor and usefulness, he died at his home, May 19, 1846, leaving a large estate to his widow, and the two children of his deceased brother. His widow died September 28, 1855, and they lie buried in the "Leg" burying-ground at Sterling, near the West Boylston line.

SAMUEL A. GREEN.

RECLAIMING MEADOW AND SWAMP LANDS.

GRADUALLY the farmers of New England are abandoning the hard, rocky hills and hillsides, and moving down into the valleys to drain and clear up the wet lowlands, which are rich in plant food, and, when properly drained and tilled, will produce large crops with a less quantity of fertilizers than is required on the high lands. Many mistakes have been made in draining swamp lands by not draining the water low enough. Especially has this been the case on land that is made up of partially decayed vegetation, and is somewhat soft. When such meadows are drained so as to draw the water twelve to eighteen inches below the surface, decomposition of the vegetable substance of which the meadow is composed is quite rapid, and in a few years the surface of the soil will sink almost as near the water as before draining. The farmer, finding the land too wet, instead of lowering the bed of the stream which is the outlet of the meadow, makes the serious mistake of trying to raise the land by carting on gravel or sand, every load of which, by its weight, sinks the land lower. The best and only certain way to make such meadows drier is to lower the outlet.

A meadow that is wet, and is made up of several feet of soft vegetable substance, should have the water drawn three feet below the surface. This will give it a chance to settle eighteen inches, and still leave it eighteen inches above the water, which is none too much. When the water is lower than this it is well to have a flume at the outlet, so the water can be raised or lowered according to the weather, and according to the wants of the particular crop under cultivation. A meadow where the water can be thus controlled is worth more than twice as much per acre as land where the water cannot be thus used. Many garden crops can be grown on such land at a large profit, especially in a dry season, when the crops on high land are a failure. They can be produced on such land for two-thirds what it can be on the hills, for two reasons; first, the gradual decomposition of the vegetable substance of which the soil is composed furnishes considerable quantities of plant food, thus reducing the cost of fertilizers; second, having control of the water, the grass will not suffer during dry weather as it will on high land.

The successful farmer will try to cultivate such land as will be pretty sure to produce good crops, when, by reason of drought, prices are high, and his product is in good demand.

Pages 40 and 41 from the 1892 *Almanac* in which the biography of Robert B. Thomas, founder and first editor of the publication, is set forth.

THE

FARMER's ALMANAC,

CALCULATED ON A NEW AND IMPROVED PLAN,

FOR THE YEAR OF OUR LORD

1793:

Being the first after Leap Year, and seventeenth of the Independence of America.

Fitted to the town of BOSTON, but will serve for any of the adjoining States.

Containing, besides the large number of ASTRO-NOMICAL CALCULATIONS and FARMER'S CA-LENDAR for every month in the year, as great a vari-ety as are to be found in any other Almanac, *Of* NEW, USEFUL, *and* ENTERTAINING MATTER,

ROBERT B. THOMAS.

"While the bright radient sun in centre glows,
The earth, in annual motion round it goes;
At the same time on its own axis reels,
And gives us change of seasons as it wheels."

Published according to Act of Congress.

PRINTED AT THE Apollo Press, IN BOSTON,

BY BELKNAP AND HALL,

Sold at their Office, State Street; also, by the *Author* and *M. Smith*, Sterling.

[*Sixpence single,* 4s. *per dozen,* 40s. *per groce.*]

This reproduction of the title page of the first issue (1793) of *The Old Farmer's Almanac* was printed in the 1892 edi-tion, which marked 100 years of publication. Oddly, whereas the title pages of the various editions spell "Almanack" with a "k" at the end, the cover pages always omit the "k". The word "Old" was added to the title in the latter part of the 1840s, and was used irregularly.

Like all almanacs, *The Old Farmer's Almanac* contains its share of poetry, humor, statistics, and advice to enhance personal living and family life. But, true to its title, its emphasis is on events and matters that concerned rural America in colonial and post-colonial days. It concentrated then, as it does now, on the activities of the New England farmer, always offering the latest agricultural information.

Here are the contents from several issues of the *Almanac* which indicate the variety of subjects treated by the editors. The first issue to carry a Table of Contents was the 1900 issue.

CONTENTS.

Contents of the 1900 ALMANAC

Contents of the 1904 ALMANAC

INDEX TO PRINCIPAL CONTENTS.

Contents of
the 1908
ALMANAC

INDEX TO PRINCIPAL CONTENTS.

Contents of
the 1912
ALMANAC

INDEX TO CONTENTS.

Contents of
the 1916
ALMANAC

INDEX TO CONTENTS.

7

In *The Best of the Old Farmer's Almanac*, we hope to recreate the "sense" of America as it was—and still is—in many parts of New England. We have, therefore, sifted through all the editions through World War I /and have highlighted the most important and most interesting articles, editorials, anecdotes and bits of helpful advice and information.

In addition, we have selected one edition—the 1850 edition—and have reproduced it in its entirety, since it is representative of most issues. As you will note, it contains the typical calendar, poetry, anecdotes, puzzles, humor, agricultural notes, and hints for self-improvement, plus news and observations about the world-at-large.

It should be noted that some editions drift away from this pattern and introduce elements that are out of character. The 1913 edition, for example, digs back into the *Almanac's* archives to retrieve and up-date a piece on war vessels. The original article was entitled, "Navy of the United States, July 1813." The 1913 article is reproduced below. What is most interesting, and why it is out of character, is that the *Almanac*, as a rule, plays down violence and war activity. One finds practically no reference to violent activities in all the editions that have appeared—even those that have been issued in the most turbulent and critical years of American history. The *Almanac* pays little attention to the life and death struggles of the American people: to the War of 1812, to the bitter war between the States, to the catastrophic World War—even as it pays little attention to the assassinations of Presidents and to the scandals that rocked the nation from time to time. Even where the editor promises, as he does in the 1862 edition, to give his readers "the complete chronological record of events connected with the rise and progress of the rebellion against the national government," no such record appears in that edition or in subsequent editions.

OUR WAR VESSELS A CENTURY AGO.

The Number of this Publication for the year 1814, No. XXII, gives the "Navy of the United States, July, 1813." This, it will be recollected, was a short time before Perry's victory on Lake Erie, Sept. 10, 1813. A list of the vessels with supplementary statements as given in that Almanack is subjoined. Of the vessels named two are now in the Navy Register, the Constitution, "Old Ironsides," which was launched at Boston, October 21, 1797, and is now out of commission at the Navy Yard, Boston, Mass., and the Constellation, which was launched at Baltimore, Md., September 7, 1797, and is now in commission and used as a stationery training ship at Newport, R. I.

NAMES	GUNS	NAMES	GUNS	NAMES	GUNS
Constitution	44	Revenge *	16	Viper	12
United States	44	Syren	14	Lady of the Lake	3
President	44	Nonsuch	14	Pert	3
Macedonian	38	Enterprise	14	Julia	2
Constellation	36	Carolina	14	Elizabeth	2
Congress	36	Comet *	14	Ontario	1
New York	36	*Duke of Gloucester*	12	Adeline	—
Essex	32	President	12	Asp	—
Adams	32	Petapsco *	12	Analostan	—
Boston	32	Isaac Hull	10	Despatch	—
General Pike	32	Conquest	8	Ferret	—
Madison	28	Hamilton	8	Neptune	—
John Adams	20	Raven	8	Perseverance	—
Louisiana	20	Scourge	8	Aetna	bomb
Alert	18	Governor Tompkins	6	Mary	do.
Argus	18	Scorpion	6	Spitfire	do.
Hornet	18	Growler	5	Vengeance	do.
Oneida	18	Fair American	4	Vesuvius	do.
Troupe	18				

Besides the above there are a number of Revenue Cutters, and about one hundred and seventy-eight Gun-Boats. Two sloops of war have lately been launched on Lake Erie. The vessels names which are in *Italics*, have been captured from the British since the commencement of the present war. Those marked thus (*) are hired by the United States.

THE SWAMP BLUEBERRY.

Despite the high esteem in which this wild fruit is held, attempts to cultivate it have until recently been unsuccessful. For several years past experiments have been in progress by the Department of Agriculture in which the conditions of growth and soil requirements of the plant have been closely studied in the greenhouse. Field experiments have also been made for several years in New Hampshire. Unlike most plants, it is found not to thrive in rich garden soil or land heavily manured or treated with lime. It requires for vigorous growth an acid soil, such as is furnished by peaty, boggy land or old pastures. With a successful method of culture, the possibilities of improvement of this fruit by selection and propagation are very large. The berries vary greatly in flavor and size, those from some bushes being a half inch in diameter. Individual plants also vary in earliness and in height and character of the bush. The plant can be propagated by grafting, budding, layering, twig cuttings, and by root cuttings, the best method being by cuttings from the root or stem, which is attended with some difficulty as yet. In field culture it is recommended to set the plants on uplands in trenches or holes filled with well-rotted peat, and mulch the surface with leaves or sand; or in a peat bog which has been drained, turfed, and deeply mulched with sand, keeping the ground water a little lower than is usual with cranberries.

A page from the 1913 edition of the *Almanac* in which a list of the war vessels of the U.S. Navy is up-dated.

2

TO PATRONS AND CORRESPONDENTS.

ANOTHER year has rolled away and we again offer you our little annual, hoping that it will prove acceptable to the sons as it has for so many years to the fathers and grandfathers. This past year we have all been shocked by the assassination of our good president, James A. Garfield. His memory is enshrined in our hearts and should animate us to renewed devotion to our glorious fatherland. The event has drawn all parts of our land closer together in a common sympathy, and may thus bring a blessing under the sorrow.

We have to thank our friends and correspondents for their favors, and to request them to continue to favor us with any suggestions or corrections. We close with the words of the founder of this Almanack:

"It is by our works, and not by our words, we would be judged: these, we hope, will sustain us in the humble though proud station we have so long held. . . ."

Robt. B. Thomas.

A page from the 70th (1862) edition of the *Almanac* in which the editor promises to keep his readers informed about events pertaining to the War between the States.

1882.	CALENDAR.	1882.
JANUARY.	**MAY.**	**SEPTEMBER.**

JANUARY.

Su.	Mo.	Tu.	We.	Th.	Fri.	Sat.
1	2	3	4	5	6	7
8	9	10	11	12	13	14
15	16	17	18	19	20	21
22	23	24	25	26	27	28
29	30	31	..	..	..	..

FEBRUARY.

Su.	Mo.	Tu.	We.	Th.	Fri.	Sat.
..	..	..	1	2	3	4
5	6	7	8	9	10	11
12	13	14	15	16	17	18
19	20	21	22	23	24	25
26	27	28	..	..	..	..

MARCH.

Su.	Mo.	Tu.	We.	Th.	Fri.	Sat.
..	..	..	1	2	3	4
5	6	7	8	9	10	11
12	13	14	15	16	17	18
19	20	21	22	23	24	25
26	27	28	29	30	31	..

APRIL.

Su.	Mo.	Tu.	We.	Th.	Fri.	Sat.
..	..	..	..	..	..	1
2	3	4	5	6	7	8
9	10	11	12	13	14	15
16	17	18	19	20	21	22
23	24	25	26	27	28	29
30	..	..	..	..	..	..

MAY.

Su.	Mo.	Tu.	We.	Th.	Fri.	Sat.
..	1	2	3	4	5	6
7	8	9	10	11	12	13
14	15	16	17	18	19	20
21	22	23	24	25	26	27
28	29	30	31	..	..	..

JUNE.

Su.	Mo.	Tu.	We.	Th.	Fri.	Sa.
..	..	..	..	1	2	3
4	5	6	7	8	9	10
11	12	13	14	15	16	17
18	19	20	21	22	23	24
25	26	27	28	29	30	..

JULY.

Su.	Mo.	Tu.	We.	Th.	Fri.	Sat.
..	..	..	..	..	..	1
2	3	4	5	6	7	8
9	10	11	12	13	14	15
16	17	18	19	20	21	22
23	24	25	26	27	28	29
30	31	..	..	..	..	..

AUGUST.

Su.	Mo.	Tu.	We.	Th.	Fri.	Sat.
..	..	1	2	3	4	5
6	7	8	9	10	11	12
13	14	15	16	17	18	19
20	21	22	23	24	25	26
27	28	29	30	31	..	..

SEPTEMBER.

Su.	Mo.	Tu.	We.	Th.	Fri.	Sat.
..	..	..	..	..	1	2
3	4	5	6	7	8	9
10	11	12	13	14	15	16
17	18	19	20	21	22	23
24	25	26	27	28	29	30

OCTOBER.

Su.	Mo.	Tu.	We.	Th.	Fri.	Sat.
1	2	3	4	5	6	7
8	9	10	11	12	13	14
15	16	17	18	19	20	21
22	23	24	25	26	27	28
29	30	31	..	..	..	..

NOVEMBER.

Su.	Mo.	Tu.	We.	Th.	Fri.	Sa.
..	..	..	1	2	3	4
5	6	7	8	9	10	11
12	13	14	15	16	17	18
19	20	21	22	23	24	25
26	27	28	29	30	..	..

DECEMBER.

Su.	Mo.	Tu.	We.	Th.	Fri.	Sat.
..	..	..	..	..	1	2
3	4	5	6	7	8	9
10	11	12	13	14	15	16
17	18	19	20	21	22	23
24	25	26	27	28	29	30
31	..	..	..	..	..	..

2

TO PATRONS AND CORRESPONDENTS.

NUMBER SEVENTY! Three score and ten! Few, few indeed, who greeted us as we started into life in 1793, now live to welcome us to their familiar firesides. We have survived the friends who first knew us and took us cordially by the hand — nay, have even renewed our youth from year to year, and now feel younger, stronger and more vigorous than ever. A hale, hearty old age to you all! We chronicled faithfully the rolling years, and your fathers and grandfathers delighted to finger our leaves, as they sat in the old chimney-corner, wondering as the great miracles were renewed in the changing seasons, bringing life out of death, bringing a living green upon the face of the cold earth, bringing the golden and crimson blush upon the fruits of autumn ; and we come to you now, as we came to them, with something new, something fresh, and something useful, from day to day through the whole year !

A prominent feature of this number will be found in the complete chronological record of events connected with the rise and progress of the rebellion against the national government, commencing with November, 1860, and extending to July, 1861, in the calendar pages. This record will be continued, and hence the importance of preserving the number for future reference.

"We are living, we are dwelling in a grand and awful time,
In an age on ages telling, to be living is sublime !"

We are happy to present our acknowledgments for communications, solutions to problems, enigmas, etc., to D. C. H., Moretown, Vt., D. E. M., Thompson, Ct., A. L. T., Roxbury, Ms., J. T. B., Brookfield, Ms., J. W. S., N. Andover, Ms., G. W. H., Middleton, Ms., J. H. C., Newton Lower Falls, Ms., W. A. B., Florida, Ms., and to numerous others.

The list of the Agricultural Societies in New England, with the name and address of the secretary of each, is a valuable feature of the Almanac ; and we earnestly request information by which any inaccuracies or omissions may be corrected in future. The stanzas at the head of the calendar pages are selected from our own sweet New England poet, JOHN G. WHITTIER.

The editor is in want of the numbers of this work for 1794, 1795, and 1796. Please overhaul that package of old papers up in the garret, and if you find those numbers, we shall be glad to pay you well for them.

All communications should be directed to me, *care of the publishers*, and sent previous to July 1st, and we will promise "that no efforts shall be spared to make the Almanack useful, pleasing, and worthy the continued patronage of its numerous friends.

Robt. B. Thomas.

MEETINGS OF FRIENDS IN NEW ENGLAND.

Yearly, beginning with select, 7th day after 2d 6th day, 6th mo., 9th hour, morn., at Newport, R. I. Public for worship, 1st day following, at Newport and Portsmouth, 10th hour, morn., and 4th, afternoon. For business, at Newport, 2d day following, 9th hour, morning.

This yearly meeting comprises the quarterly meetings of R. Island, Salem, Sandwich, Falmouth, Smithfield, Vassalboro', Dover and Fairfield, held as follows : — *R. Island:* 1st 5th d., 8th mo., Newport ; 1st 5th d., 11th mo., Somerset ; 1st 5th d., 2d mo., Providence ; 1st 5th d., 5th mo., East Greenwich. *Salem:* 4th 5th d., 5th mo., Amesbury ; 3d 5th d., 8th mo., Lynn ; 3d 5th d., 10th mo., Weare ; 3d 5th d., 1st mo., Salem. *Sandwich:* 1st 5th d., 4th and 12th mo., N. Bedford ; 1st 5th d., 7th mo., Falmouth ; 1st 5th d., 10th mo., Sandwich. *Falmouth:* 5th d. before 1st 6th d. in mo., at Windham, 2d and 9th mo. ; Westbrook, 6th ; Durham, 11th. *Smithfield:* 2d 5th d., 8th mo., Bolton ; 2d 5th d., 11th mo., Smithfield ; 2d 5th d., 2d mo., Worcester ; 2d 5th d., 5th mo., Northbridge. *Vassalboro':* 2d 6th d., 1st and 9th mo., Vassalboro' ; 5th and 11th mo., East Vassalboro'. *Dover, N. H.:* 4th 5th d. of the mo. ; Dover, 4th ; North Berwick, 8th ; Sandwich, 10th ; Rochester, 1st. *Fairfield:* Hallowell, 4th d. before 2d 6th d., 2d and 9th mo. ; Fairfield, 4th d. before last 6th d. of 5th mo. ; and 4th d. before 2d 6th d. of 11th mo. —(Corrected 1861.)

The assassination of President James A. Garfield in 1881 warranted only this brief mention in the editor's column of the 1882 edition.

A second such out-of-character example is that of a religious calendar—and a Jewish religious calendar at that! It is difficult to speculate why the Jewish calendar for 1864-1865 (at the height of the Civil War) was included, especially when one bears in mind that out of a total American population of 31,500,000 in 1860, there were only 150,000 Jews (or ½% of the total population in the country).

5625. JEWISH CALENDAR. 1864-1865.

Jan.	28, 1864.	1st of Shebat.
Feb.	27.	1st of Adar.
March	9.	Fast of Esther.
"	12.	Purim.
"	28.	1st of Nisan.
April	11.	1st day of Passover.
"	12.	2d day of Passover.
"	17.	7th day of Passover.
"	18.	8th day of Passover.
"	27.	1st day of Ijur.
May	26.	1st day of Siwan.
"	31.	1st day of Pentecost.
June	1.	2d day of Pentecost.
"	25.	1st of Tamus.
July	11.	17th of Tamus.
"	24.	1st of Ab.
Aug.	1.	9th of Ab. Fast. Destruction of the Temple.
"	23.	1st day of Elul.
Sept.	21.	1st day of Tishri. Year 5625 ends.
Sept.	22.	2d day of Tishri of New Year.
"	24.	Fast of Gedaljah.
"	30.	10th day of Tishri. Day of Atonement.
Oct.	5.	15th day of Tishri. Feast of Tabernacles. 1st day.
"	6.	2d day of Tabernacles.
"	11.	7th day of Tabernacles.
"	12.	22d day of Tishri. Feast of the 8th day.
"	13.	23d of Tishri. Rejoicing with the Law.
"	21.	1st day of Cheshwan.
Nov.	19.	1st of Kislew.
Dec.	13, 1864.	25th of Kislew. Dedication of the Temple.
"	19.	1st day of Tefes.
"	23.	10th day of Tefes. Fast. Siege of Jerusalem.

IMPORTANT SUGGESTIONS TO GUARD AGAINST FIRE.

The following suggestions by the Chief Engineer of the Boston Fire Department, to the inhabitants of that city, are so excellent, and so appropriate for all localities, that we transfer them to our pages, and trust they may be carefully heeded.

Keep matches in metal boxes, and out of the reach of children.

Wax matches are dangerous, and should be kept out of the way of rats or mice.

Fill fluid and camphene lamps only by daylight, and never near a fire or light.

Do not deposit coal or wood ashes in wooden vessels, and be sure burning cinders are extinguished before deposited.

Never place a light or ashes under a staircase.

Never take a light to examine a gas meter, or gas pipes inside a building.

Be careful never to place gas, or other lights, near curtains.

Do not read in bed by lamp-light.

Never take a light into a closet.

Place glass shades over gas lights in show windows, and do not crowd goods near them.

No smoking should be permitted in warehouses, particularly where goods are packed or cotton stored.

Where furnaces are used, the principal register should always be fastened open.

Stove pipes should be at least four inches from wood-work, and guarded.

All hatchways or openings in the floors of stores, factories, or warehouses, should always be closed at night.

All iron doors between stores should be closed at night, or when not in use.

OLD AND HOMELY PROVERBS FOR EVERY DAY IN THE MONTH.

1. Get thy spindle and thy distaff ready, and God will send thee flax.
2. Better ride an ass that carries us than a horse that throws us.
3. Everything comes in time to him who can wait.
4. Love rules without a sword.
5. Trust thyself only, and another shall not betray thee.
6. Nothing is lost on a journey by stopping to pray or to feed your horse.
7. Every vicious indulgence must be paid for cent per cent.
8. Better to be alone than in bad company.
9. To say little and perform much is noble.
10. Every man thinks his own geese are swans.
11. Circumstances alter cases: the straightest stick appears crooked in water.
12. An honest man is none the worse because a dog barks at him.
13. When you are an anvil, bear; when you are a hammer, strike.
14. He laughs best who laughs last.
15. He that can't paint must grind colors.
16. Wise distrust is the parent of security.
17. Idleness is the sepulchre of a living man.
18. The devil tempts all men; but the idle man tempts the devil.
19. Business is the salt of life.
20. Never measure other people's corn by your own bushel.
21. He who spares vice wrongs virtue.
22. Despatch is the soul of business, and method is the soul of despatch.
23. Like plays best with like: when the crane attempted to dance with the horse, she got broken legs.
24. A full vessel must be carried carefully.
25. That is often lost in an hour which costs a lifetime.
26. Keep yourself from opportunities, and God will keep you from sins.
27. The pitcher that goes often to the well gets broken at last.
28. Give a rogue an inch, and he will take an ell.
29. Many a cow stands often in the green meadow, and looks wistfully at the barren heath.
30. A handful of common sense is worth a bushel of learning.
31. The fire should burn brightest on one's own hearth.

Above is page 45 of the 1865 edition of the *Almanac* in which a Jewish holiday calendar appears, plus homey proverbs and suggestions to help guard against fire.

Now, let us move ahead to sample some of the best servings that the editors of *The Old Farmer's Alamanc* have offered America for the past two centuries.

BATTLEFIELD AMBULANCE

The new type of ambulance was introduced in the year when the Almanac was conceived. Designed in 1792 by Napoleon's personal surgeon, its spring-action, between carriage and wheels, made it possible for the wounded to be moved off the battlefield with a minimum of jostling.

THE FARMER'S CALENDAR

JANUARY, First Month. 1804.

Y E lusty sons of fair New-England's soil,
Inured to freedom, bravery and toil,
Enjoy the boon by labour earn'd so dear,
And sport amidst luxurious, brumal cheer.

M. D.	W. D.	Courts, Aspects, Holidays, Weather, &c. &c.	Farmer's Calendar.
1	A	Circumcision. *Fine* □ ♄ ♂	With a heart warm with be-
2	2	C.P. Lenox. *weather for*	nevolence and gratitude, the
3	3	C.P. Bost. & Ded. *the season.*	EDITOR once more greets each
4	4	Sir I. Newton born, 1643.	patron and friend, heartily wish-
5	5	Low tides. *Chang:*	ing them a *full tide* of joy and
6	6	Epiphany. *to cold* ☽ Apog.	prosperity throughout this new
7	7	*and boisterous.* □ ☉ H	year, and forever.
8	A	1st Sund. past Epiph. Luci.	To Him, who guides the sys-
9	2	C.P North.Len.&War. *Signs*	tems as they roll, let man look
10	3	Day increased 12m. *of rain.*	up with love and adoration, and
11	4	*Now comes*	bless his God, that he has lived
12	5	*a storm*	so long and so happy.
13	6	*of snow.*	A full purse, a full table,
14	7	Peace ratif. by Cong. 1784.	A full mow, a full stable,
15	A	2d Sund. past Epiph.	and a pleasant wife, makes win-
16	2	*High winds*	ter pass cheerly with the farm-
17	3	Dr. Franklin born, 1706.	er. In cold stormy evenings,
18	4	*at N. W.*	himself and possessions secure
19	5	Middling tides. *More* ☽ Per.	from the tempest, he enjoys
20	6	Fabian. *squalls.* [1793	more real happiness over his
21	7	Agnes. Louis XVI. behead.	cyder-mug and chequer-board,
22	A	3d Sund. past Epiph. Vincent.	than any nobleman of Europe
23	2	*Fine weather to make*	or nabob of India, amid pomp
24	3	*the ladies look fresh.*	and grandeur.
25	4	Convers. St. Paul. □ ☉ ♃	To make cattle thrive *well*,
26	5	*More moderate* ☽ ecl. vis.	look *well*, and labour *well*, you
27	6	*with snow or*	must feed them *well*.
28	7	Peter the Great died, 1725.	Now sled your year's wood;
29	A	Septuagesima Sund. *rain.*	cut and house it. To get one
30	2	*Pretty good*	load in summer, will be a day's
31	3	*sleighing.*	job, whereas in winter it will take but one quarter of that time. See then what time we gain, who get wood in winter "Time is money," and money, you know, neighbour Spriggins with us is a cash article.

1804 THE FARMER'S CALENDAR

HERE'S WISHING YOU:
A full purse,
A full table,
A full mow,
A full stable.

OH BURR

Oh Burr, oh Burr,
What hast thou done?
Thou hast shooted dead great
   Hamilton!
Thou hid among a bunch of
   thistle,
And shooted him dead,
With a great hoss pistol!

—*from the September 1804 Calendar*

WEEHAWKEN, N.J. — 1804

Alexander Hamilton is killed, on the banks of the Hudson, in a duel with Vice-President Aaron Burr.

—*from the September 1804 Calendar*

JANUARY

1850
THE
FARMER'S
CALENDAR

A WARM HEART
A warm barn in a snowstorm, shows
that the owner has a warm heart.

A mechanic who keeps but one
cow, by taking pains, can make
her yield abundantly.

JANUARY hath 31 days.   1850.

Swiftly pass the years away—
Silent is their fleetness;
And the changes of each day
Give to life its sweetness.

D. M.	D. W.	Courts, Aspects, Holidays, Weather, &c.	Farmer's Calendar.
1	Tu.	C. C. P. Boston. C. C. Lenox, Cambridge and Plym.	*Comfort.*
2	W.	Mass. Legis. meets. Mid. tides.	Well, my friend Goodyear, I am glad to see you so nicely cir-
3	Th.	♃ ☌ ☽. *Signs of*	cumstanced in 1850. You are cer-
4	Fr.	☿ greatest hel. lat. S.	tainly in a comfortable way. A
5	Sa.	Capt. J. N. Cushing, one of largest ship-owners in N. E., died, 1849.	good fire, a tight house, and all things as they should be. How is
6	F.	Epiphany. *snow.*	the farm stock? Hints enough,
7	Mo.	Jos. Barrett, Treas. of Mass., died, 1849. Low	perhaps, have been given, hereto-
8	Tu.	♃ stationary. *Finer,*	fore, on this subject. A warm
9	W.	7*s south 8h. 20m. ev.	barn, in a snow-storm, shows
10	Th.	tides. *with wind.*	that the owner has a warm heart,
11	Fr.	☽ runs low. *Great*	and cares for the comfort of his
12	Sa.	☽ in apo. ♀ ☌ ☽.	cattle. "A merciful man is mer-
13	F.	1st Sun. p. Epi. *signs*	ciful to his beast," you know.
14	Mo.	☿ ☌ ☽. *of*	What say you about a barn cel-
15	Tu.	*a storm,*	lar? Some one, not long ago,
16	W.	*unless very cold indeed.*	said something against them.
17	Th.	♀ rises 7h. 2m. morn.	Uncle Caleb cried Fudge! and
18	Fr.	Mid.	said it was all for the sake of scribbling for the paper. Their
19	Sa.	♄ ☌ ☽. *Some snow*	utility is unquestionable. A me-
20	F.	2d S. p. Epi. *tides.*	chanic who keeps but one cow,
21	Mo.	C. C. P. Crim. Worcester. *or rain at*	by taking pains, can make her yield abundantly. Keep her com-
22	Tu.	♂ south 8h. 59m. eve.	fortable, neighbor Handsaw.
23	W.	☿ in ♋. ♂ stationary.	Don't you know that she cannot
24	Th.	♂ ☌ ☽. *this time.*	take care of herself; and that the better you keep her, the more and
25	Fr.	☽ runs high. *Grows*	better milk she will yield? See
26	Sa.	☽ in peri. *warmer.*	yonder Tom Hardhack's poor
27	F.	Septuagesima S. Very	brindle; how she crimples to the
28	Mo.	C. C. P. Salem. ☿ sta. *Clouds*	wind, and curls her tail between her legs, as she turns over her
29	Tu.	Geo. 3d d. 1820. high tides. *up*	mess of meadow hay and bram-
30	W.	*for a storm.*	bles! She would fain, in her
31	Th.	♂ south 8h. 25m. eve.	rummaging, pick out a few spears of red-top.

15

1885
THE
FARMER'S
CALENDAR

LOVE
"Love thy neighbor
as thyself."
O, what a noble
principle.

MEUM and TUUM
What is mine is mine,
And I care not for thine.

GRANT'S TOMB

After dying of cancer at age 63, President Grant lay in state in New York City, where his body was viewed by mourners for 96 hours. His resting place, Grant's Tomb, on Riverside Drive and 122nd Street in New York City, is a national landmark.

FEBRUARY hath 28 days.　　　　1855

How keenly sweeps the cold wind's blast,
And fills the air with fleecy snow!
The sky above is overcast,
And dreary are the fields below.

D. M.	D. W.	Courts, Aspects, Holidays, Weather, &c.
1	Th.	☽ in apogee. ♅ � ☐ ⊙ Very
2	Fr.	Purification of Virgin Mary, or Candlemas Day. high
3	Sa.	Severe fire at Lowell, Mass., 1854. tides. Snow
4	G.	Great fire in New Orleans, 1854. Septu. Sund.
5	Mo.	C. C. P. Taunton. Tides or rain,
6	Tu.	♄ south 7h. 25m. eve.
7	W.	♀ ☌ ♂ decreasing.
8	Th.	and probably both.
9	Fr.	♄ stationary. Low tides.
10	Sa.	Strong southerly wind.
11	G.	E. Dyer, said to be richest man in Rhode Island, died, a. 83, 1854.
12	Mo.	C. C. P. Crim. Cambridge. ☽ runs low.
13	Tu.	Mid. Much
14	W.	7*s south 5h. 48m. eve.
15	Th.	☽ in perigee. tides.
16	Fr.	F. Sales, ins'r in Spanish at H. Univ., died, a. 82, 1854. cooler.
17	Sa.	♂ ☌ ☽ ♀ ☌ ☽ High
18	G.	Shrove Sund. ♀ in peri.
19	Mo.	C. C. P. Northampton tide. Changes
20	Tu.	S. J. C. Dedham. Tides to milder.
21	W.	Ash Wednesday. ♅ ☌ ☽
22	Th.	Washington born, 1732. decreasing.
23	Fr.	♄ ☌ ☽ Grows cooler,
24	Sa.	St. Mathias. Low tides.
25	G.	1st Sund. in Lent. with
26	Mo.	C. C. P. Lenox. ☽ runs high. snow
27	Tu.	Tides increasing. or rain.
28	W.	☽ in apogee. ♄ ☐ ⊙

Farmer's Calendar.

Meum and Tuum.

Mine and thine. — "Don't use Latin lingo to farmers," says Jobson. Be not offended, my friend. You see it is but two little words, and the translation immediately follows. *Mine* and *thine*, two little monosyllabics,— but think what a sway they have in the world, how constantly in use and on everybody's tongue! "What is mine is *mine*," emphatically quoth Jobson, " and I care not for *thine*." But Jobson is too " close-fisted," as he sometimes finds to his cost. The fruit of his neighbor's apple-trees fell over into Jobson's garden, and so he gathered them up and took them to himself. "They are *mine*," said Jobson. "They are not thine," said his neighbor, "but *mine*." They went to law about it, and this case of *meum* and *tuum* was decided against Jobson, and common sense said "*All right.*" What farmer ever grew fat by going to law? Our spunk, as it is called, sometimes costs us too much. We had better trim up scrub-oaks than enter into litigation. "Love thy neighbor as thyself." O, what a noble principle! How many are there who put it in practice? A certain old lady said it was a charming way to live, she had no doubt, but she had so much tewing about, that she could find no time to attend to it. Neither could Jobson.

FEBRUARY

1909
THE
FARMER'S
CALENDAR

CONSERVATION

"In these times there are conventions and conventions. Trees, coal, oil, water-power—all the natural resources—have worried people standing about them crying "conservation." This means that our boy of a nation, hitherto a wasteful boy, is beginning to think of saving for his old age."

FEBRUARY hath 28 days.   [1909

And still the earth is cold and white,
And mead and forest yet are bare;
But there's a something in the light
That says the germ of life is there.

MRS. JANE (GOODWIN) AUSTIN.

D. M.	D. W.	Aspects, Holidays, Events, Weather, Etc.	Farmer's Calendar.
1	M.	☿ stationary. ☾ runs high.	Are you realizing what an asset you have in that woodlot of yours? It will pay good days wages to you and your boys any time you happen to need a little ready money. Trim, single out, thin out. Cherish some of the bigger fellows for the saw mill. Don't try to "clear" unless you are sure the soil is right for crops. Encourage second growth pines. The match-makers, — not the hymeneal ones, — and the box board folks can't get pine enough. In these times there are conventions and conventions. Trees, coal, oil, water-power — all the natural resources — have worried looking people standing about them crying "Conservation." This means that our boy of a nation, — hitherto a wasteful boy — is beginning to think of saving for his old age. During the Winter evenings it will pay to make a few cheap nesting boxes for the birds. These bird homes can be fashioned from small boxes, hollow limbs, tin cans or gourds. The entrance hole should be not over one inch in diameter for wrens, and not over one and one-half inches for blue birds or swallows. It may be two inches or more for martens and larger birds. The entrance should face the South or West,
2	Tu.	Pur. of V. Mary, Candlemas Day. ☾☿☾	
3	W.	{ 1st. King Carlos and Crown Prince Luiz, of Portugal, assassinated at Lisbon, 1908.	
4	Th.	Cold	
5	Fr.	Medium tides. spell with	
6	Sa.	{ 6th. Charles II (Eng.) d., 1685. occasional snow.	
7	C	Septuagesima Sun. ☾♃☾	
8	M.	☾ in Apogee.	
9	Tu.	{ 8th. Battle of Eylau, Prussia, 1807. Signs of	
10	W.	☿ gr. hel. lat. N. snow.	
11	Th.	☾☿☉ inferior.	
12	Fr.	{ 12th. LINCOLN DAY, CONN. Snow, then cold	
13	Sa.	♂ in ♉. { 14th. St. Valentine. northwest	
14	C	Sexagesima Sunday. winds.	
15	M.	☾♂☾. 14th. Low tides.	
16	Tu.	☾ runs low. Weather	
17	W.	☾☿☾. moderates with	
18	Th.	☾♀☾. high winds.	
19	Fr.	☾☿☾. ☾♀♀.	
20	Sa.	☾ Perigee. in { 20th. A. C. Latimer, U. S. Sen., S. C., d. 1908, a. 57.	
21	C	Shrove Sunday. High tides.	
22	M.	☾♄☾ { 22d. WASHINGTON born, 1732. Look for	
23	Tu.	☿ stat'n'y. { 21st. Harriet G. Hosmer, (Am. Sculp., d. 1908, a. 77.	
24	W.	Ash Wed. St. Math. rapid changes.	
25	Th.	{ 25th. Indians burn buildings at Weymouth, Mass. 1676.	
26	Fr.	Medium tides. Expect rain	
27	Sa.	{ 28th. Battle Sacramento, Cal., 1847. or sleet.	
28	C	1st. Sunday in Lent. ☿♃☉.	

and each box should be put up in a shady place beyond the reach of cats, if possible. You will be more than repaid for your trouble by the increased destruction of noxious insects which will result if the birds occupy the boxes.

THE MODEL "T"
Working to create an inexpensive "universal" car, Henry Ford produced his low-priced Model T to retail for $850. By 1924, the price was reduced to $290.

17

MARCH, third Month. 1831.

Sweet Spring is approaching apace,
The fetters of winter to break;
And Sol is prolonging his race,
The earth from her slumbers to wake.

M.D.	W.D.	Courts, Aspects, Holydays, Weather, &c.	FARMER'S CALENDAR.
1	3	S. J. C. L. T. Bost. C. C.	**BIRDS.**
2	4	Frequent [Nor'p. & Gr'f.	'Who was it, that killed *cock robin?*'
3	5	Quite · *changes.*	'Twas the great wanton fool, who was
4	6	First Con. met '89. ☽Ap.	never whipt at school; but who now
5	7	low tides *Milder*	deserves a good drubbing. The present
6	B	3d Sun. in Lent. *with*	practice of destroying the feathered race
7	2	C. P. Worc. for the season.	every spring is most shameful, and de-
8	3	*showers*	serves the severest reprehension. In-
9	4	7*s set 11h. 50m. *of*	sects are very well known to be the fa-
10	5	*rain*	vorite food of the smaller birds, and thus
11	6	*if not snow.*	the immense increase of the former in
12	7	Greg. *Finer.*	years past is undoubtedly caused by the
13	B	4th Sun. in L. M. L. Sun.	vast destruction of the latter by incon-
14	2	C. P. Conc. & Taun.	siderate sportsmen, and cruel, shameless
15	3	C. C. Plym. *Cooler with*	boys. We may try our various experi-
16	4	Middling *white frost.*	ments to destroy the millions of trouble-
17	5	British evac. Bost. 1776.	some insects, but it will be all in vain.
18	6	Antar. ris.10h. 16m. ☽Per.	Nothing but the birds can aid us to ef-
19	7	tides. *Moderates.*	fect this desired purpose. They alone
20	B	5th. Sun. in L. ☌♃♅	will be able to relieve us, for which
21	2	C.P.Ips.&Spr. *Changeable*	they are formed by nature, and for
22	3	C. C. Taun. & Worc.	which " their habits, wants and capaci-
23	4	*weather for*	ties qualify them ;" and it is said that
24	5	Jup. ris. 4h. 30m. *some*	the parents of one young nest of birds
25	6	Anun. V. M. *days.*	have been calculated to destroy many
26	7	*Pleasant.*	thousands of insects in a day, which may
27	B	6th Sun. in L. P. S.	prevent the existence of as many millions!
28	2	C. P. North'p. *Great*	What then, can be done for us? The
29	3	7*s set 10h. 42m. *signs*	Legislatu e would probably esteem it tri-
30	4	*of a storm.*	fling and derogatory to be enacting *bird*
31	5	Tides low.	*laws.* Yet they have passed an act for
			the protection of *snipes* and *woodcocks.*
			Where then, I would ask, is the dishonor
			of extending it to *blackbirds, catbirds,*
			woodpeckers and *bobalincorns* ?

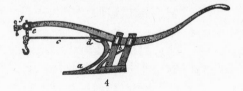

4

1831
THE
FARMER'S
CALENDAR

COCK ROBIN
Who Killed Cock Robin?
'Twas the great wanton fool,
Who was never whipt at school,
But who now deserves a good
drubbing.

NEW YORK, March 19, 1831—Using a duplicate set of keys, the City Bank of New York was broken into this morning and was robbed of $245,000. This was the first bank robbery in the United States.
Edward Smith was later apprehended and convicted, serving five years at Sing Sing prison.

MARCH

1846
THE
FARMER'S
CALENDAR

BRAYING
"March! The month
for braying
and boastin.

He is a fool
Who brays at an ass."

CONGRESS DECLARES WAR
ON MEXICO!
Is not life miserable enough; comes
not death soon enough, without resort
to the hideous enginery of war. . . .
People of the United States: Your
rulers are precipitating you into a
fathomless abyss of crime and calami-
ty. Why sleep you thoughtless on its
verge, as though this was not your
business. . . .

—Editorial of May 12, 1846
The New York Times
Horace Greeley

THE MEXICAN EAGLE BEFORE THE WAR! — THE MEXICAN EAGLE AFTER THE WAR!

Anonymous. *Yankee Doodle*, 1847.

MARCH hath 31 days.   1846.

But snow and frost forever
Will not their victims bind;
For spring their ties will sever,
And they enlargement find.

D. M.	D. W.	Courts, Aspects, Holidays, Weather, &c.	Farmer's Calendar.
1	D.	1st S. in Lent. ☌ ☾ ♃	*He is a fool who brays at an ass.*
2	2	C. P. Worc. ☌ ☉ ♀	And he is a fool who tries to out-
3	3	S. J. C. L. Bost. / C. C. Grf. North.	do an ass in strength. This is a
4	4	*Changeable, with high*	month for braying and boasting;
5	5	*winds*	the elements send forth their shouts,
6	6	Mid. tides. *at*	and the storms of old Equinox
7	7	*S. W.*	cause the heavens to crack and the
8	D.	2d Sun. in Lent. ☾ apo.	earth to tremble. Let not little,
9	2	C. P. Tau. Con.	vain man boast of *his* prowess. Say,
10	3	Not very *Frequent*	"canst thou draw out leviathan
11	4	Ben. West d. '20. *dashes*	with a hook? Canst thou put a
12	5	Greg. high tides.	hook into his nose? or bore his jaw
13	6	Plan. Her. dis. '81. *of*	through with a thorn?" "Wilt
14	7	*rain, with some*	thou play with him, as with a bird?"
15	D.	3d Sun. in Lent. *snow.*	Come, come, Mr. Rattlejaw; no
16	2	C. P. Sal. Grf.	more of your tinkling brass; the
17	3	C. C. Bri. Ply. *Cool*	season will soon be along when we
18	4	Mid. tides. *winds.*	shall make the trial; not which can
19	5	*Much finer,*	swing the heaviest plough, but
20	6	Gr. fire Bos. '60. *but*	which turns the handsomest furrow;
21	7	*cool.* ♀ stat.	not which can roll on the heaviest
22	D.	4th Sun. in Lent.	stone, but which lays the handsom-
23	2	C. P. North. *A storm*	est string of wall. Hark! 'tis the
24	3	C.C.Worc.&Tau. ☾ per	bluebird's whistle. Well, boys, it is
25	4	Ann.or Lady d. ☌ ☾ ♄	just to give us notice that we must
26	5	Pretty high *is near.*	begin to stir our stumps. Tools all
27	6	7*s set 11h. tides.	ready and in order, no doubt, as I
28	7	*Very fine*	see you have a tool-house. Some
29	D.	5th S. in Lent. ☌ ☾ ♃	depend more or less on borrowing;
30	2	*for the*	but this is a poor piece of business
31	3	*season.*	at the present day, when there is a

plenty, of every name and kind, to
be had at the stores. Your asparagus will require your attention very
soon. You know, I presume, that
it will need loosening with a fork. It
is very easily raised, and exceed-
ingly wholesome; "but it is a kind
of fodder," says Old Cider, "that I care nothing about."

19

APRIL

1849 THE FARMER'S CALENDAR

APRIL hath 30 days. 1849.

In a fitful mood the dark clouds fly,
And then cloudless leave the deep blue sky;
Again they return with treasures of rain,
Which gently distil on valley and plain.

D. M.	D. W.	Courts, Aspects, Holidays, Weather, &c.
1	G.	Palm Sund. *Frequent*
2	Mo.	State elec. Connect. ☌ ☽ ♃ *changes,*
3	Tu.	C. C. P. Barn. and Bost. C. C. Lenox. *with*
4	W.	State elec., Rhode Island. Seven stars set 10h. 53m., e. *rain.*
5	Th.	John Carver d. 1621.
6	Fr.	Good Frid. ♀ most bril.
7	Sa.	High *Cooler, but*
8	G.	East. Sun. ♃ sta. tides.
9	Mo.	C. C. P. Plym. ☿ in ♑ *fine.*
10	Tu.	S. J. C. Low. C. C. Barn., Ips. and Spring. *Cloudy,*
11	W.	*with some*
12	Th.	Henry Clay born, 1777. ☽ in apo.
13	Fr.	☽ runs low. *rain.*
14	Sa.	Lord Ashburton d. 1848, aged 74. Very
15	G.	Low Sun. low *Fre-*
16	Mo.	tides. *quent showers,*
17	Tu.	S. J. C. Wor. and Greenf. C.C.Ded. Sirius sets 9h. 52 m., eve.
18	W.	Byron died, 1824, ag. 36. *with thunder.*
19	Th.	Bat. Lex. and Conc., 1775. ☌ ☽ ♂
20	Fr.	☌ ☽ ♄ *Fine for*
21	Sa.	Ven sta. ☌ ☽ ☿
22	G.	2d. Sund. p. Easter. ☌ ☽ ♅ *the*
23	Mo.	C. C. P. Ded'm. ♀ sta. ☌ ☿ ♅
24	Tu.	S. J. C. North. and Taunton. ☽ in per.
25	W.	St. Mark. *season.*
26	Th.	☽ runs high. *Signs of*
27	Fr.	7*s set 8h. 24m. ev.
28	Sa.	J. Monroe born, 1758. Mid. *rain.*
29	G.	3d Sund. p. Easter. ☌ ☽ ♃ tides.
30	Mo.	Louisiana adm., 1812.

Farmer's Calendar.

Conservatism.

This has become a mighty fashionable word; such as we farmers, however, do not use much. I have been looking it out in the dictionary, and conclude it is about synonymous with *pre*servatism. It therefore may have something to do with husbandry. I have lately been reading an oration on this very subject, by one of our smartest scholar men. He says that the world, now-a-days, is divided into *Conservatism* and *Reform;* that is, the old and the new; and just so it is in farming. Faith, as he says, goes ahead to the new; *fear,* with eyes behind, holds on to the old. Now, I think this is completely applicable to our business; don't you, Mr. Subsoil? One man spreads his manure broadcast, another does differently, after the old fashion. The stickler for *reform* takes a small piece of land, puts what manure he has upon it, ploughs it thoroughly, tends it closely, hires but little help, and gets a good crop. The *conservator,* sticking to old customs, thinks the more land he has, the greater the produce; goes on scratching over his broad fields, hiring abundance of help, one half of which are loafers, and at last don't bring buckle and strap together; that is, he comes out at the little end of the horn.

TAXES & BORROWING

"... cities and towns are too often borrowing money to pay for things that ought to be paid for out of current taxes."

IT HAPPENED IN '49

* **Elizabeth Blackwell was the first woman to practice medicine in the United States.**
* **New York State granted women equal property rights with men.**

APRIL

1917 THE FARMER'S CALENDAR

CONSERVATISM AND REFORM

Faith goes ahead to the new Fear, with eyes behind holds on to the new.

WASHINGTON, D. C., April 1917—

On July 20, Lottery Day will be initiated. Secretary of War Newton Baker will reach into a large glass bowl and draw the lottery number of the first man to be called up in the draft. It will require 16 hours to withdraw the 10,500 capsules with their numbered slips to determine the order of the draft.

APRIL hath 30 days. [1917

Sighing, storming, singing, smiling,
With her many moods beguiling,
April walks the wakening earth;
Wheresoe'er she looks and lingers,
Wheresoe'er she lays her fingers,
Some new charm starts into birth.

JOHN CRITCHLEY PRINCE.

D. M.	D. W.	Aspects, Holidays, Heights of High Water, Etc.
1	C	Palm Sunday. ☌ ♆ ☾. {8.5 7.7
2	M.	☾ in Apo. Tides {8.5 8.0 *Showers,*
3	Tu.	Tides {8.7 8.3 *perhaps*
4	W.	Tides {8.8 8.7 *with flurries of*
5	Th.	☿ in ☊. ☾ on Eq. {9.0 9.1 *snow.*
6	Fr.	Good Friday. Tides {9.2 9.5
7	Sa.	Tides {9.2 9.8
8	C	Easter Sun. {9.2 — *Southerly,*
9	M.	Tides {9.9 9.2 *followed by*
10	Tu.	☿ in Peri. {10.0 9.1 *northerly winds.*
11	W.	Tides {10.0 8.9
12	Th.	☾ runs low. ♆ stat. Tides {10.0 8.7
13	Fr.	Tides {9.8 8.6 *Some northerly*
14	Sa.	□ ♄ ☉. Tides {9.7 8.5 *to easterly*
15	C	Low Sunday. Tides {9.6 8.7
16	M.	☌ ☿ ♃. ☌ ♅ ☾. Tides {9.6 9.1
17	Tu.	☾ in Perigee. {9.7 9.6 *winds.*
18	W.	☾ on Eq. Tides {9.9 10.2
19	Th.	PATRIOTS' DAY. Tides {10.1 10.7
20	Fr.	☿ gr. hel. lat. N. ☌ ♂ ☾. {10.3 11.1
21	Sa.	☌ ♀ ☾. {10.3 11.2 22d. □ ♆ ☉. *Dull,*
22	C	2d S. af. Easter. {10.2 — ☌ ♃ ☾.
23	M.	St. George. {11.1 9.9 22d. ☌ ☿ ☾.
24	Tu.	☾ runs high. ☿ gr. elong. E. {10.9 9.5 *possibly*
25	W.	St. Mark. Tides {10.5 9.1 *rain.*
26	Th.	☌ ♀ ☉ superior. Tides {10.0 8.7
27	Fr.	☌ ♄ ☾. Tides {9.5 8.3
28	Sa.	☌ ♆ ☾. Tides {9.0 8.0 *Spring-like*
29	C	3d Su. af. Easter. ☾ in Apo. {8.7 8.0
30	M.	Tides {8.5 8.1 *weather.*

Farmer's Calendar.

While the demand for small and medium sized driving horses for individual or family use has fallen off of late years, that for large sized draft horses has notably increased. Percherons, Clydesdales and others of the stocks of pure breed, whether imported or bred in America, bring, of course, very high prices. But large and powerful animals, the offspring of such stocks by crossing with native graded stocks, may be bought at much lower figures. Such animals are markedly docile. They are admirably adapted for the heavy work on the farm; and for that reason and because they are equally fitted to do heavy teaming in the cities they are easily saleable if the owner should desire to dispose of them.

How about the taxes in your town? Do you have a high rate on a low valuation, or a low rate on a high valuation, or a high rate on a high valuation? And do you happen to know of any city or town where they have a low rate on a low valuation? Is your house and lot assessed on a valuation a third or a half higher than you can sell it for? If so the assessors ought to cut down valuations and raise the rate. Even with high rates and high valuations cities and towns are too often borrowing money to pay for things that ought to be paid for out of current taxes.

MAY, fifth Month.   1821.

Hark! how Aurora's gentle morn,
Is hail'd with joy from ev'ry bough;
Among the trees beside the lawn,
Are heard the feather'd songsters now.

BE PATIENT
"Reckon not your chickens
before they are hatched."

M.D.	W.D.	Courts, Aspects, Holidays, Weather, &c.	FARMER'S CALENDAR.
1	3	S.J.C. North'p. High *High*	"Reckon not your chickens before they are hatched"—that is to say, be not too hasty about the enjoyment of those things which are still afar off. Wait patiently until your watermelon is ripe before you eat it. But stop! we have not planted it yet perhaps—spur up, spur up, boys! the garden must not be neglected. Three hundred and twelve years ago, the art of gardening was introduced into England; prior to which, garden produce was imported from the Netherlands. Beets, carrots, turnips, &c. common table vegetables, were imported into a country, which industry has since made one of the most fertile soils. Plough in your dung as soon as you have spread it—recollect that manure pays great interest—lime is a very excellent material for compost manure. It destroys worms as well as gives strength and body. Your early peas and beans are planted, and you must stir the ground about them. Now turn out your early calves to grass. Do not forget to give your cattle salt when they first go to grass. It is a fine month for business, and we must be as engaged as a hen and her chickens.
2	4	Gen. Elect. N Haven. tides.	
3	5	Inven. Cross. *wind and*	
4	6	Gen. El. Newp. *much rain.*	
5	7	*Quite*	
6	G	2d Sun. past Eas. *warm*	
7	2	7*s set 8h. *for the season.*	
8	3	S.J.C. Springf.& Barn. C.S.	
9	4	Low tides. *Cool* [Conc.	
10	5	*nights,*	
11	6	*but very fine*	
12	7	*days.*	
13	G	3d Sun. past Eas. ☽ apog.	
14	2	C. P. Nant. *Signs*	
15	3	S.J.C. Lenox & Plym. *of*	
16	4	*showers,*	
17	5	Gr. frost 1794. *with*	
18	6	*thunder.*	
19	7	Dark day, 1780. *Cooler*	
20	G	4th Sun. past Eas. *with*	
21	2	C. P. Edgar. *much wind.*	
22	3	*Becomes*	
23	4	C. S. Edgar. *fine* ☌ ☉ ♀	
24	5	7*s rise 4h. mor. *again.*	
25	6	*More*	
26	7	High *showers if*	
27	G	5th S. past Eas. R. S. ☽ per.	
28	2	tides. *not a storm.*	
29	3	*Grows fine*	
30	4	Ascen. D. Gen Elec. Bost.	
31	5	*again.* ☾ ☌ ☉ ☿	

MAY

1882
THE FARMER'S CALENDAR

MAN'S BRAIN
What is the use of a brain if we're not to use it?
An ox can pull as well as a man, but he can't think as much.

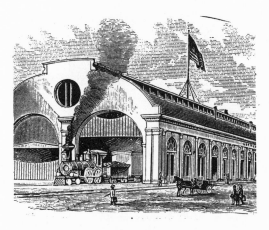

CHINESE EXCLUDED
May 6, 1882: The Chinese Exclusion Act was passed by Congress, suspend-entry into the United States of all Chinese laborers for a period of 10 years.

MAY hath 31 days.   1882.

Though I own up I like our back'ard springs
Thet kind o' haggle with their greens and things.
An' when you 'most give up, 'ithout more words
Toss the fields full o' blossoms, leaves an' birds;
Thet's Northern natur', slow, an' apt to doubt.
But when it *does* git stirred, there's no gin out!
J. R. LOWELL.

D. M.	D. W.	Aspects, Holidays, Events, Weather, &c.	Farmer's Calendar.
1	Mo.	St. Philip and St. James.	DON'T try to till too much land. Better stick to what you can do well. It is of no use to spread time and labor and manure too thin. Concentration is wiser than expansion, just as union is strength. It is the quality of work that tells in the end, just as brain work tells better than muscle. What is the use of a brain if we're not to use it? An ox can pull as well as a man, but he can't think as much. Let each one do what he can do best. To plough, to plant, to hoe, is the work which lies before us now. Make the most of the seed time. We ought to raise more seed, and not pay so much for what we know so little of. Corn sown in drills for use in its green state, can go in near the end of the month, the more of it the better. It is a great help when the grass dries up. We used to wait till the grass was well grown to turn the cows out, but it is a good plan to give them an early bite two or three hours a day. It is good for the cows, and doesn't hurt the grass. Don't forget to sow a good lot of mangold seed before the middle of the month. Some prefer the sugar beet. Either one of them is better than none.
2	Tu.	☿ in ♉. ♂ ☿ ☉ sup.	
3	W.	*Hot*	
4	Th.	♂ ☿ ♄, ♂ ☿ ♆, ♂ in Aph.	
5	Fr.	☾ r. low, ♂ ☿ ♃. High tid.	
6	Sa.	♂ ♄☉, ♂ ♆☉. 5th. Napoleon died 1821.	
7	A	4th Su. af. E. ☿ in Perih.	
8	Mo.	*for the season.*	
9	Tu.	Schiller died, 1805	
10	W.	Length of night 9h. 34m.	
11	Th.	♂ ♄♆. Low tides.	
12	Fr.	☾ in Perigee.	
13	Sa.	♂ ☿ ♃. *Fine.*	
14	A	Rogation Sunday.	
15	Mo.	16th. Conkling & Platt, U. S. senators from N.Y. resign their seats, 1881.	
16	Tu.	♂ ♆☾, ♂ ♄ ☾.	
17	W.	☉ eclipsed, inv. in Boston. ♂ ♃ ☾, ☿ Gr. Hel. lat N.	
18	Th.	Asc. Day. ☾ r.h. ♂ ☿ ☿, ♂ ♀ ☾.	
19	Fr.	Dark day, 1780. Very h. tides.	
20	Sa.	U. S. senate adjourned, 1881.	
21	A	Sun. aft. Asc. ☿ stationary.	
22	Mo.	♂ ♂ ☾. Intrigue in the army to make Washington king. He severely rebukes the proposal, 1782.	
23	Tu.		
24	W.	Queen Victoria born, 1819. *Cooler*	
25	Th.	☾ in Apogee, ♂ ☿ ☾.	
26	Fr.	25th. Very low tides. *with*	
27	Sa.	25th. R. W. Emerson born, 1803.	
28	A	Whit-Sunday. *rain.*	
29	Mo.	30th. R. I. legislature meets at Newport.	
30	Tu.	Decoration Day. ♀ in Perihelion.	
31	W.	30th. ♂ ♃☉, ♂ ☿ ♀.	

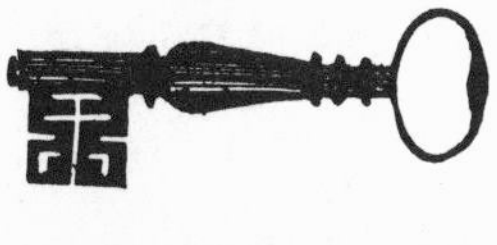

23

JUNE

1826 THE FARMER'S CALENDAR

JUNE, sixth Month. 1826.

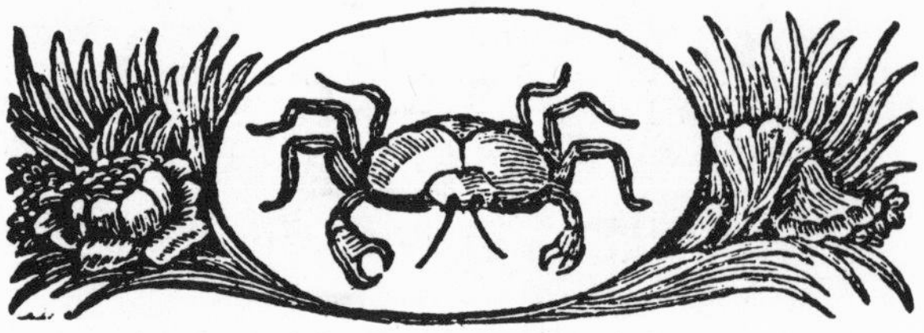

And now the sultry sun has made
His highest round : well fed
The panting flocks within the shade
Now find a cooling bed.

M. D.	W. D.	Courts, Aspects, Holidays, Weather, &c.
1	5	Nicom. *Very*
2	6	*warm.*
3	7	7*s rise 3h. 30m. ☽ apo.
4	A	2d Sun past Trin. *Some*
5	2	Art.El.Bos.Mid.☉ecl.inv.
6	3	tides. ☌ ☽ ♄
7	4	Gen.Elec.N.H. *showers*
8	5	Mahom. di. 1632. *this*
9	6	*time.*
10	7	*Pleasant for*
11	A	3d S. past T. St. B. *the*
12	2	C.P. Con. & Taun. *season.*
13	3	*Cooler with*
14	4	*frequent*
15	5	7*s rise 2h. 30m. *dashes.*
16	6	Gr.Ecl.'06. ☌ ☽ ♂ ☽ perig.
17	7	Bat.B.Hill'75.St.A. ☌ ☉ ♄
18	A	4th Sun. past T. *Fine*
19	2	C. P. Salem & Wor. Tides
20	3	decreasing. *settled*
21	4	*weather*
22	5	*for some days.*
23	6	7*s rise 2h.
24	7	Nativ. St. John B. ☌ ☉ ☿
25	A	5th Sun. past T. *Now*
26	2	S. J. C. Nant. C. P. Len.
27	3	*look out*
28	4	*for a*
29	5	St. Peter. Low *storm.*
30	6	tides. ☽ apo.

FARMER'S CALENDAR.

The Dairy.

One day last June I visited the dairy room of my cousin *Susan.* It was a part of the cellar of the dwelling house, and a neater place mortal man never set eyes on. It was well ceiled with plaister to prevent the dirt's descending. The top and sides were white-washed, to increase the light, and not a hole or chink could be seen for insects to harbor in. The floor was of stones, and she told me that she often washed it in summer with the coldest water, to keep the air cool and sweet as possible. On the northern side were two windows, and on the western, one, which could be opened and shut at pleasure. In a corner was a little stove, where she sometimes in winter burned a few coals to keep the room of an equal coolness. So her milk never grows sour in hot weather, and never freezes in cold ; of course there is no obstruction to the rising of all the cream. She has a little thermometer in the room, and endeavours to keep the air at about 50 or 55 degrees. The moment a spider spins his web there, it is death.

THE DAIRY ROOM

The moment a spider spins his web there, it is death.

1826—

THE GOLDEN ANNIVERSARY

Three of the original signers of the Declaration of Independence were alive when the year began. On July 4th, 50 years to the day, Thomas Jefferson died, and a few hours later former President John Adams died in Quincy, Mass. Now, only Charles Carroll was still alive.

JUNE

1837
THE
FARMER'S
CALENDAR

THE TWIG
"Just as the twig is bent,
The tree's inclined."
—Alexander Pope

WAR IS MURDER
Ez fer war, I call it murder,
There you have it, plain an'
flat;
I don't want to go no furder,
Than my Testyment fer that.

—James Russell Lowell
in his *Bigelow papers*, 1837

JUNE hath 30 days.　　　1837.

What can cheer the saddened heart,
If the summer season fail?
When the zephyrs play their part,
In the gentle evening gale.

M. D.	W. D.	Courts, Aspects, Holidays, Weather, &c.
1	5	Nicom.　　*Dull,*
2	6	*with*
3	7	*some* ☌ ☽ ♀ & ☿
4	A	2d Sun. p. Trin.　*rain.*
5	2	C. P. Nant. Bon.　*Quite*
6	3	C. C. North.　　*fine*
7	4	Gen.El.N.H.　*for* ☌ ☽ ♃
8	5	Low *some days.*　☽ Ap.
9	6	*Changeable*
10	7	7*s ri. 3h. tides.　*with*
11	A	3d Sun. p. Trin.　*some*
12	2	C. P. Com. & New Bed.
13	3	C. C. Greenf.　*rain.*
14	4	*More fine*
15	5	*weather*　☌ ☽ ♄
16	6	Gr.sol.Ec.'06. *for some*
17	7	St. Alb. Bat. B. H. '75.
18	A	4th Sun. p. Trin.　*days.*
19	2	C.P.Salem,Wor.& Sp'g.
20	3	C.C.Wor.& Ded. ☽ Per.
21	4	Quite high　*Great*
22	5	tides.　*heat, with*
23	6	7*s rise 1h. 50m. ☌ ☽ ♅
24	7	Nat. J. Bapt. *signs of*
25	A	5th Sun. p. Trin. *rain.*
26	2	C.P.Lenox.Geo.IV.d.'30
27	3	C.C.Springf. *Very fine*
28	4	Pr.Madison d. '36. ag.86.
29	5	St. Peter. St. Paul. *to the*
30	6	*end of the month.* ☌ ☽ ☿

FARMER'S CALENDAR.

JUNE, 1837.

"Just as the twig is bent, the tree's inclined," said Pope. But, as respects our children, we are too apt to neglect this business, having more regard for our own feelings than for their welfare. If, in bending the twig, it happens to squeak a little, it puts us all aback in our management of the tender sapling. "Poor, sweet, darling branch," cry the fond and doting parents; "it shall not be cruelly twisted and wrenched from its natural course." So that, just as this twig is inclined, thus it is suffered to grow, until, at length, it becomes an ill-shapen, crabbed, useless tree. Now, to speak without a figure, it becomes us, brother plough-joggers, to bring up our boys and girls in such way and manner, as shall make them useful to us in their minority, and afterwards respectable and beneficial to the community,—to instruct them in business as well as in amusement. Your son may be disposed to act the dandy, imagining it dishonorable to be seen holding the plough, or wielding the woodman's axe; your daughter may think to put upon her mother all the business of the kitchen, while she idles away the hours in gadding, or vainly thrumming the piano-forte, merely for fashion's sake;—but, by all means, look to this matter, and endeavor that your children's education shall not be neglected.

1875
THE
FARMER'S
CALENDAR

BEATING THE WEATHER
**The true way to go through the
  hot weather
Is to keep the mind so occupied,
That we shall not notice,
The condition of the atmosphere.**

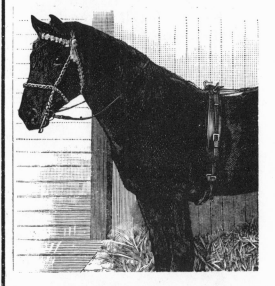

CHURCHILL DOWNS
After purchasing a parcel of land in Kentucky from the Churchill brothers, Colonel M. Lewis Clark, of Louisville, initiated the first Kentucky Derby. In the first race, there were 15 entries, and a purse of $2,850.

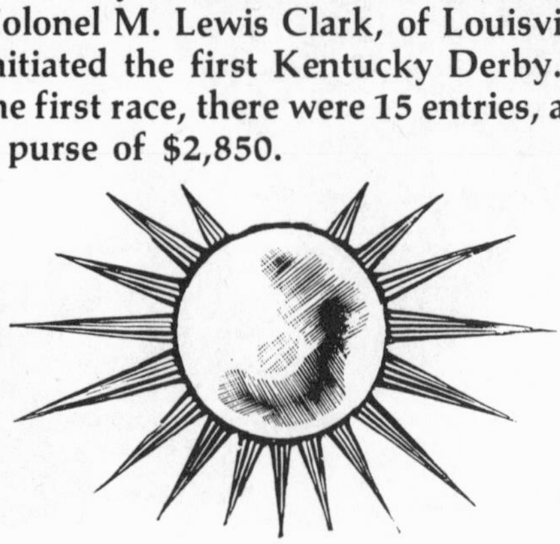

| | | JULY hath 31 days. | 1875. |

Lord, let War's tempest cease,
Fold the whole earth in peace
Under Thy wings!
Make all Thy nations one,
All hearts beneath the sun,
Till Thou shalt reign alone,
Great King of kings. — O. W. HOLMES.

D. M.	D. W.	Aspects, Holidays, Events, Weather, &c.	Farmer's Calendar.
1	Th.	☌♀☾. ☾ in Perigee.	THE true way to go through
2	Fr.	☾ru. hi. L. of ni. 8h. 49m.	the hot weather is to keep the
3	Sa.	V. hi. ti. ☉in Apo. ☌☿☾.	mind so occupied that we shall
4	C	6th Su. af. Tr. { INDEPENDENCE declared, 1776.	not notice the condition of the atmosphere. We may be up
5	Mo.	☌♅☾. Showery.	early and down late now, fill up
6	Tu.	☌☿☉ inferior.	the time with some thought or
7	W.	{ 2d. Washington takes command of the army investing Boston, 1775.	some plan, and still find plenty to do. The grasses are fit to
8	Th.	Sultry weather.	cut, but with the control over the
9	Fr.	Braddock's defeat, 1755.	haying which we now have in the
10	Sa.	☌♃☾. Thunder	use of the mowing machine, the
11	C	7th Sunday after Trinity.	tedder, the horse-rake, and the
12	Mo.	Very low tides.	horse-fork, we can still get time
13	Tu.	☾ in Apogee. showers.	to keep down the weeds in the
14	W.	{ 13th. Dogma of Papal Infal. adop. by the Œcumenical Council at Rome, 1870.	garden. No need to wait for the dew to dry off, to kill weeds in
15	Th.	St. Swithin. □♃☉. ☌♂☾.	the garden, and an hour before
16	Fr.	☾ runs low.	breakfast will take less snap out
17	Sa.	{ Middle of July to end of August good time to bud fruit trees.	of the body than a wide swath in the field, at this time of day.
18	C	8th Sunday after Trinity.	So, Up, boys, and at them! Have
19	Mo.	Good weather for	a fixed time for milking, and al-
20	Tu.	St. Margaret. ☌☿♀. ☌♄☾.	ways milk the cows in their reg-
21	W.	20th. High tides. ♀ in ☋.	ular order. The earlier they go
22	Th.	St. Mary Magdalene. the	out to pasture in the-morning the
23	Fr.	growing crops.	better. They want to fill them-
24	Sa.	Low tides. { 5th. DOG DAYS BEGIN.	selves and lie down in the shade in the middle of the day. When
25	C	9th S. af. C. St. James. ☌♀☾.	the pastures dry up, cut a little
26	Mo.	St. Anne. □♆☉.	of that green fodder-corn, once
27	Tu.	{ 26th. Terrible thunder-storm at Pitts-burg, Pa., causing a sudden freshet,	or twice a day, and feed it out in the barn. Hungarian grass is
28	W.	{ which destroyed near 200 lives and a great amount of property, 1874.	still better for milk than green corn, and a feeding of that every
29	Th.	☾in Per. ☾ runs high.	day will bridge over any common
30	Fr.	☌☿☾. Signs of	drought, keep up the flow of milk,
31	Sa.	☌♀☾. a storm.	and save the pastures.

JULY

1912 THE FARMER'S CALENDAR

LAST CHANCE

Last chance
to plant
your sweet
corn!

THE SINKING OF THE TITANIC

Making its maiden voyage, the *Titanic* struck an iceberg as it crossed the Atlantic and sank, carrying 1,500 people to a watery grave. Many prominent Americans lost their lives in the disaster.

JULY hath 31 days.   [1912

Hot July thereafter rages,
   Dog-star smitten, wild with heat;
Fierce as pard the hunter cages,—
Hot July thereafter rages.
Traffic now no more engages;
   Tongues are still in stall and street.

AUSTIN DOBSON.

D.M.	D.W.	Aspects, Holidays, Events, Weather, Etc.	Farmer's Calendar.
1	M.	☾ in Apogee. ☌ ♅ ☾.	This is the month of the national holiday. As a small part of its sane observance during its earliest days make your last planting of sweet corn, provided you do not live further north than central Massachusetts. True, frosts may harvest the crop, but there is much more than an even chance that you will be rewarded for your labor; and that most delicious of vegetables never tastes quite so delicious as in those bracing days which come in mid autumn.
2	Tu.	*Very warm and favorable*	
3	W.	4th. ⊕ in Aphelion. *for*	
4	Th.	INDEPENDENCE DAY. *showers.*	
5	Fr.	☿ ♀ ☉ superior. Low tides.	
6	Sa.	{4th. Temp. 103.5°. Highest W. B. record, 1911. *Cooler.*	
7	F	5th Sunday after Trinity.	
8	M.	*Sultry with*	
9	Tu.	*southerly winds.*	Alfalfa is now attracting the attention of many farmers who formerly believed it to be impossible to produce it. If you have not tried it this is a good month to begin the experiment. Select well drained loam and a field with sloping surface so that water will never stand upon it. After plowing, lime heavily, stock the soil abundantly with phosphoric acid and potash, work it repeatedly at intervals of a few days until you bring it into perfect tilth and about the end of this month sow the seed, which should be inoculated with a culture to supply the needed bacteria. Afalfa would be a valuable addition to New England's agricultural assets.
10	W.	☌ ♄ ☾. {10th. French army lands at Newport, R. I., 1780.	
11	Th.	Medium tides. *Pleasant*	
12	Fr.	13th. ☾ runs high. *breezes.*	
13	Sa.	☌ ♀ ♆. 14th. ☾ n Perigee.	
14	F	6th Sunday after Trinity.	
15	M.	St. Swithin. 14th. ☌ ♆ ☾. ☌ ♀ ☾.	
16	Tu.	☌ ☿ ☾. ☌ ♀ ☉. ☌ ☿ ☾.	
17	W.	*Signs of wet weather.*	
18	Th.	High tides.	
19	Fr.	☿ in ♊. {21st. Battle of Pyramids, Egypt, 1798.	
20	Sa.	St. Margaret. *Expect a few*	
21	F	7th Sunday after Trinity.	
22	M.	St. Mary Magdalene. ♀ in Perihelion.	
23	Tu.	25th. ☾ runs low. *hot days.*	
24	W.	♀ ♃ ☾. ☍ ♅ ☉.	Sweet Clover also is worth a trial, especially if you are a bee keeper, or if you have light soils poor in humus which need improvement. It demands conditions very similar to those for Alfalfa.
25	Th.	St. James. ☿ gr. elong. E.	
26	Fr.	St. Anne. 25th. DOG DAYS BEGIN.	
27	Sa.	Low tides. 28th. ☾ in Apogee.	
28	F	8th Sunday after Trinity.	
29	M.	☿ in Aphelion. 28th. ☌ ♅ ☾.	
30	Tu.	*Conditions favorable*	
31	W.	*for showers.*	

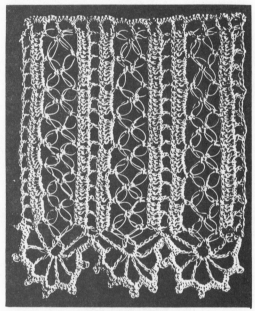

1842
THE
FARMER'S
CALENDAR

AUGUST hath 31 days. 1842.

Blossoms to fruit are ripening fast,
And fields, so lately green,
Assume a rich and yellow cast,
And golden ears are seen.
Thus Heaven bestows, with liberal hand,
All that our needful wants demand.

M. D.	W. D.	Courts, Aspects, Holidays, Weather, &c.	Farmer's Calendar.
1	2	Lam. D. *Cooler, with*	The farmer of *Uz* had three none-
2	3	C. C. Ply. *rough* Mid.	so-fair daughters, and we may pre-
3	4	Com. V. Uni. *winds.*	sume that they were brought up in
4	5	Com. Wash. Col. tides.	the good old way, honoring and re-
5	6	7*sr.11h. *Great* ☾ ☽ ☿	specting their father and mother;
6	☽	Tran'f. *heat, with*	for they were reckoned among the
7	B.	11th S. p. T. *thu'r.* ☽ P.	singular blessings of his latter days
8	2	C. P. Gr'f. & Ply. High	of prosperity. They were obedient
9	3	*Fine* tides. ☾ ☽ ♀	and obliging to their parents; and,
10	4	St. Law. *again for*	notwithstanding their distinguished
11	5	*several*	beauty and comeliness, they, doubt-
12	6	Com. Mid. *days.*	less, performed the part of farmers'
13	7	*Much* Low	daughters, without a murmur or
14	B.	12th Sun. p. T. *rain*	excuse, and gave a helping hand to
15	2	C. P. North. *in* tides.	their good mother about the affairs
16	3	*many places.* ☾ ☽ ♄	of the household. *Jemima* took her
17	4	Com. Wm. & Yale C.	turn one week; *Kezia* the next; and,
18	5	*Cooler,* [☾ ☽ ♃	lastly, the interesting *Kerenhappuch.*
19	6	*with high*	Thus everything went on in that
20	7	*winds.* Mid.	beautiful order and cheerfulness, as
21	B.	13th Sun. p. T.	ought to be done in all families.
22	2	*Some rain.* ☽ Apo.	These fair damsels not only sung,
23	3	Dr. Her. d. 1822. tides.	*Polly, put the kettle on,* but were not
24	4	St. Barth. *Signs of*	ashamed to put it in practice with
25	5	Com. Cam. Col. *frost.*	their own hands. Whenever they
26	6	7*s rise 9h. 36m.	chanted *Sweet Home,* their feelings
27	7	*Fine if* Very	always responded to the charming
28	B.	14th Sun. p. T. *not*	sentiment. We believe they were
29	2	C. P. Wor. *dry.* low	no "gadders abroad;" but were
30	3	*High* tides.	disposed to qualify themselves to
31	4	*winds at North West.*	make good farmers' wives, the best of wives, and such as the hearts of their husbands can safely trust, and fear no spoil.

Now, it has been said, that if a farmer, or any man, intends to go ahead in his business, he must first ask his wife's consent.

NEW HATS AND CAPOTES.

THE FARMER OF UZ
His and None-So-Fair
Daughters: Jemima Kezia and
Kerenhappuch

GREEN MOUNTAIN KNOT LACE.

WIFE'S CONSENT
If a farmer, or any man, intends to go ahead in his business, he must first ask his wife's consent.

AUGUST

1901 THE FARMER'S CALENDAR

ASSASSINATION

Leon Czolgosz, American-born anarchist, stalks the streets of Buffalo, N.Y., planning the assassination of President William McKinley. On September 6, 1901 he shoots the President, who dies one week later at the age of 58. Theodore Roosevelt, the 26th President, succeeds McKinley.

AUGUST hath 31 days. [1901

I see thee later by the still sea-strand,
Summer's last poppy reddening in thy hand,
And sunset's royal mystery, grand and fair,
Meshed in the glory of thy Titian hair!

PAUL HAMILTON HAYNE.

D. M.	D. W.	Aspects, Holidays, Events, Weather, Etc.	Farmer's Calendar.
1	Th.	Lammas Day.	It is a good plan, on very warm days, to go out to work early in the morning, and rest during the hottest part of the day, and work a little later at night, if necessary, to make up the time. If the weather is not too dry, this month is a good time to set a strawberry bed for another year. If you do not wish to raise strawberries for market, have a small bed for your own use; or if you have not time for this, why not give one of your boys the use of a small piece of land for a strawberry bed? Break up the land for him in the first place, then let him have the profit of the berries providing he does the rest of the work himself. Or perhaps he may prefer to cultivate some other small fruit, such as raspberries or blackberries, or even vegetables. Get him interested in the work, and he will not be as likely to leave the farm and go to the city, thinking to find a more congenial occupation. Make the home as pleasant as possible for the boys and girls by taking a kindly interest in everything which tends to the cultivation of their abilities, and the elevation of their characters. Do not allow decayed wood or vegetables to remain in the cellar, nor around the dwelling, which will give offensive odors.
2	Fr.	☿ gr. elong W.	
3	Sa.	High tides. *Southerly*	
4	F	9th Sun. af. Trin. *winds and*	
5	M.	{5th. Rev. A. J. Healy, R. C. Bishop, Me., d., 1900, aged 60. *sultry.*	
6	Tu.	Transfiguration. ☾ Per. ♂ in ♉.	
7	W.	{5th. Gen. J. D. Cox, ex-Secy. Int. d. 1900, aged 62. *Cooler*	
8	Th.	*and fine.*	
9	Fr.	☿ in ♌. ☾ runs high.	
10	Sa.	St. Lawrence. ☌ ♆ ☾.	
11	F	10th Su. after Trin. *Some*	
12	M.	Medium tides. *rain.*	
13	Tu.	☌ ☿ ☾.	
14	W.	☿ in Perihelion	
15	Th.	Assump. of V. Mary. {15th. Pekin, China cap. by allies,1900.	
16	Fr.	☌ ♀ ☾.	
17	Sa.	16th. Battle of Bennington, 1777.	
18	F	11th Su. after Trin. *Sultry*	
19	M.	☌ ♂ ☾. {16th. Ex.U.S. Senator J. J. Ingalls, d. 1900, aged 67.	
20	Tu.	☾ in Apogee. *and showers.*	
21	W.	{23d. Increase Mather died, 1723.	
22	Th.	♅ stationary. Low tides.	
23	Fr.	☌ ♅ ☾. ☾ runs low. *Cooler*	
24	Sa.	St. Bart. ☿ gr.hel.lat.N. ☌ ♃ ☾.	
25	F	12th Su. aft. Trin. ☌ ♄ ☾.	
26	M.	*and showery.*	
27	Tu.	☌ ☿ ☉ superior.	
28	W.	St. Augustine.	
29	Th.	Beheading of St. John Baptist.	
30	Fr.	♃ stationary. High tides.	
31	Sa.	{31st. John Bunyan died, 1688.	

SEPTEMBER hath 30 days.   1844.

Fixed laws control all matter and all mind;
If violated, evil must ensue;
But if obeyed, their virtue we shall find
To make life pleasant, and its ills subdue.

D. M.	D. W.	Courts, Aspects, Holidays, Weather, &c.	Farmer's Calendar.
1	F.	13th S. p. T. *Fine.*	*You cannot do better for your son, than to fit him for an employment.*
2	2	C. P. Low. & Worc.	Farmers' sons, now-a-days, are too
3	3	S. J. C. Spr. C. P. Bar. C. C. Len. Con. Gr'f. Nor. ☽ ap.	apt to imagine that their fathers' oc-
4	4	Com. Brown U. and Bowdoin Col. 7✱s r. 9h.	cupation is not befitting them. Much has been said on this subject in agri-
5	5	Dog. d. end. Low	cultural papers and public addresses;
6	6	*Changeable, with*	and there should be no ceasing to ad-
7	7	*rain.* tides.	monish silly fathers and addle-pated
8	F.	14th S. p. T. ☌ ☽ ♀	boys, about the folly and inconsis-
9	2	C. P. Tau. *Some frost.*	tency of the notions they have. Stick
10	3	S. J. C. L. Len. S. J. C. Gr'f. C. C. Worc.	him into a store, that he may learn trade; that is, that he may learn
11	4	*Unsettled* ☌ ☽ ♂	idleness, swaggering, profanity, and
12	5	*for some*	how to trim his whiskers, which are
13	6	*days.*	now just beginning to show their
14	7	Moscow bur. 1812.	brush beneath his little ears! Yes, stick him into a store, that he may
15	F.	15th S. p. T. High	measure tape, sell fish-hooks, dress
16	2	C. P. Ne'p. & Ded. ☽ per.	in buckram, and so be a *gentleman!*
17	3	Lamb. *More*	My conscience! where's the honor, compared to that of being a farmer,—
18	4	tides.	a man of muck, and a man of mind?
19	5	*rain is near.*	How pert and saucy one of these
20	6	*Much finer.*	shallow boobies will become, after
21	7	St. Matt. ☍ ☉ ♃ ☌ ☽ ♄	having "lapped 'lasses" and meas-
22	F.	16th S. p. T. [P. Wor.	ured pigtail a week or two! A fid-
23	2	S. J. C. L. Nor. C. C.	dle-stick for such an *employment!*
24	3	C. C. Tau. Ded.	Give the boy a good trade, or instruct him in the art of husbandry. And,
25	4	7✱s so.3h.20m. ☌ ☽ ♃	as to the girls, teach them that "to
26	5	*Much dull* Mid	earn their own living by laboring
27	6	♉ d. L. sou. 3h. 20m.	with their own hands, is to be reck-
28	7	tides. *weather.*	oned among female accomplish-
29	F.	17th S. p. T.	ments." A young man of spirit will be ashamed to live without an
0	2	C. P. Edg.	object.

Every vain person hath his weak side, whereby he exposes himself.

THE POLITICAL CRY OF 1844

"Fifty-four Forty or Fight" was the political slogan of candidate for the presidency James K. Polk, who took office on March 4, 1845. Polk and his supporters wanted the western territory which was held by England, Russia and Spain. Russia agreed to stay north of the 54°40' parallel—hence the slogan.

1844 THE FARMER'S CALENDAR

PREPARING CHILDREN FOR GOOD LIVING

". . . Give the boy a good trade, or instruct him in the art of husbandry."

". . . And as to girls, teach them to earn their own living by laboring with their hands."

SEPTEMBER

1855
THE FARMER'S CALENDAR

DEGENERACY

". . . a man must watch his coat hanging up in his own entry to have it safe against pilferers. Alas for the degeneracy of the times."

ALL . . . EXCEPT

Our progress in degeneracy appears to me to be pretty rapid. As a nation, we began by declaring that "all men are created equal." We now practically read it "all men are created equal except Negroes." When the Know-Nothings get control, it will read "all men are created equal except Negroes and foreigners and Catholics." When it comes to this I should prefer emigrating to some country where they make no pretense of loving liberty—to Russia, for instance, where despotism can be taken pure and without the base alloy of hypocrisy.

—Abraham Lincoln

SEPTEMBER hath 30 days.   1855.

Who but a Deity divine,
Whose kindness all His works declare,
Could make the seasons all combine
To scatter blessings everywhere?

D. M.	D. W.	Courts, Aspects, Holidays, Weather, &c.	Farmer's Calendar.
1	Sa.	2nd. New Style adopted, 1752. *Very*	*Ride and Tie.*
2	G.	13th Su. af. Tri. *pleasant.*	This was a clever, economical mode of journeying in good old times, when we could boast of rigid honesty among men. It was done after this wise. If John and James, two young farmers, both wanted to go to Boston at the same time—having but one horse between them, and neither chaise nor buggy, John would first mount the saddle and ride on, while James set off on foot. Having rode a few miles, John made fast the bridle to a post or tree, and then became the pedestrian in his turn. James coming up, took his turn to ride a bit, and in this way of *ride* and *tie* they effected their journey with ease and safety. Dobbin stood perfectly safe and secure with the saddle-bags across him, holding the cold junk and bread and cheese on one side, and a stone to balance on the other. Such a thing as thieving was not thought of, any more than in the famous good moral reign of the excellent King Alfred of England. Say, my friend, how would such a project answer now, when a man must watch his coat hanging up in his own entry, to have it safe against pilferers? Alas, for the degeneracy of the times!
3	Mo.	C. C. P. Wor. & Lowell. Low *Warm*	
4	Tu.	S.J.C.Sp'gf. C.C.P. Barn. C.C. G'nf., N'tham. & Con. C.C. Len. ☋ru. ☽hi.	
5	W.	Dog Days {4th. St. elec. end. {Vermont, '55. *tides.*	
6	Th.	5th. J. P. Norton, Prof. Ag'l Chem. in Yale Coll., d. 1852. *and*	
7	Fr.	♂ ☌ ☽ *rainy.*	
8	Sa.	♀ sta. *Unsettled for some*	
9	G.	☽ in ap. 14th Su. af. Trin.	
10	Mo.	C. C. P. {St. elec. Taun. {Maine. High *days.*	
11	Tu.	S. J. C. L. Len. S. J. C. Greenf. C. C. Worces. ♃ south 10h. 29m. eve.	
12	W.	Battle of Chapultepec, 1847. *tides.*	
13	Th.	♀ ☌ ☽ *Finer.*	
14	Fr.	Duke of Wellington died, a. 83, 1852.	
15	Sa.	Mid. *Frost in low*	
16	G.	15th Sun. af. Trin. *tides.*	
17	Mo.	C. C. P. New- {Cornwallis bury p't & Ded. {sur., 1781. *lands.*	
18	Tu.	*Becomes very*	
19	W.	☽ runs low. Very *fine.*	
20	Th.	19th. Prof. And. Norton, of H. Uni. d. 1853. *low tides.*	
21	Fr.	St. Matthew. *Uncommon-*	
22	Sa.	Autumn {23rd. Da. & ni. com. {nearly equal. *ly fine*	
23	G.	16th Sun. af. Trin. ☉ en. ♎ 10h. 16m. *for*	
24	Mo.	S. J. C. L. N'tham. C.C.P. Edgart'n. C.C.P.Cri. Wor. ☽ in p.	
25	Tu.	C. C. Taunton & Dedham. *the season.*	
26	W.	7*s ri. 7h. 52m. e. High	
27	Th.	*tides.* A storm is	
28	Fr.	*approaching.*	
29	Sa.	St. Michael, or Michaelmas Day. *High winds.*	
30	G.	17th Sun. af. Trin. ♀ in inf. ☌ ☉	

31

1807
THE
FARMER'S
CALENDAR

OCTOBER, tenth Month.   1807.

Sweet's the noise of busy labour;
Sweet the lowing o'er the farm;
Sweet the sound of pipe and tabour—
Every season has its charm.

M. D.	W. D.	Courts, Aspects, Holidays, Weather, &c.	FARMER'S CALENDAR.
1	5	Remig. *Clouds with*	*A begger's wallet is a mile to*
2	6	High tides *some rain.*	the bottom. No matter for that,
3	7	Gov. Adams died 1803 Æt 82	give him a trifle and you will get
4	D	19th Sun. past Trin. ☌ ☽ ♌	rid of him.
5	2	*Fine*	Every one should now be busy
6	3	S.J.C. Taun. C.P. Bos. & Nan.	in harvest; regardless of minor
7	4	*weather for some*	concerns. Gathering of corn
8	5	Go .Hanc. died 1793. *days.*	and potatoes will employ all
9	6	St. Denys. *Dull and*	hands.
10	7	Eagle's H. sou. 6h. 0m.	Plough your low and wet
11	D	20th Sun. past Trin. *hazy*	gardens into ridges. Husk your
12	2	*with thick air.*	corn betimes. I have thought
13	3	S.J.C. Plym. & Portl. C.S. Ips.	it cheaper to husk my own corn
14	4	Gen. Elect. Verm. ☽ Apog.	with my own hired men, than
15	5	Low tides ☌ ☉ ♀	to make a husking; for among
16	6	Queen France behead. 1793.	all the frolick, bustle and con-
17	7	Ethel. *Signs of*	fusion of a husking my corn gets
18	D	21st Sun. past Trin. *more*	mixed, crumbled and dirty;
19	2	Cornwallis taken 1781.	some husked, some half husk-
20	3	S.J.C. Barnstable. *rain.*	ed, and some not at all.
21	4	*Good weather for*	Haste makes waste, and waste
22	5	7*s sou. 1h. 44m. *the*	costs money, says cousin Tim.
23	6	Colum. disc. Amer. 1492.	Finish making cider. Gath-
24	7	*season.* ☌ ☉ ☿	er in your roots. Gather in
25	D	22d Sun. past Trin. Crisp.	your seeds, and take good care
26	2	*Becomes cooler.* □ ☉ ♃ [Tisb.	of them, that you need not have
27	3	S.J.C. Camb. & Alfred. C.P.	to beg of your neighbours next
28	4	St. Simon & St. Jude. ☽ Peri.	spring.
29	5	High tides. ☌ ☽ ♀	Heap up your summer dung,
30	6	President Adams born 1735.	or carry it into your fields and
31	7	*Changeable.*	grass lands.

Feed your turkeys if you mean to have them ready for thanksgiving.
Keep no more cats than what will catch mice.

THE WISDOM OF 1807
* A beggar's wallet is a mile to the bottom.
* Keep no more cats than what will catch mice.

Exchange Coffee House (built 1808; demolished 1853)
Congress Sq., Boston, Mass.

NEW YORK
The first crossing of the Hudson River was made by Robert Fulton in his steamboat *Clermont.* On a subsequent trip up the Hudson, Fulton made the trip from New York City to Albany in approximately 30 hours.

OCTOBER

1894
THE
FARMER'S
CALENDAR

A GREAT FARM MONTH

"While the wideawake farmer will manage to make many improvements every year during October, he will not neglect carefully to pick his winter fruit, and store it where it will be likely to keep well."

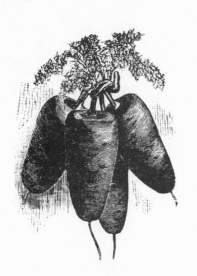

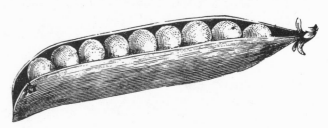

And far in heaven, the while,
The sun, that sends that gale to wander here,
Pours out on the fair earth his quiet smile—
The sweetest of the year.

D. M.	D. W.	Aspects, Holidays, Events, Weather, &c.	Farmer's Calendar.
1	Mo.	☿ in Aphel. *Pleasant,*	This is one of the best months in the year for making improvements on the farm. Clear the mowing fields of rocks, root out the bushes from under the fences and on the banks of the ditches, improve the farm roads, and build new ones where they are needed. It pays to have good roads from the public streets to the farm buildings, and from these to the cultivated portions of the land. Look the farm buildings over. If they need repairing or painting, now is the time to do it; don't wait until cold weather and short days, thus greatly increasing the cost. While the wideawake farmer will manage to make many improvements every year during October, he will not neglect carefully to pick his winter fruit, and store it where it will be likely to keep well; and he will watch his corn crop, and secure it when in the best condition to harvest. The pumpkins and squashes must not be left out to be injured by the frost, and the half-hardy shrubs around the dwelling must be looked after and protected before the weather becomes too cold. Both fruit and ornamental trees do well set this month. Set a few every year, whatever may be your age; some one will get the advantage of them if you do not. Fire-wood, if cut this month, is much better than if cut later in the season.
2	Tu.	High tides. *clear,*	
3	W.	Meeting of the legislature of Vermont.	
4	Th.	2d. Joseph Ernest Renan, French writer, died, aged 69, 1892.	
5	Fr.	☾ runs low. *and*	
6	Sa.	6th. Alfred Tennyson died, aged 83, 1892.	
7	G	20th Sunday after Trinity.	
8	Mo.	Low tides. 7th. ☾ in Apo.	
9	Tu.	St. Denis. ♀ gr. hel. lat. N.	
10	W.	10th. Celebration of the 400th anniv. of the discovery of America in New York City, 1892.	
11	Th.	*cool.*	
12	Fr.	Gen. Robert E. Lee died, 1870.	
13	Sa.	*Easterly winds.*	
14	G	21st Sun. aft. Tr. ☾ ☿ ♅.	
15	Mo.	☌ ♂ ☾. 16th. Marie Antoinette guillotined, 1793.	
16	Tu.	High tides. *Frosty*	
17	W.	Mercury vis. in the west.	
18	Th.	St. Luke, Evang. ☌ ♆ ☾.	
19	Fr.	☿ gr. el. E. ☾ runs high.	
20	Sa.	☌ ♃ ☾, ☍ ♂ ☉. *nights.*	
21	G	22d Sun. af. Tr. ☾ ♄ ☉.	
22	Mo.	☾ in Perig., ☿ gr. h. l. S.	
23	Tu.	25th. Mrs. Harrison, wife of the President, died, 1892.	
24	W.	♃ stat. Medium tides.	
25	Th.	St. Crispin. *A cold*	
26	Fr.	24th. Daniel Webster died, 1852.	
27	Sa.	☌ ♀ ☾. *rain.*	
28	G	23d Sun. a. Tr. St. Simon & St.	
29	Mo.	☌ ♅ ☾. 28th. ☌ ♄ ☾. [Jude.	
30	Tu.	☌ ☿ ☾, ☌ ♀ ♄, ☿ stat.	
31	W.	All-Hallows Eve.	

1820
THE
FARMER'S
CALENDAR

NOVEMBER, eleventh Month. 1820.

Again, o'er many a hill and plain,
Rich Ceres spreads her bounteous reign,
And waves her golden wand ;
To fill with joy the human heart,
And sweetest blessings to impart,
To man's ungrateful hand.
(Selected from J. Hawkins' Poems.)

M. D.	W. D.	Courts, Aspects, Holidays, Weather, &c.	FARMER'S CALENDAR.
1	4	All Saints. *Cool*	This is the last month of Au-
2	5	*but* ☽ apog.	tumn, and it is now the business
3	6	*pleasant.*	of the prudent man to be making
4	7	7*s sou. 0h. 52m. *A*	his calculations about winter mat-
5	A	23d Sund. past Trin. *cold*	ters. I have often mentioned the
6	2	C. P. Nant. Norr. & Edg.	importance of schooling to the ris-
7	3	S.J.C.Salem. *storm is near.*	ing generation. Few, if any coun-
8	4	*Pleasant*	tries, are blest like New-England,
9	5	*for the*	with public school establishments.
10	6	Middling tides. *season.*	No stinginess about the business.
11	7	*Cooler*	See that you have an able master,
12	A	24th Sund. past Trin. *with*	and pay him well. Here my neigh-
13	2	C. P. Greenf. *flakes*	bor Hugpurse and I can never
14	3	*of snow.* ☌ ☽ ♃	agree ; for he says, " So much of
15	4	New Stile com. 1752. ☽ per.	this here larnin is altogether useless
16	5	*Now comes*	and expensive. There is Joe Sim-
17	6	7*s sou. at midn. High *on*	ple is good enough for our school.
18	7	Gr. earthquake 1755. tides.	He has cyphered through com
19	A	25th Sun. past Trin. *a fine*	pound interest, and that's fur
20	2	C.P. N'amp. & Ply. *spell.*	enough for any man. He knows
21	3	C.P.Por.&Cast.C.S.Green.	nothing about Jogrify and Gram-
22	4	Ceciel *Much*	mar and such stuff; but he can
23	5	St. Clem. C. S. Cast. *cooler*	write as good a hand as I can ; and
24	6	*with* ☌ ☽ pol.	as for reading, he is far better than
25	7	Cath. *signs of*	Squire Puff. In spelling they say
26	A	26th Sun. past Trin. *snow.*	he is curious. I have often heard
27	4	C. P. Springf. Low tides.	that when a boy he could spell
28	3	S. J. C. Bost. *Very fine*	*Nebuchadnezzar* quicker than any
29	4	*to end of* ☽ apog.	one in school. I move, Mr. cheers-
30	5	St. Andrew. *the month.*	man, that we hire Joe Simple to keep our school this winter. Give him five dollars a month and board himself, which is all he axes."

G. Z. GLADWIN. HOLBROOK SCHOOL APPARATUS.

THE DEBATE ABOUT "LARNIN"

The con view:

" . . . I move, Mr. Cheersman, that we hire Joe Simple to keep our school this winter. Give him five dollars a month and board himself, which is all he axes."

NOVEMBER

1872
THE
FARMER'S
CALENDAR

November 5, 1872, Rochester, N.Y.
Suffragette Susan B. Anthony and her associates arrested for attempting to vote as Ulysses S. Grant is reelected president over candidate Horace Greeley.

NOVEMBER hath 30 days.　　　1872.

The piping winds sing Nature's dirge,
　As through the forest bleak they roar;
Whose leafy screen, like locks of eld,
　Each day shows scantier than before.
　　　　　　　　　　　　TRENCH.

D. M.	D. W.	Aspects, Holidays, Events, Weather, &c.	Farmer's Calendar.
1	Fr.	All Saints' Day. ☌ ☿ ☾.	THE harvest by this time ought to be nearly done. It gladdens the heart to see the barns and the cellars and the garrets. the corn bins and the root-pits, fill up till they swell with fatness at the end of the summer's growth. It is the result of faithful toil and endeavor, and he must be cold indeed who isn't getting ready for a joyful Thanksgiving. If the weather is mild the swedes will continue to grow. Most root crops that are raised for cattle make the largest part of their growth in the fall months, and so it is best to let them stay in the ground as long as it is safe, but be on the watch for cold weather. Don't fail to stall the cattle these frosty nights. Cows fall off rapidly in milk if left out, and young calves should have been taken up before this, if you want them to thrive. Pumpkins are an excellent feed for stock of all kinds this month. After the corn and other crops are well gathered, it will be time to start the plough. If you've a lot that you want to sow with oats or other spring grain, it is a good plan to plough it now, so as to have it ready earlier in April. The team is stronger now than it will be then, and you can make better work. Trim the grape vines as soon as the leaves have fallen.
2	Sa.	High tides.	
3	F	23ᵈ Su. af. Trin. ☌ ♀ ☾.	
4	Mo.	3d. ♂ gr. hel. lat. N. *Fine*	
5	Tu.	☾ runs low. ☌ ♄ ☾.	
6	W.	☾ in Per. {5th. State election in Massachusetts.	
7	Th.	5th. Presidential election in all the States.	
8	Fr.	Low tides. {6th. Admiral Charles Stewart died, 1869.	
9	Sa.	{Prince of Wales born, 1841. *but cool.*	
10	F	24th Sund. after Trinity.	
11	Mo.	St. Martin. *High winds*	
12	Tu.	☌ ♅ ☾. *with*	
13	W.	Remarkable meteoric display, 1833.	
14	Th.	☾ eclipsed, visible in U. S.	
15	Fr.	♀ in Aph. High tides.	
16	Sa.	*cold rain.*	
17	F	25th Sund. after Trinity.	
18	Mo.	☾ runs high.	
19	Tu.	*Fine for the*	
20	W.	☌ ♅ ☾. *season.*	
21	Th.	☾ in Per. ☿ gr. hel. lat. S.	
22	Fr.	St. Cecilia. ☐ ♃ ☉. ☌ ♃ ☾.	
23	Sa.	Very low tides. *Cold*	
24	F	26th Sund. after Trinity.	
25	Mo.	☌ ♂ ☾. {British evacuated New York, 1783.	
26	Tu.	*increases.*	
27	W.	☿ gr. elongation East.	
28	Th.	{Washington Irving died, 1859. *Rough,*	
29	Fr.	*with rain or snow.*	
30	Sa.	St. Andrew. ☉ eclip., invis. [in U. S.	

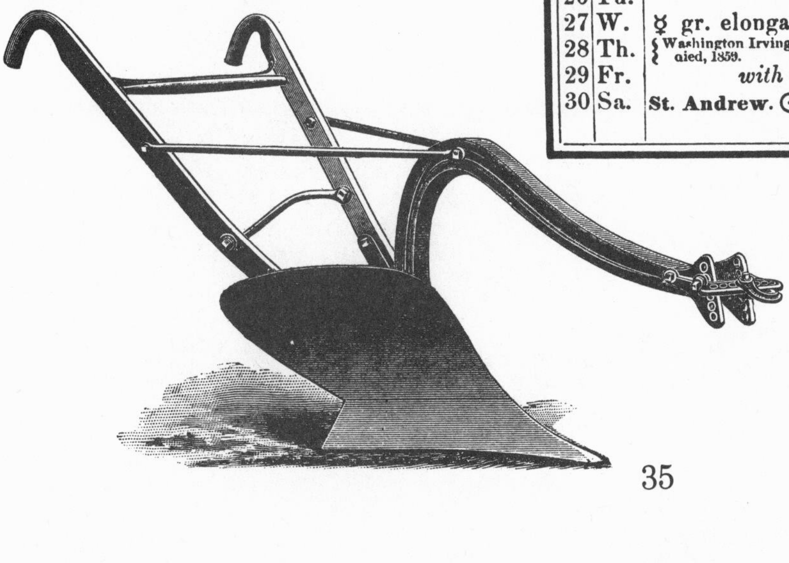

DECEMBER

1814
THE
FARMER'S
CALENDAR

DECEMBER, twelfth Month. 1814.

While Boreas around us is roaring and raging,
   Within we have matter for good winter cheer;
Books, friends, and good fires are very engaging,
   With means of supply for the ensuing year.

(Communicated)

M.D	W.D	Courts, Aspects, Holidays, Weather, &c.	FARMER'S CALENDAR.
1	5	7*s sou. 11h. even.	New-Year's day is approaching; and are you ready for it? Have you got your accounts all so well arranged that you can then settle with each neighbour without confusion, trouble and hard thoughts. The first of January is the day for balancing accounts. This most surely ought never to be neglected. You will therefore be preparing your papers in order to preserve a good neighbourhood.
2	6	*Becomes*	
3	7	Tides grow less. *cooler,*	
4	B	2d Sunday in Advent.	
5	2	C.P. Worcester. *with some*	
6	3	C.S Augusta. *snow.*	
7	4	*Changes to*	
8	5	Concep. V. Mary. *warmer*	
9	6	*with rain.*	
10	7	Gov. Sullivan died 1808.	It is all important that every man should know the history and geography of his own country.—Yet a vast many of us hardly know our right hand from our left in this respect. What more profitable employment can you have during the long winter evenings than reading Hutchinson's history of Massachusetts—Belknap's New-Hampshire—Williams's Vermont—Life of Gen. Washington—American Revolution. Morses' and other Geographies, &c.
11	B	3d Sun. in Advent. *Chilly*	
12	2	C.P. Camb. Taunt. & Aug.	
13	3	*winds but pleasant.*	
14	4	WASHING. died '99, Æt. 68.	
15	5	7*s so. 10h. ev. ♂ ☽ ♄ [♑ ap.	
16	6	Tea destroyed in Bost. 1773.	
17	7	*Now look out*	
18	B	4th Sun. in Advent. *for*	
19	2	C.P. Ips. Greenf. & Dedham.	
20	3	*a snow storm.*	
21	4	St. Thomas. *Agreeable*	It is highly proper also to improve this season in visiting your friends. You will likewise remember that now you can afford to turn a little something to assist those, whom Providence has seen fit to depress with poverty.
22	5	Shortest day. *weather*	
23	6	*for Christmas.*	
24	7	7*s set 5h. 30m.	
25	B	Christmas Day.	
26	2	C.S. Len. St. Steph. ♂ ☉ ♀	
27	3	C P. Boston. ☽ eclip. vis.	
28	4	Innocent. High tides. ☽ per.	
29	5	*Grows cooler*	
30	6	Sirius sou. midnight.	
31	7	Sylvester *with snow.* □ ☉ ♃	

RING OUT THE OLD!
RING IN THE NEW!

Ring out, wild bells, to the wild sky,
   The flying clouds, the frosty light;
   The year is dying, in the night;
Ring out, wild bells, and let him die.

Ring out the old, ring in the new;
   Ring, happy bells, across the snow;
   The year is going—let him go—
Ring out the false, ring in the true.

Ring out the grief that saps the mind
   For those that here we see no more;
   Ring out the feuds of rich and poor,
Ring in redress to all mankind.

Ring out false pride in place and blood,
   The faithless coldness and the spite;
   Ring in the love of truth and right,
Ring in the common love of good.

Ring out old shapes of foul disease,
   Ring out the narrow lust of gold;
   Ring out the thousand wars of old.
Ring in the thousand years of peace.

—LORD ALFRED TENNYSON

December 24, 1814:
The Treaty of Ghent is signed, and it brings to a close the War of 1812 which was declared by Congress against England two years earlier. The cost of the war to the government of the United States was $105 million.

36

DECEMBER

1856
THE FARMER'S CALENDAR

THE SCOTCH WIDOW'S BLESSING

"Be wi' the rich in the world that now is,
And wi' the poor in the world that's to come."

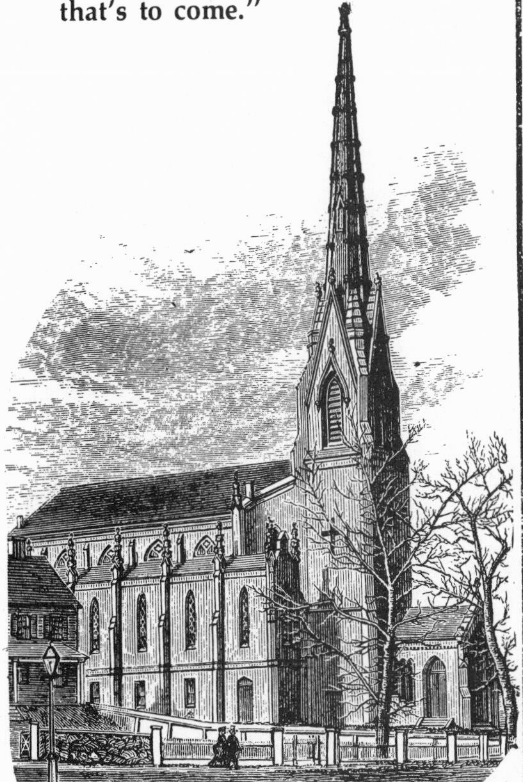

MEN OF WORTH

The men of mark,
Are the men of worth;
Let us then start in
Upon the new year,
With a will
To make the most of the time.

DECEMBER hath 31 days. 1856.

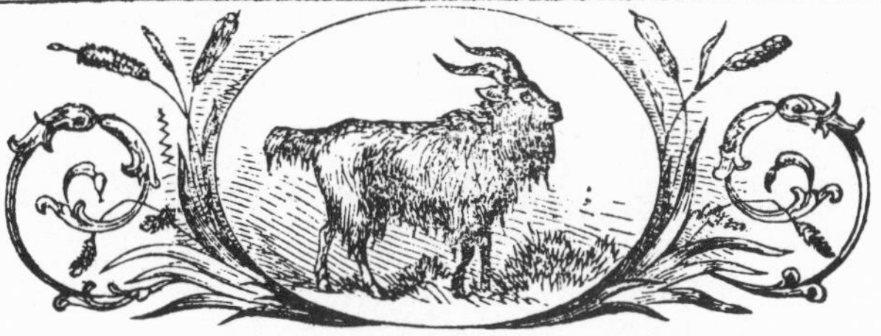

Cold December, bleak and dreary,
Stares us rudely in the face;
And the year, with all it promised,
Hastens to its close apace.

East Cambridge. J. W. D.

D. M.	D. W.	Courts, Aspects, Holidays, Weather, &c.
1	Mo.	C. C. P. Crim. Springfield. C. C. P. Plym. & Worces. ♂ ☌ ☽
2	Tu.	C. C. Northam. ♃ so. 7h. 13m. ev.
3	W.	Napoleon I. crowned emperor, 1804. *Rather*
4	Th.	7*s so. 10h. 54m. e. *finer.*
5	Fr.	Bible translated into English, 1611. Low
6	Sa.	♃ ☌ ☽ tides. *Much*
7	E.	2d Sun. in Advent. *cooler,*
8	Mo.	C. C. P. Cambridge & New Bedford. *with signs*
9	Tu.	C. C. Green. ☽ in peri. ♀ gr. hel. lat. S.
10	W.	Louis Napoleon chosen pres. of France, 1848. *of snow.*
11	Th.	♄ so. 1h. 34m. mor. *A*
12	Fr.	☽ r. h. ♂ in perih. *storm is*
13	Sa.	♄ ☌ ☽ High tides. *near.*
14	E.	3d Sun. in Advent. *Snow*
15	Mo.	C. C. P. Ipsw., or Lawr. if accom. are pro., & Ded'm. C. C. P. Cr. Northam.
16	Tu.	15th. Izaak Walton, the complete angler, d., 1683. *or rain.*
17	W.	7*s so. 9h. 57m. ev. *Fine.*
18	Th.	Horatio Greenough, the sculptor, died, 1852. *Snow*
19	Fr.	♃ south 6h. 9m. eve. *or*
20	Sa.	Low tides. *rain, again.*
21	E.	3d Su. in Ad. St. Tho. ☽ in apo.
22	Mo.	[☉ enters ♑, Wint. com. 21st, 9h. 55m. morn.] Shor. day.
23	Tu.	C. C. Salem, Newburyp't, or Ipswich, as ordered, Springfield & Worcester.
24	W.	23d. Gr. earthq. in Japan, 1854. ♄ south 0h. 39m. m.
25	Th.	CHRISTMAS DAY. *Cold, but*
26	Fr.	St. Stephen. ☽ ru. lo. *fine for*
27	Sa.	St. John the Evangelist. High *the sea-*
28	E.	Holy Innocents. ♀ ☌ ♂ tides. *son.*
29	Mo.	25th. Mr. Josiah Hall, of Walpole, Mass., celebrated his 100th year, 1853.
30	Tu.	31st. Amos Lawrence, a Bost. merch., died, aged 68, 1852. ♂ ☌ ☽
31	W.	C. C. Ded'm. ♄ ☍ ☉. ♄ so. midni.

Farmer's Calendar.

The Fleecy Snow appears!

The year has put on her night-cap, and is going to rest. Yes, as the inimitable Thomson says, "dread winter comes at last, and shuts the scene!" But it shuts not the scene to all rational pleasure and enjoyment. There is a satisfaction arising from doing our duty in every season. Now, be not too selfish in this cold, inclement portion of the year. Think of such as may not be so well provided as yourself against its cutting severities. O, there is pleasure in affording relief to the needy! I fear that the family of poor Tom Shelterless are suffering. I am told that he lies in pitiful condition with a *white swelling.* Suppose we take a turn and call upon these unfortunates? Heaven has furnished us with means, more or less, to help others, and why not use them? Well, let us all try to do our duty. But time presses; good-by, until we meet, shake hands, and wish you "Happy New Year," in our next. May you always have the Scotch widow's blessing, "Be wi' the rich in the world that now is, and wi' the poor in the world that 's to come;" and that you may never be so poor as to envy the rich, nor so rich as to *feel yourself poor,* is our sincere wish.

AGRICULTURE
&
HORTICULTURE

AGRICULTURE & HORTICULTURE

THE POSITIVE POWER OF MANURE

"The importance of manure to the farmer is such, that his success in the production of the crops he cultivates will depend on its quality, and the application of it to the crops he raises as food for stock. Those crops which are consumed on the farm are much more productive of an additional quantity of manure than the crops of grain, a part of which is carried off the farm. Vegetable and animal manure, when well mixed in the soil, gives to it the power of absorbing and transmitting moisture for the use of plants that grow in it; therefore improvement in some soils and increased energy in other."

AGRICULTURAL.

MANURES AND THEIR APPLICATIONS.

WE give the name of manure to all substances which are applied to land, for the purpose of increasing the crops we intend to cultivate; and we are satisfied that, by the application of manures to our land, greater crops are produced, until the strength of the manure be exhausted; and then we apply another quantity to keep up its productiveness. The importance of manure to the farmer is such, that his success in the production of the crops he cultivates will depend on its quality, and the application of it to the crops he raises as food for stock. Those crops which are consumed on the farm are much more productive of an additional quantity of manure than the crops of grain, a part of which is carried off the farm. Vegetable and animal manure, when well mixed in the soil, gives to it the power of absorbing and transmitting moisture for the use of plants that grow in it; therefore improvement in some soils and increased energy in other. The effects produced will continue much longer in some soils than others. The dung of animals kept on the farm with litter, is the principal manure on which the farmer should depend. Other manure he can have recourse to when an additional quantity is wanted. Well fed cattle or sheep, whether in the field, stall, or yard, produce an abundant supply of the best and most valuable manure, which will again produce an abundant crop of green food for the stock. We hold it to be an axiom in agriculture, that all the manure which can be produced should be applied to the production of green food, such as turnips, mangel-wurzel, potatoes, &c. By the application of all our manure to the production of food for stock, a very large quantity of food can thus be obtained on a small quantity of land, when compared with the old system of applying all our manure for production of corn for the market. The produce of food for the feeding of stock ought to be our first object—that of corn for sale the second: if we secure the first, the second will follow of course.

The manufacture of manure, or the art of preparing it for every kind of land, ought to be attended to. If farmers saw the advantage which they would derive from having their manure prepared for their particular kind of soil, they would pay more attention to it: this is one of the most necessary branches of the agricultural business—not only the preparation, but the means of increasing its quantity. When dung is mixed with the soil, it produces a certain degree of fermentation in the vegetable matter which the earth contains, separating its parts, dividing and pulverizing it, making it friable and porous, and in a certain degree performing what is done by tillage. As manure is of such vital importance to the farmer, every attention should be paid to the collection of the materials necessary to form it; every vegetable substance, together with the waste earth of ditches, road-sides, sides of the fields, yards, &c., will add to the compost heap, not only in quantity but also in quality, if proper care in the mixture be attended to.

Regard, in preparing composts, should be had to the nature of the soil to which we intend to apply them; for we should regard manure more as an alterative, than as food, for plants. A compost for a light soil should be formed of cold manure, the dung of animals which chew the cud, of clayey or tenacious earth, and the clearing of ditches or other water-fed earths. The compost for strong tenacious soils should, on the other hand, be formed of hot manure, the dung of animals that do not chew the cud, such as horses and pigs. These should be mixed with light, sandy earth, the sides of roads, &c. In the application of manure, the nature of the soil should be considered. If the soil be a strong one of clay or slate, the manure should be of a light, or loose porous nature, such as green stable unfermented dung; and if a compost, it should be made of a light, sandy or porous nature, which tends to keep the soil open and porous. But if the soil is light and sandy, the dung should be of a cold nature, such as well rotten cow or cattle dung.

Compost made of cattle dung and clayey loam, or any heavy substance, is best manure for light sandy land; long straw, or unfermented dung, as stable dung, or any substance which is loose and friable, should never be used on sandy soils.

Peat or swamp mud mixed with green dung and fermented, is formed into an excellent vegetable manure.—[*Morton on Soils.*]

FROM THE 1842 ALMANAC

AGRICULTURE & HORTICULTURE

FROM THE 1842 ALMANAC
BUCKWHEAT & POTATOES

—Properly cut seed potatoes.

BUCKWHEAT.

Buckwheat is a grain that will grow on most poor soils. It delights most in dry locations, a soil inclined to gravel or sand. It has many qualities that recommend it highly as an article to be grown for the purpose of filling the soil with vegetable matter, of which it has been much exhausted in the states which we have known.

In the first place, it will grow and produce a handsome layer for the plough on lands that will produce nothing else. In the second place, we do not find it an exhausting crop. We can raise it many years in succession on our poorest lands without any manure, and we very commonly save fifteen or twenty bushels of the grain from an acre. This plant has a very small fibrous root, and is easily pulled up by the hand. It has also a large branching top, that never could get its support from this root. It has therefore probably greater facilities for procuring nourishment from the atmosphere than most plants have.

All theory and all experience unite in showing that this plant takes less from the soil than any other of the same size. In the next place, it has a rapid growth; six weeks, in Massachusetts, being long enough to bring it in full blossom, when it should be ploughed in. Two crops may therefore be turned under in one season, and then it will be early enough (Sept. 1st) to sow down winter grain and grass seed. Another advantage attends the raising of this for grain or for green crops—the expense is not great. It usually bears the same price of oats, and is worth quite as much for fattening animals, and one bushel of seed is enough for an acre. When it is raised for the purpose of saving the grain, we often sow but half a bushel. The straw is also greedily eaten by young cattle and horses.—Yet we have known large piles of the straw to be burned in the field where it was thrashed.

The policy of raising so many acres of Indian corn on poor and reduced land, must be abandoned. When more buckwheat can be raised on the acre than is obtained of Indian corn, it should be substituted for corn in a great measure, for it requires not a sixth part of the expense to produce it.

Albany Cultivator.

HARVESTING POTATOES.

Never commence harvesting your potatoes till they have come to full maturity, or till the frost has killed the tops down. While the tops are green, the bulbs are growing and improving. In digging them, use either the plough or the potato hook. As soon as they are out of the ground let them be picked up. Never permit them to remain out in the sun or air longer than you can possibly help. I am well aware that this direction is at once in opposition to the rule of many farmers, which is, to allow their potatoes to remain out in the sun *drying* as long as they can, and yet have them picked up on the same day they are dug, in order that as much of the earth as possible may cleave off from them. This is very bad management for potatoes designed for table use, because it renders them strong, or bitter in taste. Every attentive observer has noticed that that part of the potato which happens to be uncovered in the hill, changes its color to a dark green. This portion is very much injured in the taste; in fact it is unfit for use, because it has imbibed from the atmosphere poisonous qualities. As soon as potatoes are dug and exposed to the light and air, this change begins. Every attentive observer has also noticed that potatoes are of the best flavor and quality after they have come to maturity and while they are yet in the ground. The longer they are dug and exposed to light and air, the more of this fine flavor is gone, till it is wholly lost and they become unpalatable and unwholesome. Potatoes that remain all winter in the earth where they grew, are in excellent condition for the table in the spring. In view, therefore, of all these facts, let us prescribe a rule in harvesting the potatoes, which will tend to *perpetuate through the season* these excellent qualities. As soon then as practicable after digging, remove the potatoes designed for the table to a dark bin in the cellar. After depositing thus the whole crop, or as many as are designed for the table, cover them over with boards, or earth, or both, and they will retain their excellent qualities till they begin to sprout in the spring, and require to be removed; when they should be removed to a dry and cool apartment above stairs, and kept from the light as much as possible.—*Albany Cultivator.*

A GRAIN FOR ALL SEASONS

"Buckwheat is a grain that will grow on most poor soils. It delights most in dry locations, a soil inclined to gravel or sand. It has many qualities that recommend it highly as an article to be grown for the purpose of filling the soil with vegetable matter, of which it has been much exhausted in the states which we have known."

SOUND ADVICE FOR POTATO PICKERS

"Every attentive observer has also noticed that potatoes are of the best flavor and quality after they have come to maturity and while they are yet in the ground. The longer they are dug and exposed to light and air, the more of this fine flavor is gone, till it is wholly lost and they become unpalatable and unwholesome. Potatoes that remain all winter in the earth where they grew, are in excellent condition for the table in the spring."

AGRICULTURE & HORTICULTURE

BARLEY'S BEST FRIEND: SANDY SOIL

FROM THE 1844 ALMANAC

A FOOD FOR THE MAN AND BEAST

"The land that produces the best barley, is generally of a salty, light, dry nature. Cold, wet soils, which are peculiarly retentive of water, are ill adapted to the growth of this grain. The whole matter of barley and its straw contains more silicous particles than that of any other grain cultivated by the farmer; and hence one reason why a sandy soil is most congenial to the growth of this plant."

"In Germany, they grind the barley, and form it into cakes, with which they feed their horses; and it is no unusual circumstance, in travelling in that country to see the driver eating a slice from the same loaf with which he feeds his horses."

AGRICULTURAL.

BARLEY.

BARLEY is a grain to be preferred to most others for laying down to grass, being less pungent than oats, but serves rather to nurse the young grass than smother it, as oats often do. There is no grain perhaps more affected, (says a noted writer on agriculture) by soil and cultivation than barley—the same species exhibiting opposite qualities, modified by the nature of the soil from which it is produced. These opposite productions of the same individual, will, if sown at the same period, on the same land, and under the same course of cultivation, exhibit corresponding differences, which are manifested during the growth of the crop, and subsequently in the quality of the sample when in hand. Thus, the finest samples, the growth of suitable and well cultivated lands, would, if sown on a poor and sterile soil, become alike coarse in appearance and indifferent in quality. This fact, however important, has hitherto but little engaged the attention of the farmer.

The land that produces the best barley, is generally of a slaty, light, dry nature. Cold, wet soils, which are peculiarly retentive of water, are ill adapted to the growth of this grain. The whole matter of barley and its straw contains more silicious particles than that of any other grain cultivated by the farmer; and hence one reason why a sandy soil is most congenial to the growth of this plant. In choice of seed, great care should be taken that it is not of a reddish hue, as in that case it is more than probable that a great part of it will never vegetate. The seed should be of a pale, lively color, and plump. In harvesting, more care is requisite than most other white crops. When the period of harvest arrives, barley must be allowed to be sufficiently ripe, but not become what is termed "dead ripe."

Barley, says one, on account of the softness of its stem, and the tendency of its ears to vegetate, is very apt to be injured, and even destroyed by wet. Barley is not only the most useful grain for making into malt, but it is the best food for promoting the fattening of hogs, after they have been fed to a certain extent with other food; from which it has been found that the meat is not only more tender, but increases in boiling. Barley is employed for various other purposes. It is excellent for fattening poultry. For feeding horses, two parts of barley are equal to three parts of oats. In Germany, they grind the barley, and form it into cakes, with which they feed their horses; and it is no unusual circumstance, in travelling in that country, to see the driver eating a slice from the same loaf with which he feeds his horses.—*Farmer's Ency.*

CANADA THISTLE.

A GREAT many devices have been resorted to for the eradication of this vilest pest, in the form of a weed, that has ever invaded American farms. Some aim at the entire removal of the roots by machines contrived to cut off and harrow up the roots. Others rely upon mowing down the thistle when they are in full bloom, as a most certain method. Not content with simply cutting down, some apply common salt to the stumps or stems of the roots, which makes the destruction more sure. Low and frequent cutting down when in full bloom will doubtless destroy plants, however tenacious of life they may be, since the roots are as much indebted for life to their leaves or lungs, as the leaves are to the roots. Neither can subsist long without the aid of the other.—*Ibid.*

To get rich.—Nothing is easier, says Mr. Paulding, than to grow rich. It is only to trust nobody, to befriend none, to get everything, and save all we get; to stint ourselves and everybody belonging to us; to be the friend of no man, and to have no man our friend; to heap interest upon interest, cent per cent.; to be mean, miserable and despised for some twenty or thirty years; and riches will come as sure as disease and disappointment. Such people live without enjoyment, having done no good to their kind, and die despised.

AGRICULTURE & HORTICULTURE

FROM THE 1846 ALMANAC

THE CULTURE OF FRUIT TREES

LAYERING FRUIT STOCKS,
SHOWING NOTCHES.

AGRICULTURAL.

The Culture of Fruit Trees; a discussion held at the State-house in Boston, Tuesday morning, Feb. 4th, 1845. Hon. Mr. Allen in the chair.

Maj. B. Wheeler, of Framingham, was called to make some remarks relative to the subject. He responded readily. He thought the cultivation of choice fruit had a tendency to promote the health and happiness of a family, affording a greater luxury, and a better, than the imported fruits. He said it was for the interest of the farmer to cultivate a succession of fruit, so as to have a supply the year round; and of all the varieties, apples were the most substantial. As to peaches, in some sections of the country they can be cultivated to good advantage, but were more difficult to raise than most fruits. While they succeeded in some sections of a town, in other portions of it the crop would fail, and he was puzzled to account for it. The plum had been much neglected, and for good reasons. When he was a boy, there were abundant crops of plums; afterwards, the trees were affected with warts or excrescences; these for many years injured the trees, and plums were very scarce; but within seven years they have succeeded better with him; they are sometimes injured by a storm while ripening, which causes them to crack open and rot. The cherry was easy to cultivate, and produced abundant crops every year.

The pear was as easily cultivated as the apple. It was thought formerly that it required a longer time to bring it into bearing than the apple, but now, when budded on the quince, the trees would bear the second or third year after transplanting; and it was very pleasant to see a small tree, no larger than a hoe-handle, with twenty or thirty fine pears upon it. An old tree could be grafted over with choice fruit, and in three years a good crop may be expected.

In grafting old trees, he cuts only a part off first, and lets the old fruit remain until the new comes into bearing—cuts off by degrees, and thinks the trees do better by so doing. The operation of grafting was very simple, and any person could do it with a little practice; but he could remember the time when it was thought a difficult operation, and very few could do it. He had tried wax for grafting, and does not fully approve of it, and has given it up; when he used it the scions seemed to make but little wood, and the limb does not appear to heal over so readily as when clay is used: he adds to the clay, cow manure, and puts in a little hair to make it bind together; does not think it necessary to apply a bandage.

Mr. Stone inquired of Mr. Wheeler, what was the best soil for the pear tree? whether it would thrive on gravelly soil? He had seen some beautiful trees—very small indeed, but full of fruit; the soil looked rich, like some sort of compost. Mr. Wheeler replied, that he had no great preference for any particular soil;—if the soil was poor, he enriched it; his soil was naturally rather light and gravelly. He put out an orchard on light gravelly soil, many years since, and his neighbors ridiculed him for so doing; but his orchard had flourished well. It has been thought that the Roxbury russet must be raised on strong clayey soils, to produce fair fruit; but his orchard, set out thirty years ago on poor soil, having been put in good condition, within a few years has renewed its youth. He thought peat mud mixed with ashes, a good manure for light soils; a townsman of his had set out between two and three hundred pear trees on sandy soil, manured with this compost, and they were doing well.

In transplanting trees, care should be taken not to set them too deep; many failed in consequence of so doing. He knew of a man who succeeded in raising quince trees from cuttings. The ground was covered about the cuttings; all grew, and some made a growth of two feet the first season, the soil having been made rich and dug deep. Mr. B. V. French remarked that he had for many years been collecting everything new, and had at this time at least two hundred and fifty or more varieties on his farm. It was too many, and he should probably settle down upon twenty or thirty. He would recommend to new beginners, to set out young and thrifty trees without regard to quality, and after they have got well under way, they may be grafted with such fruits as will give him a succession of fruit. He thought highly of the Newton pippin; it keeps well.

MAJOR WHEELER'S OBSERVATIONS ON THE CULTIVATION OF FRUIT TREES

"The cultivation of choice fruit had a tendency to promote the health and happiness of a family; affording a greater luxury, and a better, than the imported fruits. He said it was for the interest of the farmer to cultivate a succession of fruit, so as to have a supply the year round; and of all the varieties, apples were the most substantial. As to peaches, in some sections of the country they can be cultivated to good advantage, but were more difficult to raise than most fruits."

ADVICE ON TRANSPLANTING

"In transplanting trees, care should be taken not to set them too deep; many failed in consequence of so doing."

AGRICULTURE & HORTICULTURE

MILK AND THE SEASONS

The season has its effects. The milk in spring is supposed to be best for drinking, and hence it would be best suited for cheese; and, in autumn,—the butter keeping better than that of summer, —the cows, less frequently milked, give richer milk, and, consequently, more butter.

COLORING BUTTER YELLOW

It is only a few years since we had various recommendations for coloring butter to a deep golden yellow by grinding up and mixing in the pulp of the orange carrot. But the best way that we have found for giving the carrot color was to pass these roots first through the cow.

Facts about Cream and Milk.—Cream cannot rise through a great depth of milk. If, therefore, milk is desired to retain its cream for a time, it should be put into a deep, narrow dish; and, if it be desired to free it most completely of cream, it should be poured into a broad, flat dish, not much exceeding one inch in depth. The evolution of cream is facilitated by a rise and retarded by a depression of temperature. At the usual temperature of the dairy—50 degrees Fahrenheit—all the cream will rise in thirty-six hours; but, at 70 degrees, it will, perhaps, rise in half that time; and, when the milk is kept near the freezing-point, the cream will rise very slowly, because it becomes solidified. In wet and cold weather the milk is less rich than in dry and warm; and, on this account, more cheese is obtained in cold than in warm, though not in thundery weather. The season has its effects. The milk in spring is supposed to be best for drinking, and hence it would be best suited for cheese; and, in autumn,—the butter keeping better than that of summer,—the cows, less frequently milked, give richer milk, and, consequently, more butter. The morning's milk is richer than the evening's. The last-drawn milk of each milking, at all times and seasons, is richer than the first-drawn, which is the poorest.

"Paint costs Nothing."—This is the old Dutch adage, and we believe judicious economists subscribe to it in theory, and act upon it in practice. Here, in New England, we are a paint-loving people; the color, however, which we use most upon our houses (glaring white) is not the best, or most lasting. It distresses the eyes, creates a monotony in the landscape, is cold in winter, and dazzling in summer. The darker shades, neutral tints, buff, French gray, light browns, and also dark browns, are warmer in winter, and more agreeable in summer; while for the darker colors a cheaper and more lasting material may be used, which will, in buildings with ornamental work, heighten the architectural effect.

White lead in the form of a sub-carbonate, and zinc in the form of an oxide, have been the paints heretofore used; but science and enterprise have discovered, or newly applied an old discovery, by using the oxides of iron and manganese as a basis for a paint, which is not injurious, like lead, goes twice as far as zinc or lead, and does not cost more than one fourth as much as either.

These iron paints are manufactured by an Iron Mining Company, at Brandon, Vermont; are called Brandon Paints, and are for sale at the paint-stores in Boston; and for neutral tints, or dark colors, for outside work, farm-implements, etc., will be found the cheapest paints the farmer or builder can use.

It is said that an analysis of paints found in good preservation upon the walls of the recently-discovered ruins of Nineveh shows that the use of iron paints, identical in composition with those above referred to, was known to the people of ancient times. The proper time to paint is when your buildings require it; and the best time is when the buildings are thoroughly dry, and the weather is not too hot or too cold.

Carrots for Milk and Butter.—It is only a few years since we had various recommendations for coloring butter to a deep golden yellow by grinding up and mixing in the pulp of the orange carrot. But the best way that we have found for giving the carrot color was to pass these roots first through the cow. We have, with nothing more than an average decent cow, made seven pounds of butter a week, much resembling the best grass butter, besides using a small portion of the milk daily on the table. This was accomplished by the use of about a peck and a half of the white variety per day. We hope such of our readers as can, will, experiment in the use of this root, and let us know the result. — *Albany Cultivator.*

Gardening.—Gardening, or the cultivation of fruits and flowers, may, in some sort, be regarded as the test of civilization. It diffuses peace, contentment and happiness, stimulates and invigorates the mental and physical powers, promotes habits of industry and domestic frugality among the humbler classes, and places within their reach a large amount of luxury in the shape of delicious fruits and magnificent flowers.

Fixed Facts in Agriculture.—Somebody has got up the following list of "fixed facts" in agriculture, and for once, in a condensation of the sort, has hit the right nail on the head, in most of them.

1. All lands on which clover or the grasses are grown must either have lime in them naturally, or that mineral must be artificially supplied. It matters but little whether it be supplied in the form of stone-lime, oyster-lime, or marl.

2. All permanent improvement of lands must look to lime as its basis.

3. Lands which have been long in culture will be benefited by the application of phosphate of lime; and it is unimportant whether the deficiency be supplied in the form of bone-dust, guano, native phosphate of lime, composts of fresh ashes, or that of oyster-shell lime — or marl — if the land needs lime also.

4. No lands can be preserved in a high state of fertility unless clover and the grasses are cultivated in the course of rotation.

5. Mould is indispensable in every soil, and a healthy supply can alone be preserved through the cultivation of clover and the grasses, the turning in of green crops, or by the application of composts rich in the elements of mould.

6. All highly concentrated animal manures are increased in value, and their benefits prolonged, by admixture with plaster, salt, or with pulverized charcoal.

7. Deep ploughing greatly improves the productive powers of every variety of soil that is not wet.

8. Subsoiling sound land — that is, land that is not wet — is also eminently conducive to increased production.

9. All wet land should be drained.

10. All grain crops should be harvested before the grain is fully ripe.

11. Clover, as well as the grasses, intended for hay, should be mowed when in bloom.

12. Sandy lands can be most effectually improved by clay. When such lands require liming or marling, the lime or marl is most beneficially applied when made into composts with clay. In slacking lime, salt brine is better than water.

13. The chopping or grinding of grain to be fed to stock operates as a saving of at least twenty-five per cent.

14. Draining of wet lands and marshes adds to their value, by making them to produce more, and by improving the health of neighborhoods.

15. To manure or lime wet lands, is to throw manure, lime, and labor, away.

16. Shallow ploughing operates to impoverish the soil, while it decreases production.

17. By stabling and shedding stock through the winter, a saving of one fourth the food may be effected: that is, one fourth less food will answer than when the stock may be exposed to the inclemencies of the weather.

18. A bushel of plaster per acre, sown broadcast over clover, will add one hundred per cent. to its product.

19. Periodical applications of ashes tend to keep up the integrity of soils, by supplying most, if not all, of the organic substances.

20. Thorough preparation of land is absolutely necessary to the successful and luxuriant growth of crops.

21. Abundant crops cannot be grown for a succession of years unless care be taken to provide an equivalent for the substances carried off the land in the products grown thereon.

22. To preserve meadows in their productiveness, it is necessary to harrow them every second autumn, apply top-dressing, and roll them up.

23. All stiff clays are benefited by fall and winter ploughings; but should never be ploughed when wet. If, at such ploughings, the furrow be materially deepened, lime, marl, or ashes, should be supplied.

24. Young stock should be moderately fed with grain in winter, and receive generous supplies of long provenders, it being essential to keep them in a fair condition, in order that the formation of muscle, bones, &c., may be encouraged and continuously carried on.

FROM THE 1857 ALMANAC

BASIC FACTS ABOUT FARMING

DEEP PLOUGHING

Deep ploughing greatly improves the productive powers of every variety of soil that is not wet.

SHALLOW PLOUGHING

Shallow ploughing operates to impoverish the soil, while it decreases production.

STIFF CLAYS

All stiff clays are benefited by fall and winter ploughings; but should never be ploughed when wet. If, at such ploughings, the furrow be materially deepened, lime, or ashes, should be supplied.

AGRICULTURE & HORTICULTURE

FROM THE 1861 ALMANAC

BEST SOIL FOR GRAPES

Soils that contain lime are best for the grape, but all soils that are *light* and *rich, warm* and *friable,* so that the roots can penetrate in every way, will grow good grapes.

BEST PRUNING TIME

The best time to prune is early in November; but you may prune any time after the fall of the leaf till March, except when the wood is frozen. If pruned later than the first of March, the vine will bleed. In pruning or thinning out, in summer, do not remove the leaves. They are the lungs of the plant, and the hot sun must not be let in upon the fruit.

THE CULTURE OF THE GRAPE.

EVERY farmer, and every owner of a cottage with a rod of land, ought to cultivate a few choice grapes. They require but a small space; they are ornamental, either pruned as a shrub or trained as a vine; they are among the most healthy and luscious of all our fruits; and, with proper care and attention, they produce an annual crop equal to any other in money value.

SOIL.—Soils that contain lime are best for the grape, but all soils that are *light* and *rich, warm* and *friable,* so that the roots can penetrate in every way, will grow good grapes.

ASPECT.—A south aspect is best. If such is not at command, a south-west is next to be preferred, next south-east, next west, and lastly east. Protect the vines, if possible, from the north and east winds, and set them where they can feel the genial rays of the sun the whole day, or at least during the after part of the day. Light and heat are essential.

MANURES.—Stable manures, if used at all, ought to be used only as a mulching or top-dressing. Bone-dust, ashes, sulphur or plaster, are among the best fertilizers. Soap-suds from the wash-tub may be poured round the roots at any season.

PRUNING.—The best time to prune is early in November; but you may prune any time after the fall of the leaf till March, except when the wood is frozen. If pruned later than the first of March, the vine will bleed. In pruning or thinning out, in summer, do not remove the leaves. They are the lungs of the plant, and the hot sun must not be let in upon the fruit.

VARIETIES.—The Delaware, the Concord, the Diana, and the Hartford Prolific, are the best varieties for open culture. The Delaware is a small, hardy grape, of fine quality. The Concord is a good, hardy and prolific grape, earlier than the Isabella, and more reliable year after year. The Diana is a small grape, of fine flavor, but thought by some to be too liable to mildew. The Catawba and Isabella are not suited to general cultivation in New England; but in very warm and long seasons, and in very favorable locations, they yield a valuable and luxuriant crop.

MARKET DAYS.

THE chief advantage which the English farmer has over us in New England is to be found in the great market facilities existing all over England. There are no less than eleven hundred and forty markets, or market days, in a year; and more than a thousand markets, at as many different points, are established by law.

In all other respects the New England farmer is about as well situated for making farming profitable. We have a large population of consumers who are not producers, owing to the large predominance of the manufacturing and commercial interests. And yet the farmer in England has to hire his land, in many cases at a high rent,—from twenty-five to thirty dollars a year per acre being no uncommon price,—and still succeeds in making money, living well, and laying up more for future use than many of us.

An effort has been made to establish regular stated market days in Massachusetts. A committee of the State Board of Agriculture, after a full and complete survey and statement of the facts, give the following as the results of frequent markets in our midst:

"1. Greater convenience in buying and selling than we now enjoy.

"2. A great saving of time.

"3. Cash for all things sold.

"4. The removal of middle men, thus bringing the consumer and producer face to face.

"5. As a consequence of this removal, better prices to the farmer, and cheaper purchases to the consumer.

"6. The abolition of the peddling system.

AGRICULTURE & HORTICULTURE

CRANBERRIES.

THE first object of attention, after selecting a location for the cultivation of cranberries, is the means of drainage. The piece ought to be capable of being drained at least a foot and a half below the surface. It is not absolutely essential to be able to flow the plantation, yet to have water at command, so as to flash it over as occasion may require, is of great advantage. Sometimes the effects of a frost, when the plant is in blossom, may be guarded against in this way, and a thorough flooding will often destroy the insect. In fact, bogs that are kept flowed till the 20th or 25th of May are seldom molested by insects.

But drainage is more essential than flowage, and, where this is imperfect, it is very difficult to keep out the wild grasses and water-rushes that choke up the vines and make them unproductive. I could name large pieces whose value has been destroyed by bad drainage.

After fixing upon a location, the first step, of course, is to level it off. With a piece of plank a dozen feet long, a common carpenter's level, and a lot of stakes a foot long and cut square at the tops, you can begin by driving a stake leaving the top just even with the proposed surface of the piece, and then running several lines of stakes through and across the lot. The stakes show at a glance where the surface is to be taken off and where it is to be filled in, so as to bring up the whole to a uniform level. A little calculation will enable you to level up from the spots where material is to be removed. The advantage of getting this perfect level is very great, because it requires much less water to flow a piece having a level surface than it does an uneven one; so that nothing is lost by spending some time in engineering.

A certain amount of sand is best for surface filling, as it is generally free from weed seed, and gives a clean, nice surface; but if it is too thick, the vines will be slower in coming to bearing. If the peat or bog is only a foot or two deep, the sand need not be deeper than from three to five inches. A small admixture of vegetable matter with sand will make them more productive, but too much of it brings in wild grasses and weeds, and makes too much work.

The spring is the best time for setting, but the vine is hard to kill, and will generally do well set at any season. Punch holes a foot and a half apart each way, and stick in two or three vines, and press the sand down hard about them. Some make a shallow furrow with a cultivator, and lay the vines in along the furrow, leaving out the ends, and so covering the roots.

As to soil, avoid loam, clay, and gravel. The alluvial soil, as sand and fine pulverized quartz, like the deltas and intervals near the outlets of streams, the mud of narrow bogs and creeks, and the salt and fresh swales or meadows, formed of deposits of mud and by decayed vegetable matter, is of this description. All peat and mud soils, whether originally fresh or salt, are practically of the same character so far as regards the growth of the cranberry. Where beach or quartz sand lies under a foot or so of turfy peat, the best way is to subsoil, throwing up about three inches of the sand. If the peat is deep and covered with rushes and bushes, the cheapest way, in the end, would be to pave over the whole surface, down to the bottom of the roots, and top-dress with sand, when a thick coating will be required to prevent trouble from weeds.

On rich interval lands, and on a deep, pure black peat, the vine will grow with great rapidity, and perhaps bear one or two years, but then the vines will become barren. They seem to incline to run too much to wood, and become too rank. The wood will be soft and flimsy, and not tough and hard as that on productive vines. There is a great and well-marked difference between these two kinds of vine.

The miller, that produces the cranberry worm, so destructive to this fine fruit, appears about the time the berry sets, and punctures a hole in it, laying its eggs just under the skin. If small fires were set at night near the bog, at this season, it is probable that myriads would be destroyed and the fruit saved. As the period is only a week or ten days, the experiment need not be an expensive one to try.

When picked, which should be carefully done by hand, cranberries should be spread out not over five inches deep on platforms, made by laths left open so that the air that can draw through. They may remain three weeks or more in a dry and airy place, and will ripen up fast. Then, before packing for sale, they should be winnowed and the unsound berries picked out. The barrels or boxes in which they are packed for market should be dry and clean.

CRANBERRIES

THE BEST SETTING TIME

The spring is the best time for setting, but the vine is hard to kill, and will generally do well set at any season. Punch holes a foot and a half apart each way, and stick in two or three vines, and press the sand down hard about them. Some make a shallow furrow with a cultivator, and lay the vines in along the furrow, leaving out the ends, and so covering the roots.

PICKING CRANBERRIES

When picked, which should be carefully done by hand, cranberries should be spread out not over five inches deep on platforms, made by laths left open so that the air that can draw through. They may remain three weeks or more in a dry and airy place, and will ripen up fast.

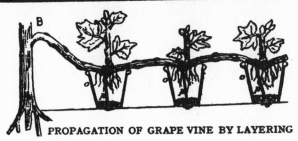

PROPAGATION OF GRAPE VINE BY LAYERING

AGRICULTURE & HORTICULTURE

ON THE NEGLECT OF THE COW

WINTERING COWS

"It cannot be denied that the general practice in wintering cows and other neat stock in New England, is one of low and insufficient feeding. Most farmers, no doubt, think this system is one of economy, and that they cannot afford to feed any grain or meal on account of the cost."

"What is the cow but a machine on which we depend for earning an income on the investment? What is the food we give her but the raw material for the manufacture of so much milk? If a cotton or a woolen manufacturer should neglect to keep up the supply of the raw material, or let it run short, so as to run on half time, or below the fair working capacity of his mill, in ordinary or prosperous times, when his goods found a ready sale in the market, what should we think of his judgment or skill as a business man? Now the farmer's position is precisely similar."

WINTER FEED OF COWS.

It cannot be denied that the general practice in wintering cows and other neat stock in New England, is one of low and insufficient feeding. Most farmers, no doubt, think this system is one of economy, and that they cannot afford to feed any grain or meal on account of the cost. But many go still farther, and neglect or refuse to supply even their best animals, on which they rely for the income of the farm, in the form of dairy products, with roots or other succulent food in winter, even when they know it will add materially to their productiveness through the whole of the succeeding summer. They forget or overlook the fact that the true system of feeding cows would lead us to induce the cow to take as much palatable food as her system is capable of assimilating.

What is the cow but a machine on which we depend for earning an income on the investment? What is the food we give her but the raw material for the manufacture of so much milk? If a cotton or a woollen manufacturer should neglect to keep up the supply of the raw material, or let it run short, so as to run on half time, or below the fair working capacity of his mill, in ordinary or prosperous times, when his goods found a ready sale in the market, what should we think of his judgment or skill as a business man? Now the farmer's position is precisely similar. He has a certain amount of capital invested in the farm buildings, the barns, the tools, and appliances, and in the cows, as the machinery. He wants to obtain the largest income from this capital and the labor applied that is consistent with the present capacity and the wear and tear of the machinery. Nothing can, therefore, be so short-sighted as to neglect to supply the requisite amount of raw material to keep the machinery running up to its full reasonable capacity for production.

The idea which some farmers appear to entertain, that a cow gives the largest yield when she is in low condition, and that this yield depends upon this state of the system, is quite absurd. To be sure, a large milker, at the time of her full flow of milk, will often fall off in condition, especially if inadequately fed, but both reason and common sense show that the abundant yield is in spite of the low condition, and not dependent on it. If the condition is low and the system emaciated, the yield of milk is of necessity small compared with what the cow would be capable of yielding on the same food if in a better condition. And if the yield is large in quantity it will be poor in quality, because much of the food which should go to yield milk will necessarily be drawn upon by the animal to maintain its bodily condition.

But let us look, for a moment, at the actual comparative cost of a little better system of feeding, and see if we are not making a mistake in feeding our cows so exclusively on dry hay, or other kinds of dry fodder, with the idea that it is the only cheap way of getting on. We will take good English hay as the standard of value, because that is the most common basis of our winter feed, and all other kinds of feeding substances are good or poor, dear or cheap, as compared with that.

We take the nutritive equivalents of different feeding substances as established by careful chemical investigation. Make whatever allowance you please for any inaccuracies in these investigations. They may not be positively and precisely accurate in every detail, but, as between each other, they furnish us with the only tolerable comparison we have, and they are, probably, not far from the truth anyhow.

According to these, the nutritive equivalent of one hundred pounds of good English or upland hay would be as follows:—

Good Linseed Meal,	22 lbs.
Indian Meal,	25 lbs.
Second quality of hay, say,	150 lbs.
Oat Straw,	260 lbs.
Carrots,	200 lbs.
Turnips,	400 lbs.

Now to get a given amount of nourishment out of good English Hay, at $20 per ton, would cost, we will say, ... $1.00

To get the same from Linseed Meal, at $60 per ton, the usual price, would cost .66

To get the same from Indian Meal, at $40 per ton, the ordinary price, would cost .50

To get it from Turnips, at $10 per ton, would cost 2.00

To get it from Carrots, at $20 per ton, would cost the same, namely, . . . 2.00

Of course the price of these articles will vary a little, according to locality, but any one can calculate for himself, from the prices in his own neighborhood. As to the roots, they are to be credited with their effect on the health of the animal, and even if they cost more they could not be given up.

Now it is clear that, making all due allowance for possible inaccuracies, there is still a very large margin in favor of a higher system of feeding. We hope every reader will consider this subject, and experiment, and give the cows the benefit of his conclusions.

AGRICULTURE & HORTICULTURE

The Strawberry.

THIS delicious fruit is so easily cultivated, so healthful, and so universally popular, that it is worth while for every farmer to raise it in quantities sufficient, at least, to supply his own family. Indeed why should not all the small fruits receive greater attention in every farmer's garden? They ripen for the most part at a season of the year when other fruits are scarce, and their free use is unquestionably conducive to health.

The old matted bed system, so common a few years ago, is now generally given up for better methods of cultivation. By that method, after the ground was thoroughly prepared, the plants were set out in rows about four feet apart and about fourteen inches in the row, as early in the spring as possible, or as soon as the soil was dry enough to handle. The weeds were carefully kept down till the runners began to spread, when the ground was levelled off, and the runners trained evenly over the bed, and they would entirely cover it by October. The next spring paths a foot wide were cut through the whole, leaving it in beds three feet wide, for convenience of access in picking. After the crop was taken off the second year, the plough was run through, breaking up the whole bed. That method gave but one crop in two years, but that was a full and very profitable one, and it was claimed that it was less work to plant a new bed than to weed an old one. But it was very expensive keeping the plants free from weeds the first year, since after the runners spread it was mostly hard work. It is admirably adapted to such varieties as throw up but one fruit stem to a plant, like Hovey's seedling, and others that must be thick to get any crop. That is called the annual system, and has been extensively adopted by the market gardeners of Belmont, Massachusetts.

A modified form of this system is to plant in rows three feet apart only, and the plants allowed to cover a space only a foot wide. It is subject to the same trouble about weeding.

Another plan is to set in hills in rows three feet apart, and a foot or a foot and a half in the rows, cutting off all runners, and throwing the whole force and vitality into the main stalks. With some varieties, like the Triomph de Gand, and similar growers, it does well, giving fruit of splendid quality.

Still another method is to set in rows two feet apart, and a foot apart in the row, cutting off all runners, and doing the weeding by hand culture. With high manuring the plants will bear two or three years without renewal, but it is all hand labor, and too expensive for field crops on a large scale.

A method which has been adopted, and practised with great success by Captain Moore, of Concord, is to plant in spring in rows four feet apart, and twelve to fourteen inches in the row. Weed with horse-hoe and cultivator till the runners start about the 1st of July. The spaces between the rows are then levelled with a rake, and two runners from each plant, one on each side, are laid in at right angles with the row, and one foot from the original plant, and all other runners are kept cut off, both from the old and the new plants. When the new plants are well rooted, the strings by which they are attached to the old plants are cut off. This leaves a bed with three rows in it one foot apart, with a space of two feet between the beds. The overhanging of the leaves will give a space but one foot for a path for the pickers. Perhaps the following diagram will give a clearer idea of it, where the large stars show the original rows of old plants, and the small ones the new plants taken from the runners and struck in a foot from the old rows : —

```
  *  12 in.  *     *     *     *     *     *     *

 ❋     ❋     ❋     ❋     ❋     ❋     ❋     ❋

  *     *     *     *     *     *     *     *

                    2 FEET PATH.

  *     *     *     *     *     *     *     *
   12 in.
 ❋     ❋     ❋     ❋     ❋     ❋     ❋     ❋

  *     *     *     *     *     *     *     *
```

This plan gives ample room to cultivate with a horse, or to use an onion hoe between the plants. The weeds can be kept down on four beds, arranged in this way, easier than on one in the annual or matted bed system. By proper care and manuring it will give three or four good crops without renewing.

Whatever method is adopted clean cultivation is essential to success, and without it no plan will avail to secure good crops. They should be hoed as often as twice in three weeks from the middle of May till the first of October. It is evident that about nine tenths of all the work they require comes in the first year, and the crops to follow will depend almost wholly upon the fidelity with which that work is done.

STRAWBERRIES

BUBACH STRAWBERRY.

EASY TO CULTIVATE

This delicious fruit is so easily cultivated, so healthful, and so universally popular, that it is worth while for every farmer to raise it in quantities sufficient, at least, to supply his own family. Indeed why should not all the small fruits receive greater attention in every farmer's garden? They ripen for the most part at a season of the year when other fruits are scarce, and their free use is unquestionably conducive to health.

AGRICULTURE & HORTICULTURE

FROM THE 1872 ALMANAC

DISCOVERING THE CABBAGE

A NUTRITIVE VEGETABLE

Cabbages are conveniently fed out late in the season, about the time that pumpkins come into use, and they not only increase the milk of cows, but are very nutritive and greatly relished by all kinds of stock. Cabbages contain a large percentage of flesh forming substances as compared with most other articles of food.

CABBAGE FOR COWS

Being much more nutritive, weight for weight than turnips, and at the same time very succulent, cabbages form a valuable food for milch cows. Cattle are very fond of cabbages, and dairy cows fed upon them and some hay produce much and rich milk; and the butter made from the latter is free from the disagreeable flavor which it always has when cows are fed upon turnips. Cabbages, for this reason, are a valuable substitute for turnips, and deserve to be more extensively cultivated than they are at present.

Cabbage as a Field Crop.

MOST farmers have been accustomed to cultivate cabbages in a small way in the garden and for family use. The methods of raising them are, therefore, well known. Now the great want of New England, and of any country where the winters are so long, and the necessity for stall feeding so imperative, is an abundance of food for stock. With more food we can keep more stock, with more stock we obtain more manure, with more manure we can increase the fertility of our land.

The farmer's chief study ought to be to see by what means he can increase his supply of animal food in the cheapest and most economical manner. His success as a farmer turns very much upon this. His grass lands should be kept in the best condition; but that is not enough. He should raise a liberal supply of root crops; and even with them most farmers who are aiming at the highest point of excellence, will still want something more.

There are certain crops that are very convenient to use in the late fall, and serve not only to prevent a too early encroachment upon the hay-mow, but to break the too sudden change from green and succulent grass to dry hay. Such are pumpkins in October and November, as they come from the field; round turnips in December, when they may be fed freely and to great advantage. After these follow ruta bagas through January and February, and then mangolds still later. Cabbages are conveniently fed out late in the season, about the time that pumpkins come into use, and they not only increase the milk of cows, but are very nutritive and greatly relished by all kinds of stock. Cabbages contain a large percentage of flesh-forming substances as compared with most other articles of food. Here is their composition: —

Water,	86.28
Flesh-forming matter,	4.75
Heat and fat-forming substances,	7.10
Inorganic matter (ash),	1.87
	100.00

It will be seen that the proportion of flesh-forming material in their composition is three times as great as that of turnips (about 1.5 per cent.), and is equal to that of clover and our common grasses. This is why this vegetable is so readily eaten by all kinds of stock, especially by young and growing animals, like lambs and calves, and by milch cows. As a summer field crop, therefore, why is it not superior to the clovers and the grasses, since, though the expense of producing it is a little greater, the yield in weight per acre is two or three times as great? Indeed, what crop is there that will yield so large an amount of nutritive food at the same cost? The distinguished agricultural chemist, Dr. Voelcker, says of it, "No kind of green food, cultivated on a large scale, in the field, contains so much nutritious matter as the cabbage. Being much more nutritive, weight for weight, than turnips, and at the same time very succulent, cabbages form a valuable food for milch cows. Cattle are very fond of cabbages, and dairy cows fed upon them and some hay produce much and rich milk; and the butter made from the latter is free from the disagreeable flavor which it always has when cows are fed upon turnips. Cabbages, for this reason, are a valuable substitute for turnips, and deserve to be more extensively cultivated than they are at present." This is the highest indorsement from the highest authority. But the testimony of the few practical men who raise cabbages as a field crop, and feed them out to dairy stock, is equally strong. They consider them the best crop they can raise for this purpose.

For a field crop the late varieties are preferable. The seed is sown about the first of May, in beds, and by the tenth or the middle of June the plants will be sufficiently large and strong to be transplanted. A piece of sod land well ploughed will answer very well, and a light clover sod is the best. The liberal supply of manure may be partly spread and ploughed under, and partly spread on the furrow and harrowed in. It is best to select wet weather, if possible, for transplanting. A smart man can easily set out five thousand plants a day. The market gardeners can set six thousand five hundred. The plants may wilt a little during the first week if the weather is dry and warm, but as soon as they get hold of the soil and hold their heads up, run a cultivator through them, to keep down the weeds and stir the soil. If the plants are set two feet by two and a half, this operation is easily performed. At those distances the number of plants will be eight thousand nine hundred to the acre. Of these it will be fair to expect six thousand heads. Some will fail to head, and others may be destroyed by disease or insects after it is too late to replace them. They will be worth, to feed out to dairy cows, say from thirty to forty dollars a thousand. The amount of feeding material on an acre of well-grown cabbages is something enormous.

The culture of this plant, for the purposes proposed, is worthy of a careful trial by every farmer. Try it under favorable circumstances, and estimate the cost of the crop as compared with other farm crops, and then report your experience for the benefit of other farmers. Farmers ought to remember that noble old precept, "Do good and communicate." It is a grand rule to follow.

50

AGRICULTURE & HORTICULTURE

FROM THE 1875 ALMANAC

WHO'S WHO IN THE WORLD OF CHICKENS

Each breed of poultry has marked traits or characteristics, and these are so well known and understood that it is an easy matter to recommend a special breed to meet the wants of each individual.

The large breeds known as *"Asiatic,"* in which are included the different *"Cochins," "Shanghaes," "Brahmas,"* etc., are not generally distinguished as great layers, and from their strong setting proclivities are most valuable as breeders of chickens.

For the Best Eggs

To the small poultry-keeper who wishes eggs only, the Brown Leghorn, Black Spanish, and White Leghorn breeds are most desirable, and most valuable in the order in which we have named them.

THE BEST BREEDS OF POULTRY

The Poultry to Keep.

THE question is often asked, "Which breeds of poultry are the best?" and it is a pretty difficult question to answer; for there are so many different conditions in which the fowls are to be kept, and so many different breeds of poultry, that almost each individual poultry-keeper will have requirements different from others, and in answering the question we can, therefore, speak in general terms only.

There are two chief classes of poultry-keepers, namely, those who, on considerable areas of land, have large flocks, and those who have but limited space, and generally keep their poultry in confinement. The requirements of these two classes are, of course, in a measure, different. Again, some large poultry-keepers raise but few chickens, and depend on eggs for profit, and others raise every chicken possible, looking to these for remuneration, while the village poultry-keeper is generally anxious to get eggs and chickens, and all he can of both.

Each breed of poultry has marked traits or characteristics, and these are so well known and understood that it is an easy matter to recommend a special breed to meet the wants of each individual.

The large breeds known as *"Asiatic,"* in which are included the different *"Cochins," "Shanghaes," "Brahmas,"* &c., are not generally distinguished as great layers, and from their strong setting proclivities are most valuable as breeders of chickens.

The Cochins are generally slow in maturing, and unless crossed with the common fowl are not very valuable to the economical poultry-breeder.

The Brahma is a valuable and favorite breed, but it is not so profitable when thorough-bred as it is when crossed; that is, when the raising of chickens is an object in view. We have had considerable experience with all the large breeds of poultry, and we have invariably found the half-breeds the most profitable. The chicks of the thorough-breds do not mature so rapidly, and they are, from their nakedness of feathers at the most critical period of their lives, more subject to disease than the half-breeds.

The latter feather out much earlier than the others, and this is largely in their favor in this climate of sudden and great changes of temperature. To the poultry-breeder, then, who wishes quick-growing and early-maturing chickens, who cares more for two pounds in a *"Fourth of July broiler"* than five pounds in September, a cross between one of the varieties of the Brahma and the common fowl is most desirable. A very popular and profitable cross has been found between the Brahma and Leghorn, the offspring maturing quickly, and the pullets being early and good layers. To the large poultry-keeper, who wishes eggs more than chickens, of course the non-incubating breeds, or their grades, are most valuable. Crosses of Leghorns, Spanish, or Polish, with the common fowl, we have found to be, on the whole, about as profitable, or, rather, good layers, as the thorough-breds, and they stand our rough climate much better.

Of course, in the foregoing, we have not intended to include the breeders of fancy fowls, to be sold at "fancy prices," but we intended to treat simply of ordinary poultry-keepers.

There are not a few practical men who are of the opinion that good selections, that is, selections of perfectly sound, healthy dunghill fowls, are as valuable to the large poultry-keepers as are the thorough-breds. Our common barn-yard fowl is a conglomeration, or rather mixture, of almost every breed that has been in existence here, and the "good points" of some of the thorough-bred ancestors are often apparent. We once owned a hen which had the five toes of the Dorking, the white face of the Spanish, the crown of the Polish, and the feathered legs of the Brahma breeds. Thus it would be a wonder if the birds uniting such a variety of good bloods were not sometimes as valuable as the carefully bred varieties. To the small poultry-keeper who wishes eggs only, the Brown Leghorn, Black Spanish, and White Leghorn breeds are most desirable, and most valuable in the order in which we have named them.

To the villager who wishes early chickens and early eggs, the Dark Brahma is, perhaps, the best, either full-bred or grade, and if he is not particular as to the purity of the blood, but wishes the greatest pecuniary returns, a cross between Brown Leghorns and White Brahmas, or White Leghorns and Dark Brahmas, will pay him better than any other stock. The half-breed feathers and matures earlier, begins to lay younger, and lays more eggs than the full-blood Brahma, is larger, more quiet and domestic than the full-blood Leghorn, and makes a good setter and mother, which the Leghorn rarely becomes.

The following table is a record, by an experienced poultry keeper, of the cost of food and returns from ten pullets, six months old, of five different breeds, each flock of ten being kept by itself:—

	Cost of Feed.	Value of Eggs.	Value of Meat.	Total Value.	Total Profit.
Brahmas	$9.22	$12.10	$14.00	$26.10	$16.28
Cochins	10.15	11.82	14.16	23.42	16.29
Dorkings	7.72	10.48	11.90	22.38	14.36
Houdans	7.35	15.26	9.10	24.76	19.51
Leghorns	5.77	16.14	7.30	23.44	17.07

AGRICULTURE & HORTICULTURE

FROM THE 1875 ALMANAC

Clover as a Fertilizer.

It is not easy for many farmers to see how it is that clover should differ so much from other plants as to be regarded as a fertilizing rather than an exhaustive crop. To most people all crops seem to be exhaustive, as all crops must live and thrive, and they must have something to live and thrive on. They do not stop to think that it makes all the difference in the world where this something comes from.

Clover can be recommended, to be sure, for its intrinsic value as a forage crop; but it is more than this. It has the wonderful power of assimilating and storing up in its roots, its stems, and its leaves, a large amount of nitrogen. It sends its roots very deeply, and pumps up a portion of its food from great depths below the surface soil, while its leaves are broad and large, to absorb materials from the atmosphere. If, therefore, the stalks and leaves were allowed to remain and decay upon the soil, they would impart a still larger proportion of food to the plants that require large amounts of nitrogen, but have less power to seek it.

But let it be borne in mind that the roots of clover always remain in the soil, that they amount in extent or weight to two thirds of the stems and leaves, so that a heavy crop of clover must leave in the ground from a hundred and fifty to two hundred pounds of nitrogen to the acre, an amount quite sufficient to meet the wants of any crop which may follow it, which may not be able to get it so readily in any other way, as the wheat crop, for instance, or any other grain crop.

Let clover, therefore, have a prominent place in the rotation on all well-managed farms. It will improve rather than injure the soil, while it is, of itself, a very profitable and remunerative crop, especially for feeding to dairy stock.

Facts about Grafting.

There are many very curious facts about vegetable life that appear in the process of grafting and budding. We know, for instance, that we can graft the apricot on the plum, the peach on the apricot, and the almond on the peach, and thus we can produce a tree having plum roots and almond leaves. Of course, the wood of the stem or trunk will consist of four varieties of wood, each distinct in its characteristics, though formed of a continuous layer. We shall have a perfect peach wood and bark below the almond wood and bark, and then below that perfect apricot wood and bark, and at the bottom of all perfect plum wood and bark, with the roots of the plum to gather and supply nourishment to the whole series.

The intimate relation between the bark and the leaf is apparent; for, if we should cut off the almond branches, we could cause the different sets of wood to push out buds and leafy branches each of its own kind. The stem is compound, each section having its source of vitality in what is called the cambium layer, from which there grow annually a layer of wood and a layer of bark, each consisting of longitudinal, fibrous and vascular tissue, and of horizontal cellular tissue; and each section of this cambium layer makes cells of its own kind out of the compound fluid which nourishes the whole plant, being originally taken up from the soil by the plum roots. This may be regarded as one of the curiosities of plant life. The study of botany will develop many others. Botany ought to be introduced, under competent instruction, in our common schools. We hope the time will soon come when our children will be taught the names and properties of all the objects that come under their daily observation.

Labels for Trees.

It is often very desirable to preserve the names of fruit trees, shrubs, and plants. The simplest, cheapest, and most durable label we know of for this purpose is a strip of corroded zinc, with the name written on it with black lead. Some chemical action takes place between the plumbago and the corroded zinc that makes the name perfectly durable and incapable of being easily erased. If no old pieces of corroded zinc are near at hand, take any zinc and cut it into the desirable shape, and expose the pieces some weeks to the atmosphere, and they are ready for use, and may be attached to the trees or shrubs with copper wire, which is almost as durable as the zinc itself.

When the name is first written on the corroded zinc, it can be erased without difficulty; but in a few weeks it becomes permanently fixed, and no ordinary rubbing can get it off. We know of labels that have been in use for thirty years, hanging on trees in Colonel Wilder's nursery, that are as perfect and as legible as the day they were put on. Sometimes the label will get coated over with a white, salty-looking substance, so as to obscure the name, but a slight rubbing with the moistened finger will bring out the name very distinctly.

This simple and permanent plan was discovered accidentally by Marshall P. Wilder, who had previously been using indelible ink; but, being in a hurry one day, and wishing to make sure of saving the names of a lot of new fruits he was setting out, he simply wrote on the labels hastily with a black-lead pencil, intending to write them over with ink. To his surprise, they never needed mending.

RED TURKEY

Mennonites from Russia, who settled in Kansas in the 1870s, brought with them a new variety of winter wheat called "Red Turkey." They planted it successfully, and as a result Kansas became the leading wheat-growing state.

TREE LABELS

The simplest, cheapest, and most durable label we know of can be written on a strip of corroded zinc (or any kind of zinc) with an ordinary lead pencil.

Indian Corn.

To produce corn cheaply, the land should be manured to give 60 to 75 bushels per acre; to do this upon poor, run-out grass land will require twenty to twenty-five loads of manure of thirty bushels each. The manure should be spread late in the fall; November is the best time, but even later, in December or January, will be more beneficial than to spread in spring. The rains of winter and early spring will dissolve the valuable parts of the manure and diffuse them through the soil so as to be ready for the spreading roots of the corn. Repeated experiments by reliable farmers show that the effect upon the next year's corn crop of manure spread in November is nearly double that of the same amount of manure applied in spring.

The land should be ploughed early in May about six inches deep, and the surface worked up fine with the harrow. For this purpose the two-horse Randall harrow is best. If manure is not to be had in sufficient quantity, a good substitute is at hand in genuine fertilizers. Professor Stockbridge has told us how much of various chemicals should be applied to the poor lands of New England to produce a given quantity of corn. He says, for 50 bushels of corn we ought to apply 64 pounds of nitrogen, 77 pounds of actual potash, 31 pounds of soluble phosphoric acid to an acre of land. The yield from an acre thus manured and properly cultivated should be 50 to 70 bushels of shelled corn. Now the laws of Massachusetts require of every manufacturer of fertilizers that each package be marked with a statement of the quantity of nitrogen, soluble phosphoric acid, and potash contained in it; so that it is not a hard matter for the farmer to compare the prices and the strength of various fertilizers offered in the market, and select such a one, or such a mixture, as will give the required amount of plant food at the cheapest price.

The application of fertilizers according to the above proportions, but in larger quantities per acre, costing thirty-three dollars per acre, has been known to produce 80 bushels of shelled corn per acre; and many cases are known where corn has been raised on fertilizers at a cost of only forty cents per bushel, allowing the stover to be worth eight dollars per ton. To produce the most economical results, the corn should be worked by horse-power, and not hand-hoed. For this purpose several tools and machines will be needed when the work is done upon a scale of ten acres or more in a field. The fertilizer can be spread by hand well enough, and a machine will hardly be needed for this purpose, unless on large farms. A machine for planting the corn, however, will be found very useful and economical in fields of much size; they are made to plant one or two rows at a time, and put in the seed with great accuracy, making the rows so straight and even that the cultivators will work close up to the corn.

The Thomas smoothing-harrow is a most essential implement in growing large fields cheaply; it is drawn by two horses, and sweeps nine feet wide. A smaller size, for one horse, works five feet. It has a large number of small sharp steel teeth slanting backwards. It should be drawn over the field every five days from planting till the corn is eight inches high; it will kill the small weeds just as they break ground, and will not injure the corn to any extent worth naming. The cultivator and double mouldboard plough will finish the cultivation without any hand-hoeing at all.

Corn raised in this way need not cost over 40 cents a bushel; and as it almost always commands 70 cents or more in our market, there is a better margin for profit here than in the West, on account of the value of the stover, which there is considered worthless, but here is usually estimated as worth about 8 dollars per ton, or about 25 dollars per acre. With corn at 40 cents a bushel, the farmer could afford to keep more stock and feed a few hogs, and thus increase his manure pile.

The exhausted land of New England must have something done to improve it, and the best way to *begin* the improvement will be found, in most cases, by raising corn upon fertilizers. The crop may be depended upon to pay expenses, with a moderate profit, and the land will be improved enough after a year or two of corn on fertilizers to raise clover. With a fair proportion of land once in clover there will be little trouble in increasing the stock and keeping up the supply of manure.

Manufactured fertilizers, unlike manure, are applied with best results in spring. They should not be applied in the hill or drill, except in very small quantities and well mixed with the soil. The chemicals are so strong that where they come in contact with the young corn in any quantity, the roots are injured.

FROM THE 1878 ALMANAC

52

AGRICULTURE & HORTICULTURE

Grass Mixtures.

THE first settlers on these shores sowed no grass-seed, but relied on the spontaneous growth of the salt marshes and the inland swamps. The first step of progress was to use the seed from the bottom of haystacks and hay-mows. Years after, a few seeds were cleaned by winnowing; but it is scarcely more than half a century since it was the custom to limit the quantity of seed to twelve quarts, of which eight quarts were usually timothy, and the balance clover. Then the most common mixture came to consist of timothy and redtop almost exclusively, some farmers adding clover, but seldom any other seed. Clover blossoms early, usually about the middle of June; but timothy and redtop are both late grasses. One objection to this mixture is that clover comes into condition to cut long before the timothy and redtop; but a far more serious objection is, that the number of species is too limited. Other things being equal, a large number of species will produce a better crop than a small number. Nature is a good guide in this respect, for, if we examine the turf of an old field or pasture, we shall find a large number of species, often fifteen or twenty, growing in close connection.

But the special point we wish to make is, that for mowing-lots, cultivated for hay, we ought to regulate the selection of seed by the time of blossoming, that period of growth being agreed upon as the time when grass ought to be cut for hay, as then it contains its maximum amount of nutriment, which rapidly diminishes after the plant has passed this stage of growth. We would earnestly recommend sowing the early grasses together, and the late ones by themselves. A few species may properly be included in both mixtures, as their usual time of blossoming is intermediate, between the early and late species.

For an early mixture, we would take orchard grass as the basis. That blossoms by the middle of June or before, and it is one of the best grasses for hay on account of its luxuriant growth, its intrinsic nutritive qualities, and its habit of starting very rapidly after being cut or fed off by stock. It endures shade, too, better than most of our grasses, and this is a valuable characteristic. To orchard-grass seed we would add June grass, which is the same as Kentucky blue grass, one of our most common and valuable pasture grasses, worth less, perhaps, for hay, as it requires three or four years to reach its perfection and form a close sward. It blossoms very early, about the same time with orchard grass, and ought to be sown with it. Then we would add also perennial rye-grass, and especially the tall oat-grass. This last (the tall oat-grass) is not appreciated as it deserves to be. On rich and mellow land it is astonishing what crops it will produce. We saw it last season growing with the utmost luxuriance nearly six feet high, and it made the best of hay. We would also add a few pounds of meadow fescue. That is a common grass with us, makes good hay, and is worthy of a far more general cultivation. With these, clover can be grown with great advantage, as it blossoms about the same time. Then we should have the mixture as follows: orchard grass, June grass, perennial rye-grass, tall oat-grass, meadow fescue, and red clover and alsike clover,—a very good mixture for early haying. All these seeds can be procured in any quantity and at reasonable prices. The seedsman can advise as to the particular quantity of each, depending a little on the soil and location.

For a late mixture there is nothing better than timothy as a basis. We would use timothy, redtop, Rhode Island bent, meadow fescue, tall oat-grass, and alsike-clover. The meadow fescue and tall oat-grass would blossom a little earlier than redtop and timothy, and a little later than orchard and June grass, but the difference would not be very great, probably; and they are excellent additions to both mixtures.

The great advantage of these mixtures is, that they would produce grasses that are fit to cut at the same time. Another great gain is, that they spread the work over a longer season: some fields will be early and some late. This gives a chance to keep along with the hoeing, and that is not to be overlooked. The hay will be better than if early and late grasses are mixed together. If you mix clover with timothy and redtop, the clover will be mostly out of blossom when the other grasses are just coming into this condition. If you mix orchard grass with timothy, the former will be dead-ripe, and worthless for hay, when the latter is in blossom, while the timothy will hardly show itself at all, when the orchard grass is in blossom and fit to cut. These mixtures are for mowing-lots. For pastures the object should be to get a constant succession of growth; and the proper way is to sow all the kinds of grasses we can get.

THE ADVANTAGE OF GRASS MIXTURES

EARLY AMERICAN SEEDS

The first settlers on these shores sowed no grass-seed, but relied on the spontaneous growth of the salt marshes and the inland swamps. The first step of progress was to use the seed from the bottom of haystacks and haymows.

THE MOST NATURAL GRASSES

Other things being equal, a large number of species will produce a better crop than a small number. Nature is a good guide in this respect, for, if we examine the turf of an old field or pasture, we shall find a large number of species, often fifteen or twenty, growing in close connection.

FROM THE 1879 ALMANAC

AGRICULTURE & HORTICULTURE

FROM THE 1881 ALMANAC

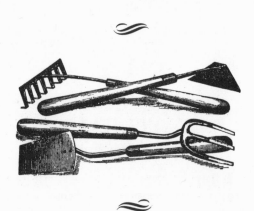

GETTING RID OF WEEDS

Weeds can be raised cheaper than most other crops, because they will bear more neglect. But they don't pay in the end. They are the little vices that beset plant-life, and are to be got rid of the best way we know how.

BE PREPARED

Don't fail to have a good tool-house, and a place for a set of carpenter's tools,—saws, chisels, hatchets, hammers, an assortment of nails, spikes, and bolts of every kind that may be needed in an emergency, to replace any breakage.

Practical Farm Hints.

For the yellows in peach trees apply potash salts to the surface under the tree, and rake it in, then put on a light mulching of old hay, straw, leaves, or any suitable materials. The German crude muriate of potash will, perhaps, be the least expensive, and one to two pounds, according to the size of the tree and the spread of its branches, a sufficient quantity. Apply a pound late in the fall, and the same quantity early in the spring, under each tree.

To sell dairy products in the form of butter is the least exhaustive system of dairy farming. Selling all the milk in its purity is parting with the farm inch by inch, and its constituents must be replaced in some form, or exhaustion will be sure to follow.

Don't try to live without labor. If necessity does not quicken the energies, keep to work as a matter of principle, for activity, mental and physical, is essential to the perfect development of human character.

To raise corn at small cost of labor, make the rows perfectly straight both ways. After the corn is well up, run a light plough as near the plants as possible, turning the furrow from the row. Do this on both sides of the row, and in both directions. The "hill" will be left standing in a little square, three or four inches higher than the bottom of the furrows. Let it stand so a few days. The roots need the heat of the sun at this time, and it will warm up the soil, and give the plants a rapid push. After a few days, run over the back furrow between the rows with a cultivator or horse-hoe. That will level the surface and throw the soil back towards the hills, and it is easy to keep the culture level. The cost of hand-hoeing with this method will be very slight.

In buying plants for the orchard or the garden, make it an inflexible rule never to buy a second-rate tree, shrub, vine, or seed of any kind, at any price, no matter how low, when you can get a first-rate article at a fair price. If you buy cheap goods of this kind because they are low-priced, you'll be sure to get what you bargain for. If you buy them below the real value of the best of their kind, you may be sure there is some "out" about them that you do not see.

As a general rule, for all hoed crops, plant in such a way that you can reach every hill, plant, or vine with the cultivator, and use this tool early and often. Where any crop needs clean culture, it will cost less to cultivate or hoe it every eight days than it will to hoe it once in fifteen days.

Weeds can be raised cheaper than most other crops, because they will bear more neglect. But they don't pay in the end. They are the little vices that beset plant-life, and are to be got rid of the best way we know how. The first thing is to avoid getting their seeds into manure. It is almost as important to keep the manure, as to keep the land, clean. The next is to take them early. It is cheaper to nip them in the bud than to pull them up, root and branch, when they get ahead. Here is where brain-work comes in. It is work that must be done, and the problem is to keep down the cost.

The time to cut grass is when the field shows the greatest number of blossoms. Nature fixes no particular day. Seasons vary several days, and some fields reach this stage of growth earlier than others. So judgment and skill will always be required to decide the question when it is best to begin. Let it be when the grass contains the most sugar, gum, starch, or other elements of nutrition, and cure it so as to preserve these constituents, and not drive them off by too much exposure to the sun.

Don't fail to have a good tool-house, and a place for a set of carpenter's tools,—saws, chisels, hatchets, hammers, an assortment of nails, spikes, and bolts of every kind that may be needed in an emergency, to replace any breakage; and duplicates of the parts of ploughs, mowing-machines, tedders, horse-hoes, &c. A liberal investment in these things will pay the highest per cent. interest of any investment you have.

STAGGERED PLANTING

Never plant the garden all at one time, but begin as early as the land is in good condition, and plant something every week until August.

AGRICULTURE & HORTICULTURE

FROM THE 1881 ALMANAC

WORK IS MATTER OF PRINCIPLE

THE YELLOW IN PEACHES

For the yellows in peach trees apply potash salts to the surface under the tree, and rake it in, then put on a light mulching of old hay, straw, leaves, or any suitable materials.

HUMAN CHARACTER

Don't try to live without labor. If necessity does not quicken the energies, keep to work as a matter of principle, for activity, mental and physical, is essential to the perfect development of human character.

ON BUYING PLANTS

In buying plants for the orchard or the garden, make it an inflexible rule never to buy a second-rate tree, shrub, vine, or seed of any kind, at any price, no matter how low, when you can get a first-rate article at a fair price. If you buy cheap goods of this kind because they are low-priced, you'll be sure to get what you bargain for.

Practical Farm Hints.

FOR the yellows in peach trees apply potash salts to the surface under the tree, and rake it in, then put on a light mulching of old hay, straw, leaves, or any suitable materials. The German crude muriate of potash will, perhaps, be the least expensive, and one to two pounds, according to the size of the tree and the spread of its branches, a sufficient quantity. Apply a pound late in the fall, and the same quantity early in the spring, under each tree.

To sell dairy products in the form of butter is the least exhaustive system of dairy farming. Selling all the milk in its purity is parting with the farm inch by inch, and its constituents must be replaced in some form, or exhaustion will be sure to follow.

DON'T try to live without labor. If necessity does not quicken the energies, keep to work as a matter of principle, for activity, mental and physical, is essential to the perfect development of human character.

To raise corn at small cost of labor, make the rows perfectly straight both ways. After the corn is well up, run a light plough as near the plants as possible, turning the furrow from the row. Do this on both sides of the row, and in both directions. The "hill" will be left standing in a little square, three or four inches higher than the bottom of the furrows. Let it stand so a few days. The roots need the heat of the sun at this time, and it will warm up the soil, and give the plants a rapid push. After a few days, run over the back furrow between the rows with a cultivator or horse-hoe. That will level the surface and throw the soil back towards the hills, and it is easy to keep the culture level. The cost of hand-hoeing with this method will be very slight.

IN buying plants for the orchard or the garden, make it an inflexible rule never to buy a second-rate tree, shrub, vine, or seed of any kind, at any price, no matter how low, when you can get a first-rate article at a fair price. If you buy cheap goods of this kind because they are low-priced, you'll be sure to get what you bargain for. If you buy them below the real value of the best of their kind, you may be sure there is some "out" about them that you do not see.

As a general rule, for all hoed crops, plant in such a way that you can reach every hill, plant, or vine with the cultivator, and use this tool early and often. Where any crop needs clean culture, it will cost less to cultivate or hoe it every eight days than it will to hoe it once in fifteen days.

WEEDS can be raised cheaper than most other crops, because they will bear more neglect. But they don't pay in the end. They are the little vices that beset plant-life, and are to be got rid of the best way we know how. The first thing is to avoid getting their seeds into manure. It is almost as important to keep the manure, as to keep the land, clean. The next is to take them early. It is cheaper to nip them in the bud than to pull them up, root and branch, when they get ahead. Here is where brain-work comes in. It is work that must be done, and the problem is to keep down the cost.

THE time to cut grass is when the field shows the greatest number of blossoms. Nature fixes no particular day. Seasons vary several days, and some fields reach this stage of growth earlier than others. So judgment and skill will always be required to decide the question when it is best to begin. Let it be when the grass contains the most sugar, gum, starch, or other elements of nutrition, and cure it so as to preserve these constituents, and not drive them off by too much exposure to the sun.

DON'T fail to have a good tool-house, and a place for a set of carpenter's tools, — saws, chisels, hatchets, hammers, an assortment of nails, spikes, and bolts of every kind that may be needed in an emergency, to replace any breakage; and duplicates of the parts of ploughs, mowing-machines, tedders, horse-hoes, &c. A liberal investment in these things will pay the highest per cent. interest of any investment you have.

AGRICULTURE & HORTICULTURE

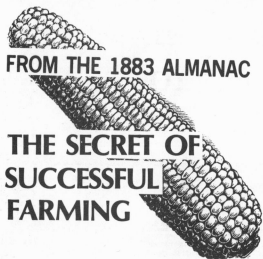

FROM THE 1883 ALMANAC

THE SECRET OF SUCCESSFUL FARMING

SUCCESS

Frequest cultivation may be regarded as the secret of success.

COTTON-SEED VS. CORN MEAL

Lawes and Gilbert, two accurate experimenters in England, fed a given number of sheep, on two acres of land, with a ton of cotton-seed meal; by the side of the same, on two similar acres, they fed to the same number of sheep, a ton of corn meal. They harvested in the first season and the first crop of the second year, fifteen hundred more pounds of hay where the cotton-seed meal was fed than where corn meal was fed. That is just about the difference in manurial value of these articles, and what might reasonably be expected in any similar experiment.

THE rain, hail, and snow that fall upon the surface of the earth hold in solution more or less of the gases of the atmosphere. The rains that fall in the country, upon our farms hold nitrogen and oxygen chiefly, with a small quantity of carbonic acid, and a still less quantity of carbonate of ammonium. They also hold some solid substances—chlorides, sulphates and nitrates of sodium, calcium, and ammonium in solution, while particles of dust, soot, etc., are held mechanically, and it is these last that give to rain-water its dirty appearance. The air of large towns is much richer in ammonia than that of the country. In northern latitudes southerly winds are richer in ammonia than those from any other quarter.

NITROGEN is a gaseous body, so that when it is spoken of as an element of plant food, it must be understood that it cannot be applied by itself, but only in combination with some salt, like sodium, ammonium, or potassium. It is in the form of nitrates that its application is most practicable, and in this form it is readily available to plants. The farmer who asked for a bag of nitrogen was surprised to find that there was no such thing.

WITH corn on the cob the proportional weight of the cob is, on an average, about one-eighth. Different varieties will vary slightly, but the general ratio will be one to seven.

TREES, shrubs and other plants may be overfed, when they will make too rank and watery a growth and not ripen their wood sufficiently. In such cases they do not resist the extremes of cold in winter and the great changes of the seasons, nor do they bear as well as they otherwise would. If underfed, on the other hand, they are apt to become stunted, and are neither useful nor beautiful. We have to use judgment as well as manures. Ripeness of woody fibre is essential to hardiness, and, indeed, it may be regarded as the source of hardiness.

THE perfect management of pear and apple orchards implies the frequent stirring of the surface with the cultivator or hoe, so as to keep it well pulverized. Once a week is none too often, and in severe and long-continued droughts, it is of the highest importance. The trees will make and maintain a better foliage for it, and perfect their fruit all the better. A soil kept well and often cultivated will show greater moisture two or three inches below the surface, which it would not show if it were allowed to harden. The influence of frequent cultivation is wonderful, and may be regarded as the secret of success.

LAWES AND GILBERT, two accurate experimenters in England, fed a given number of sheep, on two acres of land, with a ton of cotton-seed meal; by the side of the same, on two similar acres, they fed to the same number of sheep, a ton of corn meal. They harvested in the first season and the first crop of the second year, fifteen hundred more pounds of hay where the cotton-seed meal was fed than where corn meal was fed. That is just about the difference in manurial value of these articles, and what might reasonably be expected in any similar experiment.

THE Massachusetts Agricultural College at Amherst, is now, after so many years of vicissitudes, in a fair way to become a credit and an honor to the commonwealth. A farmer can now send his son there with a reasonable degree of confidence that he will be well taught, and that the tone and discipline of the college will be such as to give promise of turning out first-class citizens. It is worthy of a far more generous and extended patronage.

THE COB

With corn on the cob the proportional weight of the cob is, on an average, about one-eighth. Different varieties will vary slightly, but the general ratio will be one to seven.

AGRICULTURE & HORTICULTURE

FACTS FOR FARMERS.

Leguminous crops, like pease and beans, clover and lucerne, contain large amounts of nitrogen, twice as much as that found in the cereals. They also contain large amounts of lime and potash. The lime is found chiefly in the leaf. Silica is very nearly absent in these crops.

A good crop of red clover, cut for hay, removes a large quantity of nitrogen from the land, but, curiously enough, it leaves the surface soil actually richer in nitrogen than it was before the crop was sown. There is no mistake about this. And yet it is still true that nitrogenous manures usually produce but little effect on leguminous crops. They seem to prefer to pump up their nitrogen from the subsoil, while their broad leaves may get a little from the atmosphere.

Potash manures have more effect on leguminous crops than nitrogenous ones, but when "clover sickness" or "bean sickness" strikes the land even potash manures fail to cure it. There is no known remedy, and the only way is to grow other crops for a series of years.

Wheat requires hot and dry weather at the period of ripening, but oats will ripen in a moist atmosphere. Mangolds require heat, and can resist drought, while turnips grow and mature best in a cool, moist air.

By the growth of deep-rooting crops, like red clover, lucerne, mangolds, wheat and rye, in a rotation, the subsoil is made to contribute to the fertility of the farm and to yield up its accumulated wealth. Shallow-rooted crops, like white clover, potatoes, turnips and barley, cannot ask the subsoil to add to the products of the farm. Deep and shallow-rooted plants ought to alternate.

Potatoes are surface feeders, and require liberal general manuring to insure an abundant crop. Both root crops and potatoes require large supplies of potash, and so kainit, or the German potash salts, are very useful to both, but farmyard manure will always supply a considerable amount of potash.

Hay contains a much larger proportion of potash and lime than the cereal crops and a much smaller amount of phosphoric acid. If grass is to be cut for hay, manures containing potash, lime, and phosphoric acid will be required. Grass roots are shorter than those of the cereals and less able to collect the ash constituents from the soil.

Farmyard manure, or the feeding of cotton seed or linseed meal, grain or roots on the land, is the most appropriate manuring for permanent pasture, if quality as well as quantity of produce is considered.

Large crops of hay may be obtained by manuring with nitrate of sodium, which comes by thousands of tons from Chili and Peru, mixed with kainit from Germany, and a little superphosphate, but a continuance of such treatment is apt to promote a coarse herbage.

The natural clovers of a meadow or field are destroyed by the continued application of highly nitrogenous manures, but they are developed and encouraged by the application of manures containing potash and lime, and by pasturing instead of mowing.

Land laid down with clover is better than money in bank, drawing more interest than any bank can pay and compounding the interest oftener. The moral is, sow clover.

Deep-rooting plants like clover, wheat, the mangold and some others, are best able to resist a drought, while shallow-rooting crops, like grass, turnips, etc., are the ones that suffer most from it.

The composition of a crop is not a sufficient guide to the character of the manure suited to it, even when we know in addition the composition of the soil on which it is to be grown. It is not only the materials required to form a crop, but the power of the plants to assimilate these materials, that will enable us to judge, and that depends a good deal on tillage.

Turnips and swedes draw their food chiefly from the surface soil. Mangolds have deeper roots than turnips and a longer period of growth, and so they have greater capacity for drawing food from the soil, such as nitrogen, potash and phosphoric acid. Phosphatic manures are less important for them than for turnips. Purely nitrogenous manures, like nitrate of sodium, produce great effect on mangolds, but turnips require phosphates as well as nitrogen in their food. The special character of the manure for turnips should be phosphatic, that for mangolds nitrogenous.

The fertility of a soil is closely connected with its power of retaining plant food. Light sandy soils have little retentive power; they allow the water from rains to drain through them, and this carries off much of the constituents of plant food, and so they lose much that is applied to them. They are dependent on immediate supplies.

Nitrate of soda used alone will, in most cases, produce a large crop of mangolds; superphosphate alone, a large crop of turnips, while potash salts alone will produce a striking effect on pastures and clovers.

A living plant is composed largely of water. Many succulent vegetables, like turnips, lettuce, cucumbers and watermelons contain more than ninety per cent of water. Timber cut in the dryest time rarely contains less than forty per cent. If you burn a branch of a tree or any other plant the greater part passes off as a gas, but a small quantity of ash is left behind. The combustible part, often called organic, is largely obtained from the atmosphere; *the ash*, or mineral part, wholly from the soil.

The roots of plants will not grow in the absence of oxygen and they rot when they reach the permanent water level. Drainage, therefore, is the best remedy, since it increases the depth to which the roots of plants can penetrate, and so vastly increases their feeding ground and makes the subsoil available to them as a source of nutrition.

The pig is not a very popular animal on our eastern farms, but it is the most economical meat-making machine we have. The stomach of an ox or a sheep is very much larger in proportion to live weight than that of the pig, while the proportion of intestines is greater in the pig than in the sheep or the ox. So these latter, as ruminants generally, are best fitted to deal with food that requires long digestion, while the pig assimilates food far more rapidly. So the pig increases in weight far more rapidly than either the sheep or the ox, and not only is the rate of increase more rapid, but this increase is far greater in proportion to the food taken. To be sure his food is usually more digestible, but his capacity for assimilation is far greater and hence the more rapid increase.

SOIL FERTILITY

The fertility of a soil is closely connected with its power of retaining plant food. Light sandy soils have little retentive power; they allow the water from rains to drain through them, and this carries off much of the constituents of plant food, and so they lose much that is applied to them.

AGRICULTURE & HORTICULTURE

FARM HINTS.

THE increase of glucose manufactories has brought into the market a new feeding substance known as gluten meal. It is rich in nitrogen and comes in for economic value for feeding purposes between bran or shorts and meal or oil-cake, and compares favorably with bean and pea meal. It is deficient in mineral constituents, and ought to be fed with coarser articles of fodder, and such as are rich in these constituents. It may be mixed with shorts or bran to advantage. It is worth trying, and is cheap enough at the present market prices.

THE great mistake that most farmers make in the growth of fruit is the selection of too many varieties. For domestic or family use it is desirable to have a supply extending over the season, some early, medium, and late varieties, and a reasonable assortment of each; but for market a very limited number of the best kinds will be much more profitable than a great variety. Of the pears, when you have the Bartlett, the Seckel, the Hovey, the Sheldon, and the Beurré d'Anjou, you cover the whole season from August to March, and they are all first class. You can hardly have too many of any one of them, as they are all salable.

EVERY farmer ought to grow a liberal supply of apples, and, when he sets about it, a choice selection of a few kinds will be far better than a great variety. For family use a list extending over the season, from early to late, is, of course, admissible; but for market a few of the very best will pay better than a large number of kinds. The Baldwin, of course, is the king of all. That, as everybody knows, is a winter variety. The Gravenstein, the Hubbardston, the Porter, the Williams, the Greening, the Roxbury, or Hunt's Russet ought to be about the limit. They are all good, ripen at different times, and sell readily when they are sorted and put up properly.

THE best peach growers confine their attention to a few sorts. For domestic use or home consumption they want a few that ripen at different times, from the earliest to the latest. Few would be without both the early and the late Crawford. Both are splendid peaches when well grown, and thinned out so as not to overbear. Then comes the Mountain Rose, a superb peach, the Coolidge, and the Old Mixon. There are other fine varieties, but these are among the very best, and no one can go amiss in selecting and cultivating them. Mineral fertilizers, superphosphates, and especially muriate of potash, are better suited to the peach tree than stable manures.

THE strawberry is worthy of universal cultivation. It is not difficult to grow, is always relished in every family, and, with the exception of a few individuals who cannot eat it without injury, it is one of the most healthful of fruits. It is always readily marketable, so much so that many tons of the very poorest sort, like the Wilson's Albany, are thrown upon the market and taken up by those who hardly know what a good strawberry is. The best varieties, all things considered, are the Sharpless, the Charles Downing, the Bidwell, and the Hovey, which ought to be grown alongside a few Bostons, or Brighton Pines. On a suitable soil, the President Wilder is a superb fruit. It is a little more exacting in this respect than some other varieties.

THE BLACKBERRY

The blackberry is not so generally grown as it ought to be. It is about the most healthful of all fruits, and produces abundantly when properly treated. It is worthy of a fair share of space in every garden, and those who make a specialty of it and bring it to perfection find it a profitable market crop.

SELECTIVE PLANTING

The great mistake that most farmers make in the growth of fruit is the selection of too many varieties. For domestic or family use it is desirable to have a supply extending over the season, some early, medium, and late varieties, and a reasonable assortment of each.

THE raspberry has fewer growers than most other fruits, but it ought to be found in every garden in sufficient quantities for home consumption. It is one of the most healthful, as well as one of the most palatable of fruits, is easily grown, readily salable, and returns a good profit on the cost. A few kinds will give a better result than many, and the old Franconia, the Clark, the Brinkle's Orange, and the Fastolff are among the very best. With these most growers ought to be satisfied. It is better to leave experimenting with a great variety of fruits and with seedlings to the nurseryman, whose business it is to keep all sorts.

THE blackberry is not so generally grown as it ought to be. It is about the most healthful of all fruits, and produces abundantly when properly treated. It is worthy of a fair share of space in every garden, and those who make a specialty of it and bring it to perfection find it a profitable market crop. The varieties are not very numerous as compared with the other fruits, and we may confine our attention chiefly to the Dorchester, the Schneider, and the Kittatinny. The Lawton was a great favorite a few years ago, but we think it has not quite held its own in competition with others.

No farmhouse can afford to be without an abundant supply of currants. Till a comparatively recent date it was free from insect pests, and grew fairly well in the midst of the most utter neglect, and overrun with grass and weeds. With better care and better methods of cultivation it has been much improved, both in size and quality, while it is pretty universally appreciated, though by no means so universally consumed as it ought to be. Some families think it requires a little too much sugar, and that is expensive, but when it comes to a question of health, and it is found to take the lead of most other fruits in this respect, we might as well say, hang the expense, give us plenty of currants. The only drawback is the attack of the currant worm, but it is a very simple matter to resist it with the use of a powder known as pyrethrum, or Persian insect powder, or a powder recently introduced under the name of Buhach, that is to be applied in the same way, dusted over the leaves when they are wet with dew or rain.

IT is very clear that it is for the interest of every wide-awake farmer to improve the quality of the manure of his stables, and to make it as rich as possible. It costs no more to handle and apply a cord or a ton of the best than it does a cord or a ton of the poorest. A pound of nitrogen in rich manure is worth more than the same weight of nitrogen in a poor and low quality of manure, because it is in a condition more immediately available for plant food. It ought, therefore, to be as much a study to improve the quality as to increase the quantity of stable manures.

ESTIMATING the actual value of manure from the standpoint of the nitrogen, phosphoric acid, and potash in its composition, which is the conclusion of modern science and practice combined, it has been possible to construct a table of manurial values of the different kinds of cattle foods which go to make up the manures of our barnyards and stables. No doubt they are approximately correct. They show that of all these articles of food the decorticated cotton-seed meal, fed to animals, produced the richest and most valuable manure. Previous analysis had shown it to be richest in the chemical constituents most important for the food of plants, that is, nitrogen, phosphoric acid, and potash.

58

AGRICULTURE & HORTICULTURE

FROM THE 1886 ALMANAC

 **PEACHES & RYE**

PEACH TREES NEED BREATHING SPACE

The great mistake many peach-growers have made is in setting the trees too near together. They do well enough at first, but after a few years' growth the roots meet in the ground and rob each other of proper nourishment and plant food. A peach-tree is a gross feeder. It makes wood rapidly and it requires abundant space, though a medium or even a poor soil is to be preferred rather than one too rich. With a rather poor soil we can feed to it just what it needs, without the risk of overfeeding, and a consequent tender growth of wood that is quite liable to winterkill.

LET US RAISE PEACHES!

THE readers of this Gem of the Season will recollect that we have repeatedly recommended the use of muriate of potash to be applied around peach-trees as a preventive and remedy for the yellows, a disease which no one seems fully to understand, but which has made it so difficult, of late years, to raise such crops as we used to within the memory of most farmers who have passed the meridian of life. Prof. Goessmann is entitled to the credit of having instituted the first experiments in this direction, and his investigations have borne highly valuable fruit. Here is the testimony of a practical fruit-grower of large experience, and it is worthy of the most careful consideration. He says: "At the time of planting the first trees, the whole ground, some five or six acres, was manured with about 800 pounds of muriate of potash to the acre (probably a very heavy and unnecessary application), except on one field near the house, where some 200 trees were planted. No potash was applied there. Every year since, all of these orchards have had from five to six hundred pounds of muriate of potash per acre applied, sometimes in the fall, sometimes in the spring, and this plantation of nearly 200 trees near the house has never had any potash until this last season, in the spring. They were then five years old. Of the 5800 trees, where the potash has been applied for the last four or five years, there is just one tree that shows any trace of the yellows, and of the 200 trees that have not had an application of potash, over thirty per cent. of them are dead with the yellows, and at least twenty per cent. of the balance show traces of the yellows."

This result, which corresponds with the experience of others, seems to justify the hope that the time is not far distant when the peach will be added to the long list of fruits which flourish in our soil as it used to do half a century ago. The only drawback apart from the yellows is the borer, but with ordinary care and attention we can prevent its ravages, because we know how to treat and exterminate it.

The great mistake many peach-growers have made is in setting the trees too near together. They do well enough at first, but after a few years' growth the roots meet in the ground and rob each other of proper nourishment and plant food. A peach-tree is a gross feeder. It makes wood rapidly and it requires abundant space, though a medium or even a poor soil is to be preferred rather than one too rich. With a rather poor soil we can feed to it just what it needs, without the risk of overfeeding, and a consequent tender growth of wood that is quite liable to winterkill.

A LITTLE MORE RYE.

IT is a capital idea to sow a small patch of winter rye every fall, near the hen-house. A few square rods will furnish a real treat for the fowls in the mild days of winter, and in the early spring, when a bit of green food is not easy to find. For spring use it may be sown as late as October, but for late fall and winter it is better to sow it in August, or the first of September. It can well follow early potatoes, pease or corn, or take an old sod where the grass has run out.

It is a wonder, also, that every farmer does n't sow a patch of rye for early spring feeding for cows. If cut early, while it is tender and juicy, cows and horses are very fond of it. After it reaches its full size, and is headed out, they will often refuse it. For this reason it is not worth while to sow more than you 'll be likely to want. If you overdo the thing, and get more than the hens and the cows will consume green and tender, you may be disappointed. But that is no reason why you should n't put in a little. Sow at the rate of two bushels of seed to the acre.

AGRICULTURE & HORTICULTURE

FARM HINTS.

IF you are afraid to use Paris green to kill the Colorado beetles that swarm on your potato-vines, make a mixture of five pounds each of slacked lime and copperas in twenty gallons of water, and sprinkle the vines. If taken at just the right time, once going over the field ought to do; but, if that does n't stop their voracity, try it again. It helps the plants.

IF the "striped bug," the squash-bug, or the borer threaten the cucumbers, the squashes, or the melons, make a solution of saltpetre, an ounce to a gallon of water, and sprinkle them once a day for three or four days in succession. It won't cost much to try it, and melons and cucumbers are good things to have.

IT is easy to propagate currants and gooseberries from cuttings taken from new shoots. Put them in rich earth, leaving an inch and one bud above ground, with four or five inches below the surface.

IF you try to raise celery, give it plenty of water. It is a great drinker, and, if it has n't enough to quench its thirst, it is apt to grow tough and hollow. Keep the plants growing right along from the time they appear above ground in the seed-bed till they are transplanted to rich soil, and water as often as they need it, and you'll have it tender and plump.

THE female moth of the canker-worm is wingless, and must crawl up the trunk of the tree to deposit her eggs. Anything that will prevent her from getting up will stop the ravages of this terrible pest of our orchards, which seems to be gaining ground every year. Scrape off the rough bark three feet from the ground, and fasten bands of paper tightly round the trunk, and smear it with printer's ink from the middle of October to hard freezing, and then again for two or three weeks after the middle of March.

A cow kept by herself will generally give better results in the way of milk and cream than the same cow in a herd with others. One reason of it is, no doubt, the fact that she is better fed and cared for; but another is that most of the butter made from her comes from real cream, which is rarely the case when the milk and cream of a herd of cows are mixed before churning.

EVERY farmer has noticed a great difference in the time required for churning to bring the butter from the milk or cream of different cows. This is owing to the difference in the size of the butter-globules in the milk of cows. In some the butter-globules are very much larger, and the time required to break them and bring the butter is correspondingly short.

THERE is a constant or insensible exhalation of moisture from the leaves and foliage of growing plants something analogous to the insensible perspiration of the healthy human skin, which is always perspiring, though the sweat may not stand in drops. Of course, this evaporation, constantly going on, though unperceived, involves the exhaustion of moisture in the soil.

CLOVER, like most of the grasses, ought to be cut at the time of blossoming. If the tedder is used, it may be got ready to be cocked up the same day. The best farmers usually prefer to cure it chiefly in the cock. To handle it when the stalks and leaves are dry and brittle involves a great loss. It requires more care than ordinary hay.

A COMPOST of hard-wood ashes and oyster-shell lime enabled a Pennsylvania farmer, last year, to raise and sell over $6,000 worth of potatoes from twelve acres of land. He ploughed deep, used medium-sized, well-formed, uncut potatoes planted three feet apart, gave level culture, and cultivated often. He took forty-one fine large tubers from one hill.

AS MAN GROWS SO PLANTS GROW

THE STRIPED BUG

If the "striped bug," the squash-bug, or the borer threaten the cucumbers, the squashes, or the melons, make a solution of salpetre, an ounce to a gallon of water, and sprinkle them once a day for three or four days in succession. It won't cost much to try it, and melons and cucumbers are good things to have.

LONESOME COW

A cow kept by herself will generally give better results in the way of milk and cream than the same cow in a herd with others. One reason of it is, no doubt, the fact that she is better fed and cared for; but another is that most of the butter made from her comes from real cream, which is rarely the case when the milk and cream of a herd of cows are mixed before churning.

AGRICULTURE & HORTICULTURE

FROM THE 1888 ALMANAC

APPLE GROWING and MARKET GARDENING

FACTS FOR FARMERS.

The first fruit raised in this country was upon Governor's Island, in Boston Harbor, from which, on the 10th of October, 1639, ten fair pippins were brought up to the town. The words of the old record are, "there being not one apple or pear tree planted in any part of the country, but upon that island." The island seems to have belonged at that time to John Winthrop, the first governor of the colony of Massachusetts Bay.

The Baldwin, which must be regarded as, on the whole, the best of our New England apples, originated in the town of Wilmington, Mass., and was named from Loammi Baldwin, the engineer who laid out the old Middlesex canal from Lowell to Boston. The Hubbardston Nonsuch originated in the town of that name in Worcester county, Mass. The Minister originated on the farm of a Mr. Saunders, in Rowley, Mass. The Porter was first raised by the Rev. S. Porter of Sherburne, Mass. The Williams originated on the farm of Maj. Benj. Williams of Roxbury, Mass. All these favorites were accidental. They have, perhaps, been somewhat improved by cultivation, but they were not the product of any attempt to create new varieties.

The Red Astrachan, an apple of extraordinary beauty and one of the earliest to please the palate, was first imported into England from Sweden in 1816, and from there imported into this country. The Pound Sweeting, sometimes called the Pumpkin Sweet, seems to have been raised first in Manchester, Conn. The Early Harvest, one of our beautiful and most excellent early apples, beginning to ripen soon after the first of July and continuing through that month, is an American apple, but we do not know where it originated. It is of medium size, roundish, of a very smooth skin and of a bright straw color when ripe.

The Baldwin, like most other varieties of winter apples which originated in the northern and eastern states, when grown at the south, becomes a fall or early winter apple, and loses much of its sprightly taste and its good quality as a table fruit. But the early varieties or summer apples originating here are usually greatly improved when grown at the south.

It used to be regarded as absurd for any but a young man to set out fruit trees. A curious incident in the life of the venerable Mr. Cobb of Kingston, Mass., aptly illustrates the feeling which prevailed very generally throughout New England. He began to set out an orchard at the age of seventy. The idea seemed so ludicrous as to subject him to the ridicule of the whole neighborhood. He lived to the age of one hundred and seven and died in 1801, having enjoyed for many years the fruits of his labors.

The best time for grafting fruit trees is in the spring about the time the sap begins to move. This is earliest in the plum and the cherry, and later in the apple and the pear. The exact time, of course, varies a little with the climate and the season, but will usually be in March and April. A mild atmosphere and occasional showers are favorable to success. The scions should generally be selected beforehand, say very early in the spring, and kept in moist earth in the cellar. In other words the stock on which the scion is to be placed, ought to be a little more advanced, with the sap in more active circulation, than that of the scion.

The practice of grafting as a means of multiplying and propagating choice fruit is of very ancient date. It was well known to the ancient Greeks and Romans, and the latter adopted a great variety of methods about as ingenious as any known to our modern gardeners. The French, who are among the most expert in grafting, practising as many as fifty different methods, have succeeded perfectly in grafting annuals like the dahlia, the tomato, etc.

By grafting we can hasten the bearing of seedling varieties of fruit, and such as are slow in coming into bearing, and so obtain their fruit much sooner than we otherwise could. A seedling pear, for example, which would require at least a dozen years to produce fruit on its own stock, will begin to bear the third or fourth year if grafted on or near the ends of the branches of a mature tree.

The market garden is a specialty which many a young man thinks he can master, but in which he often fails for want of knowing the conditions requisite for sucesss. The market gardens within six miles from Boston are worth often more than a thousand dollars per acre for purposes of cultivation. Capital, therefore, is one of the great requisites for success in this business; but, in addition, there must be good soil, and that within easy reach of a good market.

The market garden implies the highest cultivation. A very large amount of manure is to be applied to a small amount of land. Twenty to thirty cords to the acre, every year, is not uncommon, and for a garden of ten or a dozen acres a two-horse team is kept going nearly every day to draw manure, to say nothing of the carting of the produce, which, if skilfully marketed, will amount to from eight hundred to a thousand dollars per acre.

With the conditions absolutely necessary for success in market gardening, one must have a natural tact for it, and this implies habits of industry and a keen eye, together with some years of experience, so as to be familiar with the infinite details of the business. Within five or six miles of a large city both the market and the manure wagon can make two trips or more a day, if necessary, and this is often the case.

The number of hands required to run a market garden within five or six miles of the city will be about one man to the acre in summer, and a horse for every three acres, and the crops most frequently produced are the bulky but valuable ones, such as lettuce, spinach, radishes, dandelions for greens, beets, early cabbages, onions, kale, horseradish, celery, the early crops being followed by later ones on the same land, such as squashes, melons, tomatoes, cauliflowers, carrots, parsnips, etc. Dandelions and rhubarb occupy the land for the whole year, but with most other things two crops are grown on the same land, and sometimes even three or four crops a year are raised on the same ground.

As to gardens, or farms devoted to market gardening, at a greater distance from market, say from eight to twelve or fifteen miles, the conditions are different. Land is cheaper, ranging from one to two hundred dollars per acre, the cost of hauling manure and produce is much greater, and the management varies accordingly. The capital required will be less, and the crops raised, such as need less manure, and are in general less bulky, like beans, pease, asparagus, early potatoes, strawberries and other small fruits, squashes, late cabbages and turnips, cucumbers for pickles. The market wagon will make fewer trips, say three or four times a week in summer, only once or twice in winter.

While market gardens near the city will require a working capital of five to eight hundred dollars per acre, to be invested in tools, teams, buildings, hot beds, manure, etc.: those lying at a greater distance may be worked with a capital of from one hundred to two hundred dollars per acre, and the force required for efficient working will be less, say on an average one man and a horse for every two or three acres.

If you hear the question asked, "Does farming pay?" you can safely answer yes, when the right man is found in the right place. Those who fail will be found to be the wrong men in the right men's place. They would as a general rule fail in any other calling for which they were no more fitted than they were for the farm. In other words, it depends more upon the energy and intelligence of the man and his love for the work, than upon the kind of business which he follows.

FIRST AMERICAN FRUITS

The first fruit raised in this country was upon Governor's Island, in Boston Harbor, from which, on the 10th of October, 1639, ten fair pippins were brought up to the town. The words of the old record are, "there being not one apple or pear tree planted in any part of the country, but upon that island."

61

AGRICULTURE & HORTICULTURE

THE QUALITY OF MILK.

It often becomes important, as in the feeding of infants or the sick, to study the quality of milk, and to see that it continues to be uniform as that from the same animal is supposed to be. The milk inspectors of our cities look after the chemical constituents, to see if the article contains the ordinary proportion of sugar, caseine and fat, and if it has a certain percentage of solids, as the law requires, but they seldom or never study the pathological conditions as exhibited in the use of the article, when, in fact, the very strongest evidence that a cow produces healthy milk is, that she has a calf that is strong and healthy at birth, and makes a rapid and vigorous development while being fed on the milk of its dam. We must go to herds where the calves are strong and healthy, and a proper inspection would include the districts from whence the milk is taken, to see the cows and their calves, to examine the food they eat, and the water they drink. There could be formed a vastly better opinion as to whether the milk is sound and healthful, than that based on the amount of solid constituents or on the amount of sugar and caseine. A milk that is first rate for calves, as shown in their thrift and rapid growth, is as good as it can be for children and for grown people too. Look, therefore, to the herds where the milk is drawn. If they are kept clean and well fed, and especially if their young show a strong and healthy growth, you may be sure their milk is good.

BAD ODORS AFFECT MILK.

Since the adoption a few years ago of the factory system of dairying, which led to the employment of a class of men whose whole time and thought were given strictly to the handling and study of milk in the butter and cheese factories, many things have been brought to light which were never before known or suspected. Many old theories and old teachings have been clearly shown to be false, and many new facts have been established as to the nature of milk and the causes which affect its quality.

Among the important facts brought to light by close and careful observation and study, is that bad odors breathed in by cows in the pasture where they feed will most seriously taint their milk. Any putrifying bodies, or carrion of any kind sending off foul odors which the cows must inhale, will surely injure the milk and make it unfit for cheese or butter, even when mixed with a large mass of milk from cows not so situated. Milk secretions are so extremely sensitive that absolute cleanliness and purity, both while the cows are at pasture and in their stalls, must be insisted upon and maintained by all farmers and dairymen who aim to produce a first class article either for home use or for the market.

PACKING BUTTER.

Butter nowadays is often sent to distant markets, and it becomes a matter of the first importance to pack it properly. The readiness of a sale will depend very much upon it. The utmost care should be taken in the first place to free the butter entirely from milk by washing and working it after churning, at a temperature so low as to prevent it from losing its granular texture and becoming greasy. Of course every good butter maker knows that the quality of the product will depend, in a great measure, on the temperature at which the milk or cream is churned and worked over, which should be from 60° to 65° of Fahr. When free from milk, eight ounces of fine salt will be enough for ten pounds. While the tub or firkin is being packed, the contents should be kept from the air by being covered with brine. No salt that is undissolved should be put in the bottom of the tub. The firkin should be made of white oak with hickory hoops, to hold about eighty pounds.

New tubs can be prepared in the shortest time, by dissolving common or bi-carbonate of soda in boiling water, as much as will dissolve, and water enough to fill the tubs. Let it stand over night and the tub can be used the next day.

ICE CREAM CONES

In 1896, Italo Marcioni, an Italian immigrant living in New Jersey, made the first ice cream cone. His special mold was patented on December 13, 1903 and became popular after it was introduced at the Louisiana Purchase Exposition in St. Louis, Mo. in 1904.

FROM THE 1889 ALMANAC

ICE CREAM

Ice cream, probably first created in 17th-century England, was popular with wealthy Americans of the 18th century. In 1790, George Washington spent $200.00 on ice cream in two months.

A NOVEL CHURN.

A delicate and fine flavored butter may be made by simply wrapping the cream in a napkin or clean cloth, and burying it a foot deep or so in the earth, from twelve to twenty-four hours. The experiment has been repeatedly tried with complete success. The butter will come out sweet and palatable, but destitute of the yellow or straw color common to most butter in summer. Of course it requires to be salted to the taste as much as butter made by any other process. A tenacious sub-soil loam would seem to be best for such an experiment. After putting the cream into a clean cloth the whole should be surrounded by a coarse towel.

ICE IN THE DAIRY.

In the management of the dairy, a good ice house and a full supply of ice for summer use are not only very convenient for controlling the temperature of the room and for preserving and keeping the butter at a proper consistency, but profitable in other respects. Ice houses are so easily constructed and the supply is so readily obtained, that no well ordered dairy should be without it. It is housed when other farm work is not pressing. Ponds are so distributed over the country, that it can generally be procured with little difficulty. In the want of ponds or streams in the immediate vicinity, an artificial pond can be easily made by damming up the outlet of some spring in the neighborhood, in which case, it is hardly necessary to say, the utmost care should be taken to keep the water perfectly clean when the ice is forming. The location of the ice-house should be above ground, in a dry and airy place. The top of a dry knoll is better than a low damp shade. Ice may be packed in sawdust, tan, shavings, or other non-conducting substances, and when wanted for use it should be taken from the top.

SPARE THE BIRDS.

It is right at all times for a man to stick up for his friends. Most of us would like to have them come and live near by, and be close neighbors, as well as friends. But judging from the wanton destruction of the birds in some sections, one would say that many a man does not know his friends when he sees them. There is no doubt that the wren, the swallow, the martin, the ground sparrow, the robin, the thrush, the blue bird, the bob-o-link, the cat-bird and other gay songsters, save us from more flies, worms and other insects, than all the nostrums and scare-crows ever invented. A pair of ground sparrows, while feeding their young, will catch and use about 3,360 caterpillars in a week. A hundred crows, that are hunted down as if they were our greatest enemies, will eat a ton and a half of grubs and worms in a single season. That sort of hobgoblin, the bat, so apt to be knocked on the head if he ventures to enter the house, will destroy its own bulk of flies in a single night. A flock of young turkeys will destroy their weight of grasshoppers every three days, while these insects cover our fields in the summer. Sixteen fresh beetles, making a pile equal to its bulk after a day of fasting, have been found at one time in the stomach of a single toad. The frog, leaving his puddle at times and traipsing over the dewy fields, gets his chief living in the same way. Let us study to find out who and what our friends are, and then lift a helping hand to protect and defend them.

PAY AS YOU GO.

Nothing is more certain than that little things make the man. As a rule, the world will gauge a man, and weigh his character, not so much by what they hear of him, as by what they see of him. Now, it is very true that at some seasons the cash seems to go faster than it comes, and it is so easy to say to the grocer, the blacksmith, the butcher, and the mechanic who mends a tool, "You may charge it," that many are apt to fall into the habit of it, and it is one of the very worst and most expensive habits in the world. Better hire fifty or a hundred dollars for a time, than to incur little debts. Never let a tradesman enter your name on his books. He'll be sure to charge for it, as he ought to.

AGRICULTURE & HORTICULTURE

ON TRIMMING HEDGES & TRANSPLANTING EVERGREENS

Mountain hemlock. Engelmann spruce. Blue spruce.

TRIMMING HEDGES.

THE close observer who fully realizes the beauties of nature, never looks on a hedge trimmed so as to show a level top and perpendicular sides, without a feeling of disgust ; and his sympathy goes out to the man who handled the shears with so little conception of either the beauties or the demands of nature. Who ever saw a tree grow naturally with a perfectly level top, and limbs reaching just as far from the trunk at the top as at the bottom? When man demands of Nature a change so great and so unnatural, she rebels, and refuses to submit. The shortened limbs at the bottom of the hedge refuse to send out leaves, and thus they die, leaving large, unsightly gaps in the hedge, which the owner makes every effort to fill up, but never succeeds so long as the top of the hedge is kept as wide as the bottom. As the gaps grow larger and larger every year, the time comes when the hedge must be cut down, hoping it will grow thicker at the bottom ; and it will for a few years, but when at the proper height, and the top spreads out so as to trim a square top and perpendicular sides, the process of decay commences again, and the result is as bad as, or even worse than, when the hedge was cut down.

This may all be avoided if nature be consulted, and the trees comprising the hedge be trimmed in a manner to conform to nature.

Let the hedge be trimmed so as to keep the bottom limbs the longest and the top the shortest. This gives the sun a chance to shine on the leaves of the lowest limbs, the same as in the natural growth. The top of the hedge should be arched.

A hedge thus trimmed will be more natural, more beautiful, and will rarely show any places bare of leaves at the bottom.

The writer has a hedge that has been trimmed thus for more than thirty years, yet it is to-day just as thick with branches and leaves at the bottom as at the top and bids fair to present a beautiful appearance for thirty years to come.

TRANSPLANTING EVERGREEN TREES.

THE large number of evergreen trees that die the first year after they are transplanted is good evidence that the work of removing them is too often done by those who do not understand the business ; for, when the work is properly performed, quite as large a proportion of evergreen trees will live as deciduous trees.

The almost universal mistake is made of selecting trees that are too large. The rule should be to select trees not more than twelve inches high.

Another mistake is made in selecting trees that grow in the shade, or partial shade. If a good growth is expected the first year, or even the second, it is important to select only such trees as grow in open spaces, where they have the full force of the heat of the sun.

Another mistake is made in lifting the trees. Many are taken up so carelessly that large portions of the roots are cut off, and the soil is all shaken from what are left. The trees thus lifted are permitted to lie in the sun unprotected, until not one out of fifty can be made to live. This is all wrong.

To be sure of success, select a cloudy day in May, and with a sharp, round-pointed shovel, dig up the small trees by cutting entirely around them with the shovel, and when this is done gently raise the tree with the shovel, in a manner so as not to disturb the soil which covers the roots. The trees, when thus lifted, should be carefully packed in a wagon and transported to where they are to be set. When there, the holes should be dug, and each tree, as it is taken from the wagon, set in the hole dug for it ; and after thus carefully placing it where it is to stand, the earth should be well packed around the roots and the earth which has been removed with the tree. If the soil be rather dry, one or two pailfuls of water may be poured around each tree.

If the soil is very dry, the tree should be well mulched after being watered. Not more than two per cent of trees thus set will die.

TRIMMING HEDGES THE NATURAL WAY

Let the hedge be trimmed so as to keep the bottom limbs the longest and the top the shortest. This gives the sun a chance to shine on the leaves of the lowest limbs, the same as in the natural growth. The top of the hedge should be arched.

A hedge thus trimmed will be more natural, more beautiful, and will rarely show any places bare of leaves at the bottom.

THE RIGHT WAY TO TRANSPLANT

To be sure of success, select a cloudy day in May, and with a sharp, round-pointed shovel, dig up the small trees by cutting entirely around them with the shovel, and when this is done gently raise the tree with the shovel, in a manner so as not to disturb the soil which covers the roots.

AGRICULTURE & HORTICULTURE

FROM THE 1896 ALMANAC

IMPROVEMENT OF FRUITS BY THE SELECTION OF SEED.

WHILE a great proportion of our larger fruits have been improved through chance productions, it is no evidence that this is the best way. A careful investigation of the subject will show that while improvement through chance production is very uncertain and very slow, through systematic and well-guarded action it is much more certain, and progresses more rapidly.

This is because when man assumes direction he not only selects seed from the trees that bear the best fruit, but he selects from trees the blossoms of which have been fertilized by the pollen of flowers from a tree that bears equally good fruit, thus securing good parentage on both sides; and he also seeks the seed of a fruit that is as many generations as possible removed from the wild fruit that is not edible. For example, he would not plant seed from the Isabella grape in preference to the Moore's Early, because the Isabella came from the wild grape, while the Moore's Early came from the Concord, making it at least removed from the wild grape two generations, and thus much more likely to be good than the seeds of either the Isabella or the Concord. In the smaller fruits we have had greater opportunities to observe the importance of obtaining seed as many generations as possible from the small wild fruit. Who would think of planting seed from the small, wild strawberry to get a seedling that would produce a better fruit than the Marshall? To work intelligently and to the best advantage, we need to be able to trace back the parentage of a fruit that we are striving to improve, and then plant the seed of those that are the farthest removed from the unimproved fruit, and at the same time come from several generations that have produced fruit of good quality.

Much time and labor have been wasted in trying to improve fruit by seeds which are from fruits of a chance production of an inferior wild fruit. As the qualities of the seedling fruit are affected by the qualities possessed by several generations which precede it, there is not one chance in a thousand that such seed will produce fruit better than that of its parent.

In breeding cattle we are very careful to breed from pedigree stock; and the longer the line, and the better the quality of the line, the more valuable is it considered. That which is true with cattle is also true with fruits and vegetables. Yet fruit-growers do not seem to realize the importance of keeping a record of the pedigree of fruits and vegetables; but in strawberries they are beginning to see that if they are to work in a systematic way, they need to have a record of the parentage, as far back as possible, of all varieties which they desire to improve.

When this is done the progress will be not only more certain, but more rapid. We shall then, by working more intelligently, produce fruit not only of a large size, but of good flavor, and of firm flesh for market purposes. We shall also produce a variety adapted for home use, of fair size, excellent flavor, and of a delicate flesh.

The time has come when we ought to drop our haphazard way of improving our fruits and vegetables, and adopt a system which will enable us to work with as much certainty of results as we now do in the breeding of cattle.

THE PEANUT.

IT does not seem to be generally known that the peanut can be grown to full perfection as far north as central Massachusetts. It should be planted in a hot-bed the middle of April, and as early as the danger of frost is over it should be set in a warm, rich, and light soil on a southern slope. The soil should not only be well fertilized, but should be thoroughly pulverized before the plants are set. They should be kept well cultivated during the growing season, and care should be taken not to disturb the plants while in blossom by lifting the branches from the ground, as the stalk on which the peanut grows penetrates the ground immediately after the blossom appears.

CORN FLAKES

Dr. William Kellogg, brother of Dr. John Kellogg (who prepared the first flaked breakfast cereal) introduced Corn Flakes in 1898. It was manufactured by the Sanitas Food Co. of Battle Creek, Michigan.

MILK AND THE WEATHER

"In wet and cold weather the milk is less rich than in dry and warm; and, on this account, more cheese is obtained in cold than in warm, though not in thundery weather."

64

AGRICULTURE & HORTICULTURE

FROM THE 1896 ALMANAC

EARLY GARDENS & LATE GARDENS

LOCATING THE GARDEN

The early garden should be located on a southern slope, with a soil of sandy loam, free from stones. The late garden should be located on level land, rather low, but well drained. The soil should be a rather heavy, rich loam, but made light by liberal dressings of manure, and by thorough cultivation before being used for the production of garden crops. In fact, the early as well as the late garden should be prepared for garden crops by growing on it field crops at least two years, and applying two or three times the amount of fertilizer that the crops consume, and at the same time cultivating so thoroughly that no weeds will mature their seeds.

GARDEN NOTES.

THE early garden should be located on a southern slope, with a soil of sandy loam, free from stones. The late garden should be located on level land, rather low, but well drained. The soil should be a rather heavy, rich loam, but made light by liberal dressings of manure, and by thorough cultivation before being used for the production of garden crops. In fact, the early as well as the late garden should be prepared for garden crops by growing on it field crops at least two years, and applying two or three times the amount of fertilizer that the crops consume, and at the same time cultivating so thoroughly that no weeds will mature their seeds.

The practice of setting a row of currant bushes or raspberries on the edge of the garden, is a very poor one. A better way is to set them in the middle. Then the plough may be run on both sides of the row, and the grass roots will not be running in from the outside, as they will when the bushes are set on the border.

When strawberries are grown in matted beds in the garden, it is best not to try to get more than one crop of fruit, but to dig the vines in and plant some late crop, thus preventing a crop of weed seeds from ripening to cover the garden the next season with weeds. If more than one crop is to be obtained, then keep the vines in hills and the ground thoroughly cultivated, cutting the runners off before they get rooted.

Never plant the garden all at one time, but begin as early as the land is in good condition, and plant something every week until August. To have sweet corn every day until the frost comes, begin early in the season and plant a row every two weeks until the Fourth of July. It is but little use to plant peas after the middle of June. They mildew so badly after the middle of July that they are of but little value. Radishes, lettuce, beets, cucumbers, and beans may be planted at different seasons and a success secured.

While it is important to apply heavy dressings of manure to the garden, it is equally important to keep the weeds out, and frequently to stir the surface of the soil, even if there are no weeds. Plants grow but slowly when the surface of the earth is covered with a hard crust; therefore, as soon after every hard shower as the surface of the soil is dry enough to crumble, it should be stirred by the hand-hoe, wheel-hoe, or horse cultivator. This starts the circulation of air in the soil, without which the plants cannot grow.

If very early potatoes are desired, whole potatoes should be planted, and two weeks before planting they should be placed in a warm room where they will sprout, care being taken, when planting, not to break off any of the sprouts.

To raise potatoes still earlier, plant them under glass the 10th of April, about five inches apart. When the danger of frost is over carefully remove them, with the surrounding earth, to a warm, rich location; but before attempting to remove them, make the earth around them very wet. In this way potatoes may be obtained full grown by the Fourth of July.

Tomatoes should be started in the hotbed the last of March, and when two inches high, thin out so as to be three inches apart. This gives a plant with more strength of stalk than if left to grow very close together. Set as early as possible and avoid the frost. Set the plants deep, in a light, dry, and rich soil.

Watermelons should be planted the last of May, in a warm, dry soil, in hills five feet apart. When a good variety is obtained, save the seed to plant the next year, and ever after select seed from the most desirable specimens. Then you will know what to expect, which you do not always know when you buy seed.

Potatoes for planting should be stored in a dry, cool place, where the temperature keeps not less than eight, and not more than eighteen degrees above the freezing point. Never keep them in a warm cellar, where the sprouts will grow several inches in length by planting time.

TOMATO PLANTS

Tomatoes should be started in the hotbed the last of March, and when two inches high, thin out so as to be three inches apart. This gives a plant with more strength of stalk than if left to grow very close together. Set as early as possible and avoid the frost. Set the plants deep, in a light, dry, and rich soil.

AGRICULTURE & HORTICULTURE

FROM THE 1897 ALMANAC

GOOD ADVICE TO CHICKEN FARMERS

THE POULTRY YARD.

LOCATION.

THE poultry house should be built on a dry, gravelly, or sandy soil, sheltered on the north and west sides by high land or evergreen trees. Avoid, if possible, low, wet land, or a high, clayey soil where the water does not readily drain off. This is important; for many have failed to make the poultry business pay because of the damp, unhealthy location of their houses. The yard should slope to the south, running down to the low land, and if to a running stream of water, so much the better.

A yard thus located gives the birds a chance to get at good water during the warm season, and also good feeding-ground in the dry season. It also gives them dry ground near the houses during the wet and cold portion of the year.

FENCES.

The yard should be kept well fenced, and at the present time the common galvanized wire netting seems to be the cheapest, if not the best. Four feet is high enough, if built right.

The posts should be the tops of cedar-trees, seven or eight feet long, and four or five inches in diameter at the end set in the ground. The top end should run up to a point, leaving nothing for the hens to see that will afford them a resting-place. A fence thus built, if only three feet high, will rarely be passed by even the lighter hens. If large, short posts are used, it is best to have them six inches below the top of the netting. Fasten the top of the fence to a narrow strip of board nailed on the side of the post next to the inclosure, and reaching only to the top of the netting, thus leaving no resting-place for the hens that have a disposition to get outside of the inclosure assigned them. The posts should be set from eight to ten feet apart, and at the bottom of them should be nailed a board about six inches in width. To this should be fastened the wire netting. This board adds very much to the strength of the fence, and also prevents the hens from passing under it. No board should be at the top of the fence, as this will permit a resting-place for the hens, and as they will readily see it, they will be very likely to fly over.

CONSTRUCTION OF HOUSE.

Ten feet is wide enough, and every ten feet in length will afford space for fifteen hens. The walls may be covered with paper, and also the roof, if kept painted, but not otherwise. The foundation should be of stone laid in cement, and the bottom of the hen-house should be of cement also, thus making the building proof against the entrance of skunks, minks, weasels, rats, and mice.

Never make the south side wholly of glass; one-third is enough. More than that makes too much difference in the temperature of cold nights and sunny days in February and March. Ventilation is important. Give sufficient air, so that when the house is opened in the morning there will be but little unpleasant odor.

BREEDS.

If the object is eggs, then select the best breed, and the best strain of blood of that breed that you can find, and if not up to what is most desirable, then begin in a systematic way to breed up to your ideal; and if you are keeping a flock of over twenty hens, do not go outside for new strains of blood, but separate your flock into families, and breed from the best specimens of your own flock. By so doing it is easy to breed to a feather, and to produce an ideal bird; but if you keep mixing up from outside sources, it can never be done.

FEEDING.

Young chicks should never be fed with fine ground Indian meal, but with cracked corn, millet, baked wheat bread, a small amount of ground bone, and a very small ration of cooked meat.

Laying hens should have a great variety of food, such as corn, wheat, oats, barley, boiled vegetables mixed with wheat bran or middlings, ground bone, oyster-shells, meat scraps, plenty of fine gravel, and in winter chopped rowen; in summer, grass in abundance.

CLEANLINESS.

The houses should be kept clean and sweet. If not cleaned every day, cover the floor with dry muck or loam often enough to keep the air sweet and pure.

ON BUILDING A POULTRY HOUSE

Build it on dry, sandy soil

Fence yard to be at least four feet high

For 15 hens, area should be at least 10 feet wide

Foundation should be of stone laid in cement

Breed from the best specimens of your own flock

Laying hens should be served a great variety of food

Houses should be kept clean and sweet.

AGRICULTURE & HORTICULTURE

FROM THE 1898 ALMANAC

IMPROVEMENT OF FRUIT AND VEGETABLES.

PERSONS who have been engaged in the business of improving farm animals have, for more than a century, kept a record of the ancestors of all animals that have shown marks of progress, and have kept the record so complete that a remarkable animal of to-day has a full record of its ancestors back for many generations; thus enabling the breeder of stock to breed from that family which shows a line of ancestors the farthest removed from the unimproved stock, and at the same time possessing the highest number of desirable points of excellence. While this is being done for the improvement of farm animals, no systematic efforts are being made to improve our fruit and vegetables, except by chance production from stock that has no pedigree.

Fruit-growers seem to be satisfied with simply crossing two varieties of fruit, and have little, if any, knowledge of more than one generation back. By this method there is probably not one chance in ten thousand of making any improvement, for they are in precisely the position that the stock-breeder would be if he should continue to breed from those only one generation removed from the unimproved wild stock.

It must be evident to every thoughtful person that, to make sure of progress in the quality of fruit, we need to get as far as possible away from the wild, undesirable fruit. When we can produce a strawberry that has come through ten generations of strawberries that possessed good qualities, we shall be reasonably sure of obtaining a seedling from it that, if not as good as the parent, would be quite likely to be a very good berry. In consequence of this pedigree, there would be a thousand chances for it to be a better berry than the parent, while there would be one chance of getting a really good berry from a seedling which came from a strawberry only one generation removed from the wild strawberry.

What is true of the strawberry is also true of the grape. If we can get a good grape that has come down from the wild grape through several generations of really good grapes, we shall have secured a good starting-point, from which we shall be able to make more rapid progress. The Moore's Early grape is said to be a seedling from the Concord, which, if true, removes it two generations from the wild grape, and thus makes it more desirable to propagate from than the Concord. If we could remove it two generations farther, and get equally as good a grape in each generation, we should be getting so far away from the wild grape that a considerable portion of the bad qualities of the wild fruit would be bred out.

The progress we have made in Indian corn shows what progress can be made in securing varieties that will reproduce their like by continuing, year after year, to plant seed that is selected and kept by itself, away from other varieties.

The potato has been bred away from the wild potato so long that it has but little resemblance to its original. This is because it was less difficult to do than in the case of fruit, and the potato does not seem so liable to run back as fruits. We usually plant the tuber, which is not the seed. There are comparatively few who plant the potato seed, and then only with the hope of making some improvement.

To improve our fruits is a work much more difficult to perform than either vegetables or grain; but the more difficult the task, the greater should be the effort, and the more systematically should the work be done, and not in a haphazard manner. This is a work that should be done by our Experiment Stations, and it should be performed in an intelligent, as well as a systematic, manner. To make much progress in our varieties of apples and pears must necessarily be a slow work; but it can be done much better by intelligent, systematic work, than by the haphazard manner of the past. There seems to be no doubt of this, and the sooner the Experiment Stations take hold of the work the sooner shall we enter upon the road which will lead to success by a much shorter route than that we have been travelling. In fact, without a continued and systematic effort, our progress in the future must rely, as in the past, principally on chance productions from parents of unknown qualities.

HEALTHY PLANT ROOTS

The roots of plants will not grow in the absence of oxygen and they rot when they reach the permanent water level. Drainage, therefore, is the best remedy.

SUGAR BEETS

Upon his return from France, in 1852, a Mormon missionary, John Taylor, brought with him seeds of the sugar beet. The first small crop of beet sugar was manufactured in 1853, and canning was first started in a home plant in Ogden in 1886. By 1891, in Lehi, Utah, sugar was being manufactured for commercial purposes.

AGRICULTURE & HORTICULTURE

PRUDENT PLANNING
and
HONEST MARKETING

PLANTING PRUDENTLY

Never plant more land than you can fertilize sufficiently to feed the crops in a manner to secure good ones. Make it a rule to apply fertilizers in such quantities as will leave the soil richer, after the crops are removed, than it was before cultivation was begun.

CARE OF LAWNS.

In towns where waterworks have been built for furnishing water for drinking and other purposes, great efforts are made by a large proportion of the people to keep the lawns around their dwellings in the best condition possible; and to the artistic eye, most of them succeed in securing a beautiful lawn; but to the æsthetic eye, those who expend the most labor on their lawns secure the most unsatisfactory results.

If we would improve Nature, we must study her. We must educate ourselves so that our eyes will see and realize the great beauty of natural forms. He who sees only geometrical forms, and studies only mechanical arts, will make sad mistakes when he enters upon the work of making a beautiful lawn, especially if he tries to ornament it with shrubs and trees. If he be a mechanic, he will trim his hedges so as to have the sides exactly perpendicular, and the top horizontal, and his shrubs the shape of a long box set on one end; and for variety some will be trimmed in the shape of pillars, and others in the shape of an umbrella. Others, who are strangers to natural beauty, will trim off all the lower limbs on the trunks of the trees as high as they can reach, if not as high as they dare to climb. While it is sometimes necessary to trim shrubs and trees, it should always be done with caution, and with an eye to natural beauty. The trimming of ornamental shrubbery should rarely, if ever, be done to an extent which will show that the knife has been used.

If a lawn is to be kept well covered with grass, it should not be cut every week close to the ground, and watered every day; it is a much better way to put on the same amount of water twice a week, or in ordinary weather once a week, and to cut the grass once in two weeks, cutting it at least an inch above the surface. If the grass roots are to be kept from being winter-killed, it is important that the grass should not be cut after the third week in September. Some try to improve their lawns by covering them in winter with a very heavy dressing of stable or barnyard manure; there are two serious objections to this; first, a person who has any regard for the health and comfort of his family will not keep them where they will be surrounded by a strong odor of the horse stable or the cowyard. The odor coming from manure thus spread is frequently so strong as to be offensive to those who pass in the street. The second objection to spreading fresh manure on a lawn is the weed-seeds it contains, making the lawn very weedy the next year. The fertility of the lawn had best be kept up by the application of commercial fertilizers containing phosphoric acid, potash, and nitrogen.

TILLING THE SOIL IN DRY WEATHER.

There is nothing, except water, that will carry a crop through a severe drought so well as the frequent stirring of the soil; but care must be taken not to stir it very deep; an inch, or an inch and a half, is deep enough. This acts as a mulch, and prevents the forming of a crust on the surface, and also prevents the hot sun from heating the ground very much. The old custom of not stirring the soil in dry weather was a wrong one, and frequently was destructive of the crop. The same land that under the old system frequently failed to produce a good crop, under the new system of cultivation does not fail to produce good crops in the dryest seasons.

AGRICULTURE & HORTICULTURE

FROM THE 1899 ALMANAC

CARING FOR SOIL & LAWN

WATERING TREES

Trees and shrubs should be looked after during dry weather, and watered whenever it seems necessary; but do not make the mistake of watering every day with a small quantity close around the trunk of the tree, but water liberally once a week, and thoroughly wet the ground at least two feet beyond where the roots reach.

FARM HINTS.

FREQUENT visits should be made to the cultivated portion of the farm during the growing season, and a close watch kept to discover insect enemies before they have done any serious injury to the young plants. No time on the farm is better spent than in looking over the crops, to decide what fields need attention first; by always being ready to do the most important work first, the farmer is generally able to do his work at the right time, and have no crops suffer for want of proper attention.

Never plant more land than you can take good care of, and no more than you can fertilize sufficiently to feed the crops in a manner to secure good ones. Make it a rule to apply fertilizers in such quantities as will leave the soil richer, after the crops are removed, than it was before cultivation was begun.

In growing most of the farm and garden crops the land should be rich enough to produce one crop without fertilizer, then in a dry season there will be a fair crop, because the growth of the crop will not have to depend on the rain to advance the crude fertilizer applied in the spring to plant-food; for that already in the soil will be so far advanced that the moisture already in the soil will be sufficient to bring it into a condition to enter the plants.

Trees and shrubs should be looked after during dry weather, and watered whenever it seems necessary; but do not make the mistake of watering every day with a small quantity close around the trunk of the tree, but water liberally once a week, and thoroughly wet the ground at least two feet beyond where the roots reach. If the ground be well mulched, it will rarely be necessary to water the trees except in a very dry location, or in a very dry season. It is sometimes as necessary to water trees in October as it is in July; and frequently forest trees need watering the second year after transplanting more than they do the first year.

Farm wagons should be kept in a dark, dry building, when not in use, and they should be painted as often as is necessary to keep the wood well covered; by so doing, they will last twice as long as if left exposed to the weather with but little paint on them. For heavy loads drawn over public roads, it is well to have tires at least four inches wide; the tires of tip-carts that are to be used on the farm should be at least five inches wide.

Whatever crop is to be grown for market should be of as good quality as possible, and before sending it to market, pick out the imperfect or undesirable portion, to be sold as second or third quality.

For success, especially in market gardening, it is important to establish a good reputation by always sending produce that is well selected, well packed in attractive packages with the quality in the middle as good as that on top, and each package marked with the name of the grower.

Good fences should be kept around the pastures if you would have your cattle quiet and at home; and especial effort should be made to secure for them good water during the driest portion of the year.

When the pasture gets run down by years of feeding, it is well to apply five hundred pounds of ground bone to the acre; it not only makes the grass grow better, but improves its quality, thus securing better health for the cattle.

Always plan to have a few good shade trees in each pasture, on high land if possible, thus securing a cool, shady place for the cattle on a hot day.

In building a barn, plan it so as to give the cattle both light and sunshine during the winter; also plan it so the manure will not be in the cellar under the barn, but in a shed by the side of it, where the swine can be kept without danger to their health. Every barn should be so constructed as to secure good ventilation.

Never borrow money to buy more land than you can keep well cultivated, nor to build a house larger than is necessary to furnish room sufficient for your family, simply because you wish to outdo your neighbor.

HONEST MARKETING

Whatever crop is to be grown for market should be of as good quality as possible, and before sending it to market, pick out the imperfect or undesirable portion, to be sold as second or third quality.

AGRICULTURE & HORTICULTURE

GOOD FENCES

Good fences should be kept around the pastures if you would have your cattle quiet and at home; and especial effort should be made to secure for them good water during the driest portion of the year.

LIVE WITHIN YOUR MEANS

Never borrow money to buy more land than you can keep well cultivated, nor to build a house larger than is necessary to furnish room sufficient for your family, simply because you wish to outdo your neighbor.

FARM HINTS.

FREQUENT visits should be made to the cultivated portion of the farm during the growing season, and a close watch kept to discover insect enemies before they have done any serious injury to the young plants. No time on the farm is better spent than in looking over the crops, to decide what fields need attention first; by always being ready to do the most important work first, the farmer is generally able to do his work at the right time, and have no crops suffer for want of proper attention.

Never plant more land than you can take good care of, and no more than you can fertilize sufficiently to feed the crops in a manner to secure good ones. Make it a rule to apply fertilizers in such quantities as will leave the soil richer, after the crops are removed, than it was before cultivation was begun.

In growing most of the farm and garden crops the land should be rich enough to produce one crop without fertilizer, then in a dry season there will be a fair crop, because the growth of the crop will not have to depend on the rain to advance the crude fertilizer applied in the spring to plant-food; for that already in the soil will be so far advanced that the moisture already in the soil will be sufficient to bring it into a condition to enter the plants.

Trees and shrubs should be looked after during dry weather, and watered whenever it seems necessary; but do not make the mistake of watering every day with a small quantity close around the trunk of the tree, but water liberally once a week, and thoroughly wet the ground at least two feet beyond where the roots reach. If the ground be well mulched, it will rarely be necessary to water the trees except in a very dry location, or in a very dry season. It is sometimes as necessary to water trees in October as it is in July; and frequently forest trees need watering the second year after transplanting more than they do the first year.

Farm wagons should be kept in a dark, dry building, when not in use, and they should be painted as often as is necessary to keep the wood well covered; by so doing, they will last twice as long as if left exposed to the weather with but little paint on them. For heavy loads drawn over public roads, it is well to have tires at least four inches wide; the tires of tip-carts that are to be used on the farm should be at least five inches wide.

Whatever crop is to be grown for market should be of as good quality as possible, and before sending it to market, pick out the imperfect or undesirable portion, to be sold as second or third quality.

For success, especially in market gardening, it is important to establish a good reputation by always sending produce that is well selected, well packed in attractive packages with the quality in the middle as good as that on top, and each package marked with the name of the grower.

Good fences should be kept around the pastures if you would have your cattle quiet and at home; and especial effort should be made to secure for them good water during the driest portion of the year.

When the pasture gets run down by years of feeding, it is well to apply five hundred pounds of ground bone to the acre; it not only makes the grass grow better, but improves its quality, thus securing better health for the cattle,

Always plan to have a few good shade trees in each pasture, on high land if possible, thus securing a cool, shady place for the cattle on a hot day.

In building a barn, plan it so as to give the cattle both light and sunshine during the winter; also plan it so the manure will not be in the cellar under the barn, but in a shed by the side of it, where the swine can be kept without danger to their health. Every barn should be so constructed as to secure good ventilation.

Never borrow money to buy more land than you can keep well cultivated, nor to build a house larger than is necessary to furnish room sufficient for your family, simply because you wish to outdo your neighbor.

"When the well's dry, we know the worth of water."

—from POOR RICHARD'S ALMANAC

AGRICULTURE & HORTICULTURE

FROM THE 1899 ALMANAC

CARING FOR SOIL & LAWN

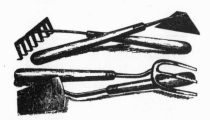

LAWN MANICURE

If a lawn is to be kept well covered with grass, it should not be cut every week close to the ground, and watered every day; it is a much better way to put on the same amount of water twice a week, or in ordinary weather once a week, and to cut the grass once in two weeks, cutting it at least an inch above the surface.

CARE OF LAWNS.

In towns where waterworks have been built for furnishing water for drinking and other purposes, great efforts are made by a large proportion of the people to keep the lawns around their dwellings in the best condition possible; and to the artistic eye, most of them succeed in securing a beautiful lawn; but to the æsthetic eye, those who expend the most labor on their lawns secure the most unsatisfactory results.

If we would improve Nature, we must study her. We must educate ourselves so that our eyes will see and realize the great beauty of natural forms. He who sees only geometrical forms, and studies only mechanical arts, will make sad mistakes when he enters upon the work of making a beautiful lawn, especially if he tries to ornament it with shrubs and trees. If he be a mechanic, he will trim his hedges so as to have the sides exactly perpendicular, and the top horizontal, and his shrubs the shape of a long box set on one end; and for variety some will be trimmed in the shape of pillars, and others in the shape of an umbrella. Others, who are strangers to natural beauty, will trim off all the lower limbs on the trunks of the trees as high as they can reach, if not as high as they dare to climb. While it is sometimes necessary to trim shrubs and trees, it should always be done with caution, and with an eye to natural beauty. The trimming of ornamental shrubbery should rarely, if ever, be done to an extent which will show that the knife has been used.

If a lawn is to be kept well covered with grass, it should not be cut every week close to the ground, and watered every day; it is a much better way to put on the same amount of water twice a week, or in ordinary weather once a week, and to cut the grass once in two weeks, cutting it at least an inch above the surface. If the grass roots are to be kept from being winter-killed, it is important that the grass should not be cut after the third week in September. Some try to improve their lawns by covering them in winter with a very heavy dressing of stable or barnyard manure; there are two serious objections to this; first, a person who has any regard for the health and comfort of his family will not keep them where they will be surrounded by a strong odor of the horse stable or the cowyard. The odor coming from manure thus spread is frequently so strong as to be offensive to those who pass in the street. The second objection to spreading fresh manure on a lawn is the weed-seeds it contains, making the lawn very weedy the next year. The fertility of the lawn had best be kept up by the application of commercial fertilizers containing phosphoric acid, potash, and nitrogen.

TILLING THE SOIL IN DRY WEATHER.

There is nothing, except water, that will carry a crop through a severe drought so well as the frequent stirring of the soil; but care must be taken not to stir it very deep; an inch, or an inch and a half, is deep enough. This acts as a mulch, and prevents the forming of a crust on the surface, and also prevents the hot sun from heating the ground very much. The old custom of not stirring the soil in dry weather was a wrong one, and frequently was destructive of the crop. The same land that under the old system frequently failed to produce a good crop, under the new system of cultivation does not fail to produce good crops in the dryest seasons.

AGRICULTURE & HORTICULTURE

BLUEBERRIES & POTATOES

BLUEBERRIES NEED SHADE

"... it may be grown successfully in the garden where it can be partially shaded by trees. It will not ripen its fruit well on cultivated land without shade, as the hot sun burns the fruit and dries it."

ON TRANSPLANTING THE BLUEBERRY

The early spring is the best time to transplant the blueberry, and a cloudy day should be selected. Young bushes which have but one stalk are the best; but one with many stalks should not be rejected, if the fruit be large and of good quality.

POTATO PICKIN' TIME

"Potatoes to be sold in the home market should be dug as soon as fully grown; for the prices in such market are usually much higher than a month later, and if dug early, the ground can be cleared in time to grow a good crop of flat turnips. ..."

THE HIGHBUSH BLUEBERRY.

AMONG the small fruits worthy of a place on every table may be classed the blueberry, which usually grows in low and somewhat wet land, but will grow very well on high land rich enough for grass to grow well; or it may be grown successfully in the garden where it can be partially shaded by trees. It will not ripen its fruit well on cultivated land without shade, as the hot sun burns the fruit and dries it. If grown in the garden, the bushes should be set within four feet of each other, that they may shade the whole surface of the ground; until they do this, the ground should be well mulched with leaves. When a plantation of blueberry bushes is to be set, it is well to select them while the fruit is on, and mark them so they can be found when wanted. The early spring is the best time to transplant the blueberry, and a cloudy day should be selected. Young bushes which have but one stalk are the best; but one with many stalks should not be rejected, if the fruit be large and of good quality. Experience proves it to be best to cut off the entire top that it may send up new and thrifty shoots. There is a great choice in the quality of the fruit: so great, that if one has time and patience, it would be best to graft from the best variety that can be found, and thus secure an entire plantation of large fruit of good quality. It requires considerable skill to graft the blueberry with success; but it can be done, and should be done much oftener than it is. It is also very difficult to propagate from the seed, but patience and perseverance will insure success. An acre of blueberry bushes, properly set and cared for, will bring a much larger profit than an acre of currants, or even strawberries; and as the fruit will be much larger and better than that grown naturally, there will undoubtedly be a demand for all that will be grown, at very high prices.

IMPROVED IMPLEMENTS FOR THE DESTRUCTION OF WEEDS.

WITHIN comparatively few years, great improvements have been made in implements for the destruction of weeds. When the first cultivator was made, it was considered almost perfection, it was such an advance over the one-horse plough; but if we look at it now, and compare it with cultivators of to-day, it looks like a very crude implement, and one which would be very undesirable to use. The horse-hoe has been made to do good work, and some of the harrows have very much lessened the work of destroying weeds in the early part of the season; but following these implements are the weeders, which have undoubtedly come to stay; for some of them are made, not only to do a great amount of work in a very short time, but to do it wonderfully well, picking out the small weeds with great rapidity, leaving the crop uninjured, and free from weeds. The various wheel-hoes have been a great help, but there has been little improvement in them for the last twenty-five years; in fact, there was one put on the market twenty-five years ago that has never been surpassed for lightness and quality of work it will do, yet the inventor went out of business, and his wheel-hoe dropped out with him. The great fault with nearly all the wheel-hoes is they are too heavy for hand use; and another serious fault is, many of them cut the weeds, and leave them standing with the surface roots in the ground.

HARVESTING POTATOES.

POTATOES to be sold in the home market should be dug as soon as fully grown; for the prices in such market are usually much higher than a month later, and if dug early, the ground can be cleared in time to grow a good crop of flat turnips, or it may be seeded down to grass. If this is not desired, then sow with winter rye for a crop of grain, or for a green crop to feed to cattle; or if the land is deficient in vegetable material, plough the rye under as soon as the ears appear the next spring, and plant with corn, potatoes, or some garden crop.

If the potatoes are to be kept for winter use, or winter market, let them remain in the ground until the middle of September.

FROM THE 1899 ALMANAC

AGRICULTURE & HORTICULTURE

THE SUGAR ORCHARD

THE ROCK MAPLE

This tree thrives best on cool, rocky uplands, and may be readily distinguished by its rough, light gray bark, its broad, five-lobed leaves with shallow depressions, and its key-winged fruit. The sugar maker speaks of his maple woods as the "sugar place," "sugar bush" or "sugar orchard." It is usually a rough, hilly, rather open forest, generally quite free from underbrush, with the sugar house or sap boiling place, located within its limits.

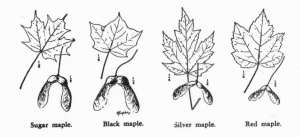

Sugar maple.   Black maple.   Silver maple.   Red maple.

TAPPING THE TREE

The tree is tapped with a bit or auger, and a metallic or wooden spout is inserted, through which the sap drains slowly into the bucket hung thereon or on a spike driven into the tree. The gathered sap is brought to the sugar house.

MAPLE SUGAR.

Statistics show that the yearly production of maple sugar in the United States exceeds $2,000,000 in value. These figures, however, have no great significance, since yields vary widely from year to year. The sap season is controlled by the weather, which may favor a long continued flow or cause but brief and irregular runs. Thus one year's product from the same trees may not be more than a third of the yield of the preceding season. New England, New York, Pennsylvania, Ohio, Michigan and Canada are the main sources of supply of pure goods. Vermont is the head centre, and produces more than any other state, her soil, climate and maple forests being well adapted to, and her men skilled in, the industry. New York and the Western Reserve in Ohio also make considerable quantities.

Sugar Orchard. Practically the entire product is derived from the sugar or rock maple. This tree thrives best on cool, rocky uplands, and may be readily distinguished by its rough, light gray bark, its broad, five-lobed leaves with shallow depressions, and its key-winged fruit. The sugar maker speaks of his maple woods as the "sugar place," "sugar bush" or "sugar orchard." It is usually a rough, hilly, rather open forest, generally quite free from underbrush, with the sugar house, or sap boiling place, located within its limits. Maple sap is, as it were, the life blood of the tree, the constructive material from which are built the wood and leaf tissues. The tree stores starch in the Summer, which in the Winter is changed to sugar, and later on is transferred to the buds to stimulate leaf growth. The sap passes both up and down the tree in Spring in the layers immediately beneath the bark. The flow is strongest in the late Winter days, when the thawing weather comes. Sap pressure on a warm day may be as high as twenty-five pounds to the square inch, increasing with warmth and lessening with cold. "Sugaring time" in Vermont may start as early as the last week in March, and may last two weeks or a month, according to the weather.

Average sap carries ninety-six per cent of water, about three per cent of sugar and more or less albuminous and mineral matters. These proportions change somewhat as the season advances. The early "runs" are apt to be nearly pure sugar and water, while later flows carry more albuminous and kindred substances which injure the quality of the goods.

The Process. The tree is tapped with a bit or auger, and a metallic or wooden spout is inserted, through which the sap drains slowly into the bucket hung thereon or on a spike driven into the tree. The gathered sap is brought to the sugar house in a large wooden tank on a sled or "stone-boat" drawn by horses or oxen over the snow, and emptied into the reservoir tank, whence it passes into the "evaporator." Old time sugar makers used great iron kettles suspended over a wood fire. This is sometimes done to-day, but smoke and ashes do not conduce to cleanliness or to good quality. Most sugar makers now use the evaporator, a shallow pan, or series of pans, longer than it is wide. A constant flow of sap is maintained in a circuitous course over the long heated surface from the front end of the evaporator to the rear, whence it is drawn from time to time as a thin syrup. This is periodically reboiled to concentrate it. Eleven pounds to the gallon is standard, if it is to be sold as syrup. If it is to be made into sugar, the syrup is still further boiled or "sugared off" over a brisk fire until it "hairs," or the thermometer shows 236° or higher, or until judgment and experience say, stop. The viscid fluid is then taken from the fire, stirred until granulation is well established, and poured into a tub, box, cake mould or brick mould to harden.

Sugar and Syrup. While most of the product is made into sugar, much is marketed as syrup, which, when hermetically sealed and properly stored, keeps well. Sugar, however, keeps on the whole better. The latter is eaten as candy and is used in confectionery, but most commonly is melted for use as table syrup. Sugar sells at from four to twenty cents a pound, according to the quantity sold, the quality of the goods, time of the year, size of crop, etc. That from early runs, light in color and fine in flavor, in small cakes, sells at top prices for a few days early in the season. The main crop, good, bad and indifferent, sells at lower prices, sometimes below the cost of production. Light colored sugars and syrups, of mild and delicate aroma, command the best prices.

AGRICULTURE & HORTICULTURE

APPLES.

The Apple has been known in cultivation from the dawn of history, and even in pre-historic times had doubtless reached a certain stage of improvement as has been shown by the discovery of identifiable remnants among the lake-dwellings of Switzerland. It was well known among the Romans, for Pliny, in the first century of the Christian Era, states that there were twenty-two varieties. In America the Apple has attained a degree of quality and productiveness far surpassing that of any other country. It reaches its greatest perfection in New England and the adjacent Canadian Provinces, where it excels in flavor and keeping qualities those grown further West and South.

The varieties of Apples now known and named number into the thousands; the greater part having been produced from seed variations, or sports from existing kinds. Almost every section of the country has evolved varieties by these means that have proved well adapted to its conditions and have been propagated by grafting and budding. But the present tendency among fruit growers is not so much to create new varieties as to improve the best existing kinds, and to study the adaptation of these to the varying conditions of soil and climate.

In planting a commercial orchard it is desirable to have few kinds, as it is easier to dispose of a large lot of one variety than small lots of several different kinds. For home use varieties that give a succession of ripening through the season should be considered. The orchard should be located on well-drained land, preferably upland, and the hillsides of New England furnish favorable situations for the establishment of apple orchards. In a young orchard open cultivation should be practised, and other crops may be grown while the trees are developing. Well-rotted barnyard manure is the best fertilizer, with an occasional dressing of wood ashes to supply the necessary potash. Clover, cow peas, or other leguminous plants can be grown as a cover crop, and allowed to die down or be turned under in the Fall. If the orchard is kept in sod, which is not recommended, the grass around the trees should be cut and left on the ground as a mulch.

From the great number of varieties of Apples in existence it is a somewhat difficult matter to select a few best adapted for the location, but the experience of many orchardists favors a selection from the following list as profitable for cultivation in the middle and southern sections of New England.

Summer Apples. July and August. Red Astrachan, Williams, Oldenburg, Sweet Bough, Early Harvest, Yellow Transparent.

Fall Apples. September to November. Gravenstein, McIntosh Red, Wealthy, Hubbardston, Washington Strawberry.

Winter Apples. November to March. Baldwin, Rhode Island Greening, Northern Spy, Tompkins King, Roxbury Russet, Spitzenburg.

The Baldwin is probably grown to a greater extent in New England than all others combined, but this and some others of the above list are not sufficiently hardy for the northern portions of Maine, New Hampshire, and Vermont. In these sections the varieties Alexander, Arctic, Bethel, Oldenburg are suggested for Fall, and Pewaukee and Wealthy for Winter Apples. Like certain other varieties, the Oldenburg changes from a Summer to a Fall Apple, and the Wealthy from a Fall to a Winter Apple, in the last named sections.

Difficulties are to be met with in commercial orcharding as in all other lines of business enterprise; there are the vicissitudes of the seasons to be encountered, and the depredations of borers and other insect pests to be watched for and overcome. But with intelligent care and treatment, a well-established orchard is an investment producing ever-increasing dividends for a long term of years, and will prove an asset of value to every farm. The possibilities in this line of work on our New England hillsides are already attracting much favorable attention, and many of the old hill farms have been brought up by new owners to a paying condition through the renovation of the old orchards or by the planting of new ones.

FROM THE 1907 ALMANAC

THE ANCIENT APPLE

VARIETIES OF APPLES

The varieties of Apples now known and named number into the thousands; the greater part having been produced from seed variations, or sports from existing kinds. Almost every section of the country has evolved varieties by these means that have proved well adapted to its conditions and have been propagated by grafting and budding.

KEEPING FLOWERS FRESH LONGER

FROM THE 1912 ALMANAC

KEEPING FLOWERS FRESH

One tablespoonful of ordinary table salt placed in the water of a common sized vase will keep flowers put therein for a much longer period than they will keep without it.

HOW TO MAKE TASTY, TENDER MEAT

A good way of cooking an inexpensive cut of beef is as follows:—Take four pounds of lean beef. Cut some narrow strips of bacon or salt pork and with a pointed knife insert them into the beef. Cut up three large onions and lay them in a bowl. Rub a little salt over the beef and lay the latter on the onions. Place the bowl in a kettle half full of boiling water and steam four hours. The result ought to be rich gravy and tender meat.

USEFUL HINTS.

One tablespoonful of ordinary table salt placed in the water of a common sized vase will keep flowers put therein for a much longer period than they will keep without it.

If 95% alcohol is applied to parts exposed to poison ivy within an hour the eruption can frequently be prevented. If the eruption has already appeared, saturate a soft white cloth with the following lotion, and apply three times a day:—Calamin, 1 teaspoonful; zinc oxide, 1 tablespoonful; carbolic acid, ¼ teaspoonful; lime water, ½ pint. Avoid the use of soap while the eruption is active. The treatment is not expected to effect a direct cure, but it diminishes the discomfort and lessens the inclination to scratch, which otherwise would tend to prolong the trouble.

While jellies are so rich in sugar that they are protected from bacteria and yeasts, they should be covered closely and carefully in order to protect them from mold spores and evaporation. After being covered they should be kept in a cool, dry, dark place.

When people sit down in an easy chair to rest they would do well to put their legs on a chair or other support. This tends to relax the muscles from tension; while the lifting of the feet and legs helps to flow from them, through the veins towards the heart, the excess of blood in them which comes from their long continued or arduous use.

Grease is removed from dry goods, clothing, etc., by benzine, ether, naptha and gasoline because the grease is dissolved by any of those fluids. But to make the treatment thorough plenty of the fluid should be applied; and in order that it may carry away the grease something absorbent, like a piece of clean woolen cloth or blotting paper, should be placed under the fabric when the fluid is rubbed in.

Raspberry and blackberry canes are biennial, that is they grow one year, fruit the next, then die. It helps the new canes to cut out the old ones, and at the same time any weak growths after the fruit is gathered. More light and air are admitted to the growing wood for next year. Neither raspberries nor blackberries should be grown too thick; by giving plenty of room the quality and quantity of fruit is improved. In old beds this is particularly necessary.

A good way of cooking an inexpensive cut of beef is as follows:—Take four pounds of lean beef. Cut some narrow strips of bacon or salt pork and with a pointed knife insert them into the beef. Cut up three large onions and lay them in a bowl. Rub a little salt over the beef and lay the latter on the onions. Place the bowl in a kettle half full of boiling water and steam four hours. The result ought to be rich gravy and tender meat.

Pour a little oil or water on one end of your cloth duster; roll it up and wring until the water or oil has spread over the whole. This will prevent the flying of the light dust over adjacent articles.

It is said that pieces of white wax put away with white cotton garments, bedding etc., will keep them from turning yellow.

When a new shoe seems tight and stiff over a joint in any particular spot, try pressing against the lining with the curve of a boot-buttoner, stretching the leather outward. Sometimes a shoe that it seems impossible to wear may be made perfectly comfortable by a few minutes of this treatment.

Don't throw away the packets in which the seeds come. In addition to containing directions for planting and cultivation they are excellent sources of information when the name of a particular flower slips the tongue and is wanted.

Mattings should always be taken up, because the dirt sifts through to the floors, but sweep it twice first. Once with a stiff broom, following the grain; then use a soft one wet with warm water, shaking well, and going across the straw.

Do not put any other kind of cake in the same jar or tin with the fruit cake, and do not raise oftener than necessary the lids which should be kept tightly closed, for the less air that gets to such pastry the longer it stays fresh and the richer it becomes in flavor.

AGRICULTURE & HORTICULTURE

GROWING PARSLEY
and
PRUDENT PRUNING

AN UNHEATED GREENHOUSE.

In the milder climate of England such structures are not uncommon; they are called Alpine houses and are used for plants which flower early in Spring or are tender. Such a house might not prove successful in northern New England, but in southern New England it would not only give a fair quantity of flowers during the Winter—Wallflowers, Violets. Daisies, etc.,—but would be a help in starting early vegetables,—Tomatoes, Lettuce, Cabbage, and, perhaps, with a hot-bed made inside, Egg Plant and Pepper. The house should be built below the surface of the ground, four to six feet, and should have a southern aspect, if possible favoring the southeast, to get the early morning sun. The glass roof should be a lean-to or three-quarters span, and made of hot-bed sash. It should be built against the cellar of a house or out building, and if this cellar is heated so much the better. In most cases the rear roof of the three-quarters span can be made of wood. Access to the cellar should be convenient to help in caring for the plants, storing soil, pots, etc., and, of course, water should be handy. It is in effect a large cold-frame which is accessible from within in all weather and in which the plants get better care than in pits or frames. If the glass is double glazed and some covering to the most tender plants is made on cold nights it is astonishing what good results are obtained. In such a house, built well below the ground, and attached to a heated cellar during the last three winters a self-registering thermometer has only recorded 10 degrees of frost. If the ground freezes it soon thaws out and no harm is done, except that growth, perhaps, is retarded. There should always be good ventilation at the top and, if possible, at the bottom, and the ventilators should be open in all good weather. Such a house should be ten feet wide at least—and twelve feet or even more is better,—and the length determined by circumstances. There should be a path two feet wide which should furnish access to the benches and to the cellar. The benches can be built on posts with board bottoms or they can be of earth. In most cases a combination of these two ways will be found convenient. Where the benches are of solid earth a covering of leaves 10 or 12 inches thick should be given the ground outside. Such a structure is useful to people living all Winter in the country. The flowers named above and many more, Hyacinths, Tulips and Narcissus for instance, can be had in quantity and cheaply.

SUMMER PRUNING CERTAIN SHRUBS.

It helps Forsythia, Double Plums and Almonds, the Plum-leafed Spiræa, etc., if they are Summer pruned. Simply remove the flowering wood as soon as the flowers fade. Not all of it, but as much as one can reasonably expect. This forces new growth from the sturdier buds at the base of the shoots. It can be supplemented by removing some of the oldest stems from the base of the plant when the shrub is five or six years old. This Summer pruning is also practised on plants like Deutzia, Weigela, Spiræa Van Houttei, etc., but as it comes much later in the season and these plants might be injured by removing too much of their foliage at once, it is well to continue the operation over a period of ten days or a fortnight so that the growth is not too much checked at any one time. The plant is relieved from the necessity of ripening its fruit and a better opportunity is given it to expand its growth.

PARSLEY.

Parsley is biennial, that is, it grows from seed the first year, it blooms, ripens its seed and dies the second. It is hardy in our climate in favorable seasons and can be gathered in good condition all Winter if given the protection of a frame,—protection more against weather than against frost. A portable cold frame three feet wide and five and one half feet long, or longer if more convenient, should be placed over the row, or part of the row, in late November. If opened on all good days to give ventilation an abundant supply of this useful vegetable is obtained all Winter. A mat thrown over the glass on cold nights helps.

ALPINE HOUSES

In the milder climate of England such structures are not uncommon; they are called Alpine houses and are used for plants which flower early in Spring or are tender. Such a house might not prove successful in northern New England, but in southern New England it would not only give a fair quantity of flowers during the Winter—Wallflowers, Violets, Daisies, etc.,—but would be a help in starting early vegetables,—Tomatoes, Lettuce, Cabbage, and perhaps, with a hot-bed made inside, Egg Plant and Pepper.

SUMMER PRUNING

It helps Forsythia, Double Plums and Almonds, the Plum-leafed Spiraea, etc., if they are Summer pruned. Simply remove the flowering wood as soon as the flowers fade. Not all of it, but as much as one can reasonably expect.

HOUSEHOLD HINTS

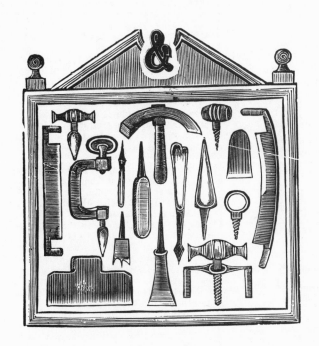

&

WORLDLY WISDOM

HOUSEHOLD HINTS

WHAT IS MAN?
45
pounds of carbon
and nitrogen
diffused through
5½
pailfuls of water.

PURE AIR
Keep the premises, particularly around the dwelling, perfectly free from every substance that will taint the air. Every decaying vegetable or animal substance should be removed a good distance, and then covered in earth for the purpose of manure.

Old Indian house built in 1704 and demolished in 1848. Deerfield, Massachusetts.

Keep the Premises Clean. — The following excellent remarks are from the *Rural New Yorker*. If they were heeded by all persons living in city and country, good health would be very much promoted.

Every cultivator should keep his premises as clean as possible, for the important purpose of saving manure, and promoting health.

Some discerning persons remark that in the hot summer, while vegetation is in a flourishing condition, it is more healthy in the country than in the city, but the reverse is the case in September and October, as at this season many vegetable productions have come to maturity, and are decaying, filling the air with noxious gases and odors, whence arise fever, dysentery, and other complaints, which are more common in the country early in the fall. We give this view of the subject which some have presented, and we will make a few remarks on subjects that claim the particular attention of every cultivator, whether this view be correct or not.

Pure Air. — Keep the premises, particularly around the dwelling, perfectly free from every substance that will taint the air. Every decaying vegetable or animal substance should be removed a good distance, and then covered in earth for the purpose of manure.

The Pig-pen, though at a respectable distance, should be supplied with loam to absorb all liquid matter. All manure in the barn-yard should be covered with loam, sand or mud, to save it from waste, and to keep the air pure, as, in the changes so common to the wind, the air is liable to be wafted from the barn to the house.

Cellars should be made as clean as possible, particularly as they communicate directly with the dwelling above, and any foul air produced in them is liable to pass into the house. All vegetables in the cellar that are tending to decay should be removed immediately. It is best to ventilate cellars thoroughly by opening doors and windows, keeping the door open as little as possible that communicates with the rooms. Ground plaster, and freshly-burnt charcoal, set in vessels, or strewed around in cellars or other places where foul air exists, or is liable to be produced, has a very healthy effect by absorbing gases.

Necessaries often produce a foul atmosphere around them ; and as the dwelling is near, the offensive air is often wafted to it, and even when not perceptible, is often operating injuriously. Some prepare these conveniences, and cover with loam or other substances all night soil, so as to do away with all unpleasant and injurious effects. When this is not the case, charcoal, plaster, chloride of lime, or other disinfectants, should be thrown into the vault to absorb all noxious odors.

Water from the Sink should be absorbed in loam, &c., for manure, instead of rising in foul gases, and being blown into the house. There are some cases of malignant and fatal disorders going through a family, while all the rest of the neighborhood are in good health. This is often owing to some local cause, some foul puddle, pool, or stagnant pond near the dwelling, or a general negligence as to keeping the premises clean.

Decaying Substances, as weeds, grass, potatoes affected with the rot, potato-tops, pumpkin and other vines, and various productions, are undergoing decomposition in the fall ; and, in the aggregate, the amount is large, and filling the air with pestilential gases. Farmers may do much good to themselves and the community by burying all such substances, and converting them into manure. Make them into a compost heap, well covered with loam, to absorb the gases.

Causes of Idiocy. — Dr. Howe has examined almost the entire number of cases of idiocy known in Massachusetts, and the result is, in all but four instances, he found the parents of those idiots were either intemperate, addicted to sensual vices, scrofulous, predisposed to insanity, or had intermarried with blood relations.

The Chemist's Answer to "What is Man ?" — The *Quarterly Review* says, chemically speaking, a man is forty-five pounds of carbon and nitrogen diffused through five and a half pailfuls of water.

**Fish and visitors
Stink after three days.**

& WORLDLY WISDOM

Science in the Kitchen. – Professor Liebig, in a letter to Professor Silliman, says: The method of roasting is obviously the best to make flesh the most nutritious. But it does not follow that boiling is to be interdicted. If a piece of meat be put into cold water, and this heated to boiling, and boiled until it is "done," it will become harder, and have less taste, than if thrown into water already boiling. In the first case, the matters grateful to the smell and taste go into the extract — the soup; in the second, the albumen of the meat coagulates from the surface inward, and envelopes the interior with a layer which is impregnable to water.

Keeping Beef Fresh. — In preserving beef, the *ribs* will keep longest, or five or six days, in summer; the middle of the *loin* next; the *rump* next; the *round* next; and the shortest of all, the *brisket*, which will not keep longer than three days in hot weather.

Want of Fresh Air. — The Hon. Horace Mann, in alluding to ill-ventilated school-houses, remarks as follows: To put children on a short allowance of fresh air, is as foolish as it would have been for Noah, during the deluge, to have put his family on a short allowance of water. Since God has poured out an atmosphere fifty miles deep, it is enough to make a miser weep to see our children stinted in breath.

Bathing. — "As a matter of health and duty," says a medical writer, "the bath is imperative; as one of ease, and comfort, and enjoyment, and lastly, of cleanliness, incomparable; if omitted from distrust in the first instance, folly; if from dilatoriness or indolence, or on the score of trouble or expense, unpardonable. Read what Armstrong says:

"Do not omit, ye who would health secure,
The daily fresh ablution that shall clear
The sluices of the skin; enough to keep
The body sacred from indecent soil.
Still to be pure, even did it not conduce
(As much it does) to health, were greatly worth
Your daily pains: 't is this adorns the rich;
The want of this is poverty's worst foe.
With this external virtue, age maintains
A decent grace; without it youth and charms
Are loathsome.

A Good Custom. — A Spanish peasant, when he eats a good apple, pear, peach or any other fruit, in a forest, or by the roadside, plants the seed; and hence it is, that the woods and roadsides of Spain have more fruit in and along them than those of any other country. Cannot we do the same?

"Scientific Farming" is the ascertaining of what substances the plants you wish to raise are made — which of these substances are wanting in your land — and what manures will supply them.

Strawberries. — No other valuable fruit can be raised so easily. An acre has produced one hundred bushels in a season. If planted early in the spring, they will bear a crop the first year. They require good corn land, a soil deep and strong, but not too rich.

Scions. — March is the time to cut them for use. Take care and select thrifty shoots; *not* from the lower branches, as these are apt to grow badly. Keep them for use in a dry cellar, and cover them with sand. If kept in sawdust, they mould; in damp earth, they decay; on bare boards, they dry too much.

Transplanting. — If your tree or shrub is dried too much, do not plunge it in water, but *moisten* the roots, cut away the branches severally, and bury the whole tree in the ground for three or four days.

Shade Trees. — There are few men whose friends will build them a monument so honorable or so durable as he builds for himself who plants an elm, maple, oak, or other good shade tree.

Shrub Fruits. — Your crop of currants, gooseberries and raspberries, will improve if you dig up the old plants once in three or four years, and plant young bushes, and weed and keep the ground open about them.

Roasting: A Most Nutritious Method of Cooking

. . . The Pros and Cons of Roasting vs. Boiling Meat

. . . Hints on Beef Preservation

. . . On the Importance of Fresh Air

. . . Towards Keeping the Body Respectfully
"The want of this
Is poverty's worst foe."

. . . Why the Countryside of Spain Is So Fruitful

. . . On the Ease of Growing Strawberries

. . . A Transplanting Hint

. . . A Shade Tree: Man's Most Durable Monument

. . . Some Advice on Shrub Fruits

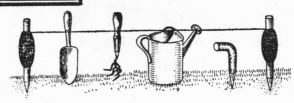

FROM THE
1871
ALMANAC

HOUSEHOLD HINTS

WINDOW PLANT

"Do not fail to have a few plants in your window in winter. They give beauty to the homeliest room, and pleasure and variety to the most monotonous life . . ."

Simple Household Products that Remove Black Spots and Stains . . .

Reducing Fever with Cooking Soda . . .

A Sore Throat Remedy . . .

Tenderizing Meat With Vinegar . . .

A Recipe for Cup-Cakes . . .

Olive Oil as a Cold Remedy . . .

The Cost of Travel in 1871 . . .

HOUSE PLANTS IN WINTER.

Do not fail to have a few plants in your window in winter. They give beauty to the homeliest room, and pleasure and variety to the most monotonous life. They need sunshine and tolerably pure air, however; and if you and your children manage to live without these, you may be sure that your plants cannot. But air which poisons plants is not fit for human beings to breathe. Prepare and mix your soil in the fall, if you have not done so before. Take the leaf-mould from a wood, if you can get it, and mix it with dust from the road, half and half, and add a little scrubbing sand. If you cannot obtain leaf-mould, take three parts of garden-mould, add one part of thoroughly rotted manure, and one part of sand. Pulverize finely and mix well. An old wooden box does very well instead of using several flower pots. A strawberry-box, half of a cocoa-nut shell, a small wooden kitchen bowl, perforated for cords, make excellent hanging baskets. A few cents' worth of flower-seeds will produce many flowers. They generally cost five cents a packet. Mignonette is valuable for its perfume. Morning-glories and Nasturtiums generally thrive and flower well in the house. Almost any one could obtain slips of Geranium or Verbena from some friend. Give plenty of sunshine, but not hot enough to wilt the plants. They sometimes need to be shaded at noon. It is best to water in the morning; not a little every day; but thoroughly whenever the surface of the earth is quite dry. The leaves should be well showered every week, to remove dust and insects.

HOUSEKEEPING HINTS.

Scouring.—In scouring knives, dip the cork in soft soap instead of water and it will take out black spots. A small potato, with one end cut off, is better than a cork to use with brick-dust. COAL-ASHES are good to scour with. WOOD ASHES scour soap-stone nicely. HARD COAL-ASHES remove very black spots from paint and plaster. WHITING applied with a damp piece of flannel will instantly remove finger-marks from paint. SALT rubbed on silver removes egg stains. DISH-WATER or MILK AND WATER is said to clean a stove better than clear water.

Kerosene Oil is said to destroy bed-bugs.

To Remove Ink Stains from White Cotton.—Put some Cream of Tartar on each spot, and tie it up with a thread; put it in a saucepan of cold water over the fire, and let it boil.

A Cooling Application for Headache or Feverishness.—Put a teaspoonful of Saleratus or Cooking Soda into a pint of warm water, and bathe with it. It takes paint from tin or wood, and must not be poured into a painted slop-pail. It also stains straw carpets; so that it must be used with some care.

For Sore Throat.—Take a teaspoonful of powdered Chlorate of Potash, mix it with an equal quantity of sugar. Take a little at a time, and let it dissolve slowly in the mouth. This can be taken in the course of the day, by a grown person; and a child three years old can take nearly as much safely. A teaspoonful of Chlorate of Potash alone, dissolved in a pint of water, makes an excellent gargle.

Wash Hair Brushes with a teaspoonful or more of powdered borax dissolved in a pint of warm water, or with saleratus and water.

A little Vinegar added to the water in which meat is stewed makes the meat more tender.

Rye Cup-Cakes.—Very good and wholesome for tea or breakfast. Take about an equal quantity of wheat flour and rye meal, a little salt, four eggs. Mix with milk, making a batter as thick as batter pudding. Bake for fifteen minutes in a slow oven, and then increase the fire. This makes about fifteen cakes baked in cups.

Olive Oil, commonly called sweet oil, is often useful in a family. A teaspoonful or two given to a child who has a cold, at bed-time, will soothe the irritation, and quiet coughing. A little oil rubbed on the chest relieves the breathing, when the lungs are oppressed. It can be rubbed over the bridge of a baby's nose, when it is stuffed, and greatly helps the breathing. A few drops, applied with a feather at the hinges, stops the creaking of a door. It must be remembered, however, that it is liable to stain clothing and straw carpets.

CARRIAGE FARES IN BOSTON.

FOR one adult, from one place to another within the city proper (except as hereinafter provided), **50 cents.** Each additional adult, **50 cents.**

For one adult from any place in the city proper, south of Dover street and west of Berkeley street, to any place north of State, Court, and Cambridge streets, or from any place north of State, Court, and Cambridge streets to any place south of Dover street and west of Berkeley street, **One Dollar.** For two or more adults, **50 cents** each.

Children under four years, with an adult, **no charge.**

Children between four and twelve years old, with an adult, **25 cents** each.

From twelve at night to six in the morning the fare for one adult is **double the preceding rates,** and **50 cents** for each additional adult.

80

& WORLDLY WISDOM

HINTS FOR THE HOUSEHOLD.

Pure Air for Children. — Children are much more susceptible than grown people to all noxious influences. That which, above all, is known to injure children seriously is foul air, and most seriously at night. Keeping the rooms where they sleep tight shut up is destruction to them; and if the child's breathing be disordered by disease, a few hours only of such foul air may endanger its life, even where no inconvenience is felt by grown persons in the same room. — FLORENCE NIGHTINGALE.

Breathing Night Air. — What air can we breathe at night but night air? The choice is between pure night air from without, and foul night air from within. Most people prefer the latter; an unaccountable choice. What will they say if it is proved to be true that fully one half of all the disease we suffer from is occasioned by people sleeping with their windows shut? — FLORENCE NIGHTINGALE.

Dark Houses. — A dark house is always an unhealthy house, always an ill-aired house, always a dirty house. Want of light stops growth, and promotes scrofula, rickets, &c., among the children. People lose their health in a dark house; and if they become ill, they cannot get well again in it. — FLORENCE NIGHTINGALE.

Soothing Syrups. — Opium should be used with great caution for children — *never* unless prescribed by a physician. A single drop of laudanum has been known to cause the death of an infant at the breast. It should be used sparingly, even in external applications; it is easily absorbed through the skin, especially by infants. Beware of soothing syrups. If a baby needs anything of the sort, it should be prescribed only by a physician, and discontinued as soon as possible. Soothing syrups vary so much in strength that a dose of the usual size may be dangerous. If it does not always endanger life, the habit of taking such medicines seriously injures a baby's digestion and general health, and has a stupefying effect upon the brain, which may be permanently injured.

Cottage Cheese. — Take sour skimmed milk, scald it, and when the whey rises to the top, pour it all into a colander; press out the whey lightly with a spoon, turn it into a bowl, and let it cool. When cold, cut it up with a knife, or crumble it with your fingers; then, to a quart bowl of curd, add one teaspoonful of salt, a sprinkling of pepper, and two large tablespoonfuls of hard butter; work this in well, tie it up loosely in a cloth, put it on a plate with another plate over it, and set a weight on it. It is better the third and fourth nights than the first. — COUNTRY GENTLEMAN.

Scalloped Oysters. — For a quart of oysters, allow a pound of crackers, half a pint of milk, a quarter of a pound of butter, one lemon, pepper and salt to taste. Roll the crackers, put a layer of oysters on the bottom of a deep dish, then a layer of crackers, with butter, pepper, salt, and small chips of the lemon; then oysters again, and so on until all are in the dish. Pour the milk over the whole, and bake forty minutes. — MRS. HUNNIBEE, *Hearth and Home.*

Sweet Potato Buns. — Boil and mash two potatoes; rub in as much flour as will make it like bread; add a little nutmeg and sugar, with a tablespoonful of good yeast. When it has risen, work in two tablespoonfuls of butter cut finely; then form it into small rolls, and bake on tins a nice brown. Serve hot; split open, and butter. — COUNTRY GENTLEMAN.

Potatoes baked with Cream. — Wash and peel some potatoes, and slice them as if for frying; fill a dripping pan with them, sprinkle with salt and pepper, put on bits of butter, and pour over all a coffee cup of sweet cream; set it in the oven, and cook from half to three quarters of an hour; stir once while cooking.

Fried Tomatoes for Dinner. — Peel half a dozen or more large tomatoes, cut transversely in large slices, salt and pepper them well; beat three or more eggs with a fork until very light; dip the tomatoes, each slice separately, into a little wheat flour, then into the egg, and fry immediately in hot lard. — HEARTH AND HOME.

Graham Apple Pies, or Apple Cakes. — Take good, juicy dried apple sauce, thoroughly cooked and properly sweetened; then stir into a pint, or any quantity of it, enough Graham flour to make a rather stiff batter, but not too stiff. Dip a spoonful of this into dry Graham flour, and mould it with your floury hands into a round, flattish biscuit. Fill your baking pans with these, and bake very thoroughly in a hot oven without turning them. Fresh apple sauce, stewed peaches, or huckleberries, can be used in the same way. It makes a good, nourishing lunch for children. — MASS. PLOUGHMAN.

Puff Balls. — One pint of sweet milk, two eggs, three and a half cups of sifted flour, and a little salt. Must be beaten thoroughly smooth. Bake in well-buttered roll pans, or in puff cups half filled, in a hot oven. — COUNTRY GENTLEMAN.

Cream Muffins. — One teacup sour cream, two eggs, one half teaspoon soda; thicken with flour, bake in a quick oven.

Soap for Chapped Hands. — In half a pint of boiling water dissolve a pound of white soap cut in shavings; add six ounces of olive oil and one drachm of pulverized camphor, and then pour it into moulds. — HEARTH AND HOME.

FRESH AIR

The choice is between pure night air from without, and foul night air from within. Most people prefer the latter; an unaccountable choice. What will they say if it is proved to be true that fully one half of all the disease we suffer from is occasioned by people sleeping with their windows shut?—

. . . How to Make Cottage Cheese

. . . Scalloped Oysters Recipe

. . . Recipe for Sweet Potato Buns

. . . Potatoes Drowned in Cream

. . . A Platter of Fried Tomatoes

. . . Apple Biscuits

. . . Puff Balls

. . . Sour Cream Muffins

. . . Making Soap for Chapped Hands

HOUSEHOLD HINTS

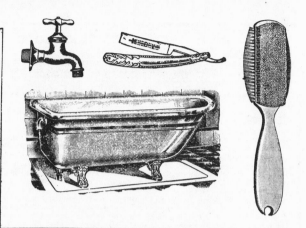

The Search Light

of investigation will prove that Wistar's Balsam of Wild Cherry positively cures Coughs, Influenza, Bronchitis, Whooping Cough, Croup, and all Throat and Lung Troubles, and that in many well attested cases Consumption has yielded to its wonderful influence. A reputation such as this remedy possesses is not obtained in one year, nor in ten. Its record for upwards of half a century is known to all, and attests its remarkable merit. Prepared by Seth W. Fowle & Sons, Boston.

Sold by Dealers generally.

Fowle's Pile & Humor Cure

For the cure of PILES, SCROFULA, ECZEMA, SALT RHEUM, CANCEROUS and ULCERATED SORES, and all diseases of the Skin and Blood. Entirely vegetable. Henry D. Fowle, Boston.

THE GREAT

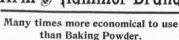

Arm & Hammer Brand

Many times more economical to use than Baking Powder.

SALERATUS. SALERATUS.

TO HOUSEKEEPERS.

IT IS IMPORTANT that the Soda or Saleratus you use should be WHITE and pure in common with all similar substances used for food. Some Soda may appear white when examined by itself, but a comparison with Church & Co.'s ARM AND HAMMER BRAND will show the difference.

FARMERS and DAIRYMEN should use only the ARM AND HAMMER BRAND for cleaning and keeping milk-pans sweet and clean.

To insure obtaining only the Arm and Hammer Brand Soda or Saleratus, it is best to buy in POUND or HALF-POUND CARTONS, which have our name and trake-mark on them, as inferior goods are sometimes substituted for the Arm and Hammer Brand when bought in bulk.

..... *Send stamp for receipt book* .....

CHURCH & CO., New York.

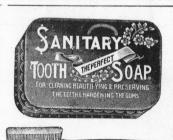

k your Grocer for

THE OVAL CAKE COLGATE & CO'S "NEW" SOAP. SAVES WASTE.

FOR LAUNDRY USE.

perior in Quality,
Moderate in Price,
Novel and Economical in Form.
Beware of Imitations!

k your Druggist for

COLGATE & CO.'S
Rosodora Toilet Soap.

[Registered.]

t is highly and exquisitely perfumed, and is universally popular.

COLGATE & CO.'S
Rosodora Toilet Water

Is a superior Toilet article, and a strong and lasting perfume for the andkerchief. Three sizes.

82

& WORLDLY WISDOM

FROM THE
1874
ALMANAC

Cures For Warts, Bee Bites and Chapped Hands

. . . The Secret of Washing Blankets

. . . Removing Iron Rust

. . . Drying Umbrellas Effectively

. . . Dissolving Warts With Washing Soda and Castor Oil

. . . Tobacco and Other Remedies for Bee and Wasp Stings

. . . Cider Vinegar Softens Chapped Hands

. . . Curing Feet-Swellings from Overexposure to Cold

. . . Making Potatoes More Mealy

. . . Preparing Oatmeal Porridge

HINTS FOR THE HOUSEHOLD.

Proper Mode of Extinguishing Kerosene Lamps. — Explosions of kerosene lamps are frequently produced in the attempt to extinguish them by blowing down the chimney. This is a very dangerous practice, and should always be avoided. The desired result will be accomplished much more certainly and safely by giving a sharp and rather prolonged puff exactly at right angles to the top of the chimney. (That is, blow across the top of the chimney.) The draft thus created draws the flame away from the wick, when the carbonic acid immediately below the departing flame also extinguishes the red-hot charred end of the wick.

To Wash Blankets. — Provide a quantity of boiling water. Take a large tub, and fill it half full of *boiling* water; dissolve and stir thoroughly into it two tablespoonfuls of powdered borax, and sufficient soap to make a good lather, but *on no account rub soap on the blankets.* Put into the tub but one blanket at a time. Shake it to and fro with the clothes-stick till perfectly wet through, then press it under the water, to remain till cool enough to use your hands in it, when each part should be examined very carefully, gently rubbing or squeezing the suds through it. Hard rubbing fulls woollens. When sure that all spots or dirt are removed, wring it into a second tub of boiling water, into which you have thoroughly stirred some bluing. If your first suds are strong enough, the blanket will retain sufficient soap for the rinsing water, which in woollens requires a little soap. Shake the blanket up and down in this water with the clothes-stick, till it has flowed through every part. Then, while the water is still hot, wring it. It requires two persons to wring and shake out a bed blanket. They should take it by the ends and snap vigorously, to remove all the water. Then carry it to the line, throw it over and pull it smooth, bringing the hems straight and true, and pin on to the line strongly. When half dry, turn it lengthwise on the line, and pull the selvages together in a straight line, so that no part may draw up in cockles, or full unevenly. It requires a fine day, and a brisk wind is desirable to dry blankets nicely. When the blanket is perfectly dry, fold very evenly, but never press or iron it.

To make Butter Cool in Hot Weather. — Set it on a bit of brick, cover with a flower-pot, and wrap a wet cloth around the pot. The evaporation cools it as well as ice.

To Remove Iron Rust. — Mix fine salt and cream of tartar, moisten with water and lay on the stain; expose to the sun, and repeat the application if necessary.

To Dry Umbrellas Properly. — After the umbrella has drained, stand it on the handle and let it dry in that position.

To Cleanse White Worsted Hoods and Clouds. — Rub them thoroughly with wheat flour, then shake well to remove the flour, and they will look nearly as well as when new.

To Cure Warts. — Dissolve as much common washing soda as the water will take up; wash the warts with this for a minute or two, and let them dry without wiping. This repeated, will, it is said, gradually destroy the largest wart. Another remedy is to rub them frequently with castor oil.

For the Sting of a Bee or Wasp. — Wet a small quantity of cut tobacco, and lay it at once on the place which was stung, holding it on tightly for four or five minutes, and the pain and swelling will be at once removed. Spirits of turpentine will reduce the swelling immediately; or, if neither that nor tobacco is at hand, honey or molasses, or fresh butter will give relief. Spirits of ammonia, too, is a good remedy.

For Chapped Hands. — Wash the hands thoroughly in cider vinegar, and let it dry in, just before going to bed. It is rather harsh the first time, but after a few applications the hands become soft and smooth. Another remedy is to smear a drop of honey over the hands after washing, and lightly wiping them.

To Relieve Chilblains. — Put some red-hot coals into an old pan, and throw a handful of corn meal upon the coals. Hold the foot in the dense smoke which will rise. One or two applications will greatly relieve the chilblains, and a persistent use of the remedy is said to cure them. Another remedy for chilblains, is to rub them every night and morning with camphorated oil, if they are unbroken, or with a mixture of one part of spirits of turpentine to three of camphorated oil. Then cover with a piece of lint or linen. To prevent chilblains, let a child always wear, in winter, warm woollen stockings, and good shoes, and avoid warming the feet by the fire, and bathing them in *hot* water.

Improvement in Boiling Potatoes. — After the potatoes have boiled till they are half cooked, pour off the water, and fill again with boiling water from another kettle, and finish boiling them. It is said to make them more mealy.

Oatmeal Porridge. — Take six tablespoonfuls of oatmeal and soak it over night in a pint and a half of water. In the morning stir it up well, and put the pail into a kettle of boiling water; let it boil for half an hour as hard as possible; then stir in a cupful of milk, and let it boil fifteen minutes. Season with salt, and eat it with cream. If soaked over night, it requires much less cooking than it would otherwise. It can be made without milk.

HOUSEHOLD HINTS

Sunshine and Pure Air Add Life to Our Years

SUNSHINE FOR THE SICK

It is found in all hospitals that those rooms facing the sun have fewer deaths, all other things considered, than those which are upon the shady side of the house; and where statistics have been kept for a period of years, it is found that the average time for recovery is less upon the sunny side than upon the shady side of the building.

—from Care of the Sick
Mutual Life Insurance Co.

Peel and Toast Prescription . . .

On Cleaning Dresses and Veils . . .

Overcoming the Rundown Feeling . .

How to Cook Onions . . .

The Bean Treatment . . .

Griddle Cakes . . .

and . . .

Hard Times Pudding . . .

FROM THE
1876
ALMANAC

HINTS FOR THE HOUSEHOLD.

Care of Children. — Use your brains upon the three subjects of air, food, and clothing for your children. If things do not seem to go well with them, think about it, search for causes in their daily lives, make changes in little things which you think you can improve, and sometimes you will find that you can substitute ease for trouble in your own lives, and health for sickness in theirs, by these same small changes. — *The Housekeeper.*

Pure Air. — Perhaps the supreme importance of giving the lungs, day and night, an unlimited supply of pure air, cannot be better impressed upon some minds than by stating that after more than twenty years' observation of the causes which produce consumption, and a familiarity with the opinions of the best physicians of the day, I am firmly of the conviction that no one need have any fear of this disease if his lungs are only nourished on good air during every hour of life. The breathing of a pure air a few hours each day will not keep off the terrible destroyer, but the lungs must have this kind of air as often as nature requires it, and this, at the least, is sixteen times every minute. — *Dr. Black.*

Sunshine for the Sick. — If possible, the sick-chamber should be the room of the house which has the most sunshine coming into it, and if the bed can be so placed that the person lying in it can see a good piece of the blue sky, so much the better it will be. It is found in all hospitals that those rooms facing the sun have fewer deaths, all other things considered, than those which are upon the shady side of the house; and where statistics have been kept for a period of years, it is found that the average time for recovery is less upon the sunny side than upon the shady side of the building. — "*Care of the Sick,*" *pub. by Mut. Life Ins. Co. of N. Y.*

Toast Water. — *A good Drink for the Sick.* — Carefully remove the crust from a slice of stale bread, and toast the slice through on both sides, but do not burn it. Break the slice into three or four pieces, and put them into a pitcher with a small piece of orange-peel or lemon-peel. Pour on a pint of boiling water, cover up with a napkin, and, when cold, strain off the water for use. It should be freshly made, especially in warm weather.

To Clean Black Dresses. — A teaspoonful of powdered borax dissolved in a quart of tepid water is good for cleaning old black dresses of silk, cashmere, or alpaca.

To Restore a Crape Veil. — Take an old piece of crape and dip it into a cup of vinegar, and sponge the veil with it; then pin the veil to a pillow carefully, and let it dry. It will look like new, and can be done whenever it looks rusty.

For a Person who is very Weak. — Take the white of an egg, a teaspoonful of brandy, and a tablespoonful of cream. Beat the egg very light. Then let somebody add the brandy, while you continue beating. Then add the cream.

Thickened Milk, for Summer Complaint. — *Especially good for Sick Children.* — Tie a pint of flour as closely as possible in a bit of strong cotton cloth, boil it four hours, well covered with water; then take it out and let it cool. This makes a hard ball of flour, which will keep for months in a dry, cool place. To cook it, boil a pint of milk over water; thicken it with a tablespoonful or more of the flour, scraped, and mixed smooth with a little cold milk. Season with salt and sugar if liked.

Improved Method of Cooking Onions. — Take off the outside skin, cut off both ends close, and let them stand in cold water an hour. Then put them into a saucepan with two quarts of *boiling* water. Cover, and boil fifteen minutes. Pour off the water, and add again two quarts of *boiling* water, and boil half an hour longer. Pour off this water, and add a cupful of cream, which has just been scalded, salt, and a little butter and flour, if the two latter ingredients are wanted. Boil up for a few minutes, and serve hot.

To Boil Shelled Beans. — After shelling the beans, let them lie in cold water for an hour. Pour this off, and put them in boiling water and let them boil for fifteen minutes; then pour this water away. Put boiling water with them again, and let them boil for fifteen minutes more. Then drain again, and fill with boiling water, and let them cook until perfectly tender. They ought to be boiled between one and two hours.

Rye Griddle Cakes. — One quart of warm water, one teaspoonful of soda, one teaspoonful of salt, two tablespoonfuls of sugar. Make a thick batter of rye meal, with a little Indian meal, which makes it less clammy, and improves the flavor.

Hard Times Pudding. — One cup of molasses, one cup of cold water, one cup of raisins chopped, one teaspoonful of salt, and one teaspoonful of soda. Flour enough to make it the thickness of soft gingerbread. Steam it two hours in a pudding mould or pail. To be eaten with sauce.

Cooking Salt Pork. — Cut slices of nice salt pork; freshen them, and then partially fry. Then dip each slice separately in a batter made of one cup of sweet milk, one egg well beaten, a little salt, and flour sufficient to make the batter of the thickness of pancakes. Then fry, in the fat that first fried out of the pork, till a light brown. — *Cor. New England Farmer.*

84

& WORLDLY WISDOM

FROM THE 1877 ALMANAC

Recipes For:
* Baked Beans without Pork
* Rhubarb Jam
* Soaked Cracker
* Cream Toast
* An Apple Drink

. . . On Caring for a Patient

. . . On Being of Good Cheer

. . . On Being Threatened by Excessive Smoke

HINTS FOR THE HOUSEHOLD.

Baked Beans without Pork. — When baked beans with pork disagree with any one, let him have the beans baked without pork, using instead a little butter or cream, which is better still. Here are the directions: For a large family, wash a quart of beans at night, and pour over them a quart of tepid water. In the morning, add two quarts of water, and when it begins to boil, turn it off and replace it with fresh boiling water. Change the water again after half an hour. Let them boil about an hour. Put them into a deep bean-pot, and pour water enough over them to cover them. Let them bake slowly four or five hours. An hour before taking them up, stir in a spoonful of salt, and a cup of cream, or of creamy milk, and a bit of butter.

Rhubarb Jam. — The rhubarb should be wiped, not washed; and it should be fresh and young. Peel the stalks, and cut them up into half-inch pieces; put into a preserving pan equal weights of rhubarb and loaf-sugar, and the juice of two lemons to every five pounds of rhubarb and sugar; or the stalks may be first boiled with half the quantity of sugar, and the other half added. Boil slowly, constantly stirring; and then boil three-quarters of an hour, skimming as long as scum rises, or till it becomes a smooth pulp and a thick jam, which leaves the bottom of the pan when stirred. The grated rind of one lemon may be added to each pound of rhubarb and sugar. A less expensive jam may be made with less sugar than the above. The jam should be put into pots and tied over.

Lime-water. — Take a piece of unslacked lime (never mind the size, because the water will only take up a certain quantity of it), put it into a perfectly clean bottle, and fill the bottle up with cold water; keep the bottle corked, and in a cool, dark place, such as a cellar. In a few minutes it is ready for use, and the clear lime-water can be poured off whenever it is needed. When the water is exhausted, fill the bottle again. This can be done three or four times, after which some new lime must be used, as in the beginning. There are many cases in which milk disagrees with a baby or child, when the addition of a little lime-water makes it digestible. In many instances, also, grown persons are able to take milk freely with benefit, by adding four tablespoonfuls of lime-water to a tumbler of cow's milk, when milk alone would cause distress or disturbance of the stomach.

Soaked Cracker. — Cover a hard pilot-biscuit, or hard cracker, with cold water, and when the water is absorbed, cover it again with water and place it in the oven; when thoroughly heated and puffed, serve it with a little salt and a few spoonfuls of sweet, rich cream.

Cream Toast. — Toast a slice of bread evenly and quickly, not allowing it to become hard, barely dip it in boiling water, then sprinkle some salt over it, and cover it with a few spoonfuls of sweet, rich cream.

Pleasant Drink in Fever. — Put half a pint of dried sour apples, washed clean, in a quart pitcher, and fill it with boiling water. When cold it is ready to drink, either with or without ice. Fresh sour apples may be used in the same way.

General Hints for the Sick Room. — Be very careful to have everything connected with the meals of the sick person as neat as possible. See that the gruel is palatable, well boiled, free from lumps, of a creamy consistency, and *hot*. Keep all medicines out of sight of the patient; have no garments hanging in the room; keep the bed well aired and clean. Do not have any cotton comforters on the bed, they are very heavy and unsuitable for sickness.

When it is not possible to sweep the sick-room, wipe the carpet with a damp cloth; pin the cloth around a broom, and clean thoroughly under all the furniture which cannot be moved.

When children are sick, drink should be given to them only from *very small* but *full* glasses. The contents of a nut-shell will satisfy them if overflowing, while a large glass, half full, would leave them unhappy.

FRETFULNESS. — All usefulness and all comfort may be prevented by an unkind, a sour, crabbed temper of mind — a mind that can bear with no difference of opinion or temperament. A spirit of fault-finding; an unsatisfied temper; a constant irritability; little irregularities in the look, the temper, or the manner; a brow cloudy and dissatisfied — your husband or your wife cannot tell why — will more than neutralize all the good you can do, and render life anything but a blessing.
REV. ALBERT S. BARNES.

THERE are two things that always pay — working and waiting. Either is useless without the other. Both united are invincible and inevitably triumphant. He who waits without working is simply a man yielding to sloth and despair. He who works without waiting is ever fitful in his strivings and misses results by impatience. He who works steadily and waits patiently may have a long journey before him, but at its close he will find his reward.

IF a person in a house on fire has the presence of mind to apply a wet cloth or handkerchief to his mouth or nostrils, a passage can be effected through the densest smoke without any serious inconvenience.

The Virtue of Working & Waiting

WORKING AND WAITING
There are two things that always pay —working and waiting. Either is useless without the other. Both united are invincible and inevitably triumphant. He who sits without working is simply a man yielding to sloth and despair. He who works without waiting is ever fitful in his strivings and misses results by impatience. He who works steadily and waits patiently may have a long journey before him, but at its close he will find his reward.

& WORLDLY WISDOM

FROM THE
1880
ALMANAC

HINTS FOR THE HOUSEHOLD.

Care of the Sick.—One of the first rules to observe is to keep the air of the room as pure as the outer air, but without chilling the sick person. The window should be open more or less all the time, and with bed-clothes and hot-water bottles at the feet, the patient can be kept comfortable. An open fireplace is invaluable, because it is constantly changing the air of the room, even without a fire, and with one it is the best ventilator possible.

Never allow a sick person to be waked, either accidentally or intentionally. After he is settled for the night, do not do or say anything to rouse his attention. If you disturb him after he has fallen asleep, he is almost sure to have a bad night.

Never speak to an invalid from behind, nor from the door, nor from any distance from him, nor when he is doing anything. Never lean against, sit upon, or unnecessarily shake, or even touch, the bed in which he lies.

Conciseness and decision are, above all things, necessary with the sick. Let your thought expressed to them be concisely and decidedly expressed. What doubt and hesitation there may be in your own mind must never be communicated to theirs, not even (I would rather say especially not) in little things. Let your doubt be to yourself, your decision to them.

It is a very common error among the well, to think that "with a little more self-control" the sick might, if they chose, "dismiss painful thoughts," which "aggravate their disease," &c. Believe me, almost *any* sick person, who behaves decently well, exercises more self-control every moment of his day than you will ever know till you are sick yourself. Almost every step that crosses his room is painful to him. Almost every thought that crosses his brain is painful to him; and if he can speak without being savage, and look without being unpleasant, he is exercising self-control.

Suppose you had been up all night, and instead of being allowed to have your cup of tea, you were to be told that you ought to "exercise self-control," what would you say? Now, the nerves of the sick are always in the state that yours are in after you have been up all night.

To leave the patient's untasted food by his side from meal to meal, in hopes that he will eat it in the interval, is simply to prevent him from taking any food at all. Let the food come at the right time, and be taken away, eaten or uneaten, at the right time; but never let a patient have "something always standing" by him, if you don't wish to disgust him with every thing.

A patient should, if possible, not see or smell either the food of others, or a greater amount of food than he himself can consume at one time, or even hear food talked about, or see it in the raw state. I know of no exception to the above rule. The breaking of it always induces a greater or less incapacity of taking food. That the more alone an invalid can be when taking food, the better, is unquestionable; and, even if he must be fed, the nurse should not allow him to talk, or talk to him, especially about food, while eating.—*From "Notes on Nursing,"* by FLORENCE NIGHTINGALE.

Weaning Children.—When the child has shown any tendency to diarrhœa, is delicate and puny, it should not be weaned till after its second summer.

When the mother furnishes an insufficient supply of milk for the child, which may be known by the constant hunger of the child and the inability of the mother to satisfy him, he may, if all his teeth are through — eight in each jaw — be either entirely or partly weaned, though summer is approaching. By partial weaning is meant that he is to be fed in part and nursed in part. By this method, if the heat of summer or any other cause produces a diarrhœa, the child can be at once confined to the breast-milk, and his chances of recovery are much greater.

It is better, if possible, to make the change from nursing to feeding a gradual, rather than a sudden one. The child should be accustomed to nurse for a shorter time as well as at longer intervals, and the number of times being reduced to one, the nursing may then be given up entirely. The child may be allowed to eat a little dry bread or cracker, and by degrees may be used to other simple articles of food, care being taken to observe whether they agree with it. In this way it may eat by the close of the second year (besides milk) bread, common and sweet potatoes (baked are better than boiled), butter, rice, soft-boiled eggs, or the yolks of eggs boiled pretty hard, and plain roasted or boiled meats. Salted or fried meat should be avoided. The diet of children like that of grown persons should be varied.—DR. PARKER.

SELF-CONTROL

It is a very common error among the well, to think that "with a little more self-control" the sick might, if they chose, "dismiss painful thoughts," which "aggravate their disease," etc. Believe me, almost *any* sick person, who behaves decently well, exercised more self-control every moment of his day than you will ever know till you are sick yourself. Almost every step that crosses his room is painful to him. Almost every thought that crosses his brain is painful to him; and if he can speak without being savage, and look without being unpleasant, he is exercising self-control.

—Doctor Parker
On the Weaning of Children

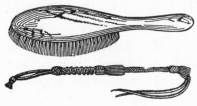

FROM THE
1881
ALMANAC

On the Care of Children

PRESCRIPTION FOR PARENTS

Remember that your happiness is bound up with that of your children. If they die young, your sorrow will be soothed by the thought that you have been loving and faithful to them always, and have filled their lives with sunshine. If they grow up, their affection will be more important to you than any other possession, and you will be richly repaid for all your efforts after self-control and unselfishness in your dealings with them.

On the Care of Children.

MANY people do not realize how much they are responsible for the health and happiness of their children. They love them dearly, work hard to support them, are full of anxiety when they are sick, and mourn them deeply if they die. But they take no pains to learn how best to keep them in health, and how to make them happy and useful members of society. To begin with the physical care. Children need an abundance of food, to build up their growing frames; and it should be of the most nourishing and wholesome kinds. It will not do to bring up a child on pork and beans, corned beef, pies, doughnuts, and coffee. Plenty of milk should be given, for that contains essential ingredients; light, sweet yeast-bread, from which the bran has not been entirely removed, oatmeal porridge, soft boiled eggs, baked apples, beef and mutton cooked rare, with such vegetables as are not hard of digestion, should form a large part of the diet. Tea and coffee should never be given to children.

Children should be dressed warmly enough; by this it is not meant that they should be oppressed by warm clothing in hot weather, so as to be kept in a constant perspiration, or that a long, thick, knit comforter should be wrapped round and round their throats in winter, by which their throats are made very sensitive.

Babies should not be allowed to wear low-necked and short-sleeved dresses, which make them liable to colds and croup, and all ages should wear flannels in winter, and keep the feet and legs warm. If there is a tendency to summer complaint, a flannel band in addition, worn around the bowels all the year round, is a great preventive. If their feet are cold at night, have them warmed before they go to bed.

Let them have enough sleep. If they have to rise for an early breakfast, be sure that they go to bed early enough to get thoroughly rested. They require considerably more sleep than grown people do. Never let them go to bed unhappy or in disgrace. Let their little minds have thoughts of love and kindness only to dwell upon, as they lie there in the dark before slumber closes their eyes.

This leads to the next point, — care of their happiness. It is not necessary to indulge and spoil children in order to make them happy. Indeed, that is one of the surest ways of making them miserable for life. Children need to be taught ready and cheerful obedience from babyhood, both for their own sakes and for all around them. But it is a great mistake to interfere continually with their pursuits, and to find fault all the time about trifles. Many little matters can be overlooked, and will come to a natural end of themselves. It is a very serious thing to irritate a child's temper constantly, and it leads to a feeling of estrangement and opposition, which is far removed from the tender love which ought to exist between mother and father and child.

It is very hard for a tired and busy mother to speak pleasantly when children are troublesome or careless, but it is a matter of duty. Reproof may be needed, but it must not be given in cross and impatient tones. Be patient with their shortcomings. Grown people are human and fallible, they are often forgetful and unwise, and how can they expect children to be always careful and considerate? Try to take a sincere interest in what interests your children, and do not make light of their little treasures and amusements. They crave sympathy, and have a right to it.

Remember that your happiness is bound up with that of your children. If they die young, your sorrow will be soothed by the thought that you have been loving and faithful to them always, and have filled their lives with sunshine. If they grow up, their affection will be more important to you than any other possession, and you will be richly repaid for all your efforts after self-control and unselfishness in your dealings with them.

It is too late to cover the well when the child is drowned.

Empty wagons make most noise.

SPOILED CHILDREN

It is not necessary to indulge and spoil children in order to make them happy. Indeed, that is one of the surest ways of making them miserable for life.

COURTS OF THE UNITED STATES.
(Corrected Sept. 1880.)

Supreme Court.—At Washington, D.C.

Court comes in 2d Monday in October.

The Supreme Court of the United States consists of one Chief and eight Associate Justices. There are nine judicial circuits, and to each of these is assigned one of the justices. There are also nine Circuit Judges, each of whom is to reside in his Circuit. The Circuits and Justices are as follows :—

First Circuit, Nathan Clifford, of Portland, Me., Asso. Justice. (Maine, N. H., Mass., R. I.)
Second " Ward Hunt, of Utica, New York, As J. (Vt., Conn., N. Y.)
Third " Wm. Strong, of Philadelphia, Pa., As. J. (Penn., N. J., Del)
Fourth " Morrison R. Waite, of Ohio, Chief Justice. (Md., Va., W. Va., N. C., S. C.)
Fifth " Joseph P. Bradley, of Newark, N. J., As. J. (Geo., Fia , Ala , Miss., La., Tex.)
Sixth " Noah H. Swayne, of Columbus, O., As. J. (Ohio, Mich., Ken., Tenn.)
Seventh " John M. Harlan, of Kentucky, As. J. (Ind., Ill., Wis.)
Eighth " Samuel F. Miller, of Keokuk, Iowa, As. J. (Min., Iowa, Mo., Kan., Ark., Neb., Col.)
Ninth " Stephen J. Field, of San Francisco, Cal., As. J. (Cal., Oregon, Nev.)
Clerk. . . . . James H. McKenney, Washington, D. C.

U. S. Circuit Courts in 1st and 2d Eastern Circuits.

Connecticut, at N. Haven, 4th Tues. in Apr., and at Hartford, 3d Tues. in Sept.
Maine, at Portland, 23d Apr. and 23d Sept.
Massachusetts, at Boston, May 15 and Oct. 15.
New Hampshire, at Portsmouth, May 8, and at Exeter, Oct. 8.
Rhode Island, at Providence, June 15, and Nov. 15.
Vermont, at Windsor, 3d Tu. May, at Rutland 1st Tu. Oct., and at Burlington, 4th Tues. in Feb.

☞ *If the days happen on Sunday, the Court comes in the Monday following.*

U. S. District Courts.
Connecticut, at Hartford, 4th Tues. in May and 1st Tues. Dec.; at N. Haven, 4th Tues. in Feb. and Aug.
Maine, at Portland, 1st Tues. in Feb. and Dec.; at Bath, 1st Tues. in Sept.; at Bangor, 4th Tues. in June.
Massachusetts, at Boston, 3d Tues. in Mar., 4th Tues. in June, 2d Tues. in Sept., and 1st Tues. in Dec.
New Hampshire, at Portsmouth, 3d Tues. in March and Sept.; at Exeter, 3d Tues. in June and Dec.
Rhode Island, at Newport, 2d Tu. in May, and 3d Tues. in Oct.; at Providence, 1st Tues. in Feb. and Aug.
Vermont, at Windsor, 3d Tu. May; at Rutland, 1st Tu. Oct.; at Burlington, 4th Tues. Feb.

U. S. District Courts have jurisdiction in bankruptcy cases, *previous to Sept. 1, '78*, and are always open for such business.

REGISTERS IN BANKRUPTCY IN NEW ENGLAND. (Corrected Sept. 1880.)

The U. S Bankrupt Law was repealed in 1878. This throws all new business in Insolvency into the hands of the state courts, on and after Sept. 1, 1878. As the closing up of the business unsettled at that date will occupy a considerable time, the list of registers is continued.

MAINE.
J. D. Fessenden, Portland.
John W. May, Auburn.
Charles Hamlin, Bangor.

NEW HAMPSHIRE.
James B. Straw, Manchester.
A. T. Batchelder, Keene.

VERMONT.
W. G. Veazey, Rutland.
John L. Edwards, Newport.
L. L. Lawrence, Burlington.

MASSACHUSETTS.
1st *District*, H. M. Knowlton, New Bedford.
2d *District*, Samuel B. Noyes, Canton.

3d *District*, F. W. Palfrey, Boston.
4th *District*, S. L. Thorndike, Boston.
5th *District*, Benj. C. Perkins, Salem.
6th *Dist.*, Edgar J. Sherman, Lawrence.
7th *Dist.*, Charles F. Howe, Lowell.
8th *Dist.*, Peter C. Bacon, Worcester.
9th *Dist.*, Charles G. Delano, Greenfield.
10th *Dist.*, Timothy M. Brown, Springfi'd.

RHODE ISLAND.
John C. Pegram, Providence.

CONNECTICUT.
1st *District*, Henry E. Burton, Hartford.
2d *District*, J. T. Platt, New Haven.
3d *District*, Robert Coit, New London.
4th *Dis.*, L N. Middlebrook, Bridgeport.

HOLIDAYS IN NEW ENGLAND. (Corrected Sept. 1880.)

The following days, *in respect to the payment of notes*, are legal holidays. On most of them, courts, banks, &c., are closed.
If the day falls on Sunday, the day following is usually kept as a Holiday.

Maine.—Jan. 1, Feb. 22, May 30, July 4, Christmas, Fast, and Thanksgiving.
New Hampshire.—Feb. 22, May 30, July 4, Christmas, Fast, and Thanksgiving.
Vermont.—Jan. 1, May 30, July 4, Christmas, Fast, and Thanksgiving.
Massachusetts.—Feb. 22, July 4, Christmas, Fast, and Thanksgiving.
Rhode Island.—Feb. 22, May 30 (or 29th if 30th is Sunday), July 4, Christmas, Fast, and Thanksgiving.
Conn.—Jan. 1, Feb. 22, May 30, July 4, Christmas, Fast, and Thanksgiving.

FROM THE
1881
ALMANAC

89

FROM THE
1882
ALMANAC

DO NOT BE STINGY WITH KISSES

A HAPPY HOME

"... Why should we not try to make our children enjoy their home? They will not, unless they are made happy there. Try to avoid all unnecessary fault-finding, and especially abstain from it at meal-times. It tends to destroy the appetite, not only of the poor offender, but of all the rest of the family. Give a pleasant greeting to all in the morning, and at night, and when meeting at the table. Do not be stingy of kisses. It is better to put them at interest than to hoard them."

IN THE SEARCH FOR THE BETTER LIFE

1. Strive for Silence
2. Resolve to Avoid Finding Fault
3. Be Free to Offer Praise

On the Treatment of Animals ...

Hints for the Household.

ONE of the elements of a happy home is a careful attention to courtesy. Family affection may be strong and devoted, but it is hard to realize it, when the manner is hasty, the speech sarcastic or fault-finding. We treat the stranger within our gates, the occasional guest, with consideration and politeness; we speak gently to him, consult his tastes and preferences, and endeavor to make him feel comfortable and at home. Why should we not try to make our children enjoy their home? They will not, unless they are made happy there. Try to avoid all unnecessary fault-finding, and especially abstain from it at meal-times. It tends to destroy the appetite, not only of the poor offender, but of all the rest of the family. Give a pleasant greeting to all in the morning, and at night, and when meeting at the table. Do not be stingy of kisses. It is better to put them at interest than to hoard them. Keep all sad depressing subjects in the background, and bring forward the cheerful and encouraging side of things. If you wish your little boy to be well-bred, treat him like a gentleman, and he will soon follow your example. Do not interrupt him when he is speaking, if you can help it, take an interest in his little plans, be patient when he seems stupid or naughty, and you will be repaid by his warmer affection.

———

EVERYBODY knows how weary and anxious it makes us to have sickness come. It would be a good plan to take a little trouble to prevent so serious a trouble. Remove decayed refuse from the premises, make sure that the well-water is unpolluted by drainage, before waiting for typhoid fever to frighten you into doing it. Put warm stockings and flannels on the children when chilly, damp weather, or suddenly cold weather comes, without waiting for them to take cold. Be careful about the baby's diet when it is teething, and so avoid the ailments which threaten and often destroy life. Of course, no care can avert all dangers, but it is better to take a good deal of care of a well family, than still more care of a sick family.

———

LET us all resolve — First, to attain to the grace of SILENCE.

Second, to deem all FAULT-FINDING that does no good a SIN; and to resolve, when we are happy ourselves, not to poison the atmosphere for our neighbors by calling on them to remark every painful and disagreeable feature of their daily life.

Third, to practice the grace and virtue of PRAISE. Parents should look out for occasions to commend their children, as carefully as they seek to reprove their faults; and employers should praise the good their servants do, as strictly as they blame the evil.

———

IT is worth while to take pains to make children kind to animals. It trains them in qualities of great importance. If calves and chickens are raised on the farm, let the children take charge of some of them, being regular and faithful in feeding them, and gentle in their treatment. If no care of this sort is practicable, make children treat the cat and dog kindly, allow no teasing or harshness, and require them to be uniformly good-tempered with them. If they behave properly to animals, they are more likely to behave rightly to their brothers and sisters and playmates. If a boy is allowed to be brutal and harsh to the cows, the dog, the cat, he will make the worse husband and father, when he grows up.

ON THE SELECTION OF THE FINEST FOODS

Meats, Poultry & Fish

TO SELECT SUPPLIES.

IT requires some knowledge and skill to select meats, poultry, fish, and groceries. Steer or heifer beef, properly fattened, is the best. It ought to be firm in texture, and have a fine grain, with a yellowish-white fat. When fresh cut it will be of a dark red color, but on a few moments' exposure to the air will change to a bright red. It must have a juicy appearance. Older beef will seem coarser in texture, be darker in color, and less juicy.

THE best mutton is quite fat, the fat parts white and hard, while the lean will be juicy and rather dark red in color. If there is little fat, and that soft and yellow, with meat coarse and flabby, it is sure to be of poor quality. Beef and mutton are improved by keeping, the time depending on temperature. Beef two or three weeks, and mutton a week old or more, is much better, if well kept, than any freshly butchered. Lamb is more juicy than mutton, and so will not keep so long. You can soon learn to judge the age of lamb by the size of the bone, which ought to be of a reddish color.

GOOD veal has flesh of a pinkish color, with the fat white and firm. Never buy veal of soft flesh with a bluish tinge. It shows that the calf was killed too young, when the bones also are soft and cartilaginous. If the meat looks white it shows that the animal was bled before being killed, and that is not only a barbarous practice, but it injures the quality of the flesh.

IT is not every fat fowl that will make a fine tender roast. It is rather late to have to judge whether a bird is tough or tender after it comes upon the table. Many a "spring chicken" turns out to be a tough old hen. The lower end of the breast-bone of a chicken is soft, and can be bent very easily. In old birds it is much less flexible. If the spurs on a fowl are hard, and the scales on the legs rough, you may be sure it is no chicken. But the head gives the best mark of age. If the under bill is stiff and hard, and cannot be easily bent down, and the comb thick and rough, the bird is sure to be old and tough, no matter how fat it may be.

To select a turkey, see that the lower end of the breast-bone is soft and easily bent. An old turkey has rough scales on the legs, long, strong claws, and callous soles on the feet. A young one is just the reverse. The best test of the age of a goose is the brittleness of the windpipe. If it breaks easily under the pressure of the finger and thumb the bird is young. If it rolls and does not break, the bird is old and tough.

THE eyes of a fish that is fresh are full and bright, the gills of a natural red color, the scales bright, the fins stiff, and the body firm. Don't buy a fish that has dim, sunken eyes, dark-colored gills, or that is soft in flesh. No animal food becomes tainted and loses quality so quickly as fish.

GRANULATED sugar is the most economical. A pound of it, being dry, contains proportionately more sweetness than that which is heavy or damp. Don't get sugar of a bluish tinge. Black tea is usually less adulterated with poisonous substances than green. The way to buy coffee is in the berry.

FOR bread select flour made by the new or Haxall process. For cake or pastry take that made by the old or St. Louis method. It is best to keep both kinds on hand, and the best flour is always the cheapest.

. . . The Best Beef

. . . The Best Mutton

. . . The Best Veal

. . . The Best Fowl

. . . A Tip on Turkeys

. . . Recognizing Fresh Fish

. . . A Word on Sugar, Tea and Coffee

. . . Two Special Types of Flour

STARTING THE DAY WITH A HEARTY BREAKFAST

THE MORNING MEAL

"... Let there be, if possible, only pleasant topics and affectionate salutations, that all may go forth their separate ways with sweet, peaceful memories of each other; for some foot may never again cross the family threshold, some eye never witness another day's dawning. This thought, if the busy world were not so clamorous as to stifle it, would often arrest the impatient, fretful words that pain so many tender hearts."

—*FANNY FERN*

HINTS FOR THE HOUSEHOLD.

OUR MORNING MEAL. — Breakfast should be the most enlivening meal of the whole day; for then we are to be nerved for another day's duties and cares, and perhaps for great sorrows also. Let there be no exciting argument, from which personalities may crop out, around the breakfast table. Let there be, if possible, only pleasant topics and affectionate salutations, that all may go forth their separate ways with sweet, peaceful memories of each other; for some foot may never again cross the family threshold, some eye never witness another day's dawning. This thought, if the busy world were not so clamorous as to stifle it, would often arrest the impatient, fretful words that pain so many tender hearts. — *Fanny Fern.*

HOW TO PUT THE CHILDREN TO BED. — *Not* with a reproof for any of that day's sins of omission or commission. Take any other time *but* bed-time for that. If you ever heard a little creature sighing or sobbing in its sleep, you could never do this. Seal their closing eyelids with a kiss and a blessing. The time will come, all too soon, when they will lay their heads upon their pillows lacking both. Let them then at least have this sweet memory of a happy childhood, of which no future sorrow or trouble can rob them. — *Fanny Fern.*

BRINGING UP CHILDREN. — The very best method to bring up a child in the way he should go is to go in that way yourself. Be yourself that which you wish your child to be. Let the father and mother be civil, considerate, patient, sweet-tempered, low-voiced, obliging, truthful, and tender, and pretty much all they would need do to their children would be to stand aside and see them grow. — *Gail Hamilton.*

CARE OF CONVALESCENTS. — The weakness and languor inseparable from long illness render convalescence sometimes a very tedious and trying time. The small stock of strength is unequal to the demands made upon it, and it should be husbanded in every possible way. At night the invalid should have something to take the last thing before going to sleep; any light nourishment will answer, — a cup of cocoa, beef tea, or thin custard. A delicate sandwich, and, if stimulant is ordered, a glass of wine taken then will prevent exhaustion during sleep.

The early morning hours, from three to five, are the most trying of the twenty-four. The powers of life are at their lowest ebb, and should be reinforced by food. If it is impossible to heat anything, a cold drink is better than nothing. Half a pint of milk, with the white of one egg beaten in it, may be given. There is usually little appetite at this early hour, and something must be chosen that can be easily taken. — *Miss E. R. Scovil, in Christian Union.*

WHAT IS EXPECTED OF WOMEN. — Observation has shown me that the majority of men expect a great deal of women, "whatever." They expect a woman will always be good-natured; will keep the whole house in order; will let nothing be wasted; will bear, and be found fault with; will never find fault; will have the children look neat; will cook three meals a day; will always have light bread; will wash and iron, make and mend, entertain company, and, if possible, get along without hired help. Yet they do not, as a general thing, exert themselves overmuch to provide her with conveniences, still less with pleasures. — *A. M. Diaz.*

QUICK TIPS FOR THE BUSY HOUSEWIFE

Testing the Quality of Butter . . .

The Secret of Preparing Oatmeal Properly

The Road to Effective Roasting . . .

Recipe for Potato Croquettes . . .

A Sandwich Spread . . .

Cleaning Kettles . . .

PRESIDENTIAL ELECTION OF 1884.

Total vote,	10,048,061	Cleveland's plurality over	
Cleveland's vote	4,911,017	Blaine	62,683
Blaine's vote	4,848,334	By State Electoral votes:	
St. John's vote	151,809	Cleveland and Hendricks	219
Butler's vote	133,825	Blaine and Logan	182

THE PRESIDENT'S CABINET.

Thomas F. Bayard (Del.), *Sec. of State.*
Daniel Manning (N.Y.), *Sec. of Treas.*
Wm. C. Endicott (Mass.), *Sec. of War.*
Wm. C. Whitney (N.Y.), *Sec. of Navy.*
L. Q. C. Lamar (Miss.), *Sec. of Interior.*
Wm. F. Vilas (Wis.), *P. M. General.*
A. H. Garland (Ark.), *Att'y General.*

THE KITCHEN.

TEST FOR BUTTER. — There is a qualitative test for butter so simple that any housewife can put it into successful practice. A clean piece of white paper is smeared with a little of the suspected butter. The paper is then rolled up and set on fire. If the butter is pure, the smell of the burning paper is rather pleasant; but the odor is distinctly tallowy if the "butter" is made up wholly or in part of animal fats. — *New York Times.*

OATMEAL. — Oatmeal, Indian meal, and hominy all require two things for perfection — plenty of water when put on to boil, and a long time for boiling. Have about two quarts of boiling water in a large stew-pan, and into it stir a cupful of oatmeal, which has been wet with cold water. Boil one hour, stirring often, and then add half a spoonful of salt, and boil an hour longer. If it should get too stiff, add more boiling water; or, if too thin, boil a little longer. You cannot boil it too much. The only trouble in cooking oatmeal is that it takes a long time; but surely this should not stand in the way, when it is so much better for having the extra time. If there is not an abundance of water at first, the oatmeal will not be very good, no matter how much may be added during the cooking. Cracked wheat is cooked in the same way. — *Miss Parloa's New Cook Book.*

ROASTING BEEF AND MUTTON. — When you roast beef, put it as near as you can to the fire till there is a crust all round. Baste first with a little butter. When the crust is formed, remove it further from the fire by degrees. Baste and turn often. Do the same for mutton.

Veal and lamb must be put further from the fire, as they will burn quick. If it be very young lamb, it may be wrapped in greased paper, set close, and basted over the paper.

POTATO CROQUETTES. — Pare, boil, and mash six good-sized potatoes. Add one tablespoonful of butter, two thirds of a cupful of hot cream or milk, the whites of two eggs, well beaten, and salt and pepper to taste. If you wish, use also a slight grating of nutmeg, or a teaspoonful of lemon juice. Let the mixture cool slightly, then shape, roll in egg and crumbs, and fry. — *Miss Parloa's New Cook Book.*

MIXED SANDWICHES. — Chop fine, cold ham, tongue, and chicken; mix with one pint of the meat half a cup of melted butter, one tablespoonful of salad oil, one of mustard if desired, the yolk of a beaten egg, and a little pepper; spread on bread cut in slices and buttered. Ham alone may be prepared in this way. — From *Practical Housekeeping.*

TO CLEAN KETTLES EASILY. — Pour a little hot water into them and put a cover on. The steam will soften the dirt so that it may be easily removed.

& WORLDLY WISDOM

THE HOUSEHOLD.

THE TABLE. — We should never speak of what is unpleasant at the table. If we have bad news to tell, this is not the place to tell it. Sickness, accident, death, and whatever is painful to hear, should not be discussed, any more than what is disagreeable. Neither is the table the place to talk of work or business details; but subjects should be chosen that all are interested in. No one should be allowed to scold or find fault at mealtime. Cheerful conversation is good for digestion as well as enjoyment. Each one should be in his best mood at the table, and the hours which families spend together there ought to be the happiest of the day. — *Lessons on Manners.*

TO KEEP THE HANDS SOFT AND SMOOTH WHILE DOING HOUSEWORK. After washing dishes, or any like work, wash the hands carefully and wipe dry. Then rinse thoroughly in vinegar and water, one half each. A bottle of the mixture should be kept handy.

TO KEEP WOOLLENS FROM MOTHS. — Brush thoroughly, then sew tightly in cotton bags. For coats or any heavy garment, hang by a hoop through the shoulders, or by loop in the usual way; and upon taking them out they are free from wrinkles, odor of camphor, etc.

TO AVOID SHRINKAGE IN WASHING ALL-WOOL GOODS. — Dissolve a sufficient quantity of soap in warm water, adding a little sal-soda to soften it.
Wash, wring, and then rinse in clean warm water, using no cold or very hot water, after which shake well and dry quickly. Do not rub on soap, or use a washboard. Avoid all patent washing powders or liquids.

EXERCISE OUT-OF-DOORS. — Every woman should take a certain amount of exercise out-of-doors. It is necessary for good health and good nature too. If by doing so you will be obliged to leave some of the work in the house undone, who will know or care one hundred years from now ? — *The Household.*

CORN MUFFINS FOR BREAKFAST. — Pour a quart of boiling milk over a pint of fine corn meal. While still hot, add a tablespoonful of butter and a little salt, stirring the batter thoroughly. Let it stand till cool, then add a small cup of wheat flour and two eggs well beaten. When mixed sufficiently, put the batter into shallow tins (or better yet, into gem pans), well greased, and bake in a brisk oven a half hour, or until of a rich brown color. Serve hot.

POTATO PIE. — Boil the potatoes until soft, then peel and rub them through a sieve; to a quarter of a pound of potatoes add one quart of milk, three teaspoonfuls of melted butter, four beaten eggs, and sugar and nutmeg to taste. Bake as you would a custard pie.

TO CLEAN OIL-CLOTH. — Use tepid skimmed milk, with an equal quantity of cold tea, and no soap.

CHOCOLATE DROPS. — Two and a half cups pulverized or granulated sugar (or maple sugar may be used), one-half cup cold water; boil four minutes; place the saucepan in cold water, and beat till cold enough to make into little balls ; take half a cake of Baker's chocolate, shave off fine, and put it in a bowl set in the top of a boiling tea-kettle to melt, and when balls are cool enough, roll them in the chocolate with a fork. This makes eighty. Or, while making into balls, mould an almond meat into the centre of each ball, roll them in coarse sugar, and you have delicious "cream almonds." Or, mould unbroken halves of walnut meats into soft sugar, and, when cold, roll them in the chocolate. When finished, take out and lay on buttered paper until cold. — *Practical Housekeeping.*

WHOLESOME TABLE TALK

"... No one should be allowed to scold or find fault at mealtime. Cheerful conversation is good for digestion as well as enjoyment. Each one should be in his best mood at the table, and the hours which families spend together there ought to be the happiest of the day."
—*Lessons on Manners*

How To:

* Keep Hands Soft

* Keep Moths Away

* Avoid Woollen Shrinkage

* Keep Healthy and Cheerful

How to Make:

* **Corn Muffins**

* **Potato Pie**

* **Sweet Chocolate**

HOUSEHOLD HINTS

DRIVING OFF OUR MOST PERSISTENT ENEMIES

... Driving Off Sour Faces and Harsh Words

... Rats, Mice and Cockroaches: How to Scare Them Off

... Eye-strengthening Exercise

... To Be Master of Well Living

... On Cleaning Blankets

... On Removing Grease Stains

... Woman's Instinct vs. Man's Reason

... The Value of Brown Sugar

... Recipe for Potato Soup ...

HINTS FOR THE HOUSEHOLD.

THE REASON. — Many a child goes astray simply because home lacks sunshine. Children need smiles as much as the flowers need sunbeams. If a thing pleases, they are apt to seek it; if it displeases, they are apt to avoid it. If home is a place where faces are sour, and words harsh, and fault-finding is ever in the ascendant, they will spend as many hours as possible elsewhere. — *A Year of Sunshine.*

To DRIVE OFF VERMIN. — If rats enter the cellar, a little powdered potash thrown into their holes, or mixed with meal and scattered in their runways, never fails to drive them away. Cayenne pepper will keep the buttery and storeroom free from rats and cockroaches. If a mouse makes an entrance into any part of your dwellings, saturate a rag with cayenne in solution, or sprinkle dry cayenne on some loose cotton, and stuff it into a hole, which can be repaired with either wood or mortar. No rat or mouse will eat that rag for the purpose of opening communication with a depot of supplies. — *Scientific American.*

SAVE THE EYES. — Many people who are obliged to use their eyes steadily in reading, writing, painting, etc., suffer much from the weakness of those organs. It will prove a relief to all and a cure in most cases to observe this rule: Every fifteen or twenty minutes give the eyes a rest by lifting the head and looking up and around for a minute or two. This allows the eyes to change their focus, and relieves the continuous strain of one adjustment. We have known people who had spent much money for glasses and eye-washes to be cured of all trouble by following this simple rule.

TRUE GREATNESS. — I honor that man whose ambition it is, not to win laurels in the state or the army, not to be a jurist or a naturalist, not to be a poet or a commander, but to be a master of living well, and to administer the offices of master or servant, of husband, father and friend. But it requires as much breadth of power for this as for those other functions, — as much or more, — and the reason for the failure is the same. I think the vice of our housekeeping is that it does not hold man sacred. — *R. W. Emerson.*

TO CLEANSE BLANKETS. — Put two large tablespoonfuls of **borax** and a pint bowl of soft soap into a tub of cold water. When dissolved, put in a pair of blankets and let them remain over night. Next day rub them out, and rinse thoroughly in two waters and hang them up to dry. Do not wring them.

TO REMOVE GREASE. — To remove grease from wall paper, lay several folds of blotting paper on the spot and hold a hot iron near it until the grease is absorbed.

HONOR THE WIFE. — He who respects his wife will find that she respects him. With what measure he metes it shall be measured to him again, good measure, pressed down, and running over. He who consults his spouse will have a good counsellor. I have heard our minister say, " Woman's instincts are often truer than man's reason." They jump at a thing at once, and are wise off-hand. Say what you will of your wife's advice, it's likely you'll be sorry you did not take it. — *John Ploughman.*

THE CHEAPEST SUGAR. — There is no economy in purchasing brown sugar. The moisture it contains more than makes up for the difference in price; but for some things, such as dark cake and mince pies, many cooks prefer it. Granulated sugar is the purest and best for ordinary uses. — *Mrs. Gilpin's Frugalities.*

POTATO SOUP. — One heaping cupful of cold mashed potatoes, one cupful of cold mashed turnips. If these vegetables are left over from dinner they will have butter in them, otherwise you must add a tablespoonful. Stir the vegetables together and add a pint of hot water in which one onion has been boiled. Put all on the stove stirring carefully. When thoroughly hot, and free from all lumps, add one quart of hot **milk** and serve at once. — *Mrs. Gilpin's Frugalities.*

HOUSEHOLD HINTS

FROM THE
1891
ALMANAC

A SMILING COUNTENANCE

Frowns and cross words not only destroy the happiness of him who dispenses them, but they cause misery to all who observe and listen to them.

WIFE-APPRECIATION

The man who cannot sit at the table opposite his wife, and eat bread that is baked too much, or not enough, without finding fault, is but little higher than the brute, and ought to be compelled to cook his own food, until he mends his manners.

. . . On Growing Your Own Seed

. . . Treating Apples Like Eggs

. . . Strawberries: A Great Staple for the Home

CHIPS.

A WEEDY garden is no honor to its owner; it shows that he lacks energy or good judgment. If two crops are to be grown on the same land, at the same time, there is no good reason why one of them should be entirely useless, and permitted to master the useful crop.

A SMILING countenance and pleasant words are wonderful helps on the farm among the workmen, as well as in the dwelling-house among the members of the household; frowns and cross words not only destroy the happiness of him who dispenses them, but they cause misery to all who observe and listen to them.

IF we would train our eyes and educate our minds so as to better understand the wonderful book of Nature, we should more fully realize the ever-presence of a Supreme Ruler, and, in our rambles over the fields, every step would bring to our view objects of the deepest interest.

THE man who is always scolding the boys, cannot build a fence high enough to keep them out of his orchard; but he who always speaks pleasantly to them, treats them with respect, and occasionally gives them a taste of his fruit, will keep them out of his orchard without any fence.

THE man who cannot sit at the table opposite his wife, and eat bread that is baked too much, or not enough, without finding fault, is but little higher than the brute, and ought to be compelled to cook his own food, until he mends his manners, or go without food until he can eat hard crusts of bread with a smiling countenance and at the same time entertain his family with pleasant words.

IF we would make the most of life, we should study not only to improve our own minds but also to improve the minds of all we come in contact with. When we succeed in making those around us happier, we make ourselves happier. It is said that happiness is never gathered faster than when we are making those around us happier, and that misery is never gathered faster than when we are trying to make those around us more miserable.

THE successful farmer will, as far as possible, grow his own seed, and will exert himself to select the very best varieties, and year after year make such improvements on them as possible. In this way he can keep in advance of those who buy their seed and depend on others for improvements. There are many kinds of garden vegetables that the farmer can improve in the direction of the particular taste of his family.

APPLES, if expected to keep well, must be picked from the trees at the right time, and handled with as much care as if they were eggs. No apple that falls to the ground should be barrelled with the first quality, but however sound it may appear, it should be classed as second quality. Winter fruit, as soon as gathered, should be stored in a cool place, where the temperature will vary but a few degrees during the entire year, and care should be taken not to disturb it until wanted to send to market.

EVERY farmer should have a few rods of strawberry vines to furnish fruit for the family. They add much to the attractions of home, especially if there are a few children to help eat the fruit. Three rods of land, properly cultivated, will furnish all the strawberries that one family will care to eat. Surely it can be no great hardship to take good care of so small a plot of land. Those who always buy their strawberries have but little conception of the flavor of a dish of this fruit when well ripened and picked from the vines but a few hours before wanted for the table. In picking a well ripened strawberry the hull should be left on the vine.

THE father of the family should exert himself to plan home amusements for the children during the long winter evenings. If the children are not amused at home, they will avail themselves of every opportunity to get away from home to seek amusements where they can find them; and very likely they will join with those who will lead them into places where the amusements are not of a high order.

& WORLDLY WISDOM

FROM THE
1892
ALMANAC

SWEETER THAN THE PERFUME OF FLOWERS

HOUSEHOLD HINTS.

Kind words can never be spoken in vain: they are like balm to the weary heart, and are sweeter than the perfume of flowers. If they should, perchance, fall unheeded on the ear, they still do a vast amount of good to the one who speaks them. They are the best weapons of defence. Be not afraid to use them freely, thus helping to make thy fellow mortals happier, as well as thyself.

Music in the household should be a comfort to each member, helping to keep the tempers sweet, and to draw them together in closer harmony. Vocal music can be enjoyed without cost: and if the farmer can afford it, do not think it a waste of money to buy a parlor organ. This has been, and may be again, a means of great good. The daughters should also be taught to cook, sew, and do well all branches of housework, while the sons should be useful and observing about the farm.

The flavor of green sweet-corn is greatly injured by boiling too long. It should be put into boiling water, and allowed to boil not over ten or twelve minutes.

An excellent way to cook asparagus is to cut it into small pieces in water, rinse well, and boil in salt water until very tender, then drain off the water, and butter the asparagus to taste.

The preserving of fruit, berries, etc., in glass cans for winter use in the household is highly recommended, thus affording a wholesome diet, as well as a great luxury, at comparatively small cost. The cans should not be filled so as to run over while the top is screwed on. Great care should be taken to have the screw and rubber entirely dry.

A few drops of ammonia put into each quart of water with which pot plants are watered will improve the color of the foliage, and greatly increase the growth.

Warm water is an excellent remedy for healing sores of all kinds, especially those on the face or lips. Take a cloth or sponge, and sop them several times a day with water as hot as can be borne. One of the best remedies for warts is to wet them with saliva several times a day, which causes them to crumble and disappear.

Small red ants can be destroyed by dipping a sponge in hot lard, and placing it on the shelf where they appear, occasionally dipping it in hot water. The large black ones may be destroyed by placing some molasses sugar in a small pitcher; when they have collected in considerable numbers, hold the pitcher over a pan of hot water and let them drop in.

In washing lamp-chimneys care should be taken to prevent scratching the inside with any hard substance, because when any glass cylinder is scratched on the inside it is sure to break on being heated, and will often break while cold. A piece of lambskin with the wool on, fastened to a stick, can be used with safety. Chimneys are often broken by permitting a cold current of air to strike on one side of them while hot.

Furs should be packed away before hot weather, or the moth miller will deposit eggs on them, and thus make it very difficult to keep them from being injured by this destructive enemy. A pretty sure way is to tie the furs up in a cotton bag, first scattering gum camphor over furs, and pack them away in a chest. Red cedar chests are considered effective, but it is safer to use the gum camphor in addition.

Woollen carpets should be taken up at least once a year, and the dust well beaten out. If kept down longer the dirt which gets under them and between the threads will wear them out very fast; besides, the health of the family requires carpets to be cleaned often. When the carpet is put down, if a small quantity of benzine be put round the edges it will prevent the moths from doing any damage. This, on trial, has been found to be better than tobacco leaves.

Wire window-screens, though the first cost is more, are really cheaper in the end than mosquito netting of cotton; and, as they do not move by the action of the wind like cotton, they are not so painful to the eye.

. . . Kind Words: A Balm to the Weary Heart

. . . Music in the Home Sets a Good Tone

. . . Don't Boil Corn Too Long

. . . Dice Asparagus for Good Results

. . . On Preserving Fruits and Berries

. . . On Healing Sores of All Kinds

. . . How to Get Rid of Ants

. . . On the Care of Lamp-Chimneys

. . . When and How to Store Furs

. . . On the Care of Woolen Carpets

HOUSEHOLD HINTS

FROM THE
1893
ALMANAC

The Refining Influence of Flowers

CULTIVATING FLOWERS

Do not think it a waste of time to cultivate a few flowers, or to let the children have a flower-bed. It is judicious for parents to cultivate a love of flowers in their children from earliest years, as flowers have a refining influence, and never lead astray, but always upward to what is purer and better. If one's time and strength are limited, a bed one yard square, with a geranium and a few nasturtiums, for instance, can give pleasure to the whole household; and these flowers will bloom all the season, until the frost blights them. A few flowers in pots are better than none.

HOUSEHOLD HINTS.

Do not think it a waste of time to cultivate a few flowers, or to let the children have a flower-bed. It is judicious for parents to cultivate a love of flowers in their children from earliest years, as flowers have a refining influence, and never lead astray, but always upward to what is purer and better. If one's time and strength are limited, a bed one yard square, with a geranium and a few nasturtiums, for instance, can give pleasure to the whole household; and these flowers will bloom all the season, until the frost blights them. A few flowers in pots are better than none.

Parents cannot be too careful in the selection of good reading for their children. They are not expected to read dry and prosy books, but such literature as will entertain, and at the same time instruct, strengthen the mind, and tend to elevate the character.

Muriatic acid will remove iron rust. Place the fabric over a cup of warm water while applying the acid with a small, soft brush. As soon as the rust disappears rinse the place in a cup of water, then rinse in two or three changes of water, and hang out in the air to dry. Do not set a hot iron on the goods, nor leave it without rinsing thoroughly, as the acid will be likely to injure the fabric if not properly removed.

If a kerosene stove smokes, take out the tubes and boil them in wood-ashes and water for one hour; clean the stove thoroughly, and put in new wicks. It is a good plan occasionally to boil kerosene-lamp tubes in the same way. A good way to extinguish the lamp in a kerosene stove is to use a common palmleaf fan.

As tuberculosis (which is really consumption) is a prevalent disease in cows, the milk should be thoroughly scalded before using, in order to avoid all danger of contracting the disease.

Furniture rubbed over with a woollen cloth slightly moistened with linseed oil will greatly improve its appearance.

The best way to preserve the teeth is to keep them clean. Clean them with a soft brush and clear water every morning after rising, then after each meal rinse them thoroughly by taking lukewarm water into the mouth. This is a very easy thing to do, and takes but a short time. It is very important, and if one will persevere in doing it the teeth will last much longer. Any preparation of soap used as a dentifrice is likely to injure the gums.

Do not try to keep out the sunlight except on very warm days, for sunlight is necessary to good health. It is better to tan the complexion and have good health than to have a delicate complexion without health.

Do not keep the parlor shut up until it becomes musty. The house and everything in it were made for use and enjoyment, and that is all the good we get from them. Keep the house neat, but do not always be scrubbing imaginary dirt; keep the strength to do something more useful.

The constant drinking of ice water during hot weather is a bad practice. It chills the stomach, retards digestion, and leads to dyspepsia. If ice water must be drunk, it should be in small quantities and very slowly; even then it tends to cause a parched and thirsty feeling in many persons.

It is convenient to have a scrap-book. One can be easily made, without expense, by taking a book which can be spared as well as not, and cutting out every other leaf; then, when you have a cooking recipe, or read a piece in the newspaper which you would like to save, cut it out and paste it in the scrap-book. A few pictures interspersed will make the book more interesting. An excellent paste is made by dissolving in water a little gum tragacanth. This paste does not show through or discolor the thinnest paper.

SHINING UP FURNITURE

Furniture rubbed over with a woollen cloth slightly moistened with linseed oil will greatly improve its appearance.

100

& WORLDLY WISDOM

USEFUL HINTS.

Do not try to preserve your name by writing it on the trunks of trees or upon the walls of old buildings, but write it in the memories and affections of your friends by your uprightness and sweetness of character.

If you have a tree that bears an inferior pear or apple, graft it with scions from a good fruit, thus making it useful to yourself and family.

Thoroughly drenching a flower bed with water once in three or four days, or even once a week, is far better than a slight watering every day.

Mock whipped cream may be made of various kinds of fruit. For example, take a medium sized apple, grate it, add one cup of sugar, the white of one egg; beat twenty minutes, using a silver fork. Bananas, strawberries, and other fruit may be used instead of apple; also, one half cup of sugar instead of one cup, if one desires a less quantity and not so sweet.

A hammock may be very useful hung out of doors in warm weather, as it enables a person to rest and take fresh air at the same time. It is also useful hung in the house in winter where one has no room for a lounge, as it can be put up and taken down at pleasure.

A little finely ground bone mixed with the soil in a flower pot is a benefit to the growth of the plant.

A very good way to cook onions is to slice them and stew them in salt water until tender, and then pour them over cracker crumbs, adding a piece of butter, and stirring all together. This will digest easier than when cooked in other ways, and consequently is better for persons who have delicate stomachs.

This earth might be a paradise if each would do his part by practising the Golden Rule in his life. It may seem a simple thing, but it embraces much, and should be among a child's first teaching.

If things go wrong in the household, and the bread is heavy, do not make it heavier by fretting and finding fault. Cheerful and encouraging words will make digestion easier.

Young girls should be thoughtful of their mothers, and lend a helping hand whenever it is possible. Do not think, because mother is smart and goes about her work cheerfully, that she can never get tired. Do not clothe yourself in laundered garments, and pile up the clothes-basket on a washing day, without ever lifting a finger to help when you can as well as not. Do not think it is not elevating or genteel to work about the house. This is a great mistake. If it is degrading for you, it certainly is for your mother. If you cannot help in the washing or ironing there are many lighter things which you can do, and many steps which you can take for her which will help her very much. Do not wait for her to insist on your doing, for it will make her very happy to have your thoughtful voluntary help; and in after years you will have it to look back upon with pleasure.

The woodbine is a favorite, and should be cultivated around buildings, and in any convenient place, for it is one of our most ornamental, hardy, and easily cultivated vines, and is readily obtained in New England. This vine, properly trained, will help to make an old house attractive, and will certainly add to the beauty of a new one.

The common yellow daisy or cone flower, planted around the house in patches, makes a very bright and pretty addition, and is especially desirable where one has neither time nor strength to cultivate a variety of flowers. These will come up year after year, and need very little care.

When setting a lawn or park with a variety of trees, the hemlock should not be overlooked. It grows to a beautiful tree, is ornamental while small, is easily cultivated in New England, and, being an evergreen, retains its beauty during the entire year.

Strive to keep a circulation of pure air through the whole house. Keep things reasonably neat and clean, but do not wash the flour barrel, or scrub the kitchen floor till it is worn so thin that you may fall through into the cellar.

If you cannot speak well of your neighbors, it is generally best to say nothing.

GROWING IN STRENGTH AND STATURE

PRESERVING YOUR NAME

Do not try to preserve your name by writing it on the trunks of trees or upon the walls of old buildings, but write it in the memories and affections of your friends by your uprightness and sweetness of character.

ON WATERING PLANTS

Thoroughly drenching a flower bed with water once in three or four days, or even once a week is far better than a slight watering every day.

PLANT GROWTH

A little finely ground bone mixed with the soil in a flower pot is a benefit to the growth of the plant.

PARADISE

This earth might be a paradise if each would do his part by practising the Golden Rule in his life. It may seem a simple thing, but it embraces much, and should be among a child's first teaching.

HOUSEHOLD HINTS

FROM THE
1893
ALMANAC

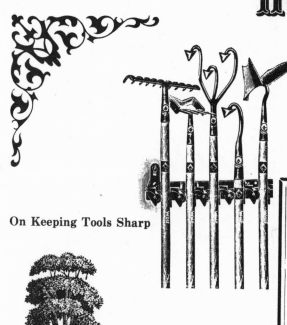

On Keeping Tools Sharp

Tree Planning or Planned Treehood

The Joy of a Water-Lily

Teaching Cats a Lesson

What Is Man That Thou Regardest Him

A Soft Answer Assuages Wrath

"Ve get Too Soon Olt Und Too late Shmot!"

The Infallible Lie Detector

Money vs. Integrity

The Slowest Learners in the World . . .

CHIPS.

WHY work with a dull hoe, when it will cut up the weeds with half the strength if kept sharp? Sharpen the upper side with a good file.

A large-sized dog will eat as much as a pig, and if his owner does not properly feed him, he will rob the neighbors of whatever he can find that suits his appetite, not excepting chickens, and even lambs.

Plant a few trees every year, until you have surrounded your home with a sufficient number to make it attractive and beautiful, but do not set them so near the dwelling-house as to shut out the sunshine, for sunshine and air are necessary for health. Too much shade causes dampness, which is very injurious to health during a considerable part of the year.

Every one who has a pond near the house should set a few water-lilies in it. They require very little care, and yet are a constant source of enjoyment during several months in the year.

Encourage the swallows to build their nests in the barn. They will destroy a large number of insects, and will afford enjoyment to all lovers of birds.

When a pet cat gets into the habit of catching birds, take one of the dead birds away from her and tie it securely under her throat with a strong string, and compel her to carry it several days. She will be so sick of it that she will never again touch a bird, though it be placed before her. This needs to be done in hot weather.

The man who thinks the world cannot get along without him would be very much surprised and mortified if he could be made to realize how little consequence he is to the world, and how soon he will be forgotten when he dies; but the man who labors so intensely as to forget himself, to create new ideas that will lift men to a higher level, will be likely to leave behind him a record of progress that will be remembered for ages.

The man who cannot govern himself cannot expect to be successful in governing others. Angry words never help a good cause, but pleasant words to an angry man often cause him to relent, and to feel ashamed of himself. Not much of a quarrel can be maintained by one person.

The more knowledge a man possesses, the more fully does he realize how little he knows, because his knowledge lifts him up to that elevation from which he can overlook the broad field of investigation not yet explored by man. The man who knows the least is the man who thinks he knows everything, and he thinks so because his knowledge does not extend beyond his vision.

Be careful to keep your promises to children, whether they be to reward or punish. A child soon learns whether a parent means to do what is promised. Exercise as much patience with a child as you have to with a sitting hen when she will not sit where you want her to, and will sit where you do not want her to. If you cannot do this, how can you expect the child to learn patience and obedience?

He who sacrifices his health, honor, or honesty for money, pays too high a price for it, but often finds it out too late.

The man who learns the most from his fellow-man is he who keeps his mouth shut and his ears open. He who is continually talking gives no one a chance to teach him. To learn to be a good listener is a trade that some men never learn, though every one they meet would like to see them keep their mouths shut long enough to try.

102

& WORLDLY WISDOM

FROM THE
1894
ALMANAC

GOOD CROPS
AND
GOOD CHARACTER

PURPLE EGG PLANT.

TWO CROPS

Do not try to raise two crops on the same plot of land the same year, and have one of them weeds. If you do, the weeds will be very likely to take the lead. The mind, with its crop of thoughts, is very much like the garden. If the bad thoughts are not rooted out at first appearance, they will be likely to overshadow and crowd out the good thoughts.

CHIPS.

IT is quite as important to keep the chambers of the memory in good order as it is the dwelling or the workshop. Ideas, although of the highest importance, are of but little practical value unless properly arranged where they can be readily brought to mind the moment they are wanted.

Wise parents try to govern their children by love, and not by fear ; by kind words, and not by the rod ; leading them to live good and useful lives by living good and useful lives themselves.

If we wish to succeed in argument we should endeavor to prove the truth of our opinions with arguments clothed in refined, as well as pleasant words. The angry man who puts forth his arguments in vulgar language rarely has the power to convince an intelligent audience that they are worth listening to.

As thoughts suggest words and acts, we should try to make them kind and generous, as well as highly intelligent ; thus fitting us to be honored members of society, and enabling us to help the world to be better for our having lived in it.

Always try to be so busy that you have no time to watch your neighbors, or to visit one of them for the purpose of finding fault with some other one. Better spend your time in trying to correct your own faults than to be going from place to place exposing the faults of others.

He who never sees anything good in others, is very likely not to have many good qualities himself. He looks through eyes that reflect on his vision the bad qualities of himself, and his great misfortune is that he does not suspect it, but believes that his vision is clear.

A wise philosopher once said, " Whatever may be said against you, take care to live so that no one will believe it." Good acts have more power to establish a good character than the best arguments from the most eloquent speaker.

Young man, do you know what would be the difference between having one thousand dollars at interest at six per cent per annum, when twenty-one years of age, and keeping it at compound interest until sixty years of age, or paying interest on the same amount of money, at the same rate, during the same time? If not, had you not better spend some winter evening to ascertain? The answer may lead you to pause before you hire much money.

Let your word be as good as your note for value received, and your note as good as gold. If your credit is good, keep it so by doing just as you agree ; for a man without credit will have to do business at a great disadvantage, though he have plenty of money.

The man who spends a large portion of his time seeking elevated positions, had better devote it to fitting himself to perform properly the duties required in a high position. It is better for a man to have the position seek him than for him to seek the position, for it is rarely that a man is sought to fill any elevated position unless he is peculiarly fitted for it.

Do not try to raise two crops on the same plot of land the same year, and have one of them weeds. If you do, the weeds will be very likely to take the lead. The mind, with its crop of thoughts, is very much like the garden. If the bad thoughts are not rooted out at first appearance, they will be likely to overshadow and crowd out the good thoughts.

As the character of the man depends very much on how he spends his leisure hours while a boy and a young man, parents should see to it that the leisure hours of the boys are well spent.

103

IMPROVING COFFEE FLAVOR AND OTHER HINTS

Keeping Cake Moist. . .

Improving Coffee Flavor. . .

Preventing Smoke Suffocation. . .

Cleaning Soiled Earthenware. . .

The Many Uses of Turpentine. . .

How to Prevent Burning When Boiling in Fat. . .

Giving Linens a Shine. . .

Use Velvet for Slipping Heels. . .

A Tip on Glass Cleaning. . .

Removing Ink Stains with Matches. . .

On Washing Milk Glasses. . .

Removing Ice Cream from Molds. . .

On Restoring Crushed Velvet. . .

Renovating Black Silk. . .

Removing Mildew from Leather. . .

Reading Aloud Good for the Health

. . . How to Remove Gloves. . .

Fruit Pits Put to Good Use. . .

Sweet Peas Anathema to Flies. . .

Removing Scorch-Marks from Linen . . .

USEFUL HINTS.

"Vinegar and brown paper" is still a good remedy for a bruise. Keep the paper, or the cloth, wet, and both swelling and discoloration will be less.

Half the benefit from a liniment is from the rubbing. Therefore rub long and gently. Do not injure the skin.

If stored seed potatoes begin to sprout, smoke them with sulphur. They will not only keep better, but will sprout quicker when planted.

Wagon grease can often be removed from cloth by the following method. Rub with lard or unsalted butter, then after fifteen minutes wash out thoroughly with hot water and soap.

Boxing a child's ears — or a dog's, for that matter — may injure the hearing, and even cause deafness. The ears should never even be pulled.

Keep the sun in the house. It is the best help to health. Air the bedding in the sun, open the closets and let good air get to them.

The best time for planting acorns, chestnuts and walnuts, is in the fall as soon as they are ripe. If they are kept long after the dead ripe state they lose their vegetating principles.

The best way to dry an umbrella, and so preserve it, is to leave it spread on the piazza or in the hall. When there is not enough room to allow that, reverse the usual method, and stand the umbrella in the corner with the handle down. The rain drips quicker off the points. The ordinary way collects all the water at one place, where the cloth dries slowly and therefore rots the quicker. Never put several wet umbrellas together in an umbrella stand.

Keep the ice chest clean by washing with soda. Do not let the waste pipe clog, and never connect it with the drainage of the house, or the worst results may ensue. Keep the butter and milk in a separate compartment.

Dry cooking-tins well before putting away. Wooden ware should not be dried near the fire, as it will warp or crack.

For cleansing tea stains, pour boiling water through the cloth.

Varnish or shellac on clothing may be removed by alcohol, paint by turpentine.

For invalids, broth may be quickly made. Mince lean meat fine, add a pint of cold water for each pound, soak for fifteen minutes, boil slowly for half an hour.

For cleaning and polishing furniture, make a mixture of one half-pint raw linseed oil, one half-pint turpentine, one tablespoonful japan. Shake each time before using, apply with a soft cloth, rub the surface dry with another. Applying this once or twice a year will keep fresh the finish on good furniture.

A thick felt under the table cloth avoids noise and saves wear on the cloth.

Give the lamp burners a good boiling often for twenty minutes in water with a little washing soda.

In breaking eggs, break them one at a time into a cup, so that a bad one may be rejected.

Use a double boiler for heating milk. It is scalded when the water in the lower pan boils.

Do not jar any rising material while it is baking. Hence, do not slam the oven door.

In spite of all the remedies offered for driving away ants from the house, the only sure way seems to be to catch and kill them. Set in the closets plates coated thick with soft lard, with little sticks leaning against them for the ants to climb. When filled, drop in a pan of boiling water, and then set the plate as before.

Soft leather gloves may be washed in the following manner. Make a strong suds of any good white soap, and to two quarts of suds add one teaspoonful of borax dissolved in half a pint of hot water. When the mixture is cold, put the gloves on the hands and wash as if washing the hands. Rinse, draw them off, and hang to dry, but not in the sun. Work gently, as the wet leather stretches. When nearly dry pull into shape.

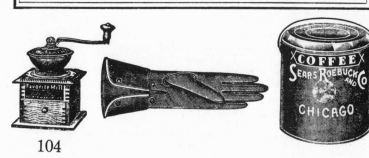

FROM THE
1900
ALMANAC

USEFUL HINTS.

Iron pillowslips lengthwise instead of crosswise if you wish to iron wrinkles out instead of in.

Save soapsuds if you have a garden, for they form a very useful manure for flowers, as well as shrubs and vegetables. It is well to have a sunk tub in every garden where the soapy water can stand till required for watering.

Do not give sick people fried foods or anything highly seasoned. Avoid hot bread and biscuits and strong tea and coffee.

Bathe the face and hands of a feverish person with warm water that has a bit of common soda dissolved in it. A few drops of alcohol or cologne is often pleasant to use to bathe the sick.

A nurse should use care that no person having wet or even damp clothing should enter the sick room. Never get out of patience with the whims of an invalid, but try to coax and soothe without irritating him.

Marble washstands and mantelpieces can be cleansed by simply washing the surface with warm water, to which a little borax has been added, polishing afterward with a dry cloth.

To take stains off the fingers, keep a piece of cut lemon on your wash stand and rub the spot with this previous to wetting. If this is not successful, try a piece of pumice soap. Even the pulp of a lemon, which has had the juice taken from it, is useful for this purpose.

Do not allow paint to be cleaned with soap or soda. Ammonia is far better. Use one tablespoon to every gallon of water required to clean the woodwork.

For use in polishing knives a good device is formed of two flat pieces of material, having polishing cushions on their opposing faces, the upper member being pivoted on the lower to admit the knife blade between the two.

To keep tortoise shell bright the best polish is rouge powder, used for brightening silver. If thus treated regularly no tortoise shell, however old, need look dull, as is so often the case.

New flatirons should be allowed to stand on the stove some time before using, in order to get off the coating of black. When they are rusted they may be cleaned with fine scouring soap, and when stored away for any length of time kerosene or vaseline should be put over them.

A good substitute for suet in puddings may be found in well clarified dripping if a little soaked, finely-crushed tapioca be added to the mixture.

A very young housekeeper frequently makes the mistake of planning for a great variety of dishes when she might for the same outlay have the very best cuts of meat and an abundance of the substantials.

To polish oilcloth, shred half an ounce of beeswax into a saucer, cover it with turpentine, and place it in the oven until melted ; after washing the oilcloth thoroughly, rub the whole surface lightly with a flannel dipped in the wax and turpentine, then rub with a dry cloth.

House cleaning should have no fixed date, but should depend entirely upon the weather. It is rarely warm enough to leave off fires until late in the spring, but many small things can be done before the real cleaning begins.

Steel kept in quicklime will not rust. The best thing for cleaning it is unslacked lime, but care should be used, as it may affect the eyes.

Tansy leaves scattered around spots infested by ants, will cause them to disappear.

KEEPING YOUR HOME SPIC AND SPAN

ON IRONING

Iron pillowslips lengthwise instead of crosswise if you wish to iron wrinkles out instead of in.

SOAPSUDS AS MANURE

Save soapsuds if you have a garden, for they form a very useful manure for flowers, as well as shrubs and vegetables. It is well to have a sunk tub in every garden where the soapy water can stand till required for watering.

FINGER STAINS

To take stains off the fingers, keep a piece of cut lemon in your wash stand and rub the spot with this previous to wetting. If this is not successful, try a piece of pumice soap. Even the pulp of a lemon, which has had the juice taken from it, it useful for this purpose.

CLEANING PAINT

Do not allow paint to be cleaned with soap or soda. Ammonia is far better. Use one tablespoon to every gallon of water required to clean the woodwork.

HOUSEHOLD HINTS

POLISHING FURNITURE
AND
OTHER USEFUL HINTS

... Treating a Bruise with Vinegar

... Removing Wagon Grease

... The Danger of Boxing Ears

... When to Plant Acorns, Chestnuts and Walnuts

... A Lesson in Umbrella Drying

... Refreshing the Ice Box with Soda

... Cleaning Tea Stains

... Broth for Invalids

... Cleaning and Polishing Furniture

... A Tip on Opening Eggs

... Don't Slam the Oven Door

... The Process of Ant-Trapping

... On Cleaning Leather Gloves

USEFUL HINTS.

CAKE is kept moist in a tin, adding (for a length of time) a piece of fresh bread daily.

A salt-spoon of salt added to a quart of coffee when made greatly improves the flavor.

Enamel-lined pans and dishes may be cleaned by scouring with eggshells, and rinsing in clean warm water. Dry with a soft cloth.

In case of fire, wet a silk handkerchief, and tie, without folding, over the face. It will prevent suffocation from smoke, permit free breathing, and exclude smoke from the lungs.

For removing the brown from earthenware, after being in the oven, rub well with salt, which will take it off almost directly.

Paint stains may be removed by applying turpentine at once. Turpentine is also good for all kinds of cuts and bruises on the human flesh, but will cause dumb animals intense pain.

When frying anything in boiling fat, if a piece of bread is put in the pan it prevents its burning, and keeps the fat at the same heat.

Linen will have a beautiful gloss, and be very stiff, if half a teaspoon of white gum arabic be dissolved in boiling water, and, when cool, added to the starch sufficient for a pint.

Bread-crumbs which may be in the bread-jar can be utilized to good advantage if dried, rolled fine and placed in a jar or can ready to use in escalloping meats, fish, oysters, vegetables or as thickening.

All closets and clothes-presses need frequent sunnings and airings. Clothing, too, should be exposed now and again, for it is one of the most sweetening measures in the world.

To prevent a boot or shoe from slipping off at the heel, gum a little piece of velvet inside the heel of the shoe. This will make it cling to the stocking, and prevent slipping.

A tablespoonful of ammonia to a quart of water is the best medium for cleaning windows, lamp chimneys, or any kind of glassware.

Ink stains may be easily and quickly removed from the fingers by rubbing them with the head of a sulphur match which has been well moistened.

To wash a glass which has held milk, plunge it first into cold water before putting it into warm. The same rule holds good for egg-cups, or spoons from which eggs have been eaten.

If ice-cream sticks to the mould, and refuses to slip out readily, put a towel wrung out of hot water around it a moment to loosen. Then if the outside seems soft, set in the icebox another moment to harden again.

When velvet gets crushed from pressure, hold the parts over a basin of hot water, with the lining of the article next the water; the pile will soon rise, and assume its original beauty.

A good renovating fluid for black silk is a little rock of ammonia and a piece of common soda; put into a bottle and dissolve into one-half pint of boiling water. Sponge with this and iron. This is also good for restoring rusty-looking black woollen goods.

Mildew on leather may be removed by gently rubbing with petroleum. Afterwards polish with a soft cloth.

Reading aloud is a beautiful practice in the home circle, and medical authorities agree that it is a most invigorating exercise. Persons who have a tendency to pulmonary disease should methodically read aloud at stated intervals, and even recite or sing, using due caution as to posture, articulation, and avoidance of excess.

Gloves must be pulled in shape as soon as they are taken off, and not put away till they are dried. They should always be removed from the hand by turning them wrong side out from the wrist up, not by tugging at the fingers, which ruins the shape, and is likely to tear the kid.

Keep all fruit stones, cooked or uncooked. Dry them slowly in the oven, put in a large jar, and in winter throw a handful on the fire of an evening. They will crack for a moment, send up a bright flame, and fill the room with a delicious odor.

The odor of the sweet pea is so offensive to flies that it will drive them out of a sick-room, though not in the slightest degree disagreeable to the patient.

Scorch marks in linen may be removed with lemon-juice and salt rubbed gently on the place and set in the sun.

The reason why large holes are found often under the crust of bread is because the gas is driven from the bottom of the loaf upward, and held by the heavy crust on top. Brush the bread thoroughly with water before putting it into the oven, prick it with a fork; if it is in large loaves it should be in ten minutes before browning. Small loaves should be baked more quickly.

& WORLDLY WISDOM

Cucumbers as Face-Cleanser

USEFUL HINTS.

To keep a spoon in position when desirous of dropping medicine into it and needing both hands to hold bottle and cork, place the handle between the leaves of a closed book lying upon a table.

Do not stuff cobwebs into a cut unless you want pus to form, as cobwebs are rich in bacteria which produce pus. Instead, stop bleeding by the use of water as hot as you can bear it, and healing will take place in half the time.

Common alum melted in an iron spoon over hot coals forms a strong cement for joining glass and metals together. It is a good thing for holding glass lamps to their stands.

Plums, peaches, lemons and similar small fruits keep best in papers. It will repay the housewife to do her perishable fruits up in paper as soon as purchased.

For insomnia a glass of hot milk, or better still hot malted milk, taken just before retiring, will often have the desired effect.

After touching poison ivy wash the parts exposed in alcohol and avoid anything greasy.

Be careful in buying second-hand books ; diseases may be easily conveyed by them, and books, moreover, are very hard to fumigate.

When beating the whites of eggs, the addition of a pinch of salt will cause the eggs to come to a froth more quickly.

A little glycerine added to tincture of iodine will enable the discoloration due to the iodine to be readily washed off.

Dental silk should be used instead of tooth picks whenever it is convenient to do so, as the former is much less injurious to the teeth.

A deposit of alkali should never be allowed to accumulate in the tea kettle. Remember that tea kettles should be washed like any other utensil.

A little vinegar put in the water when boiling fish will tend to harden the flesh and keep it firm.

It is a good plan to drop a lump or two of gum camphor in the nest of a setting hen, as it has a tendency to keep away lice.

Too frequent wearing of rubbers and rubber overshoes is a fruitful source of tender feet and soft corns. Stout shoes with heavy soles are the best for out-of-door use, except in snow and slush.

See that the playthings that the baby has are too large to be crammed into its mouth, and so avoid not only the danger of disease, but a tendency to disfigure the mouth.

Half a teaspoonful of boracic acid in two-thirds of a glass of water (if warm it will dissolve better) will relieve many cases of sore eyes in from twenty-four to thirty-six hours. Apply freely, using a fresh piece of clean, soft cloth with each application.

A slice of ripe cucumber rubbed over the face is cleansing and is excellent for the skin.

In cases of frost bite no warm air, warm water, or fire, should be permitted near the parts affected until the natural temperature is nearly restored. Rub gently the affected part with snow in a cold room, and make applications of ice water.

If the roots of trees coming from a nursery are dry, they should be allowed to stand in mud for several days before planting.

For a canker sore alcohol applied to the parts will shorten its course in a great measure.

To get comfortably fitting shoes buy them in the afternoon when the exercise of the day has stretched the muscles to their largest extent.

Do not neglect to frequently pour household ammonia, or some other disinfectant, down all waste-pipes especially in summer time.

In case a piece of the sting of a bee remains in the wound extract it with the fingers or a small pair of tweezers. The best application for the inflammation is diluted ammonia water, after which a cloth covered with sweet oil should be placed upon the part.

Milk and butter should be kept covered when in the ice chest, as they readily absorb the flavor and odor of other foods.

If table silver be washed with hot water and soap with occasionally a little ammonia, it can be kept bright without powder or paste.

A FACIAL CLEANSER

A slice of ripe cucumber rubbed over the face is cleansing and is excellent for the skin.

PRESERVING SMALL FRUITS

Plums, peaches, lemons and similar small fruits keep best in papers. It will repay the housewife to do her perishable fruits up in paper as soon as purchased.

SECOND HAND BOOKS

Be careful in buying second-hand books; diseases may be easily conveyed by them and books, moreover, are very hard to fumigate.

A FISH TIP

A little vinegar put in the water when boiling fish will tend to harden the flesh and keep it firm.

ON BUYING SHOES

To get comfortably fitting shoes buy them in the afternoon when the exercise of the day has stretched the muscles to their largest extent.

HOUSEHOLD HINTS

 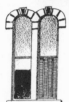

USEFUL HINTS.

Never put soda in the water in which you wash china that has any gilding on it, as the soda injures the gilding. Instead, use soap, which has no ill effects and answers just as well.

Potatoes, when cooked in their skins, should have a small piece cut from one end, in order to allow the steam to escape in cooking.

A sponge wet with alcohol and lavender placed in the dining-room just before a meal is said to keep flies away during the repast.

Add a little vinegar to the water in which you poach eggs, to prevent the whites from spreading. Breaking each egg into a cup about a quarter of an hour before it is to be used will also help.

White spots may be removed from furniture by placing over them a cloth dipped in almost boiling water, and then rubbing them with a dry soft cloth, repeating the operation if necessary.

To extract juice from a lemon without extracting the seeds, roll the lemon until soft and puncture one end of it with a fork, when the juice may be easily squeezed out.

Meat should not be washed before cooking. It may be cleaned by rubbing with a damp cloth, or by scraping with a knife. Do not pierce it while cooking, or some of the juice will be lost.

A teaspoonful of lemon juice added to boiling rice is said to make it white and keep the kernels separate.

If the water used in cleaning windows is blued, they will retain their brilliancy longer and polish more easily.

The coarseness of cake is frequently due to its standing before being put into the oven.

Gasolene cleans nickel plating quickly and well.

When removing fruit stains with boiling water, have the water fall from a distance of at least three feet, as the force thereby secured is a great help in removing the stain.

In rubbing unpolished wood, remember that the marks must be with the grain, not across it. Otherwise scratches will be inevitable.

To make a tender omelette, use hot water in the proportion of a tablespoonful to each egg, instead of the milk usually advised.

For chapped hands one may try applications to them at bed-time of a mixture of glycerine and water in about equal parts. Discontinue if the treatment does not prove beneficial, as its effect is not the same on every one. Before giving it up, however, try adding more water to the mixture.

A quick way to pulverize lumpy powdered sugar is to put it through a meat chopper.

The peculiar lifeless taste of water which has been boiled for drinking purposes can be destroyed by beating with an egg beater before using.

Never keep nickel plated articles near a gas range.

It is the present theory that one should eat a great variety of food. This does not mean that many different kinds of food must be taken at one meal, but rather that one's diet should be made up of many different wholesome things. Moreover, a wholesome article should not be permantly rejected simply because it is not liked at first. It is frequently the case that by eating such an article a few times one acquires a relish for it.

Claret stains may be removed by covering the stain while wet with salt, and after allowing it to stand a few minutes rinsing it in cold water.

To prevent the hardening of salt, mix with it a small quantity of corn-starch.

It is said that if new tinware be rubbed with lard and thoroughly heated in the oven before being used it will prevent it from rusting.

Use the potato ricer for cheese that is to be sprinkled on macaroni, which is a much easier method than grating.

When removing paint stains with turpentine, if the paint spot is surrounded with corn-starch it will prevent the turpentine from spreading.

The greatest care should be taken to thoroughly air a sleeping room in which gas has been burning during the evening before the room is slept in, as it is well known that a gas burner is a great consumer of oxygen.

USEFUL HINTS.

Green deposits on marble may be removed by applying a paste of quicklime and washing soda.

Dark furs may be cleaned with fine cedar or mahogany sawdust which has been heated in an oven. Alaska sable, seal, electric seal, fox, etc., should be beaten with a switch until free from dust, then laid with the fur side up and the hot sawdust rubbed in. Use plenty of sawdust and don't be afraid to rub. Then place the garment upon a feather pillow with the fur side down and beat it until all traces of the sawdust have disappeared. After this, hang it in a shady place.

A carpet that is turned under is almost sure to get moth-eaten. Better make it fit the floor.

When you get a new paint brush, hold it with the hair end up and the handle down, spread out the bristles and pour in a spoonful of good varnish, allowing it to become dry. This has a tendency to prevent the brush shedding its bristles when it is used and also keeps it from shrinking and falling to pieces.

Whenever you want to cut off the large limb of a tree, first saw up on the underside as far as you can easily; then saw directly above the first cut until the limb falls. This will prevent splitting down between the cut and the trunk of the tree.

If you have no storm-doors, tack dark colored oil-cloth over the wire on the inside of the screen doors and you will keep out a great deal of cold. It can be easily removed in the Spring.

When hot flannels are needed for sickness or accident, take them out of the hot water with a fork or a spoon, drop into a towel, then twist the ends of the towel until the flannel is wrung dry enough.

When the ham is hard and salty, try soaking it sliced in milk over night.

New crash does not make good tea towels. Use it first to make roller towels, cutting it two and a half yards long. After it has been used until the hardness is gone, cut in two and hem, and it will be soft but substantial.

The application of synthetic oil of Gaultheria (wintergreen) sometimes proves beneficial in cases of inflammatory rheumatism. Rub gently upon the parts affected and cover with a bandage of flannel.

Soot water is a good fertilizer for house plants.

Lemons should be kept in water until they are wanted for use, and the skin will not only be kept from hardening but their flavor will be improved.

Boil sweet potatoes until nearly done, then peel and slice the long way, lay on a baking dish, sprinkle with brown sugar, bits of butter, and a little hot water, then set in the oven till nicely browned.

To bleach handkerchiefs after washing, let them soak over night in water in which a bit of cream of tartar has been dissolved.

Spread bleached celery leaves on a plate and let them dry in a warm oven. Keep them in a glass jar and use for flavoring soups and sauces when the fresh celery is not available.

A saleratus foot-bath is most refreshing for fatigued pedestrians or elderly persons who cannot take much exercise.

The root of the Sweet-Flag placed in the drawers and on the shelves will keep moths from woollen clothes, books, etc. A decoction of this root sprinkled over skins will protect them from moths and worms.

Seeds not sufficiently ripe will swim, but when arrived at full maturity they will fall to the bottom.

It is said that a knife moistened with a strong solution of potash will cut india rubber quite easily.

Mortar and paint may be removed from window glass with hot, sharp vinegar.

Never put salt into soup when cooking till it has been thoroughly skimmed, as salt prevents the scum from rising.

When sponge-cake becomes dry it is nice to cut in thin slices and toast.

The water in which common white beans have been boiled will clean brass. A mixture of salt and vinegar will do the same.

Hang up a camphor bag to drive away mosquitos.

Use a warm knife for cutting hot bread.

HOUSEHOLD HINTS

FROM THE
1906
ALMANAC

USEFUL HINTS.

In the garden blue flowers should be placed next to orange, violet next to yellow, while red and pink should be surrounded by green or by white. White may also be dispersed among groups of blue and orange, and violet and yellow, flowers. Plants whose flowers are to produce a contrast should be of the same size.

A spoonful of elderberry juice will often stop severe coughing and insure a good night's rest.

Rose geranium leaves, when well dried, are equal to rose leaves for filling cushions and sachet bags.

Egg coffee is a drink that serves as food, and may be either hot or cold. For the former use milk and coffee at the boiling point. Beat two eggs very light. Add to them, beating well into them, half a pint of milk and a pint of strong coffee. Sweeten to taste. This, with graham crackers, makes a perfect summer lunch. If hot milk is added to the eggs, it must be done slowly, not to cook them. Egg tea and egg chocolate are prepared in the same manner.

In cold weather when using frail china or glass dishes, rinse first with tepid water before pouring into them any hot liquid.

During an electric storm, if the vessel containing milk is placed in another vessel containing water, it will be more likely to keep sweet. The water must entirely surround the milk.

Put your fresh popped corn in an air-tight fruit jar, and it will keep dry and crisp.

To set delicate colors in embroidered handkerchiefs, soak them ten minutes previous to washing in a pail of tepid water in which a dessert-spoonful of turpentine has been well stirred.

Some people like to have their turkey stuffed between the skin and the flesh. After washing in warm water, the skin over the breast and sides back to the end of the breastbone may be separated from the flesh, and the dressing packed between, making a plump and handsome bird and very much improving the flavor of the meat. This avoids the necessity of putting dressing in the inside.

Japanned trays may be cleaned by rubbing with clear olive oil. After the oil has been applied the trays should be vigorously rubbed with a flannel cloth. Also, glue can be removed, and enamelled cloth cleaned, by soaking and rubbing with olive oil.

Starched linen articles will iron easier if you let them dry after starch-ing, so that you have to sprinkle before ironing.

Before applying a poultice cover the skin lightly with glycerine to keep any particles of the poultice from adhering.

The following articles should be purchased in small quantities, as they are liable to lose flavor by keeping: — Sugar, raisins, currants, candied peel, vinegar, olive oil, macaroni, pepper, spice, and roasted coffee.

Never put boiled potatoes on the table in a covered dish. They will absorb their own moisture and become sodden.

A bit of cotton wadding pressed into the tips of the fingers of kid gloves will prevent ripping.

A pinch of granulated sugar, or a little vinegar, will make the stove polish stay on.

When through painting with lead and oil paints wipe the brush clean and wrap it in a piece of paper. Then hang it in a small, deep vessel containing linseed oil. In this way it will keep clean and always be ready for use.

If the oven is too hot for bread set a dish of cold water in it.

Save your cloth flour and salt sacks. They may at any time become useful to the thrifty housewife.

Use a pointed brush to clean tufted furniture. It will keep out the moths.

A tablespoonful of stewed tomato or catsup added to the gravy of roast meats is thought by some to improve it.

If your saws are rusty try mixing a small quantity of emery dust with sweet oil, and apply with a large corncob.

To clean finger marks from paint, wipe the spots first with a cloth dipped in warm water, then with a cloth dipped in whiting, and wipe again with a clean damp cloth.

From *Poor Richard's Almanac*:
"Little strokes fell great oaks."

& WORLDLY WISDOM

On Baking Pies and Hanging Curtains

USEFUL HINTS.

To make a rubber plant throw out branches tie a small sponge around the main stem where a leaf joins and keep the sponge moist all the time.

Warm your discolored earthenware or granite baking dishes well, then rub them with damp corn-meal. It cleans without scratching.

In putting on the bands to skirts, etc., make them long enough to turn in about an inch. Make the button-hole in this, and being doubly strong it will not pull out.

It is better to take the chill off the water given to horses or stock of any kind in the Winter.

If it is necessary to wash the face while it is smarting with sunburn, do not use cold water, but water as hot as can be borne, which will relieve the inflammation.

Do not wash oilcloth or linoleum in hot suds. Use tepid water and wipe with a cloth dampened in equal parts of cold milk and water.

To take out ink spots: — As soon as the accident happens, wet the place with juice of sorrel or lemon, or with vinegar, and the best hard white soap.

Bananas should not be put into a refrigerator, — in fact they should never be allowed to get colder than 60°. A chill turns bananas black, prevents their ever ripening properly and renders them unfit for use.

Boil 1-2 an ounce of hops and 1-2 an ounce of bruised ginger-root, in 1 1-2 gallons of water for 25 minutes; add 1 pound of brown sugar and boil 10 minutes longer; strain and bottle while hot. Keep in a cool place. A pleasant summer drink.

Mutton tallow, rubbed on the side of a stall or on the halter-rope, is said to prevent a horse from chewing them.

Juice freshly expressed from poppy stems, if promptly applied, will immediately alleviate the pain of bee stings and stop inflammation.

A little vaseline rubbed into the finger nails and the skin about them at night will prevent their becoming brittle.

Lima beans for seed should be taken from pods nearest the ground.

Hold the point of a new pen over a lighted match to remove the lacquer before using; rub the other end with a drop of oil or grease to prevent its rusting in the holder.

Do not put soda in candy; it makes it tough.

Never break eggs on the edge of a crock or pan. Use a knife instead; it is much easier.

To iron table linen: — Dampen very thoroughly and evenly, then fold and wrap in a heavy cloth. Use heavy irons, first on the wrong side until partly dry, then on the right side until dry.

By having an orange and a small onion inside the duck while roasting its flavor is said to be improved.

Keep sponges clean by washing them now and then in soda, carefully rinsing out all the powder with pure cold water.

Don't hang a carpet on the line to beat; lay it on the grass. Beat with a bamboo carpet-beater or a good stout rod until but little dust rises, then turn it over on a fresh spot and beat the other side.

Foods rich in oil should not be fed to laying hens unless in small quantities or in cold weather.

Try to have a note-book hanging in a convenient place in the kitchen to jot down any article that may be needed.

Never rub soap directly on a flannel cloth or on woolen goods of any description. Make a mild soap-suds in which to wash them.

To produce the amber clearness so much admired, cook nearly all fruits in their syrup; they are much richer and retain their shape better. Use only a granite dish to cook in. Remove carefully to the jars with a silver fork or spoon. Spread over the top of the jar a bit of white cheese cloth, and pour the syrup on to the fruit through this. This removes all the tiny floating particles and gives you a jar beautifully clear and perfect.

When your peas are all gone, pull up the old brush and vines and burn as soon as dry. All such rubbish left in the garden during Summer and Fall is only a harboring place for insect pests.

Apply flour wet with cold water to a burn.

BABY CARE

A few drops of cool water will often times soothe a crying baby. Babies should frequently be offered a little pure water, and not food every time they cry.

ON SALT

It maybe sometimes convenient to know that salt dissolves as quickly in cold water as in hot.

ON HANGING CURTAINS

In running freshly laundered curtains on the rods put a thimble on the end of the rod and it will slip through more easily.

PETTICOAT PRESERVATION

A silk petticoat hung upside down in the closet, from hangers sewed inside the bottom ruffle, will retain its freshness much longer; the ruffle will stand out and the skirt will wear better.

PIE ADVICE

In baking juicy pies try putting in each pie a teaspoonful of fine tapioca; it prevents the juice from running over and also imparts a delicate flavor.

ON THE RELIEF OF PAIN AND OTHER HINTS

On Sewing Straight Seams. . .

Common Uses of Baking Soda. . .

Preparing Preservatives. . .

Reducing Fat in Doughnuts. . .

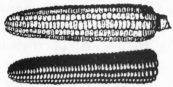

A Tip on Eating Corn. . .

Refurbishing an Eraser. . .

Hints on Freezing. . .

Treating Hoarseness. . .

Griddle Cakes Tip. . .

Getting a Fire Started. . .

Dental Care. . .

Cane Chair Care. . .

Recipe for Sherbets. . .

Sweet Orange Pudding. . .

Creating Tracing Paper. . .

Eliminating Mouse Holes. . .

Making Sugar Taste Better.

On the Handling of Silk. . .

Keeping Celery Crisp. . .

The Nap on Velvets. . .

On Papering Bedrooms. . .

USEFUL HINTS.

Never hold the skirt on your lap while basting. Remember that it is most important to keep it flat, so lay it on a table and baste from top to bottom with small even stitches, keeping your seams level and straight.

Equal parts of baking soda and common salt dissolved in warm water and well rubbed in relieve the annoyance and pain caused by the bites or stings of mosquitos and other insects.

Keep your doors and windows closed while filling preserving jars, thus avoiding drafts and breakages.

To prevent doughnuts soaking up fat, glaze the dough with the white of an egg before cutting into shapes.

When eating corn from the cob, first slit the kernels by running the point of your knife down each row of them; fewer hulls will then be taken into the mouth, and the corn will taste sweeter.

When a rubber eraser quits work or only spreads the pencil marks, rub it over a piece of sandpaper or a nail file, to make a new surface.

For freezing any mixture use salt and ice in the proportion of one part to three parts, respectively. To pack frozen dishes use one part of salt to four parts of ice.

Hoarseness may be relieved by taking a teaspoonful of the following mixture every hour: the white of one egg, one tablespoonful of lemon juice, and a tablespoonful of granulated sugar.

Mix griddle cakes with sweet cider, diluted about one-half with water. The flavor of the cider is not perceptible but it makes the cakes light and feathery.

Keep sweet potatoes where it is warm and dry.

When the fire refuses to burn on damp mornings try putting a newspaper in the ashpan under the grate and lighting it.

While it does the teeth no good to have extremely hot and cold things come in contact with them, one should especially avoid taking cold, immediately after hot, food or drink, or *vice versa*. Such severe changes in temperature cause unequal contraction or expansion of adjoining or near-by particles of enamel which makes them wrench or split apart, thereby not alone imparing the tooth, but leaving little crevices which furnish a vantage ground for decay.

Wash cane seated chairs on the under side only.

Cherry and plum juices mixed make a delicious sherbet. The juice of a lemon or two is an improvement. A syrup of sugar boiled with water enough to keep it from burning should sweeten the juices. After this mixture is frozen take out the dasher and stir in the stiffly beaten white of an egg which has been whipped light with a tablespoonful of powdered sugar.

If you do not heat the oranges when making an orange pudding it will not taste bitter.

A sheet of fine, thin, white paper dipped into a thick solution of gum arabic and pressed between two dry sheets renders the three transparent when dry. It is good for tracing, or writing, or painting.

One of the best ways to stop a mouse-hole is to fill it with common laundry soap.

Put screen door spring hinges on your chicken yard gates so that they will be self-closing, and cats and other wanderers be kept out.

Rub the lumps of sugar to be used with black coffee with lemon peel. It will impart an agreeable flavor. For tea, rub the sugar with orange peel.

When working on silk keep a piece of sand paper on the table, rubbing your hands lightly over it when they stick to the silk.

Celery can be kept for a week or longer by first rolling it up in brown paper. Then put it in a towel and keep it in a dark, cool place. Before preparing it for the table place it in a pan of cold water, and let it remain for an hour. It will then be crisp and cool.

Velvet garments should always be made with the nap inclining upwards.

In a bedroom a plain paper on the walls or ceiling is more restful for the eyes.

& WORLDLY WISDOM

FROM THE
1910
ALMANAC

The Right Way to Break an Egg

USEFUL HINTS.

To check ordinary nose bleed, hold the head up, first placing a towel a little under the nose to prevent the blood from falling upon the clothes, and draw deep inspirations. If this is not sufficient take a small strip of cotton cloth shaped into a cone, wet it with vinegar and twist it up the offending nostril, letting it remain there awhile. If bleeding continues after the cone is removed, a fresh one should be inserted.

A few drops of cool water will often times soothe a crying baby. Babies should frequently be offered a little pure water, and not food every time they cry.

It maybe sometimes convenient to know that salt dissolves as quickly in cold water as in hot.

A very hot iron should never be used for flannels or woolens.

Mice are fond of pumpkin seeds, so bait the traps with them.

To preserve rhubarb, cut in pieces, spread on a plate, and dry in a warm oven and tie up in paper bags.

Carriages should be kept in a dry place, with a moderate amount of light, otherwise the colors will be affected. Keep from the direct rays of the sun.

A silk petticoat hung upside down in the closet, from hangers sewed inside the bottom ruffle, will retain its freshness much longer; the ruffle will stand out and the skirt will wear better.

Mint vinegar is a good substitute in the Winter for mint sauce. Wash the leaves well and put them loosely into a wide mouthed bottle with good vinegar, and after it has been confined closely for three weeks, pour off clear into another bottle and keep well corked until used.

Puffs or comforts made with cotton batting which have become matted by washing or long use may be renovated and the lightness restored by hanging for several hours over a radiator or register so that the hot air may pass through them.

Do not keep leather goods where it is either too dry or too moist.

Roll the sausage in flour to prevent its going to pieces in cooking.

Puckering of seams in clothing may be avoided by soaking the spool of thread in water over night, then letting it dry before using. Colored thread may be strengthened and made smooth by soaking in olive oil.

The seeds or hulls of apple-cores are unpleasant things to happen upon in sauce, pie or pudding. Small bits and chips of bone are dangerous to the teeth when encountered in soups, stews or other food preparations.

Beds for small children should be placed out of a direct draft of air and where the morning sun will not shine into their eyes and awaken them before the proper time.

In running freshly laundered curtains on the rods put a thimble on the end of the rod and it will slip through more easily.

The white of an egg applied with a small camelhair brush will remove fly traces and soil from gilt frames; or the water in which onions have been boiled will, if rubbed over the frame, remove dust and specks and brighten the gilding.

Soak raisins in cold water before stoning.

In baking juicy pies try putting in each pie a teaspoonful of fine tapioca; it prevents the juice from running over and also imparts a delicate flavor.

Too much vinegar spoils the other flavors in a salad dressing. Vinegar may be added at the table if more is wanted; but where there is an excess of it in the original mixture the mischief has been done.

Because you have a large vaccination scar on your arm do not be deceived by the belief that you are immune. Always be revaccinated when small-pox is about, even if you have been successfully inoculated within a year or two.

In making a stew, the meat should be cut into small pieces, and put into cold, not hot, water in order that considerable of the juices and flavoring materials may be dissolved. The temperature should then be slowly raised until it reaches about 180° F. where it should be kept for some hours. Treated in this way the broth will be rich and the meat will still be tender and juicy.

NO-SCRATCH CLEANING

Warm your discolored earthenware or granite baking dishes well, then rub them with damp corn-meal. It cleans without scratching.

THE BANANA WAY

Bananas should not be put into a refrigerator,—in fact they should never be allowed to get colder than 60. A chill turns bananas black, prevents their ever ripening properly and renders them unfit for use.

BRITTLE NAILS

A little vaseline rubbed into the finger nails and the skin about them at night will prevent their becoming brittle.

BREAKING EGGS

Never break eggs on the edge of a crock or pan. Use a knife instead; it is much easier.

RUG BEATING

Don't hang a carpet on the line to beat; lay it on the grass. Beat with a bamboo carpet-beater or a good stout rod until but little dust rises, then turn it over on a fresh spot and beat the other side.

HELPFUL HINTS ON KEEPING HEALTHY

On Cleaning Eyeglasses...

To Prevent Shrinking of Woolens...

Removing Cakes from Tins...

Polishing Brass on Copper...

Making Sleeping Bags...

The Art of Sandwich-Making...

Relieving Pain of Bee-Bites...

Beware of Flies...

On the Relief of Eye-Strain...

Removing the Green...

Making Your Own Silver Polish...

Strengthening Rhubarb Plants...

Wax vs Regular Polish...

Washing Collars and Cuffs...

Home Decorating Hint...

Mental and Physical Health...

Removing Hot Fat...

Repairing Your Umbrella Handle...

Sick Room Laundry...

Foods with Excessive Acidity

USEFUL HINTS.

If the eyeglasses or spectacles do not become clear to see through after being wiped with a dry cloth or handkerchief, moisten them with warm water with which a teaspoonful or two of ammonia water has been mixed, and rub dry.

When washing anything woolen, to prevent shrinking, avoid sudden changes in the temperature of the water and the use of strong soaps. Wash and rinse in water of the same temperature.

To make small cakes turn out easily from the baking tins, dip the bottom of the tin in cold water, or set it on a dish towel wrung out in cold water.

For polishing brass or copper make a paste of rotten-stone and cotton-seed oil. If there are bad spots or stains use a little oxalic acid solution to remove them, but rinse off immediately with warm water and rub over with the cotton seed oil.

A bag for sleeping out of doors may be made of cotton-flannel with an inter-lining of seven or eight thicknesses of newspaper stitched together.

In making sandwiches, cream the butter before spreading it on the bread. If thin slices are wanted, butter the bread before cutting each slice.

Ammonia water is usually effective in relieving the pain caused by bee stings or insect bites. Apply one or more drops to the place bitten.

According to scientists the common house fly is the carrier of the germs of certain diseases, notably those of typhoid fever, and deposits them on articles of food whereby they are carried into the human system, causing infection. Flies should be exterminated, especially if there is typhoid fever in your house or neighborhood. Don't have any decomposing stuff on the premises that flies can feed on.

Reading or writing for a long time without intermission tends to bring on eye-strain and indigestion. Get up and walk about the room occasionally.

Ammonia water will remove verdigris or the green coating that forms on brass andirons or other like metallic articles.

An inexpensive silver polish may be made as follows: 5 pounds of Paris white, 2 ounces of castor oil, 1-4 of a box of pearline. Dissolve the pearline in a quart of boiling water, cool, and add the Paris white and castor oil. The mixture should be a thick paste.

A second gathering thread run just below the first will cause gathers to lay more evenly and will do away with stroking.

Break off the flower stalks from rhubarb plants and save the strength from useless seeding.

Black oak or Flemish oak and all other furniture finished with what is called a wax finish should not be cleaned with the regular furniture polish, but with a wax polish.

Run a tape through the button holes of the soiled collars and cuffs and tie loosely together. Then wash and hang to dry tying the tape on the line. By this method they will be kept together for washing and starching and not get frozen on the line in cold weather as is the case when separately pinned on.

It is always advisable to have carpets, furniture coverings and wall papers harmonize with each other. This is especially desirable where the furniture coverings and carpets have large figures.

While as a rule those who do much mental labor need physical exercise which tends to render cares and worries easier to bear, it is not good for one while feeling exhausted from mental work to take vigorous physical exercise, especially immediately before a meal.

When hot fat falls on the floor pour cold water on it at once and it will harden so that it can be easily removed with a knife.

If your umbrella has a steel rod and the handle comes off, fill the hole in the handle with powdered resin, heat the end of the rod and put it back in the handle.

It is advisable to have all bed linen and clothing from a sick room kept in boiling water for at least fifteen minutes before going to the laundry.

Tomatoes, rhubarb and early strawberries contain an excessive acid which may unpleasantly affect some people.

When roasting veal, pare some sweet and white potatoes, tuck them around it and let them cook in the juice.

FROM THE
1914
ALMANAC

Pumice & Lemon
and
Climbing Roses

USEFUL HINTS.

Newspapers are better than blankets for keeping ice from melting. When they become soaked change to dry ones.

Salt on the fingers when cleaning fowls, meat and fish, will prevent the hands from slipping.

Pour boiling water over Pecan nuts and let them stand until cold, then crack with a hammer, striking the small end of the nut. The meats can be removed without breaking.

If oriental rugs are badly creased, turn them upside down on a bare floor and wet the backs with a moistened broom. Then stretch them tight, tacking them with tinned tacks, which do not rust, and leave overnight.

It is an excellent thing to have a piece of fine pumice stone where it can be used readily, for it will remove ink and other stains from the fingers by merely wetting and rubbing over. Lemon juice is also useful for the same purpose, but should be carefully rinsed off, as the acid is drying to the skin.

Foliage plants kept near the windows in the house should be turned at least once a week in order to give all sides of them a chance at the light.

Keep a scrap basket in the kitchen. Don't throw scraps of paper, boxes, etc., into the coal hod.

A good way to destroy the sooty smell sometimes found in a room where an open fireplace or grate has been closed for the summer, is to make a fire of old newspapers and ground coffee. The coffee should be freely sprinkled among and over the newspapers before they are lighted. The heat extracts the aromatic qualities of the coffee, which purify the room, while the warmth engendered is fleeting.

Cleanse all bronze articles by rubbing with a soft cloth moistened with sweet oil; polish afterwards with an oily chamois. All dust must be removed before attempting to clean and polish.

A dress that is worn under the arms can be mended by ripping the sleeves loose from the dress well on either side of the underarm seams and setting in a new piece of the material neatly in the waist and sleeve.

The little red blood veins which sometimes show in the face are often caused by exposure of the skin to strong cold winds. Applications of warm wet cloths until the skin feels soft and a gentle rubbing with good cold cream, into which a little distilled witch hazel has been beaten, will remedy the trouble.

GARDEN HINTS.

Sow some white clover on your lawn. It withstands climatic changes, maintains itself on soil that would not be strong enough for other clovers, lies low on the ground and closely covers considerable surface. It has not too much stalk to cut well with the mower.

Borders for flowers should never be made too narrow. Five or six feet is a good width, while eight feet is better. Beds two to three feet wide suffer in dry weather and give less opportunity for grouping plants. One bed six feet wide is much better than two three feet wide.

Blank spaces occur in flower borders when bulbs like Tulips and Narcissus die down, or after such plants as Lungwort and Oriental Poppies have lost their foliage. Sow seeds of Poppies, Calendula, and Sweet Alyssum in April when the bulbous plants are just coming up, and have a reserve bed of seedlings like Zinnias or Marigolds which can be easily transplanted into the vacant spaces. Bedding plants such as Heliotrope, Salvia or Rose Geranium can also be used for this purpose.

May is the time to thin out suckers at the base of the raspberries and blackberries. The best are left for next year's fruiting canes, at least eighteen inches apart for raspberries and two feet for blackberries. Sometimes three or four canes can be left about a foot apart. They can easily be staked, but the distance between these clumps should be at least three or four feet.

Train your running vines and climbing roses on trellises or frames, attaching them to the building with long wire hooks and screw eyes. When repairs are needed the trellis can be laid on the ground without injury to the vines.

PUMICE & LEMON

It is an excellent thing to have a piece of fine pumice stone where it can be used readily, for it will remove ink and other stains from the fingers by merely wetting and rubbing over. Lemon juice is also useful for the same purpose, but should be carefully rinsed off, as the acid is drying to the skin.

HOUSEPLANTS

Foliage plants kept near the windows in the house should be turned at least once a week in order to give all sides of them a chance at the light.

WHITE CLOVER

Sow some white clover on your lawn. It withstands climatic changes, maintains itself on soil that would not be strong enough for other clovers, lies low on the ground and closely covers considerable surface. It has not too much stalk to cut well with the mower.

CLIMBING ROSES

Train your running vines and climbing roses on trellises or frames, attaching them to the building with long wire hooks and screw eyes. When repairs are needed the trellis can be laid on the ground without injury to the vines.

Bran—
the Carpet Cleaner

USEFUL HINTS.

Gold ornaments, when plain or worked and unadorned with gems, should always be washed in warm soapsuds from time to time, excellent results being obtained if a few drops of sal volatile are added to the hot water before making the lather. In the case of chains composed of close links, which are most apt to harbor dirt and dust, few remedies equal that of placing them to soak in a bottle half full of warm soapsuds mixed with a little prepared chalk.

Make a pocket out of leather, oil-cloth or demin, and tack on the outside of the refrigerator to hold the ice pick and keep it where it can be found when wanted.

As a carpet cleaner bran slightly dampened thrown on the carpet and then thoroughly swept out is unexcelled. Removes all dust and, being damp, prevents dust from flying. For sponging matting use bran water.

To keep lunch baskets from acquiring a stale odor, scald once a week in hot salt water; rinse in cold water and dry in the sunshine.

Try changing the stockings from one foot to the other every morning. It is said to greatly lessen the wear.

Do not salt down cucumbers any length of time before preparing for the table, or egg plant before cooking; it makes both of them indigestible and unpalatable.

A carpet wears better and more evenly if its position is changed every two or three years. Rip in half and sew so that the breadths formerly at the side will come in the centre of the room.

Hard food is better for poultry than soft, but soft food is an excellent invigorator when fed on cold mornings.

To remove seeds from cranberries before cooking cut them in halves, place in a colander and let the cold water run through them steadily for a minute or two.

When boiling sweet potatoes have the water bubbling hard when they are dropped in so that they will not be soggy.

Cover your plants kept in the living rooms with a thin cloth when you sweep.

A solution of equal parts of ammonia and spirits of turpentine will prove effectual in loosening dry or hardened paint in any fabric.

GARDEN HINTS.

In the February and March flower shows there is often opportunity to select plants for Spring planting. Shrubs and small trees are forced and exhibited which guide one to a wise selection.

Early April is the best time for out-of-doors grafting. Either the cleft or the crown graft are well suited to our climate. The scion should always be dormant; a slight growth on the stock is permissible, but not advisable. Apples and pears are grafted with the wood of last years growth, but if an attempt is made to graft ornamental trees the scion should be two years old with a little one year old wood on it to insure a good start.

Plants should not receive their Winter covering too early in Autumn. It is always desirable to wait until the near approach of cold weather. Have the covering material ready in early November, but do not cover until the conditions warrant;—in normal seasons between Thanksgiving and Christmas. In covering herbaceous plants do not use leaves on Strawberries, Canterbury Bells, Hollyhocks, Foxgloves, etc. Evergreen boughs or pine needles are better. Leaves do not dry out quickly, and sometimes more harm is done by moisture than by cold.

It is good economy to prepare the ground in Autumn for the Spring planting of trees and shrubs; time is saved at the busy season, fresh manure can be used as it will rot before planting time and the earth is improved by weathering during the Winter. Unless the ground is very stiff it need not be plowed or dug a second time in Spring. The trees and shrubs can be planted and a light forking afterwards is sufficient.

Utilize the midsummer days, after haying is over and the field crops have been weeded, by doing odd jobs in the home grounds. There is some time then when farm work is not pressing and numberless little improvements can be made.

CARPET CLEANING

As a carpet cleaner, bran slightly dampened thrown on the carpet and then thoroughly swept out is unexcelled. Removes all dust and, being damp, prevents dust from flying. For sponging matting use bran water.

CARPET RENEWAL

A carpet wears bettter and more evenly if its position is changed every two or three years. Rip in half and sew so that the breadths formerly at the side will come in the centre of the room.

PREPARING THE GROUND

It is good economy to prepare the ground in Autumn for the Spring planting of trees and shrubs; time is saved at the busy season, fresh manure can be used as it will rot before planting time and the earth is improved by weathering during the Winter. Unless the ground is very stiff it need not be plowed or dug a second time in Spring. The trees and shrubs can be planted and a light forking afterwards is sufficient.

AN OUNCE OF PREVENTION

Old medicines should not be preserved. Many medicines deteriorate, and what is good at one time may not be so at another. The fewer medicine bottles lying about the less risk of the wrong medicine being administered.

Tight Jars and Rubber Gloves

TIGHT JARS

To unscrew airtight jars, turn the jar upside down in enough boiling water to just cover the screw and in a minute a simple twist will take off the top.

RUBBER GLOVES

In wearing rubber gloves always pull off wrong side out and shake talcum powder into them. Leave until ready to use again.

ALMOND MEAL

Almond meal is preferred by some women to soap and acts as a pleasing alternative to soap at any time. It softens, cleanses and whitens the skin.

PRUNING TIME

Do not prune too early in autumn. Wait until the longer days come in February and March. Never prune hybrid perpetual or Rambler Roses in August and September, for then it is well to wait until April when the amount of wood which is winter killed can be determined.

USEFUL HINTS.

Old medicines should not be preserved. Many medicines deteriorate, and what is good at one time may not be so at another. The fewer medicine bottles lying about the less risk of the wrong medicine being administered.

Table linen is best mended with embroidery cotton of a number to correspond with the quality of the cloth. Under the ragged edges of the tear baste a piece of stiff paper and make over its edges, carrying the stitches about an inch beyond the tear. Thin places and breaks in linen may be run with flax or embroidery floss, and towels should be mended the same way.

To unscrew airtight jars, turn the jar upside down in enough boiling water to just cover the screw and in a minute a simple twist will take off the top.

Don't set your plates in the oven or on top of the stove. Warm them by dipping in hot water and then wipe dry.

To prevent dumplings in a stew from being tough rest them on the meat and potatoes. Do not let them sink into the broth.

It is not always the largest fowl that is the most vigorous; but it is apt to be the one with full, bright eyes, heavy bone, compact body and quick movement.

In wearing rubber gloves always pull off wrong side out and shake talcum powder into them. Leave until ready to use again.

When making strawberry jelly add some currant juice. It will improve the flavor and firmness.

Wrap your cheese in soft tissue or parafine paper with a heavier paper around it and it will not dry up.

To make apple butter fill a large kettle with cider and boil until reduced nearly one-half. Skim, and to four gallons of the boiled cider allow a half bushel of good juicy apples cored and quartered. When they are cooked soft and begin to settle, stir continuously and cook until the butter is mahogany color and the consistency of marmalade. If desired cinnamon and nutmeg may be added to taste.

To escape from a burning building creep or crawl along the floor with your face as low as possible.

Rose geranium leaves, when well dried, are equal to rose leaves for filling cushions and sachet bags.

Almond meal is preferred by some women to soap and acts as a pleasing alternative to soap at any time. It softens, cleanses and whitens the skin.

One part alcohol and three parts water is a good solution for use in freshening black goods. Sponge the material on the right side and press on the wrong side while damp.

GARDEN HINTS.

It is well known that most hardy perennials do better when planted in autumn. It is not so well understood that trees and shrubs can be advantageously transplanted in September and October. Choose a gray day. Take advantage of a wet week. Well rooted evergreens of size, especially if obtainable with a ball of earth, can be transplanted even as early as the last week in August. If the growth of deciduous trees and shrubs is mature, the drying up and falling off of the leaves is of little importance.

Do not prune too early in autumn. Wait until the longer days come in February and March. Never prune hybrid perpetual or Rambler Roses in August and September, for then it is well to wait until April when the amount of wood which is winter killed can be determined.

Remove the flower clusters from newly set strawberry plants, as soon as they appear, It weakens the growth too much to let the plant fruit or even open its flowers.

A garden of hardy perennials is more satisfactory on the whole and less expensive than one of bedding plants, and they require less care than annuals. No one need refrain from having such a garden because the area of land is limited or because expense must be considered. The first cost of the plants is small and practically they last forever.

POETRY & ANECDOTES

POETRY, ANECDOTES, &c.

LOOK BEFORE YOU LEAP.

When I was a boy I one day walked out with an old friend of my father's; and while engaged in conversation, we came to a wide ditch. The old gentleman paused; "Oliver," said he (seeing I was about springing for the other side) "look before you leap," but before the sentence was finished, I had made my leap. The other side was, as it happened, slippery, and my feet had scarce touched it, before I found myself laid at full length at the bottom, covered with mud and water. The consequence was, my new clothes were utterly spoiled, although my mother had a company of young friends that very evening. I was obliged to keep my room, and receive a severe scolding. This misfortune made a deep impression on my mind. Since that hour, I have always looked before I leaped. Yet I have never looked round me in the world without seeing many that were as thoughtless and foolish as I have been. I have seen a young man take a social glass for friendship's sake; and I have known such often to be verily laid in the ditch before they had done. I have seen young men marry wives before they were able to support themselves; and old and middle aged men indulge foolish wives and spoiled children in every finery, and knew such families to wind up their concerns in a ditch at last. When I see a mechanic about to leave his shop, and go to keeping tavern, I think good man, you had better look before you leap. The ground on the other side is slippery, and you may catch a fall. When I hear a young man resolving not to learn a trade but to get a gig, and a dandy suit, and set himself up for a rich wife, I would fain whisper in his ear, friend, look before you leap. And when I see a poor bowing and scraping young gentleman putting his neck into the yoke with a crossgrained old maid, her pocket filled with bank notes, and her head as empty as a kettle drum; I remember the boy and the grindstone, and think how often people put their noses to it. When I see a farmer adding acre after acre to his farm, though it is larger already than he can cultivate, and mortgaging the old one for payment, I would say to him, beware lest you and your farm go into the ditch together. When I see an honest cultivator of the soil, who, by hard labour, has laid up a few hundreds, getting a fine carriage and horses, buying broad cloths and Canton crapes for himself and family, I am ready to think he will find it slippery the other side of the ditch.

But when I see men or women, old or young, great or small living as if they were to live forever, without one thought of, or preparation or death. I would thunder in their ears, if I could—look before you leap for leap you must, perhaps when least you expect it and if you slip then it will be for an eternity.

Troy's Emporium.

SONG.—OLD TIMES.

Our grandmothers wore
A pocket at each side, sir,
And a stomacher before
And a hoop of two ells wide, sir,
And thus they kept their balance,
Like a stately ship at sea,
And picaroons and gallants
Were frown'd beneath their lee.

Their daughters now so prim,
In their native shapes are seen, sir,
With their persons girt as slim
As a pilgrim's walking cane, sir,
With their trinkets, if they've got 'em,
In the bag that holds their fan;
Without their breadth of bottom,
Keep your balance if you can.

Our parsons once appeared
In a wig of ample basis,
And every urchin feared
Their sober solemn faces.
And never in their teaching,
Did they think enough was said, sir,
Until they had by preaching,
Put the de'il and sun to bed, sir.

Our modern parsons use
Both dandy-dress and crop, sir,
And when they meet your view,
Scarce you know them from a fop, sir,
They back their doxies slenderly,
Both when they preach and pray,
And stroke the de'il so tenderly,
He walks in open day.

Our doctors once would mingle,
Few simples in a potion,
And empty vials jingle,
The saber to my notion,
And each disease they knew at once,
That mortal man could fancy,
And cured every sickly dunce,
With motherwort and tanzy.

Our doctors late have rode
On their gigs or ambling nags, sir,
With a thousand poisons stowed
In their bursting saddle bags, sir.
They tell you what their pills can do,
They work a certain cure, sir;
But know you what their bills can do
They kill you just as sure, sir.

N. E. Galaxy.

ORIGINAL ANECDOTES.

[Communicated.]

A person who was afflicted with a very bad humour, told another that he had begun to turn to a fish. "Well," said the other, "I always knew you to be a plaguy scaly fellow, and now you acknowledge it."

A father, who was one day wearied with the childish talk of his son, about eight years old, told him in an angry tone to "hold his tongue." "Why father," said the child, crying, "My hands are so dirty I don't want to."

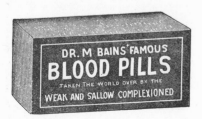

120

POETRY AND ANECDOTES

FROM THE
1837
ALMANAC

Withered Leaves
and Thorns

PROCRASTINATION IS THE THIEF OF TIME

"I'm out of all patience with these 'by and by' folks. An hour of the present time is worth a week of the future."

ROSES OF MATRIMONY

He that would gather the roses of matrimony,
Must wed in the May of life.
If you wish only the withered leaves
And the thorns
Put it off till September.

POETRY, ANECDOTES, &c.

"I WILL BY AND BY."

Zounds! sir, you may as well swear that you will never do it! I'm out of all patience with these "by and by" folks. An hour of the present time is worth a week of the future.

Why, I know a bachelor who is as well calculated for matrimonial felicity as every virtue and every accomplishment can render him;—but he has been putting off the happy time, from one year to another, always resolving that he would marry "by and by," till the best ten years of his life are gone, and he is still "resolving," and I fear "he will die the same."

He that would gather the roses of matrimony, must wed in the May of life. If you wish only the withered leaves and the thorns, why, poor Richard says, put it off till September. "Procrastination is the thief of time."

Passing by my neighbor Nodwell's the other day, I saw that his wife had made a fine garden, and the early peas were shooting above the ground. "It looks well, neighbor," said I—"but there is a hole in the fence, which you had better mend, or the hogs will ruin your garden." "I will "by and by," said he. Happening to go by there two days after, I was deafened with the cry of "Who-u, who-u, stu-boy, stu-boy,"—a drove of hogs had come along, and while my neighbor was taking a nap, they had crawled through the broken fence, and destroyed the labor of a week. "Never put off till tomorrow what you can do today," poor Richard says.

Poor Robert the Fur.

THE USURPER.—A SONG.

Tune, Yankee Doodle.

Sung at the celebration of the Fourth of July, 1836, at Jamaica Plains—without the aid of strong liquor.

In days of yore—I cannot tell
Exactly now the date, sir—
It was about the wedding day
Of good old Church and State, sir :
A fellow with a ruby nose,
Into a flagon crept, sir,
And there, in spite of all the world,
The creature lived and slept, sir.

Like other rogues he had at least
A dozen names quite handy—
Some called him Whiskey, others Rum,
And alias Cider Brandy.
And whosoever put his mouth
Unto the flagon's lip, sir,
Was sure to feel the cunning wight
Into his bosom slip, sir.

He was a stern aristocrat,
And sought to rule the roast, sir ;
The king, the pope, the d——l, too,
His fellowship did boast, sir.
He came into America,
And sought to cheat the people—
He raised a pole of hickory,
As high as any steeple.

A while the fellow had a run,
But things must turn about, sir,

The people took the thing in hand,
And turned the tyrant out, sir.
Into the flagon then they put
Some sparkling Adam's ale, sir,
And so the truth is getting plain,
And I have told my tale, sir.

But let me add a word or two—
Advice, you know, is cheap, sir—
If you would lead a pleasant life,
From whiskey ever keep, sir.
With sword and fire our fathers beat
Old England's haughty king, sir,
But we've put down King Alcohol,
And that's a glorious thing, sir

Encouraging.—A young man in the country, who had the felicity of waiting upon one of the young ladies home from a party, took the opportunity, while searching for the door-latch, to inquire whether she was *courted*. Why, replied she with ingenuousness, I'm sort o' courted, and sort o' not, but rather more sort o' not than sort o'.

A Southern Planter.—A southern planter, who had a remarkably fiery nose, sleeping in his chair, a negro boy, who was in waiting, saw a musquito hovering round his face. Quashi eyed the insect very attentively ; at last he saw him light upon his master's nose, and immediately fly off. Ah, darn you, exclaimed the negro, me darn glad to see you *burn your foot*.

[From the London Metropolitan.]

SOLID COMFORT.

I'd like to have a little farm,
And leave such scenes as these,
Where I could live without a care,
Completely at my ease.
I'd like to have a pleasant house
Upon my little farm,
Airy and cool in summer time—
In winter, close and warm.

I'd like to have a little wife—
I reckon I know who—
I'd like to have a little son,
A little daughter, too ;
And when they'd climb upon my knee,
I'd like a little toy
To give my pretty little girl—
Another to my boy.

I'd like to have a little chaise,
That we might take a ride ;
I'd like a little pony for
My boy to jog beside.
I'd like to have a little cash,
And owe no little debts ;
There's nothing in the world so much
An easy temper frets.

I should not like my wife to shake
A broomstick at my head—
For then I might begin to think
She did not love her Ned ;
But I should always like to see
Her gentle as a dove ;
I should not like to have her scold—
But be all joy and love.

POETRY AND ANECDOTES

POETRY, ANECDOTES, &c.

CHANGE OF FORTUNE,
A plain statement of facts.

Some sixty-five or seventy years ago, a vessel from Boston arrived at a wharf in London. Among the hands on board, was one named Tudor, a steady, well-looking, young man, who acted as a sailor. Very early one morning, a young, beautiful, and decently dressed female came tripping down, and enquired of Tudor for the Captain.—She was told he was not risen, but she insisted on seeing him without delay. Tudor called him up; she addressed him with,

"Good morning, Captain, I have called to see if you will marry me."

"Marry you?" believing her to be a suspicious character—"leave my vessel, instantly, if you know what is for your good." She next went to the mate, and received a similar answer, she then went where Tudor, who was engaged in handling ship tacks, and put the same question to him. "With all my heart," answered Tudor, in a jocular manner.—"Then," said she, "come along with me." Tudor left his work and followed her. By the time the principal shops were opened, the lady entered a barber's, followed by Tudor. She ordered the knight of the razor to take off his beard and hair, both he stood in need of. She faced the bills, and entered a hat store. She requested the best of beavers in the store, and told Tudor to select one,—the price was paid by the lady. Tudor threw his old tarpaulin aside. They next visited a shoe store, and selected a pair of boots, the lady paying for them. Tudor, by this time, was puzzled to divine the object the lady had in view. He solicited an explanation, but she told him to be silent. She led the way into a clothing store. Here Tudor was told to select the best suit of clothes in the store. His tar-be-daubed pants and checkered shirt, were in a few minutes metamorphosed into a fine gentleman as walks the streets. The bill, as before, paid by the lady. Tudor's amazement was now complete. He now again earnestly insisted on an explanation, the only answer he received was—Follow me, and be not alarmed—all will be explained to your satisfaction; he therefore resolved to ask no more questions. Next she conducted him into a magistrate's office, and politely requested the minister of the law to unite her and her companion in matrimony; this was rather a *damper* to Tudor, but he yielded, the ceremony over, the couple were pronounced *man* and *wife*. Without uttering a word, or exchanging a kiss, Tudor and his wife left the office, not, however, until she paid the magistrate his fee. The couple walked along in silence—Tudor hardly knowing what he was doing or what he had done. Turning the corner, Tudor saw a splendid house, towards which the wife seemed to direct her steps, and into the front door they entered: the room was furnished in a style of magnificence. She sat him down, telling him to make himself contented, while she passed into

another room. The first one who addressed her, was her uncle, calling her, demanded how she had escaped from her room, and where she had been. Her only answer was. "Thou fiend in human shape, I allow you just one hour to remove your effects from this house. You have long deprived me of my property, and meant to through life, but you are frustrated. I am mistress of my own house. I am married, and my husband is in the front room."

I must leave the newly married couple for the purpose of giving the history of Mrs. Tudor. She was the only child of a wealthy gentleman, Mr. A.—his daughter's name Eliza. Had been at great expense in her education, being the only object of his care: his wife died when she was quite young. A short time before his death he made a will, by which his brother was to have possession of all his property till his daughter was married, when it was to be given up to her husband. On condition if Eliza died without marrying, the property was to go to her uncle and his family. After the death of Mr. A., his brother removed into his house; Eliza boarded in his family. Eliza soon discovered that her uncle did not intend she should ever marry. He shut her up in one of the centre rooms in the third story and refused her associates, by telling them when they called, she had gone a journey. Three years was the unfortunate girl thus shut out from the world. Her scanty breakfast happened one morning to be carried her by her old servant Juan; Eliza seeing the face of her old friend and servant, burst into tears. Juan well understood the meaning. "hush Eliza some of your old servants have long been planning means for your escape." "What!" said Eliza, "is it possible that I am to be delivered from this vile place." It is unnecessary to detail all the minutia of her escape. Suffice it to say, that on the evening of the 4th day after the interview, she made her escape. This was about daylight. She immediately bent her steps to the wharf where the Boston vessel lay. The amazement of Tudor, and transports of his wife, at the sudden change of fortune, may possibly be conceived, but cannot be expressed. One pleasant morning, some days after the marriage, the crew of the Boston vessel's attention was drawn by a splendid carriage approaching the wharf—the driver let down the steps, and a gentleman and lady gorgeously dressed, alighted, the gentleman asked the captain what port he was from, and many other questions, (all the while avoiding the scrutiny of the captain.) at last turning to "Capt. ——, [calling him by name,] before leaving your vessel permit me to *make you acquainted with Mrs. Tudor !*" The captain and those about him had not recognized him to be their old friend and ship mate. *Tudor !* —they supposed some fatal accident had befallen him. You may judge of the congratulation that followed.

FROM THE
1840
ALMANAC

The Distressed Damsel & The Sailor

122

POETRY AND ANECDOTES

FROM THE
1845
ALMANAC

Delight Was Chasing Butterflies; and Beauty Was Watering Flowers

ON GEORGE WASHINGTON'S FARM, HE HAD:

580 acres in grass
600 bushels of oats
700 acres with wheat
150 acres with turnips
140 horses
236 working oxen, heifers and steers
500 sheep
112 cows
250 employees
24 ploughs

POETRY, ANECDOTES, &c.

A STUFFED CAT.

AN old *cheffonier* (or rag-picker) died in Paris, in a state of abject poverty. His only relation was a niece, who lived as a servant with a green grocer. The girl always assisted her uncle as far as her means would permit. When she learned of her uncle's death, which took place suddenly, she was on the point of marriage with a journeyman baker, to whom she had been long attached. The nuptial day was fixed, but Susan had not yet bought her wedding clothes. She hastened to tell her lover that the wedding must be deferred—she wanted the money for her bridal suit to lay her uncle decently in the grave. Her mistress ridiculed the idea, and exhorted her to leave him to be buried by charity. Susan refused. The consequence was a quarrel, by which the young woman lost her place and her lover, who sided with her mistress. She hastened to the miserable garret where her uncle had expired, and, by the sacrifice not only of her wedding attire, but nearly all her slender wardrobe, her pious task was fulfilled. She then sat herself down alone in her uncle's room, weeping bitterly, when the master of her faithless lover, a good-looking young man, entered.

"So, Susan, I find you have lost your place," said he. "I came to offer you one for life. Will you marry me?"

"I, sir! You are joking!"

"No, in fact, I want a wife, and I can't find a better one."

"But everybody will laugh at you for marrying a poor girl like me."

"Oh! if that is your only objection, we shall soon get over it. Come, come along; my mother is prepared to receive you."

Susan hesitated no longer; but she wished to take with her a memorial of her deceased uncle. It was a cat he had had for many years. The old man was so fond of the animal that he determined that even death should not separate them, for he had her skin stuffed, and placed it at the foot of his bed.

As Susan took down puss, she uttered an exclamation of surprise at finding her so heavy. The lover hastened to open the animal, when out fell a goodly quantity of gold coins, which had been concealed in the body of the cat; and the money, which the old miser had starved himself to amass, became the just reward of the worthy girl and her disinterested lover.

GENERAL WASHINGTON'S FARM.

THE farm of Gen. Washington, at Mount Vernon, contained ten thousand acres of land in one body, equal to about fifteen square miles. It was divided into farms of convenient size, at the distance of two, three, and five miles from his mansion-house. These farms he visited every day in pleasant weather, and was constantly engaged in making experiments for the improvement of agriculture. Some idea of the extent of his farming operations may be formed from the following facts.

In 1787, he had five hundred and eighty acres in grass; sowed six hundred bushels of oats; seven hundred acres with wheat, and as much more in corn, barley, potatoes, beans, peas, &c., and one hundred and fifty with turnips. His stock consisted of one hundred and forty horses, one hundred and twelve cows, two hundred and thirty-six working oxen, heifers, and steers, and five hundred sheep. He constantly employed two hundred and fifty hands, and kept twenty-four ploughs going during the whole year, when the earth and the state of the weather would permit. In 1786, he slaughtered one hundred and fifty hogs, for the use of his family, and provisions for his negroes, for whose comfort he had great regard.

A FAMILY A HUNDRED YEARS AGO.

I SAW Content the other day
  Set by her spinning-wheel,
And Plenty in a wooden tray
  Of wheat and Indian meal.

Health, also, at the table sat,
  Dining upon a ham;
But Appetite demanded yet
  A cabbage and a clam.

Wealth sat enthroned upon a green
  And fragrant load of hay;
And Happiness compelled a dog
  Behind his cart to play.

Delight was chasing butterflies,
  With Laughter and with Joy;
Affection gazed with ardent eyes
  Upon the sweet employ.

Beauty was watering flowers
  Beside the cottage door;
And Pleasure spoke about a tour
  To the green grocer's store.

Justice bid good morrow, and
  Invited me to tea;
But Jolly bid me stay away,
  Unless I came with Glee.

Patience sat in an easy chair
  Unravelling a skein;
While Mirth, with roguish eye and stare,
  Would tangle it again.

Benevolence had built a tower
  Of pudding, bread and meat,
And bid Compassion take it o'er
  To Want, across the street.

But I was gratified to see,
  Easy, and free, and fair,
With Innocence upon his knee,
  Old Satisfaction there.

He took me by the hand, and led
  Me down a vista green,
Where Fun and Frolic, antics,
  Two ancient oaks between.

But best of all it was to find,
  That Love, the day before,
The fopling Dress had kicked behind,
  And tossed him out of door.

And now, kind reader, if you choose
  This family to know,
A Farmer's here, I'll introduce,
  A "hundred years ago."

FROM THE
1849
ALMANAC

Hail to the Superiority of Women

M. DeTOCQUEVILLE SAYS:

"If I was asked . . . to what the singular prosperity and growing strength of that people (Americans) ought to be attributed, I should reply: to the superiority of their women."

AMERICAN WOMEN.

M. De Tocqueville, a French traveller in this country, says: " As for myself I do not hesitate to avow, that, although the women of the United States are confined within the narrow circle of domestic life, and their situation is, in some respects, one of extreme dependence, I have nowhere seen women occupying a loftier position; and if I was asked, now I am drawing to the close of this work, (" Democracy in America,") in which I have spoken of so many things done by the Americans, to what the singular prosperity and growing strength of that people ought to be attributed, I should reply—to the superiority of their women.

PROCRASTINATION AND PROMPTITUDE.

Undue procrastination indicates that a man does not see his way clearly; undue precipitation, that he does not see it at all. True promptitude and true caution lead to the same result. The wise man bides his time; but when the time comes he springs to his mark at once; therefore—

Shun delays, they breed remorse;
Take thy time while time is lent thee;
Creeping snails have weakest force;
Fly thy fault, lest thou repent thee;
Good is best when soonest wrought;
Lingering labors come to nought.

Hoist up sail while gale doth last,
Tide and wind wait no man's pleasure;
Seek not time when time is past;
Sober speed is wisdom's leisure;
After wits are dearly bought,
Let thy forewit guide thy thought.

GEN. WASHINGTON AND LORD ERSKINE.

The following note was found among the papers of the late Lord Erskine :

To General Washington,—Sir : I have taken the liberty to introduce your august and immortal name in a short sentence, which is to be found in the book I send to you.

I have a large acquaintance among the most valuable and exalted class of men, but you are the only human being for whom I ever felt an awful reverence. I sincerely pray to God to grant a long and serene evening to a life so gloriously devoted to the universal happiness of the world. T. ERSKINE.

MAGNIFICENT TELESCOPE.

An English nobleman, (Lord Rosse) has had a telescope constructed which has a reflector, whose diameter is six feet. It collects therefore all the rays of light which fall upon a circular area six feet in diameter and pours them upon the eye. It is equivalent to an eye, whose pupil is two yards across.

Parents who wish to train up their children in the way they should go, must go in the way in which they would train up their children.

Every man has in his own life follies enough, in his own mind troubles enough, in the performance of his duties deficiencies enough, without being curious about the affairs of others.

Answer to the Problem on p. 2 of our last.
157326549—the square root of which is 12543; by A. F. of P—l—m.

Answer to the New Charade in our last.
The first is *Peas*—an useful plant,
The second, an industrious *Ant,*
The whole derived from such a source
A *Peasant* then must be of course.
N. H—s of P—e.

Answer to the Anagram in our last.
Heroine: by N. H—s of P—e, and J. N. M. of B—n, and F. C. C. of J. c—y, and M. A. F. of P—t—m, and W. H. B., Jr. of L—n—g, and E. L. P. of S—n, and Al—a of W—s, and H. J. M. of S—y.

Answer to the Arithmetical Question in our last.
Circumference of outer circle 62.8318 feet; by W. H. P. of Ch—n, (R. I.) Also answered by F. C. C. of J—y, C—y, and A. F. of P—l—m, and J. N. M. of B—n.

PROBLEM A.

What proportion must the height of a cylindrical pail bear to the diameter, that the pail may contain the greatest quantity of water with the least superficies ?
F. C. C.

PROBLEM B.

A man being offered a piece of land in any shape he might choose, as large as he could enclose with a mile of fence, chose that of a square. What shape would have been most for his advantage, and what did he lose by his ignorance ? J. N. M.

PROBLEM C.

A farmer going to Boston with an 8 gallon keg was asked by two of his neighbors to procure for them four gallons of vinegar each, with which he filled the keg, agreeably to order. Upon taking it to them he found one of them had a measure holding 5 gallons and the other a measure holding 3 gallons, and there being no other measures to be had, he poured from measure to measure, using likewise the keg, until he gave each neighbor his four gallons. How did he contrive it ?

ENIGMA.

Three words, containing in all 18 letters. The 1st, 8th and 16th, An Eastern Plant.
3, 10, 17, 2, 8, 11. 1, A law term used in regard to a kind of real estate.
7, 11, 17, 3, A spice.
4, 3, 8, 1, A portion of the body used in walking.
16, 9, 3, 14, An open surface.
13, 5, 9, 12, A kind of earth.
18, 8, 3, 12, A part of a ship.
The whole an useful and entertaining publication, which the reader is sure to have seen. AL—A of Wells.

ANSWER TO PROBLEM A: The diameter must be twice the height.

ANSWER TO PROBLEM B: A circular piece of land. He lost more than 10 acres.

ANSWER TO PROBLEM C: Fill 3 from keg, and pour it into 5, then fill 3 again from keg and fill 5. Pour 5 into keg, and the 1 left in 3 into 5. Then fill 3 again from keg and pour it into 5.

ANSWER TO ENIGMA:

THE FARMER'S ALMANAC

FROM THE
1849
ALMANAC

Give Us Hard Hands and Free

GOD SAVE THE PLOUGH

Give us hard hands and free,
Culturers of field and tree,
Best friends of liberty
God save the plough!

YOUR REFLECTION

The world is a looking-glass.
Frown, and it will look sourly
upon you.

POETRY, ANECDOTES, &C.

GOD SAVE THE PLOUGH.
BY MRS. SIGOURNEY.

See how the shining share,
Maketh earth's bosom fair,
  Crowning her brow —
Bread in its furrow springs,
Health and repose it brings,
Treasures unknown to kings, —
  God save the plough!

Look — in the warrior's blade,
While o'er the-tented glade,
  Hate breathes its vow —
Wrath, its unsheathing wakes,
Love at its lightning quakes,
Weeping and woe it makes, —
  God save the plough!

Ships o'er the deep may ride,
Storms wreck their bannered pride,
  Waves whelm their prow ;
But the well-loaded wain,
Garnering the golden grain,
Gladdening the household train, —
  God save the plough !

Who are the truly great ?
Minions of pomp and state,
  Where the crowd bow ?
Give us hard hands and free,
Culturers of field and tree,
Best friends of liberty, —
  God save the plough !

THE WORLD.

"The world is a looking-glass, and
gives forth to every man the reflection of
his own face. Frown at it, and it will in
turn look sourly upon you ; laugh at it,
and it is a cheerful, kind companion ; and
so let all young persons take their choice."
—*Thackeray.*

AN ALPHABET OF SHORT RULES,
WELL WORTH REMEMBERING.

Attend well to your business.
Be punctual in your payments.
Consider well before you promise.
Dare to do right.
Envy no man.
Faithfully perform your duty.
Go not in the path of vice.
Have respect for your character.
Infringe on no one's right.
Know thyself.
Lie not, for any consideration.
Make few acquaintances.
Never profess what you do not practise.
Occupy your time in usefulness.
Postpone nothing that you can do now.
Quarrel not with your neighbor.
Recompense every man for his labor.
Save something against a day of trouble.
Treat everybody with kindness.
Use yourself to moderation.
Vilify no person's reputation.
Watchfully guard against idleness.
Examine your conduct daily.
Yield to superior judgment.
Zealously pursue the right path.

A RICH LEGACY.

Col. George Mason, of Virginia, made
the following remarks in his will, which
ought to be considered a legacy to the nation : —

"I recommend to my sons, from my
own experience in life, to prefer the happiness of independence and a private station, to the trouble and vexations of public business ; but if either their own in-
clinations, or the necessity of the time,
should engage them in public affairs, I
charge them, on a father's blessing, never
to let the motives of private interest or
ambition induce them to betray, nor the
terrors of poverty and disgrace, or of
death, deter them from asserting, the liberty of their country, and endeavoring to
transmit to their posterity those sacred
rights to which themselves were born."

HOPE.
BY J. G. WHITTIER.

The night is mother of the day,
  The winter of the spring,
And ever upon old decay
  The greenest mosses cling.
Behind the clouds the starlight lurks,
  Through showers the sunbeams fall ;
For God, who loveth all his works,
  Has left his hope with all.

GETTING STORIES MIXED.

We once heard an old fellow, famous
for his tough yarns, relate the following.
He was telling what heavy wheat he had
seen in the state of New York.

"My father," said he, "once had a
field of wheat, the heads of which were
so close together, that the wild turkeys
when they came to eat it, could walk
round on the top of it anywhere."

We suggested that the turkeys must
have been small ones.

"No, sir !" continued he, "they were
very large ones. I shot one of them one
day, and when I took hold of his legs to
carry him, his head dragged in the snow
behind me."

"A curious country you must have had,
to have snow in harvest time."

"Well, I declare," said he, looking a
little foolish, "I have got parts of two
stories mixed."

WIT.

Shrink not to aim the shaft of wit,
  At all that's low and narrow ;
But, oh ! before you bend the bow,
  Be sure it holds the arrow.

May you never be so rich as to feel
poor, nor so poor as to envy the rich.

"A thing of beauty is a joy forever."

BEAUTY
A thing of beauty
is a joy forever.

-> POETRY AND ANECDOTES <-

FROM THE
1850
ALMANAC

*"I think we are too ready
with complaint,
In this fair world
of God's."*

—Elizabeth Barrett Browning

Christ Church, Second Street, Philadelphia, Pa, in
the 1850s. Built in 1744; steeple added in 1754.

POETRY AND ANECDOTES

FROM THE
1852
ALMANAC

Counting Time By Heart Throbs

ON REAL LIVING

We live in deeds, not years; in thoughts,
  not breaths;
In feelings, not in figures on a dial.
We should count time by heart throbs.
  He most lives
Who thinks most—feels the noblest—
  acts the best.

THE BREAKFAST-TABLE.

BY HAWTHORNE.

Life, within doors, has few pleasanter prospects than a neatly-arranged and well-provisioned breakfast-table. We come to it freshly, in the dewy youth of the day, and when our spiritual and sensual elements are in better accord than at a later period; so that the material delights of the morning meal are capable of being fully enjoyed, without any very grievous reproaches, whether gastric or conscientious, for yielding even a trifle overmuch to the animal department of our nature. The thoughts, too, that run around the ring of familiar guests, have a piquancy and mirthfulness, and oftentimes a vivid truth, which more rarely find their way into the elaborate intercourse of dinner.

THE FIREMAN.

BY ELIZA COOK.

When the red sheet winds and whirls
  In the coil of frightful death;
When the bannered smoke unfurls,
  And the hot walls drink our breath;
When the crowd, with terror, nears,
  Choking in the demon glare,
And some helpless form appears
  In that furnace of despair;
Save! oh, save! the people cry;
  But who plucks the human brand?
Who will do the deed or die?
  'T is a Fireman of the land.
Then give him honor, give him fame,
A health to hands that fight the flame!

A GOOD TOAST.

At the St. Patrick's celebration in Baltimore, the following was one of the regular toasts :—
THE UNION.— A tree of majestic growth.
  "Woodman, spare that tree,
    Touch not a single bough;
  In youth it sheltered me,
    And I'll protect it now."
    AIR — " Know ye the land."
The toast was received with nine enthusiastic cheers.

THE MAN WHO LIVES.

We live in deeds, not years; in thoughts,
  not breaths;
In feelings, not in figures on a dial.
We should count time by heart throbs.
  He most lives
Who thinks most — feels the noblest —
  acts the best.

THE PLOUGH AND THE SICKLE.

BY HON. T. BURGESS.

The plough and the sickle shall shine
  bright in glory,
When the sword and the musket have
  crumbled in rust;
And the farmer shall live, both in song
  and in story,
When warriors and kings are forgotten in
  dust.

THE AMERICAN UNION.

BY PRESIDENT TAYLOR.

But attachment to the Union of the States should be habitually fostered in every American heart. For more than half a century, during which kingdoms and empires have fallen, this Union has stood unshaken. The patriots who formed it have long since descended to the grave; yet still it remains, the proudest monument to their memory, and the object of affection and admiration with every one worthy to bear the American name. In my judgment, its dissolution would be the greatest of calamities, and to avert that should be the study of every American. Upon its preservation must depend our own happiness, and that of countless generations to come.

NATIONAL SUPERSTITIONS AND OBSERVANCES.

The Ancient Romans assigned a crown of oak-leaves to be entwined around the head of any one who saved the life of a citizen. This was esteemed a high honor. The Hebrews had a saying that an old man was a great blessing in a house. The Irish have a beautiful superstition, that the cherishing of an orphan in a dwelling brings good luck to a family. The Germans have a superstition that when sudden silence takes place in a company, an angel is making a circuit around them, and the first person that speaks is supposed to have been touched by the wings of the spirit. There is another superstition among the Irish, that when an infant smiles in its sleep, an angel is whispering to it. The baptismal admonition of the Hindoos is as impressive on the bystanders as it is beautiful : "Little babe, thou enterest the world weeping, while all around you smile; contrive so to live, that you may depart in smiles, whilst all around you weep."

THE HAPPY HOME.

It is not much the world can give, with
  all its subtle art,
And gold and gems are not the things to
  satisfy the heart;
But oh, if those who cluster round the
  altar and the hearth
Have gentle words and loving smiles,
  how beautiful is earth!

ANECDOTES.

A PLEASANT COUNTRY.—A friend travelling in Florida, says of the mosquitos : Let a man go to sleep with his head in a cast-iron kettle, and their bills will make a watering-pot of it, before morning.

NOT A BAD IDEA.— A sailor went into a store and asked for "something to drink;" he was handed a glass of water, with the remark that, "that was the best thing." "I know," said he, "it is a good thing, for it has done a great deal for navigation."

POETRY AND ANECDOTES

FROM THE
1853
ALMANAC

THE COMPANY OF BOOKS.
BY CHANNING.

It is chiefly through books that we enjoy intercourse with superior minds; and these invaluable communications are in the reach of all. God be thanked for books. No matter how poor I am; no matter though the prosperous of my own time will not enter and take up their abode under my roof, * * * I may become a cultivated man, though excluded from what is called the best company where I live. Let every man, if possible, gather some good books under his roof. Nothing can supply their place.

EXCELLENT ADMONITIONS.

"Take heed of always trying to shine in company above the rest, and displaying your own understanding, or your oratory, as though you would render yourself admirable to all present. This is seldom well taken in good company. * * * In order to show, too, how free you are from prejudice, learn to bear contradiction with patience. * * * The impartial search of truth requires all calmness and serenity, all good temper and candor."—*Watts on the Mind.*

THE AMERICAN.
BY HENRY GILES.—(*An Irishman.*)

The American accepts any work *for the time,* if it pays. He does it cheerfully; he does it manfully; but if it is at the bidding of another, he does not intend to do it always, or to do it long. The American journeyman intends to be an employer. The American clerk has it in his own mind that in good time he will be a capitalist. Any man who is satisfied with perpetual dependence, any man who is void of aspiration and incapable of effort, is not in harmony with the spirit of American life, and with the genius of American society. * * I advocate, indeed, the sentiment of aspiration, but it is aspiration following its purpose with the constancy of Christian rectitude, and with the quiet of manly perseverance.

COURTESY OF AMERICANS.
BY LADY WORTLEY. (*An English Lady.*)

I like the Americans more and more. Either they have improved wonderfully lately, or else the criticisms on them have been wonderfully exaggerated. They are particularly courteous and obliging, and seem, I think, particularly anxious that foreigners should carry away a favorable impression of them. As for me, let other travellers say what they please of them, I am determined not to be prejudiced, but to judge of them exactly as I find them; and I shall most pertinaciously continue to praise them (if I see no good cause to alter my present humble opinion), and most especially for their obliging civility and hospitable attention to strangers, of which I have seen many instances.

LIBERTY.—Liberty is not safe where the people are not watchful.—*Josiah Quincy.*

YANKEE PATRIOTISM.
Told at a Fourth of July Celebration.

Captain Seth Washburn, of Leicester, grandfather of Judge Washburn, while crossing Charlestown Neck to Bunker Hill, on the memorable 17th of June, 1775, exposed to the raking fire of the British, halted his company, and gave leave to any one who chose TO GO BACK. Not a man in the company accepted the offer.

LUTHER AND THE BIRDS.—With the birds of his native country Martin Luther had established a strict intimacy, watching, smiling, and thus sweetly moralizing over their habits. "That little fellow," he said of a bird going to roost, "has chosen his shelter, and is quietly rocking himself to sleep, without a care for to-morrow's lodging, calmly holding by his little twig, and *leaving God to think for him.*" Christians, in all your situations, you must do the same. Discharge your duty, and "leave God to think for you."

A NICE MAN.—An old lady on Long Island said her idea of a nice man was, "A man what is keerful of his clothes, don't drink no spirits, kin read the Bible without spellin' the words, and kin eat a cold dinner on wash-day to save the wimmin-folks from cookin'."

CONCLUSIVE REASON FOR NOT SMOKING.—"I wish you would not smoke cigars," said a plump little dark-eyed girl to her lover. "Why may not I smoke as well as your chimney?" "Because chimneys don't smoke when they are in good order." He has quitted smoking.

THE Lowell News says that the farmer whose pigs were so lean that it took two of them to make a shadow, has been beat by another who had several so thin that they would crawl out through the cracks in their pen. He finally stopped that "fun" by *tying knots in their tails!*

WIT AND KINDNESS.—Witty sayings are as easily lost as the pearls slipping off a broken string; but a word of kindness is seldom spoken in vain. It is a seed which, even when dropped by chance, springs up a flower.

CONVERSATION.—Sir W. Temple says that the first ingredient in conversation is truth; the next, good sense; the third, good-humor; and the fourth, wit.

PROFANITY.—What ten-inch spikes would be to veneering, profane language is to conversation—splitting, shivering and defacing it. It is in bad taste, offensive to a majority, and gratifying to none.

TASTE FOR LITERATURE.—A taste for literature secures cheerful occupation for the unemployed and languid hours of life; and how many persons, in these hours, for want of innocent resources, are now impelled to coarse and brutal pleasure!

To Bear Contradiction with Patience

"In order to show how free you are from prejudice, learn to bear contradiction with patience."

LUTHER AND THE BIRDS

"The little fellow," said Luther of a bird
going to roost, *"has chosen his shelter,
and is quietly rocking himself to sleep
. . .
leaving God to think for him.*

128

POETRY AND ANECDOTES

FROM THE
1854
ALMANAC

Scatter Ye Seeds
Flowers Will Spring

NO MORE COMPLAINTS

Scatter ye seeds each passing year,
Sow amid winds and storms of rain,
Hope give thee courage,
Faith cast out fear,
God will requite thee,
With infinite gain.

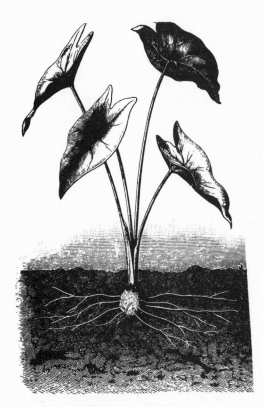

POETRY, ANECDOTES, &c.

SCATTER YE SEEDS.

To all good cultivators of land or mind.

SCATTER ye seeds, and flowers will spring;
    Strew them at broadcast o'er hill and glen ;
Sow in your garden, and time will bring
    Bright flowers, with seeds to scatter again.

Scatter ye seeds — nor think them lost,
    Though they fall amid leaves and are buried in earth ;
Spring will awake them, though heedlessly tossed,
    And to beautiful flowers those seeds will give birth.

Scatter ye seeds ; tire not, but toil ;
    'T is the work of life, 't is the labor of man ;
In the head, in the heart, and on earth's own soil,
    Sow, gather, and sow, through life's short span.

Scatter ye seeds in the field of mind, —
    Seeds of flowers, with seeds of grain ;
In the spring and summer sweet garlands ye 'll find,
    And in autumn ye 'll reap rich fruits for your pain.

Scatter ye seeds in the garden of heart,
    Seeds of affection, of truth, and of love ;
Cultivate carefully each hidden part,
    And thy flowers will be seen by angels above.

Scatter ye seeds — the seeds of Hope ;
    Plant in your bosom the Tree of Life, —
Then the flowers here budding in Heaven shall ope,
    And in Heaven will ripen the fruits of strife.

Then scatter ye seeds each passing year ;
    Sow amid winds and storms of rain,
Hope give thee courage, Faith cast out fear,
    God will requite thee with infinite gain.

THE "ROOT OF THE MATTER."

WEEP for the frail that err, the weak that fall,
Have thine own faith, but hope and pray for all.

ALL'S WELL.

BY J. G. WHITTIER.

THE clouds which rise with thunder slake
    Our thirsty soils with rain ;
The blow most dreaded falls to break
    From off our limbs a chain ;
Our very sins and follies make
    The love of God more plain ;
As through the shadowy lens of even
The eye looks furthest into heaven,
On gleams of stars and depths of blue
The glaring sunshine never knew.

CURIOUS SENTENCE.

THE following verse contains every letter in the English alphabet except " E." It is a question whether any other English rhyme can be produced (in print) without the letter " E," which is a letter employed more than any other. By inserting the word vex instead of tax, in the second line, the verse would contain all the letters of the alphabet.

A jovial swain may rack his brain,
    And tax his fancy's might,
To quiz in vain, for 't is most plain
    That what I did was right.

THE BEST MEDICINE.

GOOD, wholesome food and temperance, with pure, cold water to drink and bathe in, with fresh air, plenty of exercise, and a clear conscience, are said to do more to restore or preserve health, and prolong life, than all the doctors and medicine in the universe.

CHEERFULNESS.

BY ELIZABETH BARRETT BROWNING.

I THINK we are too ready with complaint
In this fair world of God's. Had we no hope
Indeed beyond the zenith and the scope
Of yon gray blank of sky, we might be fain
To muse upon eternity's constraint
Round our aspirant souls. But since the scope
Must widen early, is it well to droop
For a few days consumed in loss, and faint ?
O, pusillanimous heart, be comforted !
And, like a cheerful traveller, take the road,
Singing beside the hedge. What if the bread
Be bitter in thine inn, and thou unshod
To meet the flints ? At least it may be said,
" Because the way is short, I thank thee, God ! "

GOOD SENTENCES.

IT is of no consequence where these sentences were found ; they are worth treasuring up. A preacher once said :

" If you know anything that will make a brother's heart glad, *run quick and tell it ;* and if it is something that will only cause a sigh, *bottle it up, bottle it up.*"
" We never get good bread for ourselves till we begin to *ask for our brethren.*"

A BASE TEMPER.

IT is a base temper in mankind that they will not take the smallest slight at the hand of those who have done them the greatest kindness.

WEEP FOR THE FRAIL
Weep for the frail that err, the weak that fall,
Have thine own faith, but hope and pray for all.

POETRY AND ANECDOTES

POETRY, ANECDOTES, &c.

THE CORN SONG.

ABRIDGED FROM "THE HUSKERS," BY J. G. WHITTIER.

Heap high the Farmer's wintry hoard !
    Heap high the golden corn !
No richer gift has Autumn poured
    From out her lavish horn.

Let vapid idlers loll in silk,
    Around their costly board ;
Give us the bowl of samp and milk,
    By homespun beauty poured.

Where'er the wide old kitchen hearth
    Sends up its smoky curls,
Who will not thank the kindly earth,
    And bless our Farmer Girls !

Then shame on all the proud and vain,
    Whose folly laughs to scorn
The blessing of our hardy grain,
    Our wealth of golden corn !

Long let the good old crop adorn
    The hills our fathers trod ;
Still let us, for his golden corn,
    Send up our thanks to God.

BOOKS.

A learned writer says of books : "They are masters who instruct us without rods or ferules, without words or anger, without bread or money. If you approach them, they are not asleep ; if you seek them, they do not hide ; if you blunder, they do not scold ; if you are ignorant, they do not laugh at you."

THE ORGAN-GRINDER'S SONG.

Punch hits the vagabonds admirably in the following :

I roam and wander o'er the town ;
Where tan or straw I see put down,
I take my stand, and grind away,
For there my music's sure to pay.

Forth comes a servant from the door
Which I pick out to play before,
And gives me sixpence to move on,
And get myself and music gone.

He says his mistress is abed,
And that the least noise splits her head ;
Or master's near his latest breath,
And wants to die a quiet death.

So off I walk, repeat the trick
On some one else that's lying sick,
And thus my pockets often fill
By plaguing people that are ill.

DON'T ARGUE THE POINT.

An old author quaintly remarks, "Avoid argument with ladies. In spinning yarns among *silks* and *satins*, a man is sure to be worsted and twisted. And when a man is worsted and twisted, he may consider himself wound up."

OUR LAND AND FLAG.

BY GEO. P. MORRIS.

My native land, I turn to you,
    With blessing and with prayer,
Where man is brave, and woman true,
    And free as mountain air.

Long may our flag in triumph wave,
    Against the world combined,
And friends a welcome, foes a grave,
    Within our borders find.

WASHINGTON'S HIGH CHARACTER.

BY EDWARD EVERETT.

But the pure morality of Washington's character was its most important feature, and Mr. Everett, in the famous oration which he has delivered before such delighted audiences, declares it to be his decided conviction, "that it was an important part of the design of Providence, in raising up Washington to be the leader of the Revolutionary struggle, and afterwards the first President of the United States, to set before the people of America, in the morning of their national existence, a living example to prove that armies may be best conducted, just wars more successfully fought, and governments most ably and honorably administered, by men of sound moral principle ; to teach to gifted and aspiring individuals, and the parties they lead, that, though a hundred crooked paths may conduct to temporary success, the one plain and straight path of public and private virtue can alone lead to a pure and lasting fame, and the blessings of posterity."

AMERICANS, BE UNITED !

BY O. W. HOLMES.

By the name that you inherit,
    By the sufferings you recall,
Cherish the fraternal spirit ;
    Love your country first of all !

COMPENSATIONS OF LIFE.

Each has its sources of peculiar bliss ;
What one denies in that, it gives in this ;
Each boasts peculiar good, peculiar ill ;
And, strike the balance, all are equal still.

DECAY OF THE MIND IN OLD AGE.

"The failure of the mind in old age, in my opinion," says Sir Benjamin Brook, "is often less the result of natural decay than of disuse." Ambition has ceased to operate ; contentment brings indolence ; indolence decay of mental power, *ennui*, intellectual vacancy, and sometimes death.

THE IDLER.

The idler is a watch that wants both hands,
As useless when it goes as when it stands.
Want of occupation is not rest ;
A mind unoccupied is a mind distressed.

RETIREMENT
Want of occupation is not rest;
A mind unoccupied
Is a mind distressed.

The Right Man at the Right Time

THE LESSON OF
WASHINGTON'S LIFE

"... that armies may be best conducted, just wars more successfully fought, and governments most ably and honorably administered, by men of sound moral principle; to teach to gifted and aspiring individuals, and the parties they lead, that, though a hundred crooked paths may conduct to temporary success, the one plain and straight path of public and private virtue can alone lead to a pure and lasting fame, and the blessings of posterity."

FROM THE
1859
ALMANAC

Be Thankful You Broke Your Leg

THE OPTIMISTS

"Dr. Johnson used to say that a habit of looking at the best side of every event is far better than a thousand pounds a year. Bishop Hall quaintly remarks, "For every bad there might be a worse, and when one breaks his leg let him be thankful it was not his neck!"

TRUE SUCCESS

The true success in life is the attainment of a pure and exalted character.

A RECIPE FOR A WIFE.

As much of beauty as preserves affection,
As much of cheerfulness as spurns dejection,
Of modest deference as claims protection,
Yet stored with sense, with reason and reflection,
And every passion held in due subjection,
Just faults enough to keep her from perfection;
Find this, my friend, and then make your selection.

THE WAY TO ACCOMPLISH MUCH IN A SHORT TIME.

"How," said Mr. M. to Mr. Y., "do you accomplish so much in so short a time? Have you any particular plan?" "I have. When I have anything to do, I go and do it."

WOMAN'S MISSION.

'T is thine to curb the passions' maddening sway,
And wipe the mourner's bitter tear away;
'T is thine to soothe, when hope itself has fled,
And cheer with angel smile the sufferer's bed;
To give to earth its charm, to life its zest,
One only task — to bless, and to be blest.
GRAHAM.

SUCCESS IN LIFE.
BY OLIVER OPTIC.

The true success in life is the attainment of a pure and exalted character; and he who at threescore and ten has won nothing but wealth and a name, has failed to achieve the noblest purpose of his being. Wealth is success; a true life is a far nobler success. He who has won both has been doubly successful; but he who has become rich by neglecting the mind, the heart and the soul, has sacrificed the greater good to the less.

THE PAST.

I have lingered by the Past,
As by a death-bed, with unwonted love,
And such forgiveness as we bring to those
Who can offend no more.
DOBELL.

THE SUNNY SIDE.

Dr. Johnson used to say that a habit of looking at the best side of every event is far better than a thousand pounds a year. Bishop Hall quaintly remarks, "For every bad there might be a worse, and when one breaks his leg let him be thankful it was not his neck!" When Fenelon's library was on fire, "God be praised," he exclaimed, "that it is not the dwelling of some poor man!" This is the true spirit of submission — one of the most beautiful traits that can possess the human heart.

LEND A HAND.

Heed the words, thou man of wealth!
Bring back the fading hue of health
To the poor man's sunken cheek;
Thou art strong, and he is weak.
He hath neither gold nor land;
Help to raise him, — " Lend a hand ! "
Heed the words, thou poor man ! — thou
Who livest by thy sweating brow;
If a sinking brother need
Thy assistance, give him heed;
Thou mayest better understand
What his woes are, — " Lend a hand ! "
Heed the words, O thou, in whom
The softer virtues live in bloom;
If an erring sister claim
Aid and pity in her shame,
Spurn her not, but take thy stand
On higher ground, and " Lend a hand ! "

PROGRESS.

Remember, also, that whoever brings to a higher perfection any branch of noble and productive labor, does something to elevate, refine, and perfect the whole.
HUNTINGTON.

EFFORT.

Never admit that the good that is desirable is not attainable. LOTHROP.

COMPENSATIONS.
BY J. G. WHITTIER.

Forever, from the hand that takes
One blessing from us, others fall,
And soon or late our Father makes
His perfect recompense to all.

EATING AND FIDGETING.

Dr. Abernethy divided what he was pleased to call "the complicated madness of the human race" into two branches; the first consisted "in fidgeting about what could not be helped," and the second was "gormandizing."

THE LADY WHO WAS HURT.

"O, madam," said a gentleman, as he helped up a lady who had accidentally fallen in the street, "I hope you have not hurt yourself?" "Hurt myself," said she; "I am almost killed!" "Madam," again said the gentleman, "may I ask the favor of a daguerreotype of you? You are the first woman I have known *who ever acknowledyed that she was hurt.*"

WIT AND GENIUS.

True wit is like the brilliant stone,
Dug from the Indian mine,
Which boasts two different powers in one,
To cut as well as shine.

Genius, like that, if polished right,
With the same gifts abounds,
Appears at once both keen and bright,
And sparkles while it wounds.

POETRY AND ANECDOTES

FROM THE
1865
ALMANAC

To Bake and Brew and Draw a Pail of Water

The use of time is a debt we contract from birth, and it should only be paid with the interest that our life has accumulated.

CONTENTMENT
A little house,
  well filled;
A little wife,
  well willed;
A little land,
  well tilled.

AN END TO CIVIL STRIFE
The heart-sick faintness of hope delayed,
The waste, the woe, the bloodshed and the tears
That washed with terror many rolling years—
All was forgot in that blithe jubilee!

Sir Walter Scott

POETRY, ANECDOTES, ETC.

THE FARMER'S CHOICE;
OR, RURAL FELICITY AND INDEPENDENCE.

A little house, well filled — a little wife, well willed — a little land, well tilled.

Give me a snug little farm, with sufficient learning; a cheerful wife, that can milk the cow and rock the cradle; that can sleep all night and work all day; that can discourse music on the spinning wheel, and that can cook, wash, and tend the poultry and the dairy, instead of dressing at the toilet, or playing on the piano. The present times are too unnatural, fashionable, and luxurious.

Our ancesters lived on bread and broth,
  And woo'd their healthy wives in homespun cloth;
Our mothers, nurtured to the nodding reel,
  Gave all their daughters lessons on the wheel;
Though spinning did not much reduce the waist,
  It made their food much sweeter to the taste!
They plied, with honest zeal, the mop and broom,
  And drove the shuttle through the noisy loom.
They never once complained, as we do now,—
  "We have no girls to cook, or milk the cow."
Each mother taught her red-cheeked son and daughter
To bake and brew, and draw a pail of water;
No damsel shunned the wash-tub, broom, or pail,
To keep unsoiled a long-grown finger-nail.
They sought no gaudy dress, no wasp-like form,
But ate to live, and worked to keep them warm;
No idle youth, no tight-laced, mincing fair,
Became a living corpse for want of air;
No fidgets, faintings, fits, or frightful blues;
No painful corns from wearing Chinese shoes.

MAXIMS FOR HUSBANDS.

Resolve in the morning to be patient and cheerful during the day. Laugh heartily on finding all the buttons off your shirt — as usual. Say, merrily, "Boys will be boys," when you discover that the children have emptied the contents of the water jug into your boots. On gashing your chin with a razor, remember that beauty is but skin deep; and in order to divert your thoughts from the pain, recite a speech from Hamlet, or indulge in the harmonies of our native land. If breakfast is not ready for you, chuckle and grin at the menials, remembering that a merry heart is a continual feast, and depart to your daily business, imagining yourself a sufferer from indigestion.

COMPENSATIONS.
WHITTIER.

And light is mingled with the gloom,
  And joy with grief;
Divinest compensations come,
Through thorns of judgment mercies bloom
  In sweet relief.

A BIT OF ADVICE FOR BOYS.

"You are made to be kind," says Horace Mann, "generous and magnanimous. If there is a boy in the school who has a club foot, don't let him know that you ever saw it. If there is a poor boy with ragged clothes, don't talk about rags when he is within hearing. If there is a lame boy, assign him some part of the game which does not require running. If there is a hungry one, give him part of your dinner. If there is a dull one, help him to get his lesson. If there is a bright one, be not envious of him; for if one boy is proud of his talents, and another boy is envious of them, there are two great wrongs, and no more talents than before. If a larger or stronger boy has injured you, and is sorry for it, forgive him, and request the teacher not to punish him. All the school will show by their countenance how much better it is than to have a great fist."

ACROSTIC.

This is a queer and very difficult specimen of the acrostic family:

U-nite and untie are the same — so say yo-U.
N-ot in wedlock; I ween, has the unity bee-N.
I-n the drama of marriage, each wandering gou-T
T-o a new face would fly — all except you and I,
E-ach seeking to alter the *spell* in the scen-E.

TIME.

Be avaricious of time; do not give any moment without receiving it in value; only allow the hours to go from you with as much regret as you give to your gold; do not allow a single day to pass without increasing the treasure of your knowledge and virtue. The use of time is a debt we contract from birth, and it should only be paid with the interest that our life has accumulated.

THE LOVED AND LOST.
On the Death of a Classmate.
BY O. W. HOLMES.

Fast as the rolling seasons bring
  The hour of fate to those we love,
Each pearl that leaves the broken string
  Is set in Friendship's crown above;
As narrower grows the earthly chain,
  The circle widens in the sky;
These are our treasures that remain,
  But those are stars that beam on high.

READING.
EDITOR O. F. A.

Always have a good book handy, to take up and read at odd, unemployed minutes: if you have read all you own, borrow of some friend or of a library — but have a good book, and thus read it. It will save you from many a temptation, and you will be surprised to see how much information you will acquire by persisting in this plan.

THE CURSE AND THE REMEDY
For every evil under the sun,
There is a remedy—or there is none!
If there is one, try and find it;
If there isn't, never mind it.

POETRY AND ANECDOTES

FROM THE
1866
ALMANAC

Waste, Woe, Bloodshed and Tears

POETRY, ANECDOTES, &C.

THE NATIONAL REJOICING.
WALTER SCOTT.

O, who that shared them ever shall forget
Th' emotions of the spirit-rousing time,
When, breathless in the mart, the people met,
Early and late, at evening and at prime —
When the loud cannon and the merry chime
Hailed news on news, as field on field was
won! —
When Hope, long doubtful, soared at length
sublime,
And our glad eyes, awake as day begun,
Watched Joy's broad banner rise, to meet the
rising sun!

O, those were hours when thrilling joy repaid
A long, long course of darkness, doubts, and
fears! —
The heart-sick faintness of the hope delayed,
The waste, the woe, the bloodshed, and the
tears
That washed with terror many rolling years;
All was forgot in that blithe jubilee! —
Her downcast eye e'en pale Affliction rears,
To sigh a thankful prayer amid the glee
That hailed the despot's fall, and Peace and
Liberty!

LOOKING UP AND LIFTING UP.

It is horrible for a man to envy and writhe
when he regards those above him, scorn and
loathe when he regards those beneath him.
Alas, for the man who hates upward, instead
of revering; despises downward, instead of
commiserating! Gazing on our superiors,
we ought to admire and aspire; gazing on
our inferiors, we ought to pity and help.
Then our mood and posture in society will
redeemingly sublime and soften into the
twofold attitude of *looking up* to those better
off than we, and *lifting up* those worse off
than we.

THE INFLUENCE OF NEWSPAPERS.
DANIEL WEBSTER.

Daniel Webster once remarked, "Small
is the sum that is required to patronize a
newspaper, and amply rewarded is its pa-
tron, I care not how humble and unpretend-
ing the gazette which he takes. It is next
to impossible to fill a sheet with printed
matter without putting into it something
that is worth the subscription price. Every
parent whose son is away from home at
school should supply him with a newspaper.
I well remember what a marked difference
there was between those of my schoolmates
who had and those who had not access to
newspapers. Other things being equal, the
first were always superior to the last in de-
bate, composition, and general intelligence."

BEARING TROUBLE.
THE TRUE PHILOSOPHY.

For every evil under the sun
There is a remedy — or there's none!
If there is one, try and find it;
If there isn't, never mind it.

VIGILANCE AND ENERGY.

A distinguished general in the U. S. army,
in his order respecting the contest over Fort
Steadman, said, "Two lessons can be learned
from these operations — one, that no forti-
fied position, however strong, will protect an
army from an intrepid and audacious enemy,
unless vigilantly guarded; the other, THAT
NO DISASTER OR MISFORTUNE IS IRREPARABLE
WHERE ENERGY AND BRAVERY ARE DISPLAYED
IN THE DETERMINATION TO RECOVER WHAT IS
LOST, and to promptly resume the offensive."

HYMENEAL POETRY.
MINISTER.
This woman wilt thou have,
And cherish her for life?
Wilt thou love and comfort her,
And seek no other wife?
HE.
This woman I will take,
That stands beside me now;
I'll find her board and clothes,
And have no other frow.
MINISTER.
And for your husband will
You take this nice young man?
Obey his slightest wish,
And love him all you can?
SHE.
I'll love him all I can,
Obey him all I choose,
If when I ask for funds
He never does refuse.
MINISTER.
Then you are man and wife,
And happy may you be;
As many be your years
As dollars be my fee.

YANKEE NOSHUNS.
BY JOSH BILLINGS.

The noshun that skeuel heouses are cheaper than staits prisons.
The noshun that a people who have brains
enough kant be governed by anybody but
themselves.
The noshun that men are a better crop to
raise than anything else.
The noshun that if you kant make a man
think az you do, try and make him do az you
think.
The noshun that the United States is liable
at enny time to be doubled, but ain't liable
at enny time to be divided.
The noshun that Unkle Sam can thrash
his own children when they need it.
The noshun that the Yankees are a foreor-
dained rase, and kant be kept from spred-
ding and striking in, enny more than tar-
pentine when it wunce gets luce.

THE SICK DYER.

My patrons all, both far and nigh,
Wish I may longer live to dye;
When well, to them my work I'll give —
For I must dye that I may live.

IT CAN ALWAYS BE WORSE

From the day you were born,
Till the day you die,
There is nothing that happens,
Which couldn't be worse.

POETRY AND ANECDOTES

APRIL DAYS.

Twice in the year the maple tree
Grows red beneath our northern skies;
Once when October lights the lea
With splendid flames and Tyrian dyes,
And once when April and the bee
First greet us with their glad surprise,
And on the budding twigs we see
The first faint color rise.

These morning hours blend joy with grief
That draw the fuller spring-time near,
And hint the tender opening leaf,
And pour the robin's carol clear;
For not the time of ripened sheaf,
And rainbow woods, is half so dear
As this, the boyhood, bright and brief,
The earliest of the year.

CHRISTIAN COURTESY.

Every man has his faults, his failings, his peculiarities. Every one of us finds himself crossed by such failings of others from hour to hour; and if he were to resent them all, or even notice all, life would be intolerable. If for every outburst of hasty temper, and for every rudeness that wounds us in our daily path, we were to demand an apology, require an explanation, or resent it by retaliation, daily intercourse would be impossible. The very science of social life consists in that gliding tact, which avoids contact with the sharp angularities of character, which does not argue about such things, which does not seek to adjust or cure them all, but covers them as if it did not see. So a Christian spirit throws a cloak of love over these things. It knows when it is wise not to see. That microscopic distinctness in which all faults appear to captious men, who are forever blaming, dissenting, complaining, disappears in the large, calm gaze of love. And it is this spirit which our Christian society lacks, and which we shall never get until each one begins with his own heart.

TRUE COURAGE.

If, in years of fierce endeavor,
All your efforts have been vain,
Struggle on, believing ever
That the victory you will gain.

Are you friendless? you can conquer
Foes without and foes within;
What are trials, pain, and hunger,
When there is a prize to win?

Noble natures prove ascendant
In the world's ignoble strife
And true courage is descendant
Of the dauntless souls in life.

On life's changeful scene of action
Though defeat may oft appear,
Laurels, prizes, wealth, and station
Are for those who persevere.

THE PROBLEM OF THE STOICS.

When a man says "I lie," does he lie, or does he speak the truth? If he lies, he speaks the truth; if he speaks the truth, he lies.

UNDER THE CLOUD.

BY CHARLES G. AMES.

O, beauteous things of earth!
I cannot feel your worth
    To-day;

O, kind and constant friend!
Our spirits cannot blend
    To-day;

O, Lord of truth and grace!
I cannot see Thy face
    To-day;

A shadow on my heart
Keeps me from all apart
    To-day;

Yet something in me knows
How fair creation glows
    To-day;

And something makes me sure
That love is not less pure
    To-day;

And that th' Eternal Good
Minds nothing of my mood
    To-day;

Fed from a hidden bowl,
A lamp burns in my soul
    All days!

If thou workest at that which is before thee, following right reason seriously, vigorously, calmly, without allowing anything else to distract thee, but keeping thy divine part pure, as if thou shouldst be bound to give it back immediately; if thou holdest to this, expecting nothing, fearing nothing, but satisfied with thy present activity according to nature, and with heroic truth in every word and sound which thou utterest, thou wilt live happy. And there is no man who is able to prevent this.
The Emperor MARCUS ANTONINUS.

PITHY CORRESPONDENCE.

The following is given as the substance of a correspondence between the late W. H. Crawford, Secretary of the Treasury under Monroe, and an agent of the department in the State of Alabama.

Dear Sir: Please inform this department, by return of mail, how far the Tombigbee River runs up.
Respectfully,
W. H. CRAWFORD, Sec'y, &c.
REPLY.
Mobile, ———
HON. W. H. CRAWFORD, *Dear Sir*: In reply to your letter, just at hand, I have the honor to say that the Tombigbee River doesn't run up at all.
I have the honor to be, &c.
The agent's joke cost him his place.

FAITH.

WHITTIER.

Yet love will dream, and faith will trust,
That somehow, somewhere meet we must.
Alas for him who never sees
The stars shine through his cypress trees;
Who hath not learned in hours of faith,
The truth to flesh and sense unknown,
That life is ever Lord of death,
And love can never lose its own.

FROM THE
1870
ALMANAC

The Healthy Blend of Joy and Grief

LIFE WOULD BE INTOLERABLE

AN APOLOGY

If for every outburst of hasty temper, And for every rudeness that wounds us, We were to demand an apology . . . , Daily intercourse would be impossible.

WHAT'S A LIE?

When a man says, "I lie," does he lie, or does he speak the truth?

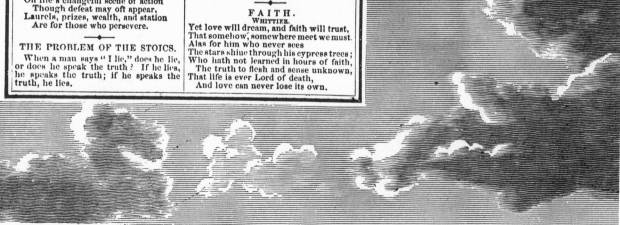

-- POETRY AND ANECDOTES --

FROM THE 1872 ALMANAC

ROCHESTER, N.Y. November 5, 1872—Ulysses S. Grant is reelected President of the United States, sending his opponent, Horace Greeley, down to defeat. Susan B. Anthony and her sister suffragettes are arrested in Rochester, New York, for attempting to vote.

POETRY, ANECDOTES, ETC.

FROM THE PERSIAN.

Lord! who art merciful as well as just,
Incline thine ear to me, a child of dust!
Not what I would, O Lord! I offer thee;
    Alas! but what I can.

Father, Almighty, who hast made me man,
And bade me look to heaven, for thou art there,
Accept my sacrifice and humble prayer.

Four things which are not in thy treasury,
I lay before thee, Lord, with this petition:
My nothingness, my wants, my sins, and my contrition.

TABLE CONVERSATION. — A great deal of character is imparted and received at the table. Parents too often forget this; and, therefore, instead of swallowing your food in sullen silence, instead of brooding over your business, instead of severely talking about others, let the conversation at the table be genial, kind, social, and cheering. Don't bring disagreeable things to the table in your conversation any more than you would in your dishes. For this reason, too, the more good company you have at your table, the better for your children. Every conversation with company at your table is an educator of the family. Hence the intelligence, and the refinement, and the appropriate behavior of a family which is given to hospitality.

[Lines found under the pillow of a soldier who died in a hospital near Port Royal, South Carolina.]

I lay me down to sleep,
    With little care
Whether my waking find
Me here or there, —

A bowing, burdened head
    That only asks to rest,
Unquestioning, upon
    A loving breast;

My good right hand forgets
    Its cunning now;
To march the weary march,
    I know not how.

I am not eager, bold,
    Nor strong — all that is past;
I am ready not to do,
    At last, at last.

My half-day's work is done,
    And this is all my part—
I give a patient God
    My patient heart;

And grasp his banner still,
    Though all the blue be dim;
These stripes as well as stars
    Lead after him.

Sheridan was once staying at the house of an elderly maiden lady in the country, who wanted more of his company than he was willing to give. Proposing, one day, to take a stroll with him, he excused himself on account of the badness of the weather. Shortly afterwards she met him sneaking out alone. "So, Mr. Sheridan," said she, "it has cleared up." "Just a little, ma'am," said he, "enough for one, but not enough for two."

SELECTIONS.

A thing of beauty is a joy forever.
                                Keats.

O, what a tangled web we weave
When first we practise to deceive.
                                Scott.

We live in deeds, not years; in thoughts, not breaths.
                                Bailey.

                    Strongest minds
Are often those of whom the world
Hears least.   *Wordsworth.*

How blessed is he who leads a country life,
Unvexed with anxious care, and void of strife!
                                Dryden.

Where men of judgment creep and feel their way,
The positive pronounce without dismay.
                                Cowper.

It is better to fight for the good than to rail at the ill.   *Tennyson.*

I dare do all that may become a man,
Who dares do more is none.
                                Shakespeare.

The aids to noble life are all within.
                                Matthew Arnold.

Time, that should enrich the noble mind,
Neglected, leaves a dreary waste behind.
                                Cowper.

Other men's sins we ever bear in mind;
None sees the fardel of his faults behind.
                                Herrick.

Care to our coffin adds a nail, no doubt,
And every grin, so merry, draws one out.
                                Dr. Wolcot.

Angry looks can do no good,
    And blows are dealt in blindness;
Words are better understood
If spoken but in kindness.
                                Burbridge.

Any one who can say "Shoes and socks shock Susan," with rapidity and faultless pronunciation four times running, may claim a large reward.

ON WOODHULL'S CAMPAIGN
"You might as well have the undressed women of North Street on stage there."
—the Governor of Massachusetts

·- POETRY AND ANECDOTES -·

ON VICTORIA WOODHULL'S CANDIDACY

Gibbery, gibbery, gab,
The women had a confab,
And demanded the rights
To wear the tights
Gibbery, gibbery, gab.

—Horace Greeley

FROM THE 1872 ALMANAC

VICTORIA CLAFLIN WOODHULL   *Mathew B. Brady   From the photograph in the New-York Historical Society, New York*

TRUE BEAUTY.

He that loves a rosy cheek,
    Or a coral lip admires,
Or from star-like eyes doth seek
    Fuel to maintain his fires,
So his flames must waste away.
But a smooth and steadfast mind,
    Gentle thoughts and calm desires,
Hearts with equal love combined,
    Kindle never-dying fires:
Where these are not, I despise
    Lovely cheeks, or lips, or eyes.
                    T. CAREW, 1589-1639.

VARIETIES.—Look most to your spending. No matter what comes in, if more goes out you will always be poor. The art is not in making money, but in keeping of it: little expenses, like mice in a barn, when they are many, make great waste. Hair by hair heads get bald; straw by straw the roof goes off the cottage; and drop by drop the rain comes into the chamber. A barrel is soon empty if the tap leaks but a drop a moment.

DON'T WORRY.

Either grief will not come ; or, if it must,
    Do not forecast:
And while it cometh, it is almost past.
    Away distrust;
My God hath promised ; he is just.
                    GEO. HERBERT.

TAKING HIS TIME.—A Scotchman, who had hired himself to a farmer, had a cheese set down before him, that he might help himself. The master had occasion to remark some time afterwards, "Sandy, you take a long time to breakfast." "In truth, master," answered he, "a cheese o' this size is nae sae soon eaten as ye may think!"

It is no great matter to associate with the good and gentle; for this is naturally pleasing to all, and every one willingly enjoyeth peace, and loveth those best that agree with him. But to be able to live peaceably with hard and perverse persons, or with the disorderly, or with such as go contrary to us, is a great grace, and a most commendable and manly thing.—THOMAS A KEMPIS.

VESPERS.

That which the gairish day had lost,
    The twilight vigil brings,—
While softlier the vesper bell
    Its silver cadence rings,—
The sense of an immortal trust,
    The hush of angel wings !

Drop down behind the solemn hills,
    O Day, with golden skies !
Serene above its fading glow
    Night, starry-crowned, arise !
So beautiful may heaven be
    When life's last sunbeam dies !
                    MISS C. M. PACKARD.

STICK TO IT.

. . . "Therefore, if any young man has embarked his life in the pursuit of knowledge, let him go on without doubting or fearing the event; let him not be intimidated by the cheerless beginnings of knowledge, by the darkness from which she springs, by the difficulties which hover around her, by the wretched habitation in which she dwells, by the want and sorrow which sometimes journey in her train. But let him ever follow her as an angel that guards him, and as the genius of his life. She will bring him out at last into the light of day, and exhibit him to the world, comprehensive in acquirement, fertile in resources, rich in imagination, strong in reasoning, prudent and powerful above his fellows in all the relations and in all the offices of life."—SYDNEY SMITH.

LIFE AND DEATH.

Life ! I know not what thou art,
But know that thou and I must part;
And when, or how, or where we met,
I own to me's a secret yet.
Life ! we've been long together,
Through pleasant and through cloudy
        weather,
'Tis hard to part when friends are dear;
Perhaps 'twill cost a sigh, a tear.
Then steal away, give little warning,
Choose thine own time;
Say not good night, but in some brighter
        clime,
Bid me good morning.
                    MRS. BARBAULD.

A HEALTHY FRUIT.—A lazy dyspeptic was bewailing his own misfortunes, and speaking with a friend on the latter's hearty appearance. "What do you do to make you so strong and healthy ?" inquired the dyspeptic. "Live on fruit alone," answered the friend. "What kind of fruit ?" "The fruit of industry ; and I am never troubled with indigestion."

TRUE FREEDOM.

Stone walls do not a prison make,
    Nor iron bars a cage;
Minds innocent and quiet take
    That for a hermitage.
If I have freedom in my love,
    And in my soul am free,
Angels alone that soar above
    Enjoy such liberty.
                    R. LOVELACE, 1618-1658.

KEEP COOL.—Don't keep in a constant fret about things that may be annoying, or worry about things you can't help. Troubles are not lightened by fretting. The true remedy is to keep cool, and try to master difficulties, and not let them master you.

I will listen to any one's convictions, but pray keep your doubts to yourself.—GOETHE.

Stone Walls Do Not a Prison Make

TRUE FREEDOM

Stone walls do not a prison make,
    Nor iron bars a cage;
Minds innocent and quiet take
    That for a hermitage.

KEEP COOL

Don't keep in a constant fret about things that may be annoying, or worry about things you can't help. Troubles are not lightened by fretting. The true remedy is to keep cool, and try to master difficulties, and not let them master you.

FROM THE
1875
ALMANAC

I Always Murmur...
..Yet, I Never Weep

FLOWERS WITHOUT FRUIT.

PRUNE thou thy words, the thoughts
control,
That o'er thee swell and throng:
They will condense within thy soul,
And change to purpose strong.

But he who lets his feelings run
In soft, luxurious flow,
Shrinks when hard service must be done,
And faints at every woe.

Faith's meanest deed more favor bears,
Where hearts and wills are weighed,
Than brightest transports, choicest
prayers,
That bloom their hour and fade.
J. H. NEWMAN.

A TRAVELLER, on his arrival in the city, stopped for a moment to examine a coat hanging in front of a clothing-store, when the proprietor rushed out, and asked, "Wouldn't you try on some coats?" "I dunno but I would," responded the traveller, consulting his time-killer; and he went in and began to work. No matter how often he found his fit, he called for more coats, and after he had tried on thirty, he looked at his watch, again resumed his own garment, and walked off, saying, "I won't charge a cent for what I've done. If I'm ever around this way again, and you've got any more coats to try on, I'll do all I can to help you."

A SCHOOL-BOY, being requested to write a composition upon the subject of "Pins," produced the following : "Pins are very useful. They have saved the lives of many men, women, and children, in fact, whole families." "How so?" asked the puzzled teacher; and the boy replied, "Why, by not swallowing them." This matches the story of the other boy, who defined salt as "the stuff that makes potatoes taste bad when you don't put on any."

JOSH BILLINGS was asked, "How fast does sound travel?" His idea is, that it depends a good deal upon the noise you are talking about. "The sound of a dinner-horn, for instance, travels half a mile in a second, while an invitashun tew get up in the morning I have known to be three quarters uv an hour going two pairs uv stairs, and then not hev strength enuff left to be heard."

A POLITICIAN, in writing a letter of condolence to the widow of a deceased member of the legislature, says, "I cannot tell you how pained I was to hear that your husband had gone to heaven. We were bosom friends; but now we shall never meet again."

IF your neighbor's hens are troublesome,
And steal across the way,
Don't let your angry passions rise,
But fix a place for them to lay.

ANSWERS TO ENIGMAS, CONUNDRUMS, &c., IN LAST YEAR'S ALMANAC.

ANSWERS TO ENIGMAS. —
1. Hay.   2. Cod.

ANSWER TO CHARADE.—Peerless.

ANSWER TO GEOMETRICAL QUESTION.—Six circles will enclose another circle of equal radius. For only six equilateral triangles can be constructed around the centre of the inner circle as an apex. Each side of the triangle will be twice the radius of the given circle.

ANSWER TO PROBLEM. — The unlucky hatter lost $42 and the hat.

ANSWERS TO CONUNDRUMS.
1. Your *mother*.
2. A *ditch*.
3. What does Y E S spell?
4. When they make 22.
5. Just before *eve*.

ENIGMAS.
1.
I always murmur, yet I never weep;
I always lie in bed, yet never sleep;
My mouth is wide, and larger than my head,
And much disgorges, though 'tis never fed.
I have no legs nor feet, yet swiftly run,
And the more falls I get, move faster on.
2.
Enough for one, too much for two, and nothing at all for three.

CHARADES.
1.
My *first* is tall, and lean, and thin,
My *second* once was Eve,
My *whole* smokes on the farmer's board;
'Tis not of sheep or beeve.

Rich, brown, and luscious, tender fare
For every worthy soul;
You and your *second*, when you dine,
Should never *first* my *whole*.
2.
If you are able to do my *first* as well as my *second* can, you will soon be a good player at my *whole*.
3.
In my *first*, my *second* sat; my *third* and *fourth* I ate.

LOGOGRAPH.
Take away one letter, and I murder: take away two, and I am dying, if the whole does not save me.

GEOMETRICAL PROBLEM.
A pavement is to be formed of tiles of the same regular figure. Show what are the only figures that can be used.

CONUNDRUMS.
1. What makes all women alike?
2. What word is that to which, if you add a syllable, it will make it shorter?
3. Why does a miller wear a white hat?
4. Which letter of the alphabet is most useful to a deaf old woman?

I ALWAYS MURMUR
—An Enigma—

I always murmur, yet I never weep
I always lie in bed, yet never sleep;
My mouth is wide, and larger than my head,
And much disgorges, though 'tis never fed.

I have no legs nor feet, yet swiftly run,
And the more falls I get, move faster on.

YOUR NEIGHBOR'S HENS
If your neighbor's hens are troublesome,
And steal across the way,
Don't let your angry passions rise,
But fix a place for them to lay.

POETRY AND ANECDOTES

FROM THE
1879
ALMANAC

An Honest Man is the Noblest Work of God

WHAT SHALL I TEACH MY CHILD?

Teach him that:
It is better to die
  than to lie;
It is better to starve
  than to steal;
It is better to be a scavenger
  or a woodchopper;
Than to be an idler
  and dead-beat;
That labor is the price
Of all honest possessions,
That an honest man
Is the noblest work of God.

POETRY, ANECDOTES, &C.

LABOR.

Ho! ye who at the anvil toil,
  And strike the sounding blow,
Where from the burning iron's breast
  The sparks fly to and fro,
While answering to the hammer's ring
  And fire's intenser glow, —
Oh! while ye feel 'tis hard to toil
  And sweat the long day through,
Remember it is harder still
  To have no work to do.

Ho! ye who till the stubborn soil,
  Whose hard hands guide the plough,
Who bend beneath the summer sun,
  With burning cheek and brow, —
Ye deem the curse still clings to earth
  From olden time till now;
But while ye feel 'tis hard to toil
  And labor all day through,
Remember,.it is harder still
  To have no work to do.

Ho! all who labor — all who strive —
  Ye wield a lofty power:
Do with your might, do with your
    strength:
  Fill every golden hour!
The glorious privilege to do
  Is man's most noble dower.
Oh! to your birthright and yourselves,
  To your own souls be true!
A weary, wretched life is theirs
  Who have no work to do.
                    CAROLINE F. ORNE.

DESPATCH OF BUSINESS.

BEWARE of stumbling over a propensity which easily besets you from not having your time fully employed, — I mean what the women call *dawdling.* Your motto must be, *Hoc age* (Do this). Do instantly whatever is to be done, and take the hours of recreation after business, never before it. When a regiment is under march, the rear is often thrown into confusion because the front does not move steadily and without interruption. It is the same with business. If that which is first in hand is not instantly, steadily, and regularly dispatched, other things accumulate behind, till affairs begin to press all at once, and no human brain can stand the confusion.
                    SIR WALTER SCOTT.

PERISH policy and cunning,
  Perish all that fears the light;
Whether losing, whether winning,
  Trust in God, and do the right.

WHAT TO TEACH A CHILD.

WHAT shall I teach my child? Teach him that it is better to die than to lie; that it is better to starve than to steal; that it is better to be a scavenger or wood-chopper than to be an idler and dead-beat; that labor is the price of all honest possessions; that no one is exempt from the obligation to labor with head, or hands, or heart; that "an honest man is the noblest work of God;" that knowledge is power; that labor is worship, and idleness is sin; that it is better to eat the crust of independent poverty than to luxuriate amid the richest viands as a dependant. Teach him these facts till they are woven into his being and regulate his life, and we will insure his success, though the heavens fall.

THE WOMAN.

NOT as all other women are
  Is she that to my soul is dear;
Her glorious fancies come from far,
  Beneath the silver evening star;
  And yet her heart is ever near.

Great feelings hath she of her own,
  Which lesser souls may never know;
God giveth them to her alone,
And sweet they are as any tone
  Wherewith the wind may choose to
    blow.

Yet in herself she dwelleth not,
  Although no home were half so fair;
No simplest duty is forgot;
Life hath no dim and lowly spot
  That doth not in her sunshine share.

She doeth little kindnesses,
  Which most leave undone or de-
    spise;
For naught that sets one heart at ease,
And giveth happiness or peace,
  Is low esteemed in her eyes.

She hath no scorn of common things;
  And, though she seem of other birth,
Round us her heart entwines and
    clings,
And patiently she folds her wings,
  To tread the humble paths of earth.
                    JAMES RUSSELL LOWELL.

NEATNESS is a point in minor morals which deserves much more attention than it receives. There is such a comfort in order and tidy habits, that as a source of refined pleasure they should be taught, encouraged, and persisted in.

THE DEFINITION OF "DAWDLING"

". . . stumbling over a propensity which easily besets you from not having your time fully employed."
SIR WALTER SCOTT

POETRY AND ANECDOTES

FROM THE
1883
ALMANAC

Do White Sheep Furnish More Wool Than Black Ones?

(see next page for answer to all charades, enigmas and conundrums on this page)

DO IT NOW.

If ever you find yourself where you have so many things pressing upon you that you hardly know how to begin, let me tell you a secret: take hold of the first one that comes to hand, and you will find the rest all fall into file, and follow after, like a company of well-drilled soldiers; and though work may be hard to meet when it charges in a squad it is easily vanquished if you can bring it into line. You have often seen the anecdote of the man who was asked how he had accomplished so much in his life? "My father taught me," was the reply, "when I had anything to do, to go and do it." There is a secret — the word *now*.

AWAY, THOU VAIN PHILOSOPHY.

Away, haunt thou not me.
　Thou vain Philosophy!
Little hast thou bestead,
Save to perplex the head,
And leave the spirit dead,
Unto thy broken cisterns wherefore go,
While from the secret treasure-depths
　below,
Fed by the skyey shower,
And clouds that sink and rest on hill-
　tops high,
Wisdom at once, and Power,
Are welling, bubbling forth, unseen,
　incessantly!
Why labor at the dull mechanic oar,
When the fresh breeze is blowing,
And the strong current flowing,
Right onward to the Eternal Shore?
　　　　　　　A. H. CLOUGH.

WIT AND HUMOR.

The farmer's surest speculations will be in live stock and ploughshares.

A Protestant bishop was declaiming to a Roman Catholic on the folly of a belief in purgatory. "My Lord," was the reply, "you may go farther and fare worse."

A father fearing an earthquake in the region of his home, sent his two boys to a distant friend's until the peril should be over. A few weeks after the father received this letter from his friend: "Please take your boys home and send down the earthquake."

A certain doctor going to visit one of his sick patients, asked him how he had rested during the night. "Oh, wondrous ill, sir," replied he, "for mine eyes have not come together these three nights." "What is the reason of that?" said the other. "Alas! sir," says he, "because my nose was betwixt them."

Lord Cockburn was seated one day on the hillside of Bonally with a Scotch shepherd, and observing the sheep reposing in the coldest situation, he observed to him, "John, if I were a sheep I would lie on the other side of the hill." The shepherd answered, "Ay, my lord, but if ye had been a sheep ye wad have had mair sense."

A cockney tourist met with a Scotch lassie going barefoot toward Glasgow. "Lassie," said he, "I should like to know if all the people in this part go barefooted?" "Part of 'em do, and the rest of 'em mind their own business," was the reply.

ANSWERS TO CHARADES, ENIGMAS, ETC., IN LAST YEAR'S ALMANACK.

ANSWERS TO CHARADES.

1. Penmanship.
2. Leap-frog.
3. Hap-hazard.

ANSWERS TO ENIGMAS.

1. The letter O.
2. Eye.

ANSWERS TO CONUNDRUMS.

1. It grows *down*.
2. Because he is above committing a bad action.
3. Adriatic (a dry attic).
4. Plague—ague.

CHARADES.

1. My *whole* is my second,
　My *whole* saves my *first*;
My *first* can be taken
　By hunger or thirst.

2. The beginning of eternity.
　The end of time and space;
The beginning of every end,
　And the end of every place.

3. My *third* are sometimes my *whole*, their occupation being to catch my *first*.

ENIGMAS.

1. The schoolboy likes me well,
For healthful sport I bring,
Yet I can harm create,
Though such a little thing;
Connubial bliss is formed by me,
My nature is equality.

2. Emblem of innocence and truth,
Too soon, alas, I fade!
Pure and unspotted as the truth
　Though of two falsehoods made.

CONUNDRUMS.

1. Why do white sheep furnish more wool than black ones?

2. What two letters make a county in Massachusetts?

3. Why is Ireland likely to become very rich?

4. What most resembles a cat in a hole?

5. What is that which lives in winter, dies in summer, and grows with its root upward?

DO IT NOW!

"If ever you find yourself where you have so many things pressing upon you that you hardly know how to begin, let me tell you a secret: take hold of the first one that comes to hand, and you will find the rest all fall into file."

FROM THE
1884
ALMANAC

DON'T WORRY ABOUT THE FUTURE.

Do not disturb thyself by thinking of the whole of thy life. Let not thy thoughts at once embrace all the various troubles which thou mayest expect to befall thee; but on every occasion ask thyself: "What is there in this which is intolerable and past bearing?" For thou wilt be ashamed to confess.

In the next place, remember that neither the future nor the past pains thee, but only the present. But this is reduced to a very little, if thou only circumscribest it, and chidest thy mind, if it is unable to hold out against even this. MARCUS ANTONINUS.

WIT AND HUMOR.

JUMP IN.—A dandy, wishing to be witty, accosted an old rag-man as follows: "You take all sorts of old trumpery in your cart, don't you?" "Yes, jump in, jump in!"

TOO LONG TO WAIT.—"When are you going to make me that pair of new boots I ordered?" asked a fop of his shoemaker. "When you pay for the last pair I made for you." "Whew! I can't wait so long as that!"

THE HAT STORY.—It is time the hat story was set a-going again. It is quite simple and the answer plain, but in a company of half a dozen you will probably get three different answers and you may get four or five. This is the story: —A man came in to a hat store and bought a hat for seven dollars and a half. In payment he offered a fifty-dollar bill. The hatter, not having so much money by him, took it to a neighbor, got it changed, and gave his customer the balance due him, with which and with his hat he departed in good humor. Soon after in comes the hatter's neighbor with the fifty-dollar bill, which has proved to be a counterfeit, demanding good money for it. Finding no help for it, the hatter is obliged to pay this demand. The question is: What is the hatter's loss?

THE CARDINAL.—Cardinal Manning relates this incident. One night I met a poor man carrying a basket and smoking a pipe. I thought over this: He who smokes gets thirsty; he who is thirsty desires to drink; he who drinks too much gets drunk; he who gets drunk endangers his soul. This man is in danger of mortal sin. Let us save him. I affectionately addressed him:—
"Are you a Catholic?"
"I am, thanks be to God."
"Where are you from?"
"From Cork, your reverence."
"Are you a member of the total abstinence society?"
"No, your reverence."
"Now," said I, "that is very wrong. Look at me; I am a member."
"Faith, may be your reverence has need of it."
I shook hands with him and left him.

ANSWERS TO CHARADES, ENIGMAS, ETC., IN LAST YEAR'S ALMANACK.

ANSWERS TO CHARADES.
1. Life-boat.
2. The letter E.
3. Fishermen.

ANSWERS TO ENIGMAS.
1. Match.   2. Lily.

ANSWERS TO CONUNDRUMS.
1. Because there are more of them.
2. S. X. (Essex).
3. Because its capital is always *doubling* (Dublin).
4. A cat *out of* a hole.
5. An icicle.

CHARADES.

1. My *first* is a name oft borne by my *second*;
And a noisy girl my *whole* is reckoned.

2. Safe on my fair one's arm my *first* may rest,
And raise no tumult in a lover's breast;
My *second* does the want of legs supply
To those that neither creep, nor walk, nor fly;
My *whole*'s a rival to the fairest toast,
And when it's most admired it suffers most.

3. I sent my *second* to my *first*, but many a *whole* passed ere I saw him again.

ENIGMA.

Formed half beneath and half above the earth,
We, sisters, owe to art a second birth;
The smiths' and carpenters' adopted daughters,
Made on the earth to travel o'er the waters;
Swifter we move, as tighter we are bound,
Yet neither touch the water, air, nor ground;
We serve the poor for use, the rich for whim,
Sink when it rains, and when it freezes swim.

PROVERB.

(Each line contains one word of a well-known proverb.)
Faint not should sorrow thee assail;
Your heart keep always right;
In danger never quake nor quail,
Strive till you've won the fight;
And fair let all your dealings be,
Show to a lady courtesy.

CONUNDRUMS.

1. How many sticks go to the building of a crow's nest?
2. Why is the letter N like a hot summer day?
3. Why is a baker a most improvident man?
4. What is that which occurs once in a minute, twice in a moment, and not once in a thousand years?

ANSWERS TO CHARADES, ENIGMAS AND CONUNDRUMS

Charades: 1. Tom-boy
2. Muff, Fin-Muffin
3. Season
Enigma: Skates (make of wood and iron).
Conundrums:
1. Not any, They are all carried.
2. Because it makes ice nice.
3. Because he sells what he needs (kneads) himself.
4. The letter M.

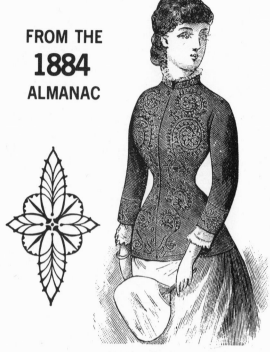

BE NATURAL.

It was not very long before I made two very useful discoveries: first, that all mankind were not solely employed in observing me (a belief that all young people have); and next, that shamming was of no use; that the world was very clear-sighted, and soon estimated a man at his just value. This cured me, and I determined to be natural, and let the world find me out.

SYDNEY SMITH.

SHE WAS A PHANTOM OF DELIGHT.

She was a phantom of delight
When first she gleamed upon my sight;
A lovely Apparition, sent
To be a moment's ornament;
Her eyes as stars of Twilight fair;
Like Twilight's, too, her dusky hair;
But all things else about her drawn,
From May-time and the cheerful dawn;
A dancing shape, an image gay,
To haunt, to startle, and waylay.

I saw her upon nearer view,
A Spirit, yet a Woman, too!
Her household motions light and free,
And steps of virgin liberty;
A countenance in which did meet
Sweet records, promises as sweet;
A creature not too bright or good
For human nature's daily food;
For transient sorrows, simple wiles,
Praise, blame, love, kisses, tears, and smiles.

And now I see with eye serene
The very pulse of the machine;
A Being breathing thoughtful breath,
A Traveller between life and death;
The reason firm, the temperate will,
Endurance, foresight, strength, and skill;
A perfect woman, nobly planned,
To warn, to comfort, and command;
And yet a Spirit still, and bright
With something of an angel light.

W. WORDSWORTH.

BOOKS.

Consider what you have in the smallest chosen library. A company of the wisest and wittiest men that could be picked out of all civil countries, in a thousand years, have set in best order the results of their learning and wisdom. The men themselves were hid and inaccessible, solitary, impatient of interruption, fenced by etiquette; but the thought which they did not uncover to their bosom friend is here written out in transparent words to us, the strangers of another age. EMERSON.

The great principle of being happy in this world is not to be affected with small things.

Polite behavior and refined address, like good pictures, make the least show to ordinary eyes.

Magnanimity is not to be disturbed by anything.

SIR JOSHUA REYNOLDS.

WORDS OF WISDOM FROM GOETHE.

RULE OF LIFE.

Would'st thou be a happy liver?
Let the past be past forever!
Fret not, when prigs and pedants bore you;
Enjoy the good that's set before you;
But chiefly hate no man; the rest
Leave thou to God, who knows what's best.

KNOWLEDGE OF MEN.

No man fears men, but he who knows them not;
And he who shuns them may not hope to know them.

THE WISDOM OF LIFE.

Use well the moment: what the hour
Brings for thy use is in thy power;
And what thou best canst understand,
Is just the thing lies nearest to thy hand.

GOETHE.

FAITHFUL IN LITTLE THINGS.

The Searcher of all hearts may make as ample a trial of you in your conduct to one poor dependent as of the man who is appointed to lead armies and administer provinces. Nay, your treatment of some animal entrusted to your care may be a history as significant for you as the chronicles of kings for them. The moral experiments of the world may be tried with the smallest quantities.

HELPS.

LOVE OF COUNTRY.

Breathes there a man, with soul so dead,
Who never to himself hath said,
This is my own, my native land!
Whose heart hath ne'er within him burned,
As home his footsteps he hath turned,
From wand'ring on a foreign strand!
If such there breathe, go, mark him well;
For him no minstrel raptures swell;
High though his titles, proud his name,
Boundless his wealth as wish can claim;
Despite those titles, power, and pelf,
The wretch concentred all in self,
Living, shall forfeit fair renown,
And, doubly dying, shall go down
To the vile dust from whence he sprung,
Unwept, unhonored, and unsung.

SIR WALTER SCOTT.

A man is a pedant, who, having been brought up among books, is able to talk of nothing else. The same of a soldier, lawyer, painter, etc.

Humility is not to despise anything, especially mankind.

SIR JOSHUA REYNOLDS.

Two ears and but a single tongue
By Nature's law to man belong!
The lesson she would teach is clear—
"Repeat but half of what you hear."

—From the Persian of Hafiz.

FROM THE 1884 ALMANAC

Is Not Victoria, Empress of India?

Writing to California suffragette and labor organizer, Marietta Stow, in the early 1880s, Belva Ann Lockwood observed that despite the legal disenfranchisement of women, there were no laws prohibiting women from seeking elected office. "Why not nominate women for important places?" Mrs. Lockwood asked. "Is not Victoria Empress of India? Have we not among our countrywomen persons of as much talent and ability? Is not history full of precedents of women rulers?"

With these words, Mrs. Lockwood unwittingly opened the way to becoming the second woman to run for president. Inspired by her correspondent's observations, Mrs. Stow banded with other suffragettes in her state to organize the National Equal Rights Party and, in 1884, was chairman of the San Francisco convention where party delegates unanimously nominated Mrs. Lockwood as their first candidate for president.

FROM THE
1886
ALMANAC

Tom Telltruth Vs. Crafty Charlie

BE LIKE A CLOCK

Let your face and hands, like the church clock, always tell how your inner works are going. Better be laughed at as Tom Telltruth than be praised as Crafty Charlie. Plaindealing may bring us trouble, but it is better than shuffling.

* * *

"Only the actions of the just smell sweet, and blossom in their dust."

* * *

"It is refreshing, in these days of speculation and dishonest dealings to know that a man can live according to principles and yet make money. It shows that honesty and business can go hand in hand."

GOOD BUSINESS RULES.

Business men, especially those who are thorough, prompt, and methodical, are guided by certain elementary principles. In some cases these principles are formulated into simple rules, which cover even the details of conduct.

A prominent banker attributes his success in business to the care with which he has obeyed these plain rules:

Take time for eating, sleeping, and digestion. Don't worry. Be satisfied with your work after doing it well.

Never ask another to do what you ought to attend to personally.

Shun the slightest appearance of dishonesty as you would shun the plague.

Always meet your appointments on time; never late; if possible, not much ahead of the moment.

Don't talk too much: let your actions speak for yourself.

Be honest, even if you lose money by it.

Never let business interfere with home duties.

Remember that money alone cannot buy peace, nor true friends, nor a loving family.

It is refreshing, in these days of speculation and dishonest dealings to know that a man can live according to the above principles and yet make money. It shows that honesty and business can go hand in hand.

UPRIGHTNESS.

Depend upon it, friends, if a straight line will not pay, a crooked one won't. What is got by shuffling is very dangerous gain. It may give a moment's peace to wear a mask, but deception will come home to you and bring sorrow with it. Honesty is the best policy. Be as true as steel. Let your face and hands, like the church clock, always tell how your inner works are going. Better be laughed at as Tom Telltruth than be praised as Crafty Charlie. Plaindealing may bring us trouble, but it is better than shuffling.

JOHN PLOUGHMAN'S TALK.

CARING FOR YOUR EYES.

Keep a shade on your lamp or gas-burner.

Avoid all sudden changes between light and darkness.

Never begin to read, write, or sew for several minutes after coming from darkness to a bright light.

Never read by twilight or moonlight.

Never read or sew directly in front of the light, window, or door.

It is best to let the light fall from above obliquely, over the left shoulder.

Never sleep so that, on first awaking, the eyes shall open on the light of a window.

Do not use the eyesight by light so scant that it requires an effort to discriminate.

The moment you are instinctively prompted to rub your eyes, that moment stop using them.

SOCIETY IN NATURAL OBJECTS.

I experienced sometimes that the most sweet and tender, the most innocent and encouraging society may be found in any natural object, even for the poor misanthrope and most melancholy man. There can be no very black melancholy to him who lives in the midst of nature and has his senses still. There was never yet such a storm but it was Æolian music to a healthy and innocent ear. Nothing can rightly compel a simple and brave man to a vulgar sadness. While I enjoy the friendship of the seasons, I trust that nothing can make life a burden to me. The gentle rain which waters my beans, and keeps me in the house to-day, is not drear and melancholy, but good for me too. Though it prevents my hoeing them, it is of far more worth than my hoeing. If it should continue so long as to rot in the ground and destroy the potatoes in the low-lands, it would still be good for the grass on the uplands, and, being good for the grass, it would be good for me.

THOREAU.

THE HEALTH OF CHILDREN.

The health of children depends very much on their mental condition and freedom from strain. The former ought to be easy and happy, and the latter an unknown quantity, at all events until they are seven years old. Consequently mothers and nurses ought to strive to avoid all unnecessary irritation and thwarting of the small people committed to their keeping, and this commands much self-control and suppression of their own worries and weaknesses. The child who is always contradicted is likely to be either contradictory or spiritless, according to its temperament; and neither of these states of mind is conducive to health, while the one who is looked upon as a nuisance is likely to become so in reality. But the child who is comfortably clothed and fed, and has plenty of amusement of a wholesome kind, is pretty sure to be innocently happy, and this serene frame of mind is the very thing productive of robust health.

EVANGELICAL MESSENGER.

MENTAL CULTURE.

Life is certainly not worth living if it has nothing better to bring than the excitement of business and wealth. It is a very low motive to urge upon a boy — the neglect of mental culture in order to obtain wealth.

LOVE.

Vain is the glory of the sky,
The beauty vain of field and grove,
Unless, while with admiring eye
We gaze, we also learn to love.

WORDSWORTH.

Only the actions of the just
Smell sweet, and blossom in their dust.

J. SHIRLEY.

FROM THE
1889
ALMANAC

I Don'd Vas Preaching Voman's Righdts

"Budt I vants to gondradict dot shap
Dot made dis leedle shoke:
"A voman vas der glingling vine,
Und man der·shturdy oak."

THE WELL BRED GIRL—WHAT SHE DOES NOT DO.

There are some things that a well bred young lady never does.

She never turns round to gaze at any one when walking on the street.

She never accepts a seat from a gentleman in a street car without thanking him.

She never snubs other young ladies even if they happen to be less popular or well favored than herself.

She never laughs or talks loudly in public places.

She never wears clothing so singular or striking as to attract particular attention in public.

She never speaks slightingly of her mother, and says she "don't care whether her behavior meets with maternal approbation or not."

THE DUTY OF HAPPINESS.

I have fallen into the hands of thieves —what then? They have left me the sun and moon, fire and water, a loving wife and many friends to pity me, and some to relieve me, and I can still discourse; and unless I list, they have not taken away my merry countenance and my cheerful spirit and a good conscience. . . . And he that hath so many causes of joy, and so great, is very much in love with sorrow and peevishness who loses all these pleasures, and chooses to sit down on his little handful of thorns.
JER. TAYLOR.

THE DUKE OF MARLBOROUGH AND HIS TEMPER.—There is an anecdote told of the Duke, that, riding one day with the Prince Eugene, a storm of rain came on, and they sent for their cloaks. Prince Eugene received his immediately. Marlborough's servant did not appear for some time. The Duke asking why he did not bring the cloak before, the answer was sulkily given: "I came as soon as I could." The Duke turned to Prince Eugene and said, "Now, I would not have that fellow's temper for the whole world."
TEMPLE BAR.

WIT AND HUMOR.

A CLEAR CASE.—"My case is just here," said a citizen to a lawyer. "The plaintiff will swear that I hit him. I will swear that I did not. Now, what can you lawyers make out of that if we go to trial?" "A hundred dollars, easy," was the reply.

REST AND CHANGE.—"Rest and change are good," said the wife as she rose in the night to rifle her husband's pockets. "I've had a rest and now I think I'll have a little change."

A MONEYED MAN WANTED.—A strong-minded woman was heard to remark, the other day, that she would marry a man who had plenty of money, though he was so ugly she had to scream every time she looked at him.

DER OAK UND DER VINE.

I don'd vas preaching voman's righdts,
Or any ding like dot,
Und I likes to see all beoples
Shust gondented mit dheir lot,
Budt I vants to gondradict dot shap
Dot made dis leedle shoke:
"A voman vas der glinging vine,
Und man der shturdy oak."

Berhaps, somedimes, dot may be drue,
Budt, den dimes oudt off nine,
I find me oudt dot man himself
Vas been der glinging vine;
Und vhen hees friendts dhey all vas gone,
Und he vas shust "tead proke,"
Dot's vhen der voman shteps righdt in,
Und been der shturdy oak.

Shust go oup to der paseball groundts
Und see dhose "shturdy oaks"
All planted roundt upon der seats—
Shust hear dheir laughs und shokes!
Dhen see dhose vomens at der tubs,
Mit glothes oudt on der lines,
Vhich vas der shturdy oaks, mine friendts,
Und vhich der glinging vines?

Vhen sickness in der householdt comes,
Und veeks und veeks he shtays,
Who vas id fighdts him mitoudt resdt,
Dhose veary nighdts und days?
Who beace und gomfort alvays prings,
Und cools dot fefered prow?
More like id vas der tender vine
Dot oak he glings to now.

In helt und sickness, shoy und pain,
In calm or shtormy veddher,
'Tvas beddher dot dhose oaks und vines
Should alvays gling togeddher.
CHARLES FOLLEN ADAMS.

A UNANIMOUS OPINION.—Lovers are prone to self-depreciation. Said he, tenderly, as they sat looking at the stars: "I do not understand what you can see in me that you love me." "That's what everybody says!" gurgled the ingenuous maiden. Then the silence became so deep that you could hear the stars twinkling.

DOMESTIC ANXIETIES.—"I feel so tired every night, John," said a farmer's wife, as she took up her darning after the day's work was done. "My bones ache, and I have fits of dizziness, and no appetite; and I'm worried, too, about the heifer, John. When I was feeding the stock to-night she acted very strangely, and refused to eat. I'm afraid she's going to die."

"Yes," said John, with an anxious look upon his face, "I'm worried about that heifer myself."

A CRACK SHOT.—"I never shot a bird in my life," said a fellow to his friend, who replied: "For my part, I never shot anything in the shape of a bird except a squirrel, which I killed with a stone, when it fell into the river and was drowned."

CLEVELAND RIBBON (SMITHSONIAN)
Used in 1888 campaign. He was defeated.
Led Democrats again in 1892 and won.
CAMPAIGN RIBBON

POETRY AND ANECDOTES

De Human Heart Am Like a Wallet

DE HUMAN HEART

"De human heart am like a wallet. It often gets low down. Kind words am its cash capital. De mo' capital it has, de harder it tries to make spring outer winter an' sunshine outer gloom an' sorrer."

On a controlled, passionate man:
"He thought worse than he spoke."

On a verbose, angry man:
"He spoke worse than he thought."

POETRY AND PROSE.

CROSSING THE BAR.

SUNSET and evening star,
  And one clear call for me!
And may there be no moaning of the bar,
  When I put out to sea,

But such a tide as moving seems asleep,
  Too full for sound and foam,
When that which drew from out the
  boundless deep
  Turns again home.

Twilight and evening bell,
  And after that the dark!
And may there be no sadness of fare-
  well,
  When I embark;

For tho' from out our bourne of Time
  and Place
The flood may bear me far,
I hope to see my Pilot face to face
  When I have crossed the bar.
                    TENNYSON.

OUR OWN.

IF I had known in the morning
  How wearily all the day
The words unkind would trouble my
  mind,
  That I said when you went away,
I had been more careful, darling,
  Nor given you needless pain;
But we vex our own with look and tone
  We may never take back again.

For though in the quiet evening
  You may give me the kiss of peace,
Yet it well might be, that never for me
  The pain of the heart should cease!
How many go forth at morning,
  Who never come home at night!
And hearts have broken for harsh words
  spoken,
  That sorrow can ne'er set right.

We have careful thought for the stran-
  ger,
  And smiles for the sometime guest;
But oft for our own the bitter tone,
  Though we love our own the best.
Ah! lips with the curve impatient,
  Ah! brow with the shade of scorn
'Twere a cruel fate, were the night too
  late
To undo the work of the morn!
                    MARGARET E. SANGSTER.

TWO KINDS.

LORD BACON was wont to say of a passionate man, who suppressed his anger, "That he thought worse than he spoke;" and he said of an angry man, who vented his passion in words, "That he spoke worse than he thought."

PLEASANT WORDS.

"I DOAN' believe," began the old man, as he crumpled up a leaf of tobacco to fill his pipe; "I doan' believe dat a sartin' amount of flattery eber hurt anybody. I know dat Poo' Richard an' a hundred others have tole us to bewar' of folks dat flatter, but ole as I ar', an' homely as I be, I sometimes kinder long fur somebody to say dat I'm lookin' young for one o' my age, or dat I'm holdin' up wonderfully well considerin' dat I've been blode up on a steamboat, fell outer a tree, wrecked on de lake, shot in de army, an' had de small-pox.

"When I crawls out on de doorstep of a mawnin', feelin' ole an' blue an' used up, an' long comes Parseverance Jones an' calls out 'Hello!' an' says I ze got de biggest wood-pile in town, an' folks am all talkin' 'bout our buyin' a seven-dollar bedstead, an' dat de boys want me to run fur offis, why, sah, it limbers me up like a bottle of liniment: my cloze doan' look half so bad, de ole woman seems ten y'ars younger, an' I begin to look aroun' to see how much it would cost fur a silver doah-plate on de front doah.

"It's the same wid de ole woman," continued the elder as he filled his pipe. "She's ole, an' gray, an' about worn out wid hard work, an' yit when I say to her dat she can roast a 'possum a little de nicest of any woman in de country, an' dat she am young 'nuff to look for a second husband, you doan' know how she chirks up.

"An' it's jest so wid my naburs. When Deakun Jackson gits sorter 'shamed of his ole cloze, an' he sots on a log by de gate an' wonders what's de use of a poo' man tryin' to git 'long, I slips out and tells him dat I nebber see sich cabbages as he grows; dat his ole hoss am pickin' up; dat his chill'en am comin' up genteel; dat he orter be proud of his ole woman — why, sah, all de medicine in de world wouldn't help de Deakun like sich talk. De blues fly away, he begins to whistle, an' he slants his hat over his ear, an' goes on his way wid a new heart in him.

"I'ze been watchin' arqun' an' it am my opinyun dat ye can hurt a human bein' a great deal mo' by indifference dan ye kin by flattery. De only way to make a man sumbody am to let him know dat he am sumbody. De human heart am like a wallet. It often gets low down. Kind words am its cash capital. De mo' capital it has, de harder it tries to make spring outer winter an' sunshine outer gloom an' sorrer."

THE following is the reply to a bill from a bookseller: "I never ordered the book; if I did, you didn't send it; if you sent it, I never got it; if I got it, I paid for it; if I didn't, I won't"

"Shust Poot Your Shoulder to Der Vheel"

"Shust poot your shoulder to der vheel,
Eef you vould vin a name,
Und eef der Vhite House needs you
You vill get dhere shust der same.

HARD TIMES.

SANTA CLAUS (in Florida, gasping).—Phew! If it wasn't for disappointing the children, bless me if I'd come down to this pesky climate at all! No snow for my reindeers, the thermometer at '90, and forced, by tradition, to climb up to the roof and down through the chimney. Drat it!

POETRY, ANECDOTES, HUMOR, ETC.

HE GETS DHERE SHUST DER SAME.

OLDT Æsop wrote a fable vonce,
  Aboudt a boasting hare,
Who say, "Vhen dhere vas racing
  You can always find *me* dhere!"

Und how a tortoise raced mit him,
  Und shtopped hees leedle game,
Und say, "Eef I don'd been so shpry,
  I gets dhere shust der same."—

Dot vas der cases eferyvhere :
  In bolidics und trade
By bersbiration of der brow
  Vas how soocksess vas made.

A man may somedime "shdrike it rich,"
  Und get renown und fame,
Budt dot bersbiration feller, too,
  He gets dhere shust der same.

Der girl dot makes goot beeskits,
  Und can vash und iron dings,
Maybe don'd been so lofely
  As dot girl mit diamondt rings.

But vhen a *rife* vas vanted,
  Who vas id dot's to blame
Eef dot girl mitoudt der shewels
  Should get dhere shust der same ?

Dot schap dot leafes his peesniss,
  Und hangs roundt "bucket shops,"
To make den tollars oudt of von,
  Vhen grain und oil shtock drops,

May go away vrom dhere, somedimes,
  Mooch poorer as he came.
"Der mills off God grind shlowly,"
  Budt dhey get dhere shust der same.

Dhen neffer mindt dhose mushroom schaps,
  Dot shpring oop in a day ;
Dhose repudations, dhey vas made
  By york, und not by blay.

Shust poot your shoulder to der vheel,
  Eef you vould vin a name,
Und eef der Vhite House needs you
  You vill get dhere shust der same.
  CHARLES FOLLEN ADAMS.

"Now," said the clairvoyant to her group of visitors, "I will describe a person known and loved by everybody in this room. The person has the characteristic of always being in a hurry and always being delayed; will run two blocks for a waiting street car, and then stop to wait for the next one ; generally stands on the wrong side of the crossing, and is invariably unable to find change. Does any one recognize this person ?" And every man in the room got up and shouted, "It's my wife !"— *Chicago News Record.*

WITHOUT the door let Sorrow lie ;
  And if for cold it hap to die,
We'll bury it in a Xmas pie,
  And evermore be merry.
        George Wither.

LIFE'S EPITOME.

A BURST of light and song and stars,
Of hopes and dreams and sometime
    glory—
          Day's begun !

A little praise, a little blame,
A little floating breath of fame,
A little sitting in the sun, a little sigh
  —and
          Day is done !
          ANNIE E. P. SEARING.

"ALWAYS pay as you go," said an old man to his nephew. "But, uncle, suppose I have nothing to pay with."— "Then don't go."

"PLENTY of milk in your cans this morning?" the customer asked a milkman the other day. And the milkman nodded gravely, as, without a wink in his eye, he made reply, "Chalk full."

"WHAT are the wild waves saying?" asked a flip young man of a sharp girl on the beach at Old Point. "They are saying they are glad they are not fresh," she answered sweet and low.

She : "I hear that you have lost your valuable little dog, Mr. Sissy."
He : "Ya'as, in a railroad accident. I was saved but the dawg was killed."
She : "What a pity !"

THE sunshine of life is made up of very little beams that are bright all the time. In the nursery, in the playground, and in the schoolroom there is room all the time for little acts of kindness that cost nothing, but are worth more than gold or silver. To give up something, where giving up will prevent unhappiness ; to yield, when persisting will chafe and fret others ; to go a little around rather than come against another ; to take an ill word or cross look rather than resent cr return it ; these are the ways in which clouds and storms are kept off, and pleasant, smiling sunshine secured, even in the humble home, among very poor people, as in families in higher stations. Much that we term the miseries of life would be avoided by adopting this rule of conduct.

"AVARICE in old age," says Cicero, "is foolish ; for what can be more absurd than to increase our provisions for the road, the nearer we approach our journey's end."

BE not stingy of kind words and pleasant acts, for such are fragrant gifts, whose perfume will gladden the heart and sweeten the life of all who hear or receive them.

HOOT away despair ; never live in sorrow ;
Darkest clouds may wear a sunny face to-morrow.

NEW HAMPSHIRE had a congressman who used to open his speeches with, "Fellow citizens, I was born in Portsmouth. I was always born in Portsmouth."

—1894

HE DIDN'T WANT TO WORK

HE DIDN'T WANT TO WORK. — Mrs. Murray was reading a story to her son, Justin, aged five years.

Mrs. Murray: "Now, Justin, if your father was to die would *you* work to help mamma?"

Justin: "Why, mamma, what for? Haven't we got a nice house to live in?"

Mrs. Murray: "Yes, Justin, but we can't eat the house, you know."

Justin: "Well, mamma, haven't we got a whole lot of good things in the pantry?"

Mrs. Murray: "Certainly, pet, but we would soon eat them up, and then what should we do?"

Justin: "Well, mamma, isn't there enough to last until you could get another husband?" — *Brooklyn Life.*

NO FOOLING. — Aunt Hizzie, a colored woman, having been converted, Parson Tappitoes wanted to baptize her in winter, but the convert objected, through fear for her health. "Doan ye trust in de Lawd?" asked the parson. "Aw, yaas, brudder," said Aunt Hizzie; "I does trust pintedly in the Lawd, but I ain't gwine to fool wid him."

THE hermit turned pale at the sound of a human voice near his lonely abode. His heart chilled with foreboding as he listened.

"Is my hat on straight?"

"That everlasting woman question again," he snarled, and plunged yet deeper into the wilderness.

PATIENCE. — "I remember," says the celebrated Wesley, "hearing my father say to my mother, 'How could you have the patience to tell that blockhead the same thing twenty times over?'—'Why,' said she, 'if I had told him only nineteen times, I should have lost all my labor.'"

"If I were so unlucky," said an officer, "as to have a stupid son, I would certainly make him a parson." A clergyman, who was in the company, calmly replied, "You think differently from your father."

A WOULD-BE poet thus criticises some church-going people:

"Attend your church," the parson cries.
To church each fair one goes,
The old go there to close their eyes,
The young to eye their clothes.

AN old clergyman, more distinguished for his piety than for the elegance of his oratorical delivery, once read aloud from his pulpit a hymn in which occurs this line, "Life's like a shadow, how it flies." But, pausing in the middle of the word "shadow" to take breath, the venerable parson astonished his hearers by what seemed to read, "Life's like a shad—oh, how it flies!"

LAUGH. — A joyous smile adds an hour to one's life; a heartfelt laugh, a day; a grin, not a moment.

MUCH as we prize the highest good in life,
We would not wish an angel for a wife;
But be content with what is far more common,
A genial-hearted, true, and loving woman.

AN old woman met in the street a friend whom she had not seen for a long time. "O, my friend," she cried, "how is it since I have seen you? Was it you or your sister that died some months ago? I saw it in the papers." "It was my sister," replied Simplicity; "we were both sick. She died, but I was the worse."

A SCEPTIC, meeting a clergyman of one of our large cities, with a view probably of showing his wit, asked, "If we are to live after death, why have we not some certain knowledge of it?" The clergyman, feeling it well sometimes to answer a fool according to his folly, asked in return, "Why didn't you get some knowledge of this world before you came into it?"

A PROFESSOR GUNNING, up in Michigan, is lecturing on, "After Man, What?" A Fort Wayne editor, who has been there, rises to remark that it is generally the sheriff or some woman. — *Hawkeye.*

IN the churchyard at Langtown, in Cumberland, is the following:—

"Life's like an inn where travellers stay:
Some only breakfast and away;
Others to dinner stay, and are full fed,
The oldest only sup and go to bed.
Long is his bill who lingers out the day;
Who goes the soonest has the least to pay.

THE *Niagara Falls Gazette* tells a story of two young ladies who were promenading along the street, when one of them slipped and came down on the icy pavement "like a thousand of bricks." Jumping quickly up, she exclaimed, *sotto voce,* "Before another winter, I'll have a man to hang to, see if I don't."

BE not stingy of kind words and pleasing acts, for such are fragrant gifts, whose perfume will gladden the heart and enliven the life of all who hear or receive them.

To illustrate the wasting of the moments that make up the year, Sydney Smith remarked to a young lady, "Do you ever reflect how you pass your life? If you live to seventy-two, which I hope you may, your life is passed in the following manner. An hour a day is three years, that makes twenty-seven years sleeping; nine years dressing; nine years at table; six years playing with children; nine years walking, drawing, and visiting; six years shopping, and three years quarrelling.

POETRY AND ANECDOTES

On An Expansionist Binge

EXPANSIONIST BINGE

At the request of President McKinley, Congress passed a joint resolution demanding Spain's withdrawal from Cuba. This was the first step of expansionism which, by the end of the century, found the U.S. driving Spain out of Cuba, swallowing up Hawaii, the Philippines, Puerto Rico, Guam, Wake Island, and a piece of Samoa.

The Cares of a Growing Family

J. Campbell Cory. *The Bee*, 1898.

Victory

If I can keep one heart from break-
ing,
   I shall not live in vain.
If I can ease one life the aching,
   Or cool one pain,
Or help one fainting robin into his
nest again,

I shall not live in vain.

               Emily Dickinson

Over-Extension

When Mr. Lincoln was a young lawyer practising in the courts of Illinois, he was once engaged in a case in which the lawyer on the other side made a speech to the jury full of wild statements. Lincoln opened his reply by saying, "My friend who has just spoken to you would be all right if it were not for one thing, and I don't know that you ought to blame him for that, for he can't help it. What I refer to is his reckless statements without any ground of truth. You have seen instances of this in his speech to you. Now the reason of this lies in the constitution of his mind. The moment he begins to talk all his mental operations cease, and he is not responsible. He is, in fact, much like a little steamboat that I saw on the Sangamon River when I was engaged in boating there. This little steamer had a five-foot boiler and seven-foot whistle, and every time it whistled the engine stopped."

MADE A REPUTATION.

SOME men are naturally such teachers, and so full of benevolence, especially toward the young, that they cannot help spreading wisdom wherever they go. That the seed may fall on stony ground is proved by a story which a gentleman, who went hunting far into the interior of Nova Scotia, tells in a letter.

The hunter was carried sixteen miles at night by a boy 16 years old and a horse 15 years old. The ride was tedious, and the boy-driver was inclined to fall asleep. The hunter, therefore, thought to interest him in something. "I see we are going due west," he said. "How do you know that?" asked the boy. "Were you ever here before?" "No; but there is the North Star." "How do you know it's the North Star?" "Why, there are the pointers." "What pointers?" The hunter explained, and told the boy how to find the North Star. Then he pointed out two of the planets. The boy seemed wide awake now; and the hunter went on to give him his first lesson in astronomy, telling him how Jupiter was 1,300 times as large as the earth, and how Mars showed changes of seasons — how it had bays and apparent canals, and so forth, and how it was supposed by many to have intelligent inhabitants.

When, after his hunting, the stranger returned to the town where he had hired the conveyance and the boy, he found that the people seemed to have a certain humorous interest in him. It was so evident that he was the object of some curiosity or joke that he made inquiries, and finally found a man who could tell him. "Why," said his informant, "you've made a great reputation for yourself around here." "In what way?" "Oh, the kid that drove you over to —— the other night came back the next day and told all the 'setters' at the hotel that of all the liars he ever heard, you were the slickest." "What lie did I tell him?" "The boy said that you pretended to know the number of miles to the sun, and that you pointed to a star that you said was called 'Jumpter,' and that you said it was 1,300 times bigger than this world, and that you pointed to another star that you said was one where folks lived." "'Oh,' says that boy, 'you just ought to hear him! He's a peach. Old Haskins ain't in it with that feller for lyin'. I tell you he's the biggest liar in Nova Scotia. I'll point him out to you when he comes back.'"

The boy had pointed him out, and he was at that moment enjoying the reputation of the champion of all the liars who had ever come to Nova Scotia. — *The Country Gentleman.*

AN anecdote of the late Wm. E. Gladstone at the time of his greatest rivalry with Disraeli is told in the Jewish *World.* At a dinner-party the subject of Judaism cropped up. " Admitted," said Gladstone, "that the Hebrews have given the world a philosopher in Spinoza, musicians in Mendelssohn and Meyerbeer, a poet in Heine, the fact remains that they have not produced a single statesman." There was silence for a moment. Every one knew, of course, that this was a direct allusion to his Jewish rival Disraeli. Then one of the company stepped into the breach. "Mr. Gladstone," he said, "as a matter of fact, the Hebrews have produced a statesman, and one of the greatest the world has seen." The fighting instinct of Mr. Gladstone surged up at once. "May I ask, sir," he said pointedly, "who was this Hebrew statesman?" Every one, anticipating a more than lively scene, waited in tense expectation for the answer. It came in the quietest tones: "Moses, sir." Every one smiled, and Mr. Gladstone joined in the laugh.

SOME years ago, when Mr. Gladstone was staying in Scotland, he attended church where the minister made the following allusion to his presence: "We pray thee, Lord, of thy goodness, to bless the prime minister of this great nation, who is now worshipping under this roof in the third pew from the pulpit. We feel ourselves to be the richer for the privilege of his company." Another minister of the same church was opening an outside function with prayer when a great personage had failed to keep an engagement to be present. He thus began his supplication: "In consequence of the rain, O Lord, and by reason of the regretted absence of the Princess of Lochnagar, I do not purpose to address thee at any length."

A MAN who went away from home some time ago to attend a convention of church people was struck with the beauty of the little town in which the gathering was held. He had plenty of time, and while wandering about, walked into the village cemetery. It was a beautiful place, and the delegate walked around among the graves. He saw a monument, one of the largest in the cemetery, and read with surprise the inscription on it : —

"A Lawyer, and an Honest Man."

The delegate scratched his head, and looked at the monument again. He read the inscription over and over. Then he walked all around the monument, and examined the grave closely. Another man in the cemetery approached and asked him, —

"Have you found the grave of an old friend?"

"No," said the delegate; "but I was wondering how they came to bury those two fellows in one grave." — *St. Joseph News.*

"WHAT are your views as to a future state, brother?" said the clergyman to a resident of the parish.

"Well, parson," said the brother, "I am still open to conviction on the subject, but, as at present advised, I'm agin the annexation of any outlying territory."

FROM THE 1899 ALMANAC

A Lawyer and An Honest Man

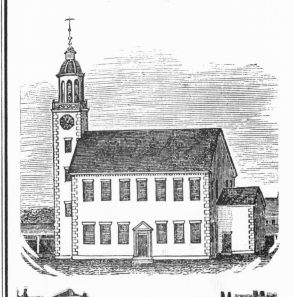

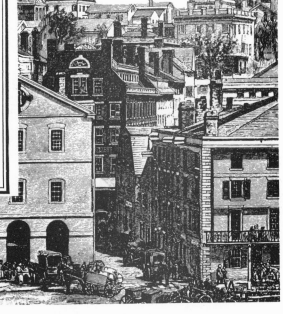

POETRY AND ANECDOTES

FROM THE
1903
ALMANAC

EVER READ
SHERLOCK HOLMES?

LEFT THE TEA KETTLE.

There was a man riding on the rear platform of a car with a package between his feet, that attracted the attention of a little man. Presently he queried:

"Ever read Sherlock Holmes?"

"Yes, sir."

"Great hand to deduce and conclude, wasn't he?"

"Yes."

"But no greater than I am. For instance, you have a tea kettle in that paper. It follows that you are a married man. Being a married man it follows that your wife has been asking you about four times a week for the last year to buy that kettle. Having been a year in buying it, the inference is that you are absent-minded in a general way, and have little concern for things around the house. The chances are that you will leave the tea kettle in the car when you get off and forget that you ever bought it. Am I correct?"

"You are an ass!" was the blunt reply.

"My dear sir, I have every reason to believe that ——"

"You have lots of gall to talk to me as you have," interrupted the tea kettle man.

"I was simply trying to prove to you that Sherlock Holmes only ——"

"What do I care about Sherlock Holmes? Who are you, sir, that you presume to be so familiar?"

"My name is Horntackle, and I like to deduce and conclude. Being an irascible man, it naturally follows that your poor wife has ——"

"If I had you on the sidewalk I'd punch your head, sir. You have said quite enough. I'll remember your mug, and if I ever catch you on the ground I'll teach you manners!"

With that he got off. He not only got off, but left his tea kettle. The little man held it up to him and waved it on high and yelled to him, and the conductor stopped the car, but the man would not return for it. After having been told that he would leave that tea kettle behind, and after having left it, he would not have claimed it for a million dollars. — *Selected.*

A BOOK FOR REFERENCE.

PAPA — Here! I told you never to go near that bookcase without permission.

WILLIE — I jest want to look at the history of the United States.

PAPA — What for?

WILLIE — This paper says the Chicagos was champeens of the league in 1887 and I don't believe it.—*Phil. Press.*

"Why, Uncle 'Rastus, you don't expect to loaf all the time, do you?"

"O no, not all de time; got to sleep some o' de time."— *Selected.*

For virtue's self may too much zeal be had;
The worst of madmen is a saint run mad. — *Pope.*

The judgment of Solomon was nearly enacted by a civil justice in Georgia, in *ante-bellum* days. Two parents claimed the same negro baby, and the evidence was so even that the puzzled judge suddenly thought of the wise king's experiment. He seized the baby, pulled out a bowie-knife from his belt, and started to halve the child. Both claimants reached forward simultaneously, crying, "Boss, don't kill him. You may have him." — *Green Bag.*

HALLOWE'EN.

Cloudy skies and low —
Not a wind to go
Whispering to the yellow woods
All that winds may know.
Here a berry drops,
There a leaf hangs still;
Melancholy gathers slowly
Over holt and hill.

While the darkening day
Deepens duskier gray,
Stealthy shadows softly steal
Down the woodland way;
Feeble flowers, unwept,
Fade along the field,
With the mystery of their history
Perished, unrevealed.

If we two to-night,
In the uncertain light,
Meet, touch hands — half shadowy
Each to other's sight —
Sudden thrill may loose
Lips from silence' thrall,
Sweetest vision find fruition,
Love be all in all.
M. C. Gillington
in Frank Leslie's Popular Monthly.

"Harry!"

"What is it, Dorothy?"

"Did you give me that parlor lamp last Christmas, or did I give it to you?" — *Indianapolis Journal.*

ONE OF THEM MIGHT.

A certain doctor, when only a beginner in practice, had occasion to attend a trial as a witness. The opposing counsel in cross examining the young doctor made several sarcastic remarks, doubting the ability of so young a man to understand the profession.

"Do you know the symptoms of concussion of the brain?"

"I do," replied the doctor.

"Well," continued the attorney, "suppose my learned friend, Mr. Baging, and myself were to bang our heads together, should we get concussion of the brain?"

"Your learned friend, Mr. Baging, might," was the reply. — *Selected.*

As the Spanish Proverb says, "He who would bring home the wealth of the Indies, must carry the wealth of the Indies with him." So it is in travelling; a man must carry knowledge with him if he would bring home knowledge. — *Dr. Johnson.*

FROM THE
1905
ALMANAC

The World Is A Comedy

THINKING & FEELING
The world is a comedy
To those that think;
A tragedy
To those who feel.

Horace Walpole

ON HEAVENLY AND EARTHLY HOPE.

Reflected on the lake, I love
To see the stars of evening glow,
So tranquil in the heaven above,
So restless in the wave below.

Thus heavenly hope is all serene,
But earthly hope, how bright so'er,
Still fluctuates o'er this changing scene
As false and fleeting as 'tis fair.
Bishop Heber.

ANECDOTE OF SHERIDAN.

Sheridan, the dramatist and orator, was once spending a few days at Bristol, and wanted a pair of new boots, but had not the wherewithal to pay for them. Shortly before he left he called upon two boot makers and ordered a pair of each, promising payment on delivery. He fixed the morning of his departure for the tradesmen to send in their goods. When the first pair arrived he tried on the boots, and, complaining that that for the right foot pinched, ordered the man to take it back, stretch it, and bring it again at nine the next morning. The second pair arrived soon after the first, and this time it was the boot for the left foot which pinched. The same complaint was made and the same order given; each of the men had taken away only the pinching boot and left the other behind. The same afternoon Sheridan left in his new boots for London. The two shoemakers called promptly at nine the next day, only to find that their customer had departed, having victimized them both with entire impartiality.

AN ANSWER NOT EXPECTED.

The teacher had given her pupils an account of the once popular belief in the Philosopher's Stone, by means of which, it was thought the baser metals might be changed to gold. The day after the lecture, in order to see how well they had remembered it, she addressed them as follows:—
"Children, you have heard a description of something which for centuries many people, some of them learned men of the period, thought to exist; of the large expenditure of money and of human labor in the attempt to discover it; of the great amount of literature, both in the assertion, and in the denial, of its existence; how it has been the only human idea of its kind; and how if it existed, he who should acquire and possess it would reap untold wealth and undying fame. Now, who of you can tell me the name of this mythical thing which, though it has never been shown to exist, has yet so excited the curiosity of mankind and exercised so potent an influence on human endeavor?"
And then cherub faced little Tommy Wilson, holding up his right hand cried out, "I know; please, ma'am, it's the sea serpent."

Poverty is in want of much, but avarice of everything. — *Publius Syrus.*

THOUGHT TELEGRAPH WOULD DO IT ALL.

In the early days of the telegraph, an aged colored man stepped into the telegraph office in Philadelphia and handed the operator a telegram from his employer to a dealer in Baltimore, requesting the latter to send him a peck of soft-shelled crabs. The man after delivering the message did not leave the office, but stood about in an expectant sort of way until the operator said, "What are you waiting for?" "I'se waiting for dem crabs," replied the negro.

A fellow living in western Pennsylvania, having gone pretty nearly through all the follies of life, took it into his head to hire a bully to do his fighting. He made a contract with the stoutest bruiser he could find, and they started on a journey down the Ohio and Mississippi. At every landing a quarrel was picked by one, and the battle fought by the other. It was tough work sometimes, but on the whole rather enjoyable. At last they reached New Orleans. On the levee they found a stout, brawny stevedore. After some chaffing a row started, and the two began to pummel each other. They were well matched, but aided by his experience the bruiser beat the stevedore. The next day the young fellow's fighting man said to him, "I say, boss, I give up this job. You expect too much of me. I don't see any reason in that ere last fight."

The world is a comedy to those that think, a tragedy to those who feel.
Horace Walpole.

A TEAR.

Oh! that the Chemist's magic art
Could crystallize this sacred treasure!
Long should it glitter near my heart,
A secret source of pensive pleasure.

The little brilliant, ere it fell,
Its lustre caught from Chloe's eye;
Then, trembling, left its coral cell —
The spring of Sensibility!

Sweet drops of pure and pearly light!
In thee the rays of Virtue shine,
More calmly clear, more mildly bright,
Than any gem that gilds the mine.

Benign restorer of the soul!
Who ever fly'st to bring relief,
When first we feel the rude control
Of Love or Pity, Joy or Grief.

The sage's and the poet's theme,
In every clime, in every age,
Thou charm'st in Fancy's idle dream,
In Reason's philosophic page.

That very law which moulds a tear,
And bids it trickle from its source,
That law preserves the Earth a sphere,
And guides the planets in their course.
Samuel Rogers.

151

NEW ENGLAND.

FOR A CELEBRATION IN KENTUCKY OF THE LANDING OF THE PILGRIMS.

Clime of the brave! the high heart's
   home,
   Laved by the wild and stormy sea!
Thy children, in this far-off land,
   Devote to-day their hearts to thee;
Our thoughts, despite of space and time,
To-day are in our native clime,
Where passed our sinless years, and
   where
Our infant heads first bowed in prayer.

Stern land! we love thy woods and rocks,
   Thy rushing streams, thy winter
   glooms,
And Memory, like a pilgrim gray,
   Kneels at thy temples and thy tombs:
The thoughts of these, where'er we
   dwell,
Come o'er us like a holy spell,
A star to light our path of tears,
A rainbow on the sky of years.

Above thy cold and rocky breast
   The tempest sweeps, the night-wind
   wails,
But Virtue, Peace, and Love, like birds
   Are nestled mid thy hills and vales;
And Glory, o'er each plain and glen,
Walks with thy free and iron men,
And lights her sacred beacon still
On Bennington and Bunker Hill.
       George Denison Prentice.

The following from *Farmer & Moore's Collections* tells of an accident happening nearly two hundred years ago of the same deplorable character as so many of recent occurrence:

James Rogers, the father of Major Robert Rogers, who commanded a company of rangers in the last French and Indian war, was one of the first settlers of Dunbarton, New Hampshire. Mr. James Rogers met his death under the following circumstances. He was proceeding to a hunter's camp in the woods in order, it was said, to invite some gentlemen who were making surveys near by to dine with him. The hunter saw him approaching through the bushes at a distance, and, not expecting to see any other beings than wild animals, and the color of his clothes being black, he supposed him to be a bear, and accordingly fired upon him and killed him.

It is reported of Major Rogers, that while in London after the French war, being in company with several persons, it was agreed that the one who should tell the most improbable story or the greatest falsehood should be exempt from paying his fare. When his turn came, he related that his father was shot in the woods of America by a person who supposed him to be a bear; and that his mother was once followed several miles through the forest by hunters, who mistook her track for that of the same kind of an animal. It was acknowledged by all that he was entitled to the prize, although he had told nothing but the truth.

A man somewhere in New England was negotiating with a dealer for the purchase of a horse. A fine looking animal was led out of the stable for him to examine. "Oh," said he, "that horse has a fine head—I won't run him down with so fine a head: it is astonishing how much that head reminds me of a horse my father owned twenty years ago. Well, that is a good shoulder, too; forelegs well formed. How much they do remind me of that horse father owned twenty years ago."

Passing along the animal he continued:—"And those hind quarters are good; and what a beautiful fine tail! It is really wonderful how they remind me of a horse father owned twenty years ago."

Going round to see the other side of the horse, he said:—"Fine mane, nice ears, splendid eyes. I declare it is marvellous how much they remind me of a horse my father owned twenty years ago." And then opening the mouth and looking at the teeth, he quietly said, "I guess it's the same horse."—*From "Funny Stories," by P. T. Barnum.*

In beauty, faults conspicuous grow;
The smallest speck is seen on snow.
       John Gay.

Without error there could be no such thing as truth.—*Chinese Proverb.*

SERENADE.

Look out upon the stars, my love,
   And shame them with thine eyes,
On which, than on the lights above,
   There hang more destinies.
Night's beauty is the harmony
   Of blending shades and light:
Then, lady, up,—look out, and be
   A sister to the night!

Sleep not!—thine image wakes for aye
   Within my watching breast;
Sleep not!—from her soft sleep should
   fly,
Who robs all hearts of rest.
Nay, lady, from thy slumbers break,
   And make this darkness gay,
With looks whose brightness well might
   make
   Of darker nights a day.
       Edward Coate Pinkney.

"You've been a great traveller, Mr. Bunsby."

"Yes; but I wish I had travelled less and seen more."

"How many rascals are there on this street besides yourself?" asked Jokesby of one of his friends.

"Besides myself," he replied in a rage; "do you mean to insult me?"

"Well, then," said Jokesby, "how many are there including yourself?"

—— "Sometimes," said Uncle Eben, "a man gives hisse'f credit foh bein' resigned to fate, when he has simply settled down to bein' good an' lazy."—*Washington Star.*

POETRY AND ANECDOTES

Old Levi Crazyman

SMOOTHING THE ROAD

Patiently smoothing for other men
The highways he'd never tread
again.
Small wonder the thrifty eyed his
plan
And dubbed him "Old Levi
Crazyman."

FOR OTHER MEN.

New England oldsters maybe can
Remember old "Levi Crazyman."
He used to lean on his old crook-cane,
And limp from Connecticut 'way to
Maine.
They called him daft in the olden days,
And faith! he did have curious ways!
For up and down and to and fro
He tramped, nor ever did people know
Who he had been or whence he came,
Or what was hidden beneath that name.
But he trudged with a smile for all he
met,
Vowed to a thankless task, self-set,
Rolling the stones from the travelled
road
Along which the careless passers
strode;
Patiently smoothing for other men
The highways he'd never tread again.
Small wonder the thrifty eyed his plan
And dubbed him "Old Levi Crazyman."
Perhaps! but give him a bit of praise
In that "he helped us mend our ways!"
For such was his well-worn little joke—
His sole response when the passers
spoke.
A poor, old tramp! Yet I've sometimes
thought
God sends such lessons as Levi taught:
That selfish man and the arrogant "I"
Might gaze and be humbled as he
passed by,
Smoothing the road before their door—
Asking no guerdon — seen no more.
Holman Day.

A colored boot-black, who kept a
small shop, became bankrupt. The
next day a gentleman called and asked
for his boots, which he had left to be
blacked. The bankrupt, hearing his
knock at the door, looked out of the
second story window, and said : — " I'se
bankrupt; but I pays fifty cents on the
dollar. Here's one of your boots!"
throwing it out of the window.—*Funny
Stories by Phineas T. Barnum.*

THE NUMBER NINE.

The singular properties of the number nine are well known to arithmeti-
cians. The following is one of the
most interesting. If the cardinal numbers from 1 to 9 inclusive, omitting 8,
be used as a multiplicand, and any one
of them multiplied by 9 be used as a
multiplier, the result will present a
succession of figures the same as that
multiplied by the 9. For example, if
we wish a series of fives, we take 5
times 9, equal to 45, for a multiplier : —

```
    1 2 3 4 5 6 7 9
              4 5
    ---------------
    6 1 7 2 8 3 9 5
    4 9 3 8 2 7 1 6
    ---------------
    5 5 5 5 5 5 5 5
```

A similar result will be obtained by
using all the other numbers, including
8 (72) ; but the 8 must in all cases be
omitted in the multiplicand.—*Gleanings
from the Harvest Fields of Literature.*

Another good way to get tanned is to
roll up your sleeves and hoe the weeds
in your back yard.—*Boston Globe.*

A WHITE LAD, AN INDIAN AND A BEAR.

In 1786 a lad named Francis Downing
was living in a fort at a place in the
Ohio Valley, subsequently known as
the Slate Creek Works. One day in
August of that year, he went out with
his friend, Yates, to find the latter's
horse which had been lost. When about
six miles from the fort, finding they
were followed by two Indians, they
started to run back. They became separated in their flight, one Indian following Downing, the other pursuing Yates.
Downing had attempted to shoot one
of the Indians, but, having missed him,
had thrown away his gun. The Indian
following Downing, in attempting to
intercept him close to the root of a
large poplar which had fallen to the
ground, stumbled upon a great she
bear which was lying there with her
two cubs. The bear sprang upon the
Indian, and, though the latter drew
his knife, he was borne to the ground
where the strugle continued. Downing,
while naturally wishing success to the
bear, did not wait to see the result
of the contest but ran on to the fort,
where he found that Yates had already
arrived, having eluded his pursuer.—
Sketches of Western Adventure.

TO A WAVE.

List, thou child of wind and sea!
Tell me of the far-off deep,
Where the tempest's wind is free,
And the waters never sleep!
Thou perchance the storm hast aided,
In its work of stern despair,
Or perchance thy hand hath braided,
In deep caves, the mermaid's hair.

Wave! now on the golden sands,
Silent as thou art, and broken,
Bear'st thou not from distant strands
To my heart some pleasant token?
Tales of mountains of the south,
Spangles of the ore of silver;
Which, with playful singing mouth,
Thou hast leaped on high to pilfer?

Faded wave! a joy to thee,
Now thy flight and toil are over!
Oh, may my departure be
Calm as thine, thou ocean rover!
When this soul's last joy or mirth
On the shore of time is driven,
Be its lot like thine on earth,
To be lost away in heaven!
James Otis Rockwell.

AT THE SUPPER TABLE.

This mince pie is a dream.
What ! so soon ?

AMERICAN HEIRESS. O, Auntie!
how literally these Europeans take
everything.
AUNT. Such as ?
AMERICAN HEIRESS. Why yester-
day Count Slicky Zinky proposed to
me, and I tried to turn it off the easiest
way and told him I'd be a sister to him ;
whereupon he exclaimed, " Impossible,
Madam! It is only by becoming my
wife that you can acquire any of the
Schlickzi-Tzinsjnxky titles."

153

POETRY AND ANECDOTES

I Hear The Voices Call

POETRY, ANECDOTES, HUMOR, Etc.

THE VOICES.

Whether landward or seaward,
  I hear the Voices call—
The Voices of the Masters
  That hold my heart in thrall!

I heard them first in childhood,
  When the world was dawn and dew,
And today, as in the old time,
  They are magical and new.

They brought the revelation
  That fills the dark with stars—
The message of the Human,
  With its glories and its scars.

They touch'd my heart to wonder,
  That winters cannot chill;
And tonight, tho' youth's behind me,
  Those stars are shining still.
      William Roscoe Thayer.

A great man quotes bravely, and will not draw on his invention when his memory serves him with a word as good.—*Ralph Waldo Emerson.*

AN INSTANCE OF INDIAN PLEASANTRY.

Gov. Winthrop, in his Journal under date of August 12, 1634, tells the following story about the Sagamore Osamekin, better known as Massasoit:

One pleasant passage happened, which was acted by the Indians. Mr. Winslow, coming in his bark from Connecticut to Narigansett—and he left her there,—and intending to return by land, he went to Osamekin the Sagamore, his old ally, who offered to conduct him home to Plymouth. But, before they took their journey, Osamekin sent one of his men to Plymouth to tell them that Mr. Winslow was dead; and directed him to show how and where he was killed. Whereupon there was much fear and sorrow at Plymouth. The next day, when Osamekin brought him home, they asked him why he sent such word, etc. He answered, that it was their manner to do so that they might be more welcome when they came home.

The house of every one is to him as his castle and fortress, as well for his defence against injury and violence, as for his repose.—*Sir Edward Coke.*

Therefore, they thought it good you
  hear a play,
And frame your mind to mirth and
  merriment,
Which bars a thousand harms, and
  lengthens life.
      Shakespeare.

AMONG THE MOUNTAINS.

ARRIVING GUEST.—But there are so few of your guests on the piazza experiencing the inspiration of the glorious panorama.

HOTEL CLERK.—Yes. Bridge Whist.

The Good are better made by Ill,
As odours crushed are sweeter still.
      Samuel Rogers.

To those who see only with their eyes, the distant is always indistinct and little, becoming less and less as it recedes, till utterly lost; but to the imagination, which thus reverses the perspective of the senses, the far off is great and imposing, the magnitude increasing with the distance.—*Mrs. Anna Jameson.*

JUST A PLACE TO SLEEP IN.

HUBSBY.—Where do the Speedwells live now-a-days?
CHUBSBY.—Don't live anywhere. They hire a small flat and own a big auto.

SILENCE.

That silence is one of the great arts of conversation is allowed by Cicero himself, who says there is not only an art, but even an eloquence in it.—*Hannah More.*

HEAVEN'S MAGNIFICENCE.

Since o'er thy footstool here below
  Such radiant gems are strown,
Oh, what magnificence must glow,
  My God, about thy throne!
So brilliant here these drops of light,
  There the full ocean rolls, how bright!

If night's blue curtain of the sky,
  With thousand stars inwrought,
Hung like a royal canopy
  With glittering diamonds fraught,
Be, Lord, thy temple's outer veil,
  What splendor at the shrine must
    dwell!

The dazzling sun at noontide hour,
  Forth from his flaming vase
Flinging o'er earth the golden shower
  Till vale and mountain blaze,
But shows, O Lord, one beam of thine:
What, then, the day where Thou dost
    shine!

Ah, how shall these dim eyes endure
  That noon of living rays!
Or how my spirit, so impure,
  Upon thy brightness gaze!
Anoint, O Lord, anoint my sight,
And robe me for that world of light.
      William Augustus Muhlenberg.

It is chiefly through books that we enjoy intercourse with superior minds, and these invaluable means of communication are in the reach of all. In the best books, great men talk to us, give us their most precious thoughts, and pour their souls into ours.—*William Ellery Channing.*

While you are doing one piece of work don't be thinking of another.

They touch'd my heart to wonder,
That winters cannot chill;
And tonight, tho' youth's behind me,
Those stars are shining still.
    —William Roscoe Thayer

-»- POETRY AND ANECDOTES -»-

I HEARD THE WIND THIS MORNING

POETRY, ANECDOTES, HUMOR, Etc.

AT DADDY DAN'S.

I heard the wind this morning when the Brahma rooster crew;
It whistled at the window with a sigh and soft "Wher-ew-w-w!"
It whistled till it woke me, and it seemed to me to say,
"Oh, Daddy Dan, get up, my man! The folks are on the way!"

A golden wedding for Daddy Dan!
Yes, gold in the life of a common man.
Gold fresh-coined from the Bank of Bliss,
With the pat of a hand or a smile or kiss
Making their mint-marks day by day;
And somehow the years have slipped away,
While wife and I have bought success
With the coin of the realm of happiness.
Is it legal tender for pomp and pride?
No, but it's gold full-weight and tried.
And all that an honest life can hold
Can be purchased, friends, by that kind of gold.

Whatever our fortunes at Daddy Dan's,
Joyful triumphs or shattered plans,
Plenty or poverty, smiles or tears,
We have trudged together adown the years!
And if two good comrades, hand in hand,
Grope through the shadows and safely stand
In the light at last, yes, somehow we
Find matters about as they ought to be.
We'll strike the average, eh, good wife?
After all, 'tis a worth-while life!

Come! Stand here at the window, Mother! Rest a little while.
It's time the boys were coming. Why, that's most a girlish smile!
Let me put my arm about you in our good, old, loving way.
Hold up your face! Thank God's good grace for our golden wedding day.

Holman Day.

FROM "THE GRAMMAR OF PAINTING & ENGRAVING."

Nature is a poem, but a poem obscure, of unfathomable depth, and of a complexity that seems to us sublime disorder. All the germs of beauty are contained in it, but only the human mind can discover them, set them free, and create them a second time, by bringing them into order, proportion, and harmony,—that is to say, unity. Nature gives us all sounds, but man alone has invented music. She possesses all woods and marbles; man alone has drawn from them architecture. She unrolls before our eyes countries bristling with mountains and forests, bathed by rivers, cut by torrents; he alone has found in them the grace of gardens. Every day she gives birth to innumerable individuals and forms of endless variety; man, alone, capable of recognizing himself in this labyrinth, draws thence the elements of the ideal he has conceived, and in submitting these forms to the laws of unity, he, sculptor or painter, makes of it a work of art.—*Charles Blanc. From the French by Kate N. Doggett.*

Conversation enriches the understanding, but solitude is the school of genius.—*Edward Gibbon.*

They never taste, who always drink;
They always talk, who never think.
Matthew Prior.

MR. TODKINS. — "So you finish your college course next June. Am afraid you've wasted a lot of time on Latin and Greek."

JACK TODKINS. — "Don't be concerned, Dad. The classics are on the dusty shelf. Athletics and sociology are all our minds have been occupied with."

·» POETRY AND ANECDOTES «·

FROM THE
1916
ALMANAC

COURAGE & TIME AND CONSTANCY

SONG.

When Love came first to Earth, the
Spring
Spread rose-buds to receive him,
And back he vow'd his flight he'd
wing
To Heaven, if she should leave
him.

But Spring departing, saw his faith
Pledged to the next new-comer—
He revell'd in the warmer breath
And richer bowers of Summer.

Then sportive Autumn claim'd by
rights
An Archer for her lover,
And even in Winter's dark cold
nights
A charm he could discover.

Her routs and balls, and fireside joy,
For this time were his reasons—
In short, Young Love's a gallant boy,
That likes all times and seasons.

Thomas Campbell.

ANECDOTE OF WANNALANCET.

The following is in "Memoir of the Pawtuckett Tribe of Indians," added to the Rev. Wilkes Allen's History of Chelmsford, Mass., 1820. Wannalancet was always peaceable and true to the English; * * * of which the following traditionary anecdote is corroborative.

At the conclusion of Philip's war, or some of those Indian wars, which proved destructive to many English settlements, and extremely embarrassed and perplexed the frontiers, Wannalancet after a long absence called on the Rev. Mr. Fiske and congratulating him on the restoration of peace, solicitously enquired after the welfare of the people in Chelmsford, and whether they had suffered greatly during the war. Mr. Fiske replied that they had been highly favored, for which he desired to thank God. "Me next," said the sagacious sagamore, intimating that through *his influence* this town had been exempted from the calamities, that had befallen many others.

VERY MUCH ALIKE.

Yes, Charles, the builders of the Tower became so confounded in speech that no two or three of them could understand each other and nobody else could understand them.

Why, Mama, that's just like the men that made the income tax law that I have heard Papa and lawyer Cokesby talk about.

ANECDOTE OF DANIEL WEBSTER.

During one of the college vacations, Daniel and his brother returned to their father's in Salisbury. Thinking he had a right to some return for the money he had expended on their education, Mr. Webster put scythes in their hands and ordered them to mow. Daniel made a few sweeps and, resting his scythe, wiped the sweat from his brow. His father said, "What's the matter, Dan?" "My scythe don't hang right, sir," he answered. His father fixed it, and Dan went to work again but with no better success. His scythe was again tinkered. But before long it wanted fixing again and the father said in a pet, "Well, hang it to suit yourself." Daniel, with great composure, hung it on the next tree; and, putting on a grave countence, said, "It hangs very well, sir, I am perfectly satisfied."

From "American Anecdotes."

Most men who want the Earth would ubject to payin' taxes on ten acres.—*Joe Cone.*

SIM.—Brixleigh must have known he had no show of being elected. Why then did he strive so for the nomination?

SAM.—Says he just wanted to get his name into "Who's Who in Politics."

Whether through the Pre Primary or otherwise the Direct Primary seems likely to become the Indirect Secondary.

TO LOVE.

Young tyrant of the bow and wings,
Thy altar asks three precious things;
The heart's, the world's most precious three,
Courage, and Time, and Constancy!
And Love must have them all, or
none:
By Time he's wearied, but not won;
He shrinks from Courage hot and
high;
He laughs at tedious Constancy;
But all his raptures, tender, true,
sublime,
Are given to Courage, Constancy,
and Time.

George Croly.

POETRY AND ANECDOTES

Fetching Phrases and Fundamental Truths

FROM THE 1916 ALMANAC

From the *New York Sun*

INNOCENT AMUSEMENT OF A GROWN-UP

From the *Indianapolis News*

FIXIN' IT

FROM THE HISTORY OF THE DECLINE AND FALL OF THE ROMAN EMPIRE.

Falsehood and insincerity, unsuitable as they seem to the dignity of public transactions, offend us with a less degrading idea of meanness than when they are found in the intercourse of private life. In the latter, they discover a want of courage; in the other, only a defect of power; and, as it is impossible for the most able statesmen to subdue millions of followers and enemies by their own personal strength, the world, under the name of policy, seems to have granted them a very liberal indulgence of craft and dissimulation.

Edward Gibbon.

Vain, very vain, my weary search
   to find
That bliss which only centres in
   the mind:
Why have I stray'd from pleasure
   and repose,
To seek a good each government
   bestows?
In every government, though
   terrors reign,
Though tyrant kings or tyrant laws
   restrain,
How small of all that human hearts
   endure,
That part which laws or kings can
   cause or cure!
Still to ourselves in every place
   consign'd,
Our own felicity we make or find:
With secret course, which no loud
   storms annoy,
Glides the smooth current of
   domestic joy,

Oliver Goldsmith.

FROM "AMERICAN ART—HOW IT CAN BE MADE TO FLOURISH."

Art has always flourished where it was asked to flourish, and never elsewhere. If we wish for a renaissance of art in America we must be students and patrons of endeavors which seem humble, but are in truth of the utmost importance, here at home. If American art does not flourish it will not be because we are too rich, or unduly sordid, or insincere; but because we refuse to become discriminating patrons of the every-day good things our fellow citizens can produce if a kindly interest stimulate them thereto.—*J. C. Dana.*

FROM VERSES TO THE COMET OF 1811.

Stranger of heaven! I bid thee hail!
   Shred from the pall of glory riven,
That flashest in celestial gale,
   Broad pennon of the King of
     heaven.
Art thou the flag of woe and death,
   From angel's ensign staff un-
     furled?
Art thou the standard of His wrath
   Waved o'er a sordid, sinful world?

*   *   *   *   *

Whate'er protends thy front of fire,
   Thy streaming locks so lovely
     pale—
Or peace to man, or judgment dire
   Stranger of heaven, I bid thee
     hail!

*   *   *   *   *

O on thy rapid prow to glide,
   To sail the boundless skies with
     thee,
And plough the twinkling stars
   aside,
   Like foambells on a tranquil sea;
To brush the embers from the sun,
   The icicles from off the pole;
Then far to other systems run,
   Where other moons and planets
     roll.

James Hogg.

FROM "CALVINISM.'

Our human laws are but the copies, more or less imperfect, of the eternal laws so far as we can read them, and either succeed and promote our welfare, or fail and bring confusion and disaster, according as the legislator's insight has detected the true principal, or has been distorted by ignorance or selfishness.

James Anthony Froude.

Fetching phrases are not always the expression of fundamental truths.

SHE MISUNDERSTOOD.

CARNEGIE LIBRARY.—"What, to exterminate them? Why, there's a bookworm comes in here every day, and he's a real nice old gentleman."

STUDENT-MAN.—"I didn't say *bookworm*, I said *hookworm*. I asked if you knew of a good treatise on the extermination of the *hookworm*."

LIBRARY.—"Oh! Ring up the Rockefeller Institute."

157

THE COMPLETE
1850 ALMANAC

THE COMPLETE 1850 ALMANAC

THE

FARMERS' ALMANAC

FOR THE YEAR OF OUR LORD

1850.

BY ROBERT B. THOMAS.

THOMAS GROOM,

STATIONER,

Blank Book Manufacturer and Importer of English and French Stationery.

82, STATE ST., BOSTON.

ON THE FOLLOWING pages is a complete typical *Farmers' Almanac* featuring all the facets of information and inspiration to be found in most issues of the *Almanac.*

THE GIFT OF SILENCE

Silence is said to be "a gift without peril, and a treasure without enemies."

THE COMPLETE 1850 ALMANAC

COUNTING-HOUSE
ALMANAC.
1850

JANUARY.

Su.	M.	Tu.	W.	Th.	Fr.	Sa.
..	..	1	2	3	4	5
6	7	8	9	10	11	12
13	14	15	16	17	18	19
20	21	22	23	24	25	26
27	28	29	30	31	..	..

MAY.

Su.	M.	Tu.	W.	Th.	Fr.	Sa.
..	..	..	1	2	3	4
5	6	7	8	9	10	11
12	13	14	15	16	17	18
19	20	21	22	23	24	25
26	27	28	29	30	31	..

SEPTEMBER.

Su.	M.	Tu.	W.	Th.	Fr.	Sa.
1	2	3	4	5	6	7
8	9	10	11	12	13	14
15	16	17	18	19	20	21
22	23	24	25	26	27	28
29	30	..	..	..	..	..

FEBRUARY.

Su.	M.	Tu.	W.	Th.	Fr.	Sa.
..	..	..	..	..	1	2
3	4	5	6	7	8	9
10	11	12	13	14	15	16
17	18	19	20	21	22	23
24	25	26	27	28	..	..

JUNE.

Su.	M.	Tu.	W.	Th.	Fr.	Sa.
..	..	..	..	..	..	1
2	3	4	5	6	7	8
9	10	11	12	13	14	15
16	17	18	19	20	21	22
23	24	25	26	27	28	29
30	..	..	..	..	..	..

OCTOBER.

Su.	M.	Tu.	W.	Th.	Fr.	Sa.
..	..	1	2	3	4	5
6	7	8	9	10	11	12
13	14	15	16	17	18	19
20	21	22	23	24	25	26
27	28	29	30	31	..	..

MARCH.

Su.	M.	Tu.	W.	Th.	Fr.	Sa.
..	..	..	..	..	1	2
3	4	5	6	7	8	9
10	11	12	13	14	15	16
17	18	19	20	21	22	23
24	25	26	27	28	29	30
31	..	..	..	..	..	..

JULY.

Su.	M.	Tu.	W.	Th.	Fr.	Sa.
..	1	2	3	4	5	6
7	8	9	10	11	12	13
14	15	16	17	18	19	20
21	22	23	24	25	26	27
28	29	30	31	..	..	..

NOVEMBER.

Su.	M.	Tu.	W.	Th.	Fr.	Sa.
..	..	..	..	..	1	2
3	4	5	6	7	8	9
10	11	12	13	14	15	16
17	18	19	20	21	22	23
24	25	26	27	28	29	30

APRIL.

Su.	M.	Tu.	W.	Th.	Fr.	Sa.
..	1	2	3	4	5	6
7	8	9	10	11	12	13
14	15	16	17	18	19	20
21	22	23	24	25	26	27
28	29	30	..	..	..	..

AUGUST.

Su.	M.	Tu.	W.	Th.	Fr.	Sa.
..	..	..	..	1	2	3
4	5	6	7	8	9	10
11	12	13	14	15	16	17
18	19	20	21	22	23	24
25	26	27	28	29	30	31

DECEMBER.

Su.	M.	Tu.	W.	Th.	Fr.	Sa.
1	2	3	4	5	6	7
8	9	10	11	12	13	14
15	16	17	18	19	20	21
22	23	24	25	26	27	28
29	30	31	..	..	..	..

NUMBER FIFTY-EIGHT.

THE
(OLD)
FARMER'S ALMANACK,

CALCULATED ON A NEW AND IMPROVED PLAN,

FOR THE YEAR OF OUR LORD

1850;

Being 2d after *Bissextile* or *Leap Year*, and (until July 4) 74th of Am. Independence.

Fitted for the City of Boston, but will answer for all the New England States.

Containing, besides the large number of Astronomical Calculations, and the Farmer's Calendar for every month in the year, as great a variety as any other Almanack of

NEW, USEFUL, AND ENTERTAINING MATTER.

ESTABLISHED IN 1793,

BY ROBERT B. THOMAS.

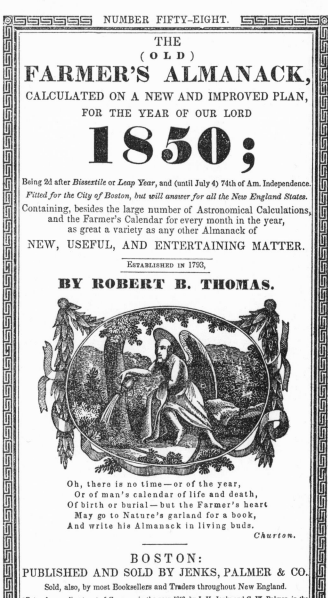

Oh, there is no time—or of the year,
Or of man's calendar of life and death,
Of birth or burial—but the Farmer's heart
May go to Nature's garland for a book,
And write his Almanack in living buds.

Churton.

BOSTON:
PUBLISHED AND SOLD BY JENKS, PALMER & CO.

Sold, also, by most Booksellers and Traders throughout New England.

[Entered, according to act of Congress, in the year 1849, by J. H. Jenks and G. W. Palmer, in the Clerk's Office of the District Court of the District of Massachusetts.]

THIS IS THE YEAR IN WHICH . . .

. . . Daniel Webster was appointed Secretary of State by President Fillmore. Previously, he served in that same capacity under Presidents Tyler and W. H. Harrison.

THE COMPLETE 1850 ALMANAC

Page 2

THE LAST HALF CENTURY IN THE UNITED STATES.

TO PATRONS AND CORRESPONDENTS.

We have again the pleasure of making our annual appearance before our kind friends, and of presenting the Old Farmer's Almanac, for 1850. As the hand of time marks this year as a half century, upon his dial plate, we have thought, "with heart poor in thanks, but rich in thankfulness," rather than fill our page with rendering formal acknowledgments to those friends who have kindly assisted us to keep up the interest of our work so long, and whose favors we gratefully feel, and hope to deserve and receive in future years, we would present a glance at events in the United States since the year 1800. Let us see in what our progress and advantages consist.

In this half century the *Individual* has been better *fed*. Our varied latitudes and Agriculture now give us the native and naturalized produce of a world, rich, abundant and cheap. Our Commerce brings us all growing things of every clime, profuse and at little price, to our very doors. The luxuries preceding this century are now necessaries of life, and there is no privileged class in eatables in our favored land.

The individual has become better *clad*. Our Manufactures surpass the fabrics of fifty years since, at one eighth the cost, and give cloth to the daily laborer that formerly the richest could hardly have compassed. There is no such thing as native rags in the United States, but as the punishment of a man's own wrong.

All are better *lodged*. In the broad circle of our land there is hardly an uncomfortable house inhabited by a sober, native-born American. The furniture of the humble now more than equals, in convenience and quantity, that of the majority of the rich in 1799. Within a few years, taste is making Domestic Architecture beautiful and appropriate; more in our villages and country towns even than in our cities, where buildings are less frequently changed. The gardens and front yards of our whole spreading population have made the desert bloom as the rose.

The individual has been better *taught*. Three months' schooling, in winter, at reading, writing, and arithmetic — truancy, freezing, mending pens and ruling writing-books deducted — was the most ever stickled for by the patriotism of the last age. Now, ten months in a year of good schools, good text-books, school-houses and appliances, teachers taught for the work, apparatus, cabinets and school libraries, — all these are fast spreading over our land. A Public School System is a part of the government; and a free school is becoming an American birthright. There is a Sabbath-school for every Sunday; professional schools; schools for teachers; the army, the navy — though, unfortunately as yet, none for Agriculture, which represents eighty per cent. of our whole population; none for commerce, for the arts, for manufactures. These we begin to talk about, and their claims may soon obtain state and private funds to establish them.

Now, too, is not only the individual's positive good cared for, but his misery is lightened and removed. Insurance against Fire, and Wreck, and of Life, is now ample in our country. Public Asylums for the Blind and the Deaf, and for the Insane, and Hospitals for the disabled and the ailing, where chloroform literally smiles at the extremity of pain.

And *Society*, too, has gone on in the last fifty years. Associations, Societies, Clubs, assist their fellows in sickness and sorrow — in their necessities and comforts, amusements, and luxuries. Go back over the increase of facilities for Business in our United States, in only Currency, and Intercourse, and Transportation — all the growth of the last fifty years — and you will be astonished.

We would have you to look at a list of some of the points of improvement. You will find instances of everything that can possibly make up individual, social, national, or human progress. With Steamboats, Railroads, Telegraphs, Ether, Improved Implements of Machinery, and of Agriculture, of almost every kind, Temperance movements, &c. &c., our country, this century, has far surpassed whole previous centuries. All the other ages of the world together cannot show such a list. It will afford subjects for many an hour of thought, conversation, inquiry and reading.

And now, how does the aggregate of all that has been done here, in the last half century, tell in our *Nation*? To this nation it has been indeed gain. In 1800, there were *thirteen* states; in 1850, there are *thirty* states. In 1800, we had 1,000,000 square miles of territory; in 1850, we have 3,000,000. In 1800, we had 5,309,758 people; in 1850, we have 24,000,000.

We will, then, say no more, Friends and Patrons, old and new, than to bid you God speed for the next fifty years, and quote the words of the Editor used heretofore, in that time should we or our readers see the last of earth, "may we receive the reward of the pure in heart, may our sins be forgiven us, and may our virtues be held in fond remembrance.

Rob't. B. Thomas."

Page 3

ECLIPSES OF THE SUN, FOR 1850.

This year there will be only two eclipses, consequently both will be of the Sun.

I. — There will be an *annular eclipse* of the Sun, commencing Feb. 11th, 10h. 42m., evening, mean time, at Boston, in longitude 39° 22′ E. of Greenwich, and latitude 11° 21′ S. The eclipse will end Feb. 12th, 4h. 49m., morning, in longitude 126° 37′ E. of Greenwich, and latitude 14° 50′ N. It will be invisible to the whole of the western continent.

II. — There will be a *total eclipse* of the Sun, Aug. 7th, invisible at Boston. It will be visible in California, Texas, Mexico, West Indies, and the Gulf of Mexico.

NAMES AND CHARACTERS OF THE PLANETS.

☉ The Sun.	♂ Mars.	♄ Saturn.	⚵ Juno.
☾ ● ☽ ○ The Moon.	♃ Jupiter.	♅ Herschel.	⚴ Pallas.
☿ Mercury.	⊕ The Earth.	⚶ Vesta.	⚳ Ceres.
♀ Venus.			

NAMES AND CHARACTERS OF THE ASPECTS.

☌ Conjunction, or in the same degree.	☍ Opposition, 180 degrees.
✱ Sextile, 60 degrees.	☊ Dragon's Head, or Ascending Node.
□ Quartile, 90 degrees.	☋ Dragon's Tail, or Descending Node.
△ Trine, 120 degrees.	

THE NAMES AND CHARACTERS OF THE TWELVE SIGNS OF THE ZODIAC.

0 ♈ Aries, head.	4 ♌ Leo, heart.	8 ♐ Sagittarius, thighs.
1 ♉ Taurus, neck.	5 ♍ Virgo, belly.	9 ♑ Capricornus, knees.
2 ♊ Gemini, arms.	6 ♎ Libra, reins.	10 ♒ Aquarius, legs.
3 ♋ Cancer, breast.	7 ♏ Scorpio, secrets.	11 ♓ Pisces, feet.

COMMON NOTES FOR 1850.

Golden Number,	8	Dominical Letter,	F	Roman Indiction,	8
Cycle of the Sun,	11	Epact,	17	Julian Period,	6563

MOVEABLE FASTS AND FEASTS FOR 1850.

Septuag. Sunday,	Jan. 27	Good Friday,	March 29	Holy Thursday,	May 9
Shrove Sunday,	Feb. 10	Easter Sunday,	" 31	Whit Sunday,	" 19
Ash Wednesday,	" 13	Low Sunday,	April 7	Trinity Sunday,	" 26
First Sun. in Lent,	" 17	Rogation Sunday,	May 5	Advent Sunday,	Dec. 1

HINTS AND HOME QUESTIONS FOR 1850.

I suppose that in dressing your land, you bear in mind that there is no true economy in doing without that which is profitable? Before you "go ahead" had not you better see how far you have got a head to go? I presume you are aware that if you do not look pretty sharply into your own affairs, your creditors will. Have you any straw-cutters, scythes, loaded guns, friction matches, &c., about your premises, that the children can get at? If so, would not it be well to *secure* either the tools, guns, &c., or the children? Do you bear in mind that if you do not improve your opportunities, you have no right to grumble about your bad luck? If, in looking back upon your past life, you "see where you have missed it," don't commit the same blunder again. When you have nothing to say, for pity's sake, say nothing! They say that we Yankees can never be satisfied to see a beautiful article without handling it — I hope your eyes are not in your fingers' ends. High living is said to be where one eats and drinks inordinately, and throws away his money, and constitution, and character oftentimes, freely! Is not this *low* living? It is certainly a low way to live. Silence is said to be "a gift without peril, and a treasure without enemies." "There is a charm in cheapness," but the cheapest things in the beginning are not always the most economical in the end. I suppose you do not count those as friends who merely come to see you when they want something? If troubles come upon you, remember that great minds are never discouraged! Are not you aware that the less a man knows, the more he suspects? Ignorance, suspicion and prejudice go hand in hand. I hope you always speak the truth, though never offensively! I presume you know that you can often bring those around you to your own standard. See that it is a high one, — never let it be low! When a friend sends you fruit, flowers, or other presents, the least you can do is to return promptly whatever the gift is sent in, even if it is an old basket. I hope, whether rich or poor, you go on the principle that you cannot afford to be careless! I trust your barn and sheds are disconnected with your house. If not, cannot you have them detached, or have a brick and slated connection, so that all may not "go," in case of fire. Speaking of fires, are you prepared for a sudden one? Have you proper articles handy, such as coffee, tea, chocolate, crackers, &c., so that you can keep up the firemen's spirits, and nerve their generous arms by timely and innocent refreshments?

IN THIS HALF CENTURY . . .

In this half century the *individual* has been better fed. Our varied latitudes and Agriculture now give us the native and naturalized produce of a world, rich, abundant and cheap. Our Commerce brings us all growing things of every clime, profuse and at little price, to our very doors.

COLLEGE COMMENCEMENTS, ANNIVERSARIES, AND VACATIONS.

HARVARD. — Com., 3d Wed. in July. Vaca., 1st, from end of first term, 6 w.; 2d, from end of second term (commencement week,) 6 w.; the academical year being divided into two terms, of twenty weeks each, and beginning at commencement.

AMHERST. — Com., 2d Thurs. in Aug. Vaca., 4 w. from com.; 6 w. from the Wed. preceding the annual Thanksgiving; 2 w. from the 3d Wed. in May.

ANDOVER THEOL. SEM. — Anniv., 1st Wed. in Sept. Vaca., 7 w., and 5 w. preceding last Wed. in May.

YALE. — Com., 3d Thurs. in Aug. Vaca., 6 w. from com. From 1st Wednes. in Jan., 2 w. Last Wed. in April, 4 w.

BURLINGTON. — Com., 1st Wed. in Aug. Vaca., com. 4 w., 1st Wed. in Dec. 8 w., and 1 w. from 2d Wed. in May.

DARTMOUTH. — Com., last Thurs. in July. Vaca., 4 w. from com., 7 w. beginning in Nov., and two weeks in May.

PROVIDENCE. — Com., 1st Wed. in Sept. Vaca., Dec. 10th, 3 w. March 31st, 3 w. July 21st, till com.

WILLIAMS. — Com., 3d Wed. in Aug. Vaca., com. 4 w. Wed. after 3d Wed. in Dec., 6 w. 1st Wed. in May, 3 w.

MIDDLEBURY. — Com., 4th Wed. in July. Vaca., com. 4 w. Last Wed. in Nov. 8 w. 1 w. from 4th Wed. in April.

BOWDOIN. — Com., 1st Wed. in Sept. Vaca., at com., 3 w. Friday after 3d Wed. in Dec., 8 w. Friday after 3d Wed. in May, 2 w.

WATERVILLE. — Com., 2d Wed. in Aug. Vaca., at com., 4 w. From 2d Wed. in Dec., 8 w. From 1st Wed. in May, 1 w.

CAMBRIDGE THEOL. SEM. — Vaca. same as Harvard College.

MAINE WESLEYAN SEMINARY. — Annual Exhibition, last Wed. of June. Vaca. from do. to 3d Mond. in Aug. From last week in Nov. to 1st Monday in March.

BANGOR THEOL. SEM. — Anniv., last Wed. in Aug. Vaca., from do. 6 w. From 4th Wed. of April, 5 w.

NEWTON THEOL. SEM. — Anniv. last Wed. but one in Aug. Vaca., 6 w. from anniv., and also 6 w. from last Wed. in March.

EXECUTIVE GOVERNMENT OF THE UNITED STATES, (July, 1849.)

ZACHARY TAYLOR,	Louisiana,	President,	$25,000
Millard Fillmore,	New York,	Vice President,	5,000
John M. Clayton,	Delaware,	Secretary of State,	6,000
William B. Preston,	Virginia,	Secretary of the Navy,	6,000
George W. Crawford,	Georgia,	Secretary of War,	6,000
William M. Meredith,	Pennsylvania,	Secretary of the Treasury,	6,000
Jacob Collamer,	Vermont,	Postmaster General,	6,000
Reverdy Johnson,	Maryland,	Attorney General,	4,000
Thomas Ewing,	Ohio,	Secretary of Home Department,	6,000

AMERICAN PRESIDENTS.

	Where born.	Date of Birth.	Inaug.	Term expired.
George Washington,	Virginia,	Feb. 22, 1732,	1789,	66th year of age.
John Adams,	Massachusetts,	Oct. 19, 1735,	1797,	do. " "
Thomas Jefferson,	Virginia,	April 2, 1743,	1801,	do. " "
James Madison,	"	Mar. 5, 1751,	1809,	do. " "
James Monroe,	"	April 2, 1759,	1817,	do. " "
John Quincy Adams,	Massachusetts,	July 11, 1767,	1825,	63d " "
Andrew Jackson,	South Carolina,	Mar. 15, 1767,	1829,	70th " "
Martin Van Buren,	New York,	Dec. 5, 1782,	1837,	59th " "
William H. Harrison,	Virginia,	Feb. 9, 1773,	1841,	69th " "
John Tyler,	"	Mar. 29, 1790,	1841,	51st " "
James K. Polk,	North Carolina,	Nov. 2, 1795,	1845,	54th " "
Zachary Taylor,	Virginia,	Nov. 24, 1784,	1849,	

LEGAL TENDER OF GOLD AND SILVER COIN.

American Eagle, coined prior to July 31, 1834, 270 gr., is	$10 66	Central American, 17 dwt. 7 gr., is	1 00
Half Eagle, 135 gr., is	5 33	Florin of Southern German States,	40
Eagles coined since July,'34, 257gr.,	10 00	Florin of Austrian Empire,	48½
Parts in proportion.		Specie Dollar of Sweden and Norway,	1 06
Doubloons, 17 dwt. 8 gr., is	15 58	" " Denmark,	1 05
Half Johannas, 9 dwt., is	8 53	Thaler of Prussia and Germany,	69
British Sovereign, 5 dwt. 3½ gr., is	4 87	Pound of Nova Scotia, New Brunswick, Newfoundland and Canada,	4 00
French Napoleon, 4 dwt. 3½ gr., is	3 86	Franc of France and Belgium, and	
Spanish Dollar, 17 dwt. 7 gr., is	1 00	Livre of Sardinia,	18 6-10 cts.
Mexican Dollar, 17 dwt. 7 gr., is	1 00	Ducat of Naples,	80 "
Peruvian Dollar, 17 dwt. 7 gr., is	1 00	Piastre of Turkey,	4 2-5 "
Chilian Dollar, 17 dwt. 7 gr., is	1 00	5 Franc Piece, (French,)	93 "

WORTHLESS AND UNCURRENT BANK NOTES IN NEW ENGLAND.

Corrected by Wetherbee, Brothers, 29 State Street, Boston. July, 1849.

MASSACHUSETTS.

Worthless.

American Bank,
Commercial Bk.
Commonwealth Bk.
Franklin Bk.
Fulton Bk.
Lafayette Bk.
Middling Interest Bk.
Oriental Bk.
(Boston.)
Amherst Bk, Amherst.
Berkshire Bk., Pittsfield.
Chelsea Bk, Chelsea.
Essex Bk., Salem.
Farmers Bk., Belchertown.
Farmers & Mechanics Bk., South Adams.
Hampshire Bk., Northampton.
Mendon Bk., Mendon.
Newburyport Bk., Newburyport.
Nahant Bk., Lynn.
Phoenix Bk., Charlestown.
Phoenix Bk., Nantucket.
Roxbury Bk., Roxbury.
Sutton Bk., Wilkinsville.
City Bk., Lowell, fraud.

Uncurrent.

Citizens Bk., Nantucket.
Cohannet Bk., Taunton.
Manufacturers & Mechanics Bk., Nantucket.
Norfolk Bk., } Roxbury.
Winthrop Bk., }
Greylock Bk.

NEW HAMPSHIRE.

Worthless.

Claremont Bk., Claremont.
Concord Bk., Concord.
Hillsboro' Bk., Hillsboro'.
Wolfborough Bk., Wolfborough.

Uncurrent.

Grafton Bk., Haverhill.
New Hampshire Bk., Portsmouth.
Pemigewasset Bk, Plym'th.

CONNECTICUT.

Worthless.

Derby Bk., Derby.
Eagle Bk., New Haven.
Conn. Mining Co., Hartf'd.

Uncurrent.

Housatonic Railroad Bank, Bridgeport.

MAINE.

Worthless.

Agricultural Bk., Brewer.
Bangor Bk., of Bangor.
Bath Bk., Bangor.
Castine Bk., Castine.
Citizens' Bk., (new plate,) Augusta.
Damariscotta Bk., Nobleborough.
Exchange Bk., Portland.
Frankfort Bk., Frankfort.
Georgia Lumber Co., Portland.
Globe Bk., Bangor.
Hallowell and Augusta Bk., Hallowell.
Kennebec Bk., Hallowell.
Kennebunk Bk., Kennebunk.
Lafayette Bank, Bangor.
Machias Bk.
Bank of Old Town, Orono.
Oxford Bk., Fryeburg.
Passamaquoddy Bk., Eastport.
Penobscot Bk., Bangor.
Peoples' Bk., Bangor.
Saco Bk., Saco.

St. Croix Bk., Calais.
Stillwater Canal Bk., Orono.
Waldo Bk., Belfast.
Washington Co., Calais.
Waterville Bk., Waterville.
Wiscasset Bk., Wiscasset.
Winthrop Bk., Winthrop.

Uncurrent.

Bangor Commercial Bank, Bangor.
City Bk., Portland.
Citizens' Bk., (old plate,) Augusta.
Calais Bk., Calais.
Mercantile Bk., Bangor.
Westbrook Bk., Westbrook.
Maine Bk., Portland.

VERMONT.

Worthless.

Agricultural Bk., Troy.
Bank of Bennington, Bennington.
Commercial Bank of Vermont, Poultney.
Essex Bk., Guildhall.
Vermont State Bank, (and branches.)
Windsor Bk., of Windsor.

Uncurrent.

St. Albans Bk., of St. Albans.

RHODE ISLAND.

Worthless.

Franklin Bk., Providence.
Burrillville Bk., Burrillville.
Eagle Bk., Newport.
Farmers' Exchange Bank, Gloucester.
Farmers' and Mechanics' Bk., Pawtucket.
Mount Hope Bk., Bristol.
R.I. Agricul'l Bk., Johnston.
Hamilton Bk., Scituate.

Uncurrent.

Pascoag Bk., Pascoag Vil.

FOR OLD AND NEW STYLE, SEE ALMANAC FOR 1846.

YEARLY AND QUARTERLY MEETINGS OF FRIENDS IN NEW ENGLAND.

Yearly meeting, beginning with select do., 7th day after 2d 6th day, 6th month, 9th hour, morn., at Newport, R. I. — Public meeting for worship, 1st day following, at Newport and Portsmouth, 10th hour, morn., and 4th, aftern. Meeting for business at Newport, 2d day following, 9th hour, morn.

This yearly meeting comprises the Quarterly Meetings of Rhode Island, Salem, Sandwich, Falmouth, Smithfield, Vassalborough, Dover and Fairfield, held as follows, viz., *Rhode Island.* — On the 1st 5th day, 8th month, Portsmouth; 1st 5th day, 11th month, Somerset; 1st 5th day, 2d month, Providence; 1st 5th day, 5th month, East Greenwich. *Salem.* — On the 4th 5th day, 5th month, Saybrook; 3d 5th day, 8th month, Lynn; 3d 5th day, 10th month, Ware; 3d 5th day, 1st month, Salem. *Sandwich.* — On the 1st 5th days, 4th and 12th months, New Bedford; 1st 5th day, 7th month, Sandwich; 1st 5th day, 10th month, Sandwich. *Falmouth.* — On the 5th day before the 1st 6th day in the month, at Windham, in the 2d and 9th months; at Falmouth, in the 6th, and at Durham in the 11th. *Smithfield.* — On the 2d 5th day, 8th month, Bolton; 2d 5th day, 11th month, Smithfield; 2d 5th day, 2d month, Worcester; 2d 5th day, 5th month, Northbridge. *Vassalborough.* — On the 2d 6th day, 2d, 9th, and 11th months; and on the 4th day before the last 6th day, 5th month, Vassalborough. *Dover, N. H.* — On the 4th 5th day in the month; at Dover, in the 4th; at North Berwick, in the 8th; at Sandwich in the 10th; and at Rochester, upper meeting, (Meaderborough,) in the 2d month. *Fairfield.* — At Hallowell, on the 4th day before the 2d 6th day, in the 11th month; at Fairfield, on the 4th day before the 2d 6th days, in the 2d and 9th months; and at Hallowell on the last 6th day in the 5th month.

IN THIS HALF CENTURY . . .

The individual has become better *clad.* Our manufacturers surpass the fabrics of fifty years since, at one eighth the cost, and give cloth to the daily laborer that formerly the richest could hardly have compassed.

THE COMPLETE 1850 ALMANAC

Page 6

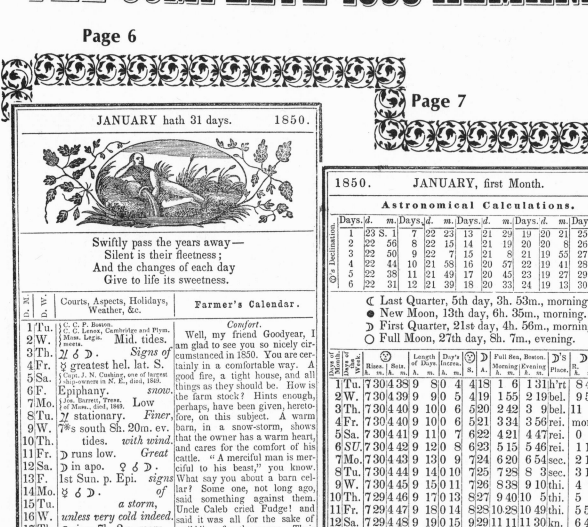

JANUARY hath 31 days. 1850.

Swiftly pass the years away—
Silent is their fleetness;
And the changes of each day
Give to life its sweetness.

D. M.	D. W.	Courts, Aspects, Holidays, Weather, &c.
1	Tu.	C. C. P. Boston. C. C. Lenox, Cambridge and Plym.
2	W.	Mass. Legis. meets. Mid. tides.
3	Th.	♃ ☌ ☽. *Signs of*
4	Fr.	☿ greatest hel. lat. S.
5	Sa.	Capt. J. N. Cushing, one of largest ship-owners in N. E., died, 1849.
6	F.	Epiphany. *snow.*
7	Mo.	Jos. Barrett, Treas. of Mass., died, 1849. Low
8	Tu.	♃ stationary. *Finer,*
9	W.	7*s south 8h. 20m. ev.
10	Th.	tides. *with wind.*
11	Fr.	☽ runs low. *Great*
12	Sa.	☽ in apo. ♀ ☌ ☽.
13	F.	1st Sun. p. Epi. *signs*
14	Mo.	☿ ☌ ☽. *of*
15	Tu.	*a storm,*
16	W.	*unless very cold indeed.*
17	Th.	♀ rises 7h. 2m. morn.
18	Fr.	Mid.
19	Sa.	♄ ☌ ☽. *Some snow*
20	F.	2d S. p. Epi. tides.
21	Mo.	C. C. P. Crim. Worcester. *or rain at*
22	Tu.	♂ south 8h. 59m. eve.
23	W.	☿ in ☊. ♂ stationary.
24	Th.	♂ ☌ ☽. *this time.*
25	Fr.	☽ runs high. *Grows*
26	Sa.	☽ in peri. *warmer.*
27	F.	Septuagesima S. Very
28	Mo.	C. C. P. Salem. ☿ sta. *Clouds*
29	Tu.	Geo. 3d d. 1820. high tides. *up*
30	W.	*for a storm.*
31	Th.	♂ south 8h. 25m. eve.

Farmer's Calendar.

Comfort.

Well, my friend Goodyear, I am glad to see you so nicely circumstanced in 1850. You are certainly in a comfortable way. A good fire, a tight house, and all things as they should be. How is the farm stock? Hints enough, perhaps, have been given, heretofore, on this subject. A warm barn, in a snow-storm, shows that the owner has a warm heart, and cares for the comfort of his cattle. "A merciful man is merciful to his beast," you know. What say you about a barn cellar? Some one, not long ago, said something against them. Uncle Caleb cried Fudge! and said it was all for the sake of scribbling for the paper. Their utility is unquestionable. A mechanic who keeps but one cow, by taking pains, can make her yield abundantly. Keep her comfortable, neighbor Handsaw. Don't you know that she cannot take care of herself; and that the better you keep her, the more and better milk she will yield? See yonder Tom Hardhack's poor brindle; how she crimples to the wind, and curls her tail between her legs, as she turns over her mess of meadow hay and brambles! She would fain, in her rummaging, pick out a few spears of red-top.

Page 7

1850. JANUARY, first Month.

Astronomical Calculations.

☉'s Declination.

Days.	d.	m.	Days.	d.	m.	Days.	d.	m.	Days.	d.	m.	Days.	d.	m.
1	23 S.	1	7	22	23	13	21	29	19	20	21	25	18	58
2	22	56	8	22	15	14	21	19	20	20	8	26	18	43
3	22	50	9	22	7	15	21	8	21	19	55	27	18	28
4	22	44	10	21	58	16	20	57	22	19	41	28	18	12
5	22	38	11	21	49	17	20	45	23	19	27	29	17	56
6	22	31	12	21	39	18	20	33	24	19	13	30	17	40

☾ Last Quarter, 5th day, 3h. 53m., morning.
● New Moon, 13th day, 6h. 35m., morning.
☽ First Quarter, 21st day, 4h. 56m., morning.
○ Full Moon, 27th day, 8h. 7m., evening.

Days of Month.	Days of the Week.	☉ Rises. h. m.	☉ Sets. h. m.	Length of Days. h. m.	Day's Increa. h. m.	☉ S.	☽ A.	Full Sea, Boston. Morning h. m.	Full Sea, Boston. Evening h. m.	☽'s Place.	☽ R. S. h. m.	☽ Souths. h. m.
1	Tu.	7 30	4 38	9 8	0 4	4	18	1 6	1 31	h'rt	8 48	2 41
2	W.	7 30	4 39	9 9	0 5	4	19	1 55	2 19	bel.	9 57	3 38
3	Th.	7 30	4 40	9 10	0 6	5	20	2 42	3 9	bel.	11 4	4 30
4	Fr.	7 30	4 40	9 10	0 6	5	21	3 34	3 56	rei.	morn	5 20
5	Sa.	7 30	4 41	9 11	0 7	6	22	4 21	4 47	rei.	0 8	6 7
6	*SU.*	7 30	4 42	9 12	0 8	6	23	5 15	5 46	rei.	1 10	6 53
7	Mo.	7 30	4 43	9 13	0 9	7	24	6 20	6 54	sec.	2 12	7 38
8	Tu.	7 30	4 44	9 14	0 10	7	25	7 28	8 3	sec.	3 11	8 23
9	W.	7 30	4 45	9 15	0 11	7	26	8 38	9 10	thi.	4 8	9 9
10	Th.	7 29	4 46	9 17	0 13	8	27	9 40	10 5	thi.	5 5	9 56
11	Fr.	7 29	4 47	9 18	0 14	8	28	10 28	10 49	thi.	5 57	10 43
12	Sa.	7 29	4 48	9 19	0 15	9	29	11 11	11 30	kn.	6 47	11 31
13	*SU.*	7 28	4 49	9 21	0 17	9	●	11 46	——	kn.	sets	ev. 18
14	Mo.	7 28	4 50	9 22	0 18	9	1	0 5	0 22	legs	6 1	1 6
15	Tu.	7 27	4 51	9 24	0 20	10	2	0 39	0 57	legs	6 59	1 52
16	W.	7 27	4 53	9 26	0 22	10	3	1 11	1 28	legs	7 55	2 38
17	Th.	7 26	4 54	9 28	0 24	10	4	1 44	2 1	feet	8 56	3 23
18	Fr.	7 26	4 55	9 29	0 25	11	5	2 16	2 35	feet	9 55	4 8
19	Sa.	7 25	4 57	9 32	0 28	11	6	2 54	3 11	h'd	10 57	4 53
20	*SU.*	7 24	4 58	9 34	0 30	11	7	3 32	3 52	h'd	11 59	5 40
21	Mo.	7 23	4 59	9 36	0 32	12	8	4 15	4 38	n'k	morn	6 28
22	Tu.	7 22	5 0	9 38	0 34	12	9	5 6	5 37	n'k	1 4	7 20
23	W.	7 22	5 2	9 40	0 36	12	10	6 10	6 49	arm	2 11	8 15
24	Th.	7 21	5 3	9 42	0 38	12	11	7 24	8 4	arm	3 18	9 14
25	Fr.	7 20	5 4	9 44	0 40	13	12	8 45	9 19	arm	4 26	10 15
26	Sa.	7 20	5 5	9 45	0 41	13	13	9 49	10 19	br.	5 32	11 18
27	*SU.*	7 19	5 6	9 47	0 43	13	○	10 48	11 14	br.	6 30	morn
28	Mo.	7 18	5 8	9 50	0 46	13	15	11 40	——	h'rt	rises	0 20
29	Tu.	7 17	5 9	9 52	0 48	13	16	0 7	0 33	h'rt	7 36	1 20
30	W.	7 16	5 10	9 54	0 50	14	17	0 56	1 18	bel.	8 44	2 16
31	Th.	7 15	5 12	9 57	0 53	14	18	1 41	2 2	bel.	9 52	3 9

IN THIS HALF CENTURY . . .

All are better *lodged*. In this broad circle of our land, there is hardly an uncomfortable house inhabited by a sober, native-born American. The furniture of the humble now more than equals, in convenience and quantity, that of the majority of the rich in 1799.

THE COMPLETE 1850 ALMANAC

1850. FEBRUARY, second Month.

Astronomical Calculations.

☉'s Declination. Days.	d.	m.	Days.	d.	m.	Days.	d.	m.	Days.	d.	m.	Days.	d.	m.
1	17 S.	7	7	15	19	13	13	22	19	11	17	25	9	6
2	16	49	8	15	0	14	13	2	20	10	56	26	8	44
3	16	32	9	14	41	15	12	41	21	10	34	27	8	21
4	16	14	10	14	22	16	12	21	22	10	12	28	7	59
5	15	56	11	14	2	17	12	0	23	9	51			
6	15	38	12	13	42	18	11	39	24	9	28			

☾ Last Quarter, 3d day, 8h. 34m., morning.
◉ New Moon, 12th day, 1h. 45m., morning.
☽ First Quarter, 19th day, 3h. 26m., evening.
○ Full Moon, 26th day, 7h. 17m., morning.

Days of Month.	Days of the Week.	☉ Rises. h. m.	Sets. h. m.	Length of Days. h. m.	Day's Increa. m.	☉ S.	☽ A.	Full Sea, Boston. Morning. h. m.	Evening. h. m.	☽'s Place.	☽ R. h. m.	S. h. m.	☽ Souths. h. m.
1	Fr.	7 14	5 14	10 0	0 56	14	19	2 24	2 46	rei.	10 57		3 59
2	Sa.	7 13	5 15	10 2	0 58	14	20	3 7	3 27	rei.	morn		4 47
3	SU.	7 11	5 16	10 5	1 1	14	21	3 48	4 11	sec.	0 0		5 34
4	Mo.	7 10	5 18	10 8	1 4	14	22	4 34	4 56	sec.	1 2		6 20
5	Tu.	7 9	5 19	10 10	1 6	14	23	5 24	5 55	sec.	2 0		7 6
6	W.	7 8	5 20	10 12	1 8	14	24	6 32	7 8	thi.	2 58		7 53
7	Th.	7 7	5 22	10 15	1 11	14	25	7 45	8 25	thi.	3 52		8 40
8	Fr.	7 6	5 23	10 17	1 13	14	26	9 2	9 37	kn.	4 43		9 27
9	Sa.	7 5	5 25	10 20	1 16	15	27	10 4	10 26	kn.	5 30		10 15
10	SU.	7 4	5 26	10 22	1 18	15	28	10 48	11 10	legs	6 12		11 2
11	Mo.	7 2	5 27	10 25	1 21	15	29	11 29	11 47	legs	6 52		11 49
12	Tu.	7 1	5 28	10 27	1 23	15	◉	—	0 3	legs	sets		ev. 36
13	W.	7 0	5 30	10 30	1 26	15	1	0 22	0 37	feet	6 50		1 21
14	Th.	6 58	5 31	10 33	1 29	14	2	0 53	1 8	feet	7 49		2 7
15	Fr.	6 57	5 32	10 35	1 31	14	3	1 24	1 40	h'd	8 50		2 52
16	Sa.	6 55	5 33	10 38	1 34	14	4	1 57	2 13	h'd	9 52		3 38
17	SU.	6 54	5 35	10 40	1 36	14	5	2 31	2 48	h'd	10 56		4 25
18	Mo.	6 52	5 35	10 43	1 37	14	6	3 8	3 27	n'k	morn		5 15
19	Tu.	6 51	5 37	10 46	1 42	14	7	3 47	4 9	n'k	0 1		6 7
20	W.	6 50	5 38	10 48	1 44	14	8	4 34	5 1	arm	1 6		7 2
21	Th.	6 48	5 40	10 52	1 48	14	9	5 35	6 13	arm	2 12		8 0
22	Fr.	6 47	5 41	10 54	1 50	14	10	6 56	7 37	br.	3 16		9 0
23	Sa.	6 45	5 42	10 57	1 53	14	11	8 21	9 4	br.	4 14		10 1
24	SU.	6 44	5 44	11 0	1 56	13	12	9 40	10 11	h'rt	5 10		11 1
25	Mo.	6 42	5 45	11 3	1 59	13	13	10 40	11 6	h'rt	5 56		11 58
26	Tu.	6 40	5 46	11 6	2 13	○		11 30	11 53	bel.	rises		morn
27	W.	6 38	5 47	11 9	2 15	13	16	—	0 17	bel.	7 29		0 53
28	Th.	6 37	5 48	11 11	2 7	13	16	0 38	1 0	rei.	8 37		1 45

Venus will be a *morning star* until Feb. 13th; then an *evening star* until Dec. 15th; and then a *morning star* the rest of the year. **Jupiter** will be a *morning star* until March 11th; then an *evening star* until Sept. 24th; and then a *morning star* the rest of the year.

IN THIS HALF CENTURY . . .

FEBRUARY hath 28 days. 1850.

When the winter's stormy blast
Roars and rages round us,
Pleasures with it come and last
Long when they have found us.

D. M.	D. W.	Courts, Aspects, Holidays, Weather, &c.	Farmer's Calendar.
1	Fr.	7✳s south 6h. 39m. eve.	*The Spinning-Wheel.*
2	Sa.	*Moderates.*	I suppose this good old-fash-
3	F.	Sex. Sun. *Much more*	ioned machine must be given up,
4	Mo.	{ Revolutionary war ceased, 1783. *Low*	since every working girl has posted off to Lowell. So aunt
5	Tu.	tides. *comfortable.*	Celia says. Every *working girl,*
6	W.	☿ greatest hel. lat. N.	did I say? Is there none then to
7	Th.	☿ in inf. ☌ ☉.	join the mother in her domestic
8	Fr.	☽ runs low. ☽ in apo.	duties? Poh! girls, think again
9	Sa.	{ Pope Pius IX. deposed, and Repub. Government declared at Rome, 1849.	on this matter, and think better. No one will despise you for know-
10	F.	Shrove Sun. *Rain*	ing and practising the business
11	Mo.	{ C. C. P. Crim. ◉ eclip. inv. Cambridge.	of housewifery. What better ac-
12	Tu.	{ Peace with Gr. *or snow.* Britain, 1815.	complishments would you, or could you, have, than to be able
13	W.	Ash Wednesday.	to manage well the affairs of a
14	Th.	St. Valentine. Mid.	family? Yet some are so illy
15	Fr.	♄ ☌ ☽ . tides. *Pleas-*	informed in these duties, that they
16	Sa.	*ant for*	can hardly cook a potato. Then there is the bread; let it not be of
17	F.	1st S. in Lent. *the*	the kind of which Hood says,
18	Mo.	{ C. C. P. *season.* Northam.	"Who hath not heard of family bread,
19	Tu.	{ S. J. C. ☿ sta. Tides Dedham.	An indigestible compound of putty and lead?"
20	W.	{ Hon. T. Farrar, oldest grad. Harv. { Uni., died, ag. 101 y. 7 m. 10 d., 1849.	Give me the girl that knows how
21	Th.	*increasing. Showers.*	to do up the dough and the dough-
22	Fr.	Washington born, 1732.	nuts, the pudding and the pot- luck. Our grandmothers were up
23	Sa.	*Rough winds.*	to all these things. They never
24	F.	{ 2d Sun. in Lent. ☽ per. { France dec. Repub. 1848.	scowled at having something to do, but, keeping good temper on
25	Mo.	{ C. C. P. *Finer.* Lenox.	their side, carried on, with steady
26	Tu.	{ Napoleon left *High Some* Elba, 1815.	hand, the whole process of boiling
27	W.	♃ ☌ ☽. *snow or rain.*	and baking, turning the spinning- wheel and rocking the cradle, in
28	Th.	♄ sets 8h. 2m. ev. tides.	one forenoon. I suppose now your

father and the boys are hard at it in the thirty-acre lot, wood-cutting. Well, girls, suppose, on their return, you try your best, and cook them something warm and good.

The individual has been better *taught.* Three months' schooling in winter at reading, writing, and arithmetic—truancy, freezing, mending pens and ruling writing books deducted—was the most ever stickled for by the patriotism of the last age. Now, ten months in a year of good schools, good text-books, school-houses and appliances, teachers taught for the work, apparatus, cabinets and school libraries—all these are fast spreading over our land.

THE COMPLETE 1850 ALMANAC

Page 10

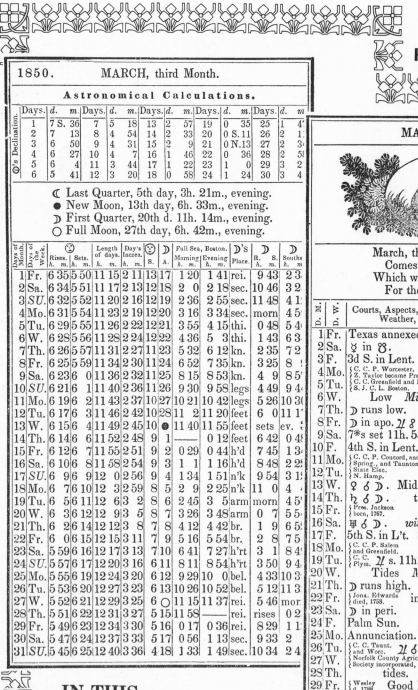

1850. MARCH, third Month.

Astronomical Calculations.

☉'s Declination.

Days.	d. m.	Days.	d. m.	Days.	d. m.	Days.	d. m.	Days.	d. m
1	7 S. 36	7	5 18	13	2 57	19	0 35	25	1 4
2	7 13	8	4 54	14	2 33	20	0 S. 11	26	2 1
3	6 50	9	4 31	15	2 9	21	0 N. 13	27	2 3
4	6 27	10	4 7	16	1 46	22	0 36	28	2 5
5	6 4	11	3 44	17	1 22	23	1 0	29	3 2
6	5 41	12	3 20	18	0 58	24	1 24	30	3 4

☾ Last Quarter, 5th day, 3h. 21m., evening.
● New Moon, 13th day, 6h. 33m., evening.
☽ First Quarter, 20th d. 11h. 14m., evening.
○ Full Moon, 27th day, 6h. 42m., evening.

Days of Month.	Days of the Week.	☉ Rises. h. m.	☉ Sets. h. m.	Length of days. h. m.	Day's Increa. h. m.	☉ S.	☽ A.	Full Sea, Boston. Morning h. m.	Full Sea, Boston. Evening h. m.	☽'s Place.	☽ R. S. h. m.	☽ Souths h. m
1	Fr.	6 35	5 50	11 15	2 11	13	17	1 20	1 41	rei.	9 43	2 3
2	Sa.	6 34	5 51	11 17	2 13	12	18	2 0	2 18	sec.	10 46	3 2
3	*SU.*	6 32	5 52	11 20	2 16	12	19	2 36	2 55	sec.	11 48	4 1
4	Mo.	6 31	5 54	11 23	2 19	12	20	3 16	3 34	sec.	morn	4 5
5	Tu.	6 29	5 55	11 26	2 22	12	21	3 55	4 15	thi.	0 48	5 4
6	W.	6 28	5 56	11 28	2 24	12	22	4 36	5 3	thi.	1 43	6 3
7	Th.	6 26	5 57	11 31	2 27	11	23	5 32	6 12	kn.	2 35	7 2
8	Fr.	6 25	5 59	11 34	2 30	11	24	6 52	7 35	kn.	3 25	8
9	Sa.	6 23	6 0	11 36	2 32	11	25	8 15	8 53	kn.	4 9	8 5
10	*SU.*	6 21	6 1	11 40	2 36	11	26	9 30	9 58	legs	4 49	9 4
11	Mo.	6 19	6 2	11 43	2 37	10	27	10 21	10 42	legs	5 26	10 3
12	Tu.	6 17	6 3	11 46	2 42	10	28	11 2	11 20	feet	6 0	11 1
13	W.	6 15	6 4	11 49	2 45	10	●	11 40	11 55	feet	sets	ev.
14	Th.	6 14	6 6	11 52	2 48	9	1	——	0 12	feet	6 42	0 4
15	Fr.	6 12	6 7	11 55	2 51	9	2	0 29	0 44	h'd	7 45	1 3
16	Sa.	6 10	6 8	11 58	2 54	9	3	1 1	1 16	h'd	8 48	2 2
17	*SU.*	6 9	6 9	12 0	2 56	9	4	1 34	1 51	n'k	9 54	3 1
18	Mo.	6 7	6 10	12 3	2 59	8	5	2 9	2 25	n'k	11 0	4
19	Tu.	6 5	6 11	12 6	3 2	8	6	2 45	3 5	arm	morn	4 5
20	W.	6 3	6 12	12 9	3 5	8	7	3 26	3 48	arm	0 7	5 5
21	Th.	6 2	6 14	12 12	3 8	7	8	4 12	4 42	br.	1 9	6 5
22	Fr.	6 0	6 15	12 15	3 11	7	9	5 16	5 54	br.	2 8	7 5
23	Sa.	5 59	6 16	12 17	3 13	7	10	6 41	7 27	h'rt	3 1	8 4
24	*SU.*	5 57	6 17	12 20	3 16	6	11	8 11	8 54	h'rt	3 50	9 4
25	Mo.	5 55	6 19	12 24	3 20	6	12	9 29	10 0	bel.	4 33	10 3
26	Tu.	5 53	6 20	12 27	3 23	6	13	10 26	10 52	bel.	5 12	11 3
27	W.	5 52	6 21	12 29	3 25	6	○	11 15	11 37	rei.	5 46	mor
28	Th.	5 51	6 22	12 31	3 27	5	15	11 58	——	rei.	rises	0 2
29	Fr.	5 49	6 23	12 34	3 30	5	16	0 17	0 36	rei.	8 29	1 1
30	Sa.	5 47	6 24	12 37	3 33	5	17	0 56	1 13	sec.	9 33	2
31	*SU.*	5 45	6 25	12 40	3 36	4	18	1 33	1 49	sec.	10 34	2 4

Page 11

MARCH hath 31 days. 1850.

March, the harbinger of Spring,
Comes with warm winds blowing,
Which will soon new verdure bring,
For the streams are flowing.

D. M.	D. W.	Courts, Aspects, Holidays, Weather, &c.
1	Fr.	Texas annexed, 1846.
2	Sa.	☿ in ♉. *Frequent*
3	F.	3d S. in Lent. *changes.*
4	Mo.	C. C. P. Worcester. Z. Taylor became Presid. U. S., 1849.
5	Tu.	C. C. Greenfield and Northampton. S. J. C. L. Boston.
6	W.	Low *Milder, with*
7	Th.	☽ runs low.
8	Fr.	☽ in apo. ♃ ☍ ☉. tides.
9	Sa.	7*s set 11h. 55m. eve.
10	F.	4th S. in Lent. *rain*
11	Mo.	C. C. P. Concord, and Spring., and Taunton. ☿ ☌ ☽.
12	Tu.	State Elec. N. Hamp. *or snow.*
13	W.	♀ ☌ ☽. Mid. *Finer.*
14	Th.	♄ ☌ ☽. tides.
15	Fr.	Pres. Jackson born, 1767. *Cooler,*
16	Sa.	♅ ☌ ☽. *with white*
17	F.	5th S. in L't. St. Pat'k.
18	Mo.	C. C. P. Salem and Greenfield. *frosts.*
19	Tu.	C. C. Plym. ♃ s. 11h. 25m. ev.
20	W.	Tides *Moderates.*
21	Th.	☽ runs high. *Change-*
22	Fr.	Jona. Edwards died, 1758. incr. *able*
23	Sa.	☽ in peri. *weather*
24	F.	Palm Sun. *for some*
25	Mo.	Annunciation. *days.*
26	Tu.	C. C. Taunt. and Worc. ♃ ☌ ☽. High
27	W.	Norfolk County Agricultural Society incorporated, 1849.
28	Th.	tides. *Great*
29	Fr.	Wesley d. 1788. Good Friday.
30	Sa.	*signs of a storm.*
31	F.	EASTER SUN. ♄ ☌ ☉.

Farmer's Calendar.

Training.

Friendly reader, I have nothing to do here about *soldier training*; but for the proper discipline of our sons and daughters I have a heart-felt interest. "Train them up," says Solomon, "in the way they should go." An important inquiry, then, is the *way*. How should they go, and where should they go? Shall they be under any regulation, or shall they go whensoever and wheresoever they list, like the idle wind? Who shall *train* them? As to parents, there are some who incline to take the guidance of their children's education, and would train them for heaven; while others have little care about it, and let them train themselves for quite a different place. I feel a special concern for farmers' boys. You, my young friends, who may be accustomed to peruse this little calendar, in candlelight evenings, will do well to consider (in case your parents have given it up) the danger that approaches you when allowed to have your own way, as you please, like a wild colt without bridle or halter. Think not that to labor is disgraceful, as some foolishly do. "If you do not need labor for food, it is capital for physic," and not costly either.

IN THIS HALF CENTURY...

We would have you to look at a list of some of the points of improvement. You will find instances of everything that can possibly make up individual, social, national or human progress. With Steamboats, Railroads, Telegraphs, our country, this century has far surpassed whole previous centuries.

THE COMPLETE 1850 ALMANAC

Page 12

Page 13

1850. APRIL, fourth Month.

Astronomical Calculations.

☉'s Declination. Days.	d.	m.	Days.	d.	m.	Days.	d.	m.	Days.	d.	m.	Days.	d.	m.
1	4	N.31	7	6	48	13	9	1	19	11	9	25	13	10
2	4	54	8	7	11	14	9	23	20	11	29	26	13	29
3	5	17	9	7	33	15	9	44	21	11	50	27	13	48
4	5	40	10	7	55	16	10	6	22	12	10	28	14	7
5	6	3	11	8	17	17	10	27	23	12	30	29	14	26
6	6	25	12	8	39	18	10	48	24	12	50	30	14	45

☾ Last Quarter, 4th day, 11h. 0m., morning.
● New Moon, 12th day, 8h. 3m., morning.
☽ First Quarter, 19th day, 5h. 23m., morning.
○ Full Moon, 26th day, 6h. 36m., morning.

Days of Month.	Days of the Week.	☉ Rises. h. m.	☉ Sets. h. m.	Length of Days. h. m.	Day's Increa. h. m	☉ S.	☽ A.	Full Sea, Boston. Morning h. m.	Full Sea, Boston. Evening h. m.	☽'s Place.	☽ R. S. h. m.	☽ Souths. h. m
1	Mo.	5 43	6 26	12 43	3 39	4	19	2 9	2 27	thi.	11 32	3 37
2	Tu.	5 42	6 27	12 45	3 41	4	20	2 43	3 1	thi.	morn	4 26
3	W.	5 40	6 28	12 48	3 44	3	21	3 20	3 39	kn.	0 28	5 14
4	Th.	5 38	6 29	12 51	3 47	3	22	4 2	4 24	kn.	1 13	6 2
5	Fr.	5 36	6 30	12 54	3 51	3	23	4 50	5 22	kn.	2 3	6 50
6	Sa.	5 34	6 31	12 57	3 53	2	24	6 4	6 45	legs	2 47	7 37
7	*SU.*	5 32	6 32	13 0	3 56	2	25	7 28	8 7	legs	3 25	8 23
8	Mo.	5 31	6 33	13 2	3 58	2	26	8 43	9 18	feet	3 58	9 10
9	Tu.	5 29	6 34	13 5	4 1	2	27	9 43	10 8	feet	4 31	9 56
10	W.	5 27	6 35	13 8	4 4	1	28	10 28	10 48	feet	5 2	10 42
11	Th.	5 26	6 36	13 10	4 6	1	29	11 5	11 22	h'd	5 32	11 28
12	Fr.	5 24	6 37	13 13	4 9	1	●	11 38	11 58	h'd	sets	ev. 16
13	Sa.	5 23	6 38	13 15	4 11	1	1	——	0 14	n'k	7 41	1 6
14	*SU.*	5 21	6 39	13 18	4 14	0	2	0 32	0 49	n'k	8 51	1 58
15	Mo.	5 19	6 40	13 21	4 17	0	3	1 8	1 26	arm	9 58	2 52
16	Tu.	5 18	6 41	13 23	4 19	F.	4	1 44	2 5	arm	11 3	3 49
17	W.	5 16	6 42	13 26	4 22	0	5	2 25	2 48	br.	morn	4 47
18	Th.	5 14	6 43	13 29	4 25	1	6	3 9	3 35	br.	0 4	5 46
19	Fr.	5 13	6 44	13 31	4 27	1	7	4 3	4 33	h'rt	0 59	6 44
20	Sa.	5 11	6 45	13 34	4 30	1	8	5 10	5 51	h'rt	1 48	7 39
21	*SU.*	5 10	6 47	13 37	4 33	1	9	6 34	7 17	h'rt	2 32	8 33
22	Mo.	5 8	6 48	13 40	4 36	2	10	7 59	8 40	bel.	3 12	9 25
23	Tu.	5 6	6 49	13 43	4 39	2	11	9 11	9 40	bel.	3 45	10 15
24	W.	5 5	6 50	13 45	4 41	2	12	10 5	10 30	rei.	4 19	11 4
25	Th.	5 3	6 52	13 47	4 43	2	13	10 53	11 14	rei.	4 50	11 52
26	Fr.	5 2	6 53	13 51	4 47	2	○	11 32	11 54	sec.	5 22	morn
27	Sa.	5 1	6 54	13 53	4 49	2	15	——	0 12	sec.	rises	0 40
28	*SU.*	4 59	6 55	13 56	4 52	3	16	0 31	0 50	thi.	9 20	1 21
29	Mo.	4 58	6 57	13 59	4 55	3	17	1 6	1 23	thi.	10 18	2 17
30	Tu.	4 56	6 58	14 2	4 58	3	18	1 40	1 58	thi.	11 11	3 6

APRIL hath 30 days. 1850.

April, fickle as the moon,
Gay, but changing ever;
Thy warm showers, a precious boon,
Fail to bless us never.

D. M.	D. W.	Courts, Aspects, Holidays, Weather, &c.
1	Mo.	State Elec. Connecticut. *Fine for*
2	Tu.	C. C. P. Bost. & Barnst. C. C. Lenox. *the*
3	W.	State Elec. R. Island. ☽ r. l. *season.*
4	Th.	Pres. Harrison died, 1841. Very
5	Fr.	Goldsmith died, 1784. low *A storm*
6	Sa.	♀ ☌ ♅. tides. *is at*
7	F.	Low Sunday. *hand.*
8	Mo.	C.C.P. Plym. ♃ s. 9h. 58m. ev.
9	Tu.	C. C. Barnst., Ips. and Springf. S. J. C. Low. *High*
10	W.	☿ ☌ ♄. Tides *winds.*
11	Th.	♄ ☌ ☽, ☿ ☌ ☽. incr.
12	Fr.	♅ ☌ ☽. *Finer.*
13	Sa.	♀ ☌ ☽. Mid.
14	F.	2d S. p. Easter. tides.
15	Mo.	7*s set 9h. 40m. eve.
16	Tu.	C. C. Dedham. S. J. C. Worc. & Greenf. ♅ ☌ ☉.
17	W.	☽ runs high. ♅ ☌ ☿.
18	Th.	☽ in peri. ♂ ☌ ☽.
19	Fr.	Battles Lex. and Conc., 1775. *Finer for*
20	Sa.	♂ sets 1h. 1m. morn.
21	F.	3d S. p. Easter. *some*
22	Mo.	C. C. P. Dedham. ♃ ☌ ☽. *days.*
23	Tu.	S. J. C. Northamp. and Taunton. High
24	W.	First paper pr. at Bost., Mass., called "Boston News Letter," 1704.
25	Th.	☿ in peri. tides.
26	Fr.	J. Kirkland, Pres. Harv. Univ., died, 1840. *Signs*
27	Sa.	*of rain.*
28	F.	4th S. p. East. Tides
29	Mo.	7*s set 8h. 47m. eve.
30	Tu.	S. J. C. Ipswich and Springfield. decreasing.

Farmer's Calendar.

Business.

This is peculiarly a *business* month. Hear now how the little birds are telling us of it! The ground is all open for our improvement, and he that thinks of having crops in Autumn must commence the preparation in good earnest. Come, Jacob and Jonas, Zenas and Zebulon, where are ye? Yare, boys, yare! as old Shakspeare says in the play; that is, be dexterous and be nimble, as a cat after a weasel. When all nature is on the spring, man should certainly be engaged. Come, put the steers between the mare and old oxen, and see how they work. Chains, chains, man! never let them rust; and the ploughs, too. As for borrowing, that's out of all fashion in these agricultural times. Let every man handle his own tools. What a choice we have! *Ruggles, Nourse & Mason; Prouty & Mears; J. Breck & Co.*, and not all told. It was scratching business for our forefathers, of olden time, with their strange kind of implements, when they used to farm it. An agricultural warehouse was not known in those times, from Passamaquoddy to Georgia. How would they have wondered at a store filled with hay-cutters, corn-shellers, fanning-mills, rakes, cradles, &c. &c.

IN THIS HALF CENTURY . . .

And now, how does the aggregate of all that has been done here, in the last half century, tell in our Nation? To this nation it has been indeed gain. In 1800, there were *thirteen* states; in 1850, there are *thirty* states. In 1800, we had 1,000,000 square miles of territory; in 1850, we have 3,000,000. In 1800, we had 5,309,758 people; in 1850, we have 24,000,000.

THE COMPLETE 1850 ALMANAC

Page 14

Page 15

1850. MAY, fifth Month.

Astronomical Calculations.

☉'s Declination.

Days.	d.	m.	Days.	d.	m.	Days.	d.	m.	Days.	d.	m.	Days.	d.	m.
1	15	N. 3	7	16	47	13	18	22	19	19	45	25	20	56
2	15	21	8	17	4	14	18	36	20	19	58	26	21	7
3	15	39	9	17	20	15	18	51	21	20	10	27	21	17
4	15	56	10	17	36	16	19	5	22	20	22	28	21	27
5	16	14	11	17	52	17	19	19	23	20	34	29	21	37
6	16	31	12	18	7	18	19	32	24	20	45	30	21	46

☾ Last Quarter, 4th day, 6h. 2m., morning.
● New Moon, 11th day, 6h. 25m., morning.
☽ First Quarter, 18th day, 11h. 8m., morning.
○ Full Moon, 25th day, 7h. 24m., evening.

Days of Month.	Days of the Week.	☉ Rises. h. m.	☉ Sets. h. m.	Length of Days. h. m.	Day's Increa. h. m.	☉ F.	☽ A.	Full Sea, Boston. Morning h. m.	Full Sea, Boston. Evening h. m.	☽'s Place.	☽ R. S. h. m.	☽ Souths. h. m.
1	W.	4 54	6 59	14 5	5 1	3	19	2 15	2 32	kn.	11 59	3 54
2	Th.	4 53	7 0	14 7	5 3	3	20	2 50	3 11	kn.	morn	4 43
3	Fr.	4 52	7 1	14 9	5 5	3	21	3 31	3 55	legs	0 43	5 30
4	Sa.	4 50	7 2	14 12	5 8	3	22	4 18	4 45	legs	1 23	6 17
5	*SU.*	4 49	7 3	14 14	5 10	3	23	5 17	5 58	legs	1 57	7 3
6	Mo.	4 48	7 4	14 16	5 12	4	24	6 37	7 13	feet	2 31	7 48
7	Tu.	4 47	7 5	14 18	5 14	4	25	7 49	8 25	feet	3 2	8 33
8	W.	4 46	7 6	14 20	5 16	4	26	8 54	9 23	h'd	3 31	9 19
9	Th.	4 45	7 7	14 22	5 18	4	27	9 46	10 3	h'd	4 2	10 6
10	Fr.	4 44	7 8	14 24	5 20	4	28	10 26	10 48	n'k	4 33	10 55
11	Sa.	4 43	7 9	14 26	5 22	4	29	11 7	11 24	n'k	5 8	11 47
12	*SU.*	4 42	7 10	14 28	5 24	4	●	11 46	——	n'k	sets	ev. 41
13	Mo.	4 41	7 11	14 30	5 26	4	1	0 6	0 26	arm	8 10	1 39
14	Tu.	4 40	7 12	14 32	5 28	4	2	0 47	1 6	arm	9 56	2 38
15	W.	4 39	7 13	14 34	5 30	4	3	1 28	1 50	br.	10 56	3 39
16	Th.	4 38	7 14	14 36	5 32	4	4	2 12	2 37	br.	11 48	4 39
17	Fr.	4 37	7 15	14 38	5 34	4	5	3 3	3 30	h'rt	morn	5 36
18	Sa.	4 36	7 16	14 40	5 36	4	6	4 0	4 30	h'rt	0 35	6 31
19	*SU.*	4 36	7 17	14 41	5 37	4	7	5 5	5 40	bel.	1 15	7 22
20	Mo.	4 35	7 18	14 43	5 39	4	8	6 24	7 1	bel.	1 49	8 12
21	Tu.	4 34	7 19	14 45	5 41	4	9	7 35	8 10	rei.	2 22	9 0
22	W.	4 33	7 20	14 47	5 43	4	10	8 44	9 14	rei.	2 54	9 47
23	Th.	4 32	7 21	14 49	5 45	4	11	9 40	10 4	sec.	3 23	10 35
24	Fr.	4 31	7 22	14 51	5 47	4	12	10 27	10 49	sec.	3 55	11 22
25	Sa.	4 30	7 23	14 53	5 49	3	○	11 11	11 31	sec.	4 29	morn
26	*SU.*	4 29	7 24	14 55	5 51	3	14	11 50	——	thi.	rises	0 10
27	Mo.	4 28	7 25	14 57	5 53	3	15	0 9	0 26	thi.	9 4	0 59
28	Tu.	4 28	7 26	14 58	5 54	3	16	0 46	1 2	kn.	9 55	1 48
29	W.	4 27	7 27	15 0	5 56	3	17	1 18	1 37	kn.	10 40	2 36
30	Th.	4 26	7 27	15 1	5 57	3	18	1 54	2 11	kn.	11 20	3 24
31	Fr.	4 26	7 28	15 2	5 58	3	19	2 29	2 48	legs	11 56	4 12

MAY hath 31 days. 1850.

May, the month of birds and flowers,
Is the poet's treasure;
We, too, love thy sunny hours,
For they give us pleasure.

D. M.	D. W.	Courts, Aspects, Holidays, Weather, &c.
1	W.	Connecticut Legis. meets. ☽ runs low.
2	Th.	☽ in apo. ☿ ☌ ♀.
3	Fr.	Columbus discov'd Jamaica, 1495. *Cool, but*
4	Sa.	Very low *pleasant.*
5	F.	Rogation Sun. tides.
6	Mo.	7th. Gen. W. J. Worth died, 1849. *Rain,*
7	Tu.	S. J. C. Barnstable. R. I. Leg. meets, Provid. *with*
8	W.	Maine Legis. meets. Tides *wind.*
9	Th.	Holy Thurs. ♄ ☌ ☽.
10	Fr.	♅ ☌ ☽. ♃ sta. incr.
11	Sa.	*Much finer.*
12	F.	Sun. p. Ascen. *Cooler,*
13	Mo.	*with some*
14	Tu.	S. J. C. Lenox and Plymouth. Mid.
15	W.	Daniel O'Connell died, 1847. tides.
16	Th.	*frost.*
17	Fr.	♂ sets 0h. 3m. morn.
18	Sa.	19th. Dark day, 1780. *Signs*
19	F.	Whit Sunday. *of*
20	Mo.	C. C. P. Crim. Springfield. *rain.*
21	Tu.	Maria Edgeworth d. '49, aged 83. *Very*
22	W.	C. C. Edgartown. *fine.*
23	Th.	♀ sets 9h. 3m. even.
24	Fr.	Victoria b. 1819. *More*
25	Sa.	Paley died, 1805.
26	F.	Trin. Sun. *signs of*
27	Mo.	C. C. P. Newbp't & Edg. C. C. P. Crim. Worc. High
28	Tu.	☽ r. low. tides. *showers.*
29	W.	☿ stationary.
30	Th.	☽ in apo. *Good*
31	Fr.	Dr. Chalmers died, 1847. *weather.*

Farmer's Calendar.

Mayflowers.

Our forefathers, the pilgrims, had a great fondness for them, if we may judge from the name they gave to the noble ship that brought them to this "rock-bound shore." We will copy them in their love of flowers, and their love of liberty, honesty and industry. Yes, we love the flowers of the field, the flowers of the sky, and would rejoice in all the beauties and all the grandeurs of nature. Sure, 't is a beautiful world, and we would "use it as not abusing it." Now, is not this a good setting-out? Tell me, ploughmen, corn-planters, wood-cutters, hedgers and ditchers. If so, let us proceed and prosecute our good resolutions. Seeds, seeds! It is time they were in the ground; especially in the garden. Farmers are too apt to think that gardening comes not much in their line of business. They will plough it up, indeed, but after that it is too much neglected. Peradventure they will have a little beet bed, and a few cabbages. But the man who is particular to have a good garden of various vegetables, well knows how favorably it operates upon the butcher's bill, as well as upon the health and spirits of his family. Are you looking out for a premium in the fall? That is well enough.

AND NOW, FINALLY . . .

Bear in mind that if you do not improve your opportunities, you have no right to grumble about your bad luck. If, in looking back upon your past life, you "see where you have missed it," don't commit the same blunder again.

Page 16

1850. JUNE, sixth Month.

Astronomical Calculations.

☉'s Declination.

Days.	d. m.	Days	d. m.	Days.	d. m.	Days.	d. m.	Days.	d. m.
1	22 N. 3	7	22 45	13	23 13	19	23 26	25	23 25
2	22 11	8	22 51	14	23 16	20	23 27	26	23 [illegible]
3	22 19	9	22 56	15	23 19	21	23 27	27	23 [illegible]
4	22 26	10	23 1	16	23 22	22	23 27	28	23 [illegible]
5	22 33	11	23 5	17	23 24	23	23 27	29	23 [illegible]
6	22 39	12	23 9	18	23 25	24	23 26	30	23 [illegible]

☾ Last Quarter, 2d day, 11h. 3m., evening.
● New Moon, 10th day, 2h. 36m., morning.
☽ First Quarter, 16th day, 5h. 39m., evening.
○ Full Moon, 24th day, 9h. 26m., morning.

Days of Month.	Days of the Week.	☉ Rises. h. m.	☉ Sets. h. m.	Length of Days. h. m	Day's Increa. h. m	☉ F.	☽ A.	Full Sea, Boston. Morning h. m.	Full Sea, Boston. Evening h. m.	☽'s Place.	☽ R. S. h. m.	☽ Souths. h. m.
1	Sa.	4 25	7 29	15 4	6 0	3	20	3 8	3 30	legs	morn	4 58
2	*SU.*	4 24	7 29	15 5	6 1	2	21	3 53	4 16	feet	0 29	5 43
3	Mo.	4 24	7 30	15 6	6 2	2	22	4 42	5 9	feet	1 0	6 27
4	Tu.	4 23	7 31	15 8	6 4	2	23	5 44	6 22	feet	1 28	7 12
5	W.	4 23	7 32	15 9	6 5	2	24	6 54	7 25	h'd	1 58	7 57
6	Th.	4 23	7 33	15 10	6 6	2	25	7 57	8 26	h'd	2 27	8 44
7	Fr.	4 22	7 33	15 11	6 7	2	26	8 56	9 22	n'k	3 0	9 33
8	Sa.	4 22	7 34	15 12	6 8	1	27	9 48	10 11	n'k	3 38	10 26
9	*SU.*	4 22	7 35	15 13	6 9	1	28	10 35	10 58	arm	4 19	11 23
10	Mo.	4 22	7 35	15 13	6 9	1	●	11 21	11 43	arm	sets	ev. 22
11	Tu.	4 22	7 36	15 14	6 10	1	1	——	0 8	br.	8 43	1 24
12	W.	4 22	7 37	15 15	6 11	1	2	0 29	0 54	br.	9 39	2 37
13	Th.	4 22	7 37	15 16	6 12	0	3	1 17	1 41	h'rt	10 30	3 27
14	Fr.	4 22	7 38	15 16	6 12	0	4	2 5	2 32	h'rt	11 12	4 25
15	Sa.	4 22	7 38	15 16	6 12	S.	5	2 57	3 23	bel.	11 50	5 19
16	*SU.*	4 22	7 38	15 16	6 12	0	6	3 51	4 20	bel.	morn	6 10
17	Mo.	4 22	7 38	15 16	6 12	0	7	4 51	5 23	rei.	0 24	6 59
18	Tu.	4 23	7 39	15 16	6 12	1	8	5 57	6 33	rei.	0 54	7 46
19	W.	4 23	7 39	15 16	6 12	1	9	7 5	7 36	rei.	1 25	8 33
20	Th.	4 23	7 39	15 16	6 12	1	10	8 9	8 39	sec.	1 56	9 19
21	Fr.	4 23	7 39	15 16	6 12	1	11	9 9	9 37	sec.	2 28	10 7
22	Sa.	4 23	7 39	15 16	6 12	2	12	10 3	10 25	thi.	3 3	10 55
23	*SU.*	4 23	7 40	15 17	6 13	2	13	10 50	11 10	thi.	3 42	11 43
24	Mo.	4 24	7 40	15 16	DEC.	2	○	11 30	11 50	kn.	4 26	morn
25	Tu.	4 24	7 40	15 16	0 1	2	15	——	0 9	kn.	rises	0 32
26	W.	4 24	7 40	15 16	0 1	2	16	0 26	0 45	kn.	9 20	1 20
27	Th.	4 25	7 40	15 15	0 1	3	17	1 3	1 20	legs	9 57	2 8
28	Fr.	4 25	7 40	15 15	0 2	3	18	1 36	1 54	legs	10 31	2 54
29	Sa.	4 25	7 40	15 15	0 2	3	19	2 10	2 29	feet	11 2	3 39
30	*SU.*	4 25	7 40	15 15	0 2	3	20	2 48	3 6	feet	11 31	4 23

A Spanish peasant, when he eats a good apple, pear, peach or any other fruit, in a forest or by the roadside, plants the seed; and hence it is that the woods and roadsides of Spain have more fruit in and along them than those of any other country. Cannot we do the same?

Page 17

JUNE hath 30 days. 1850.

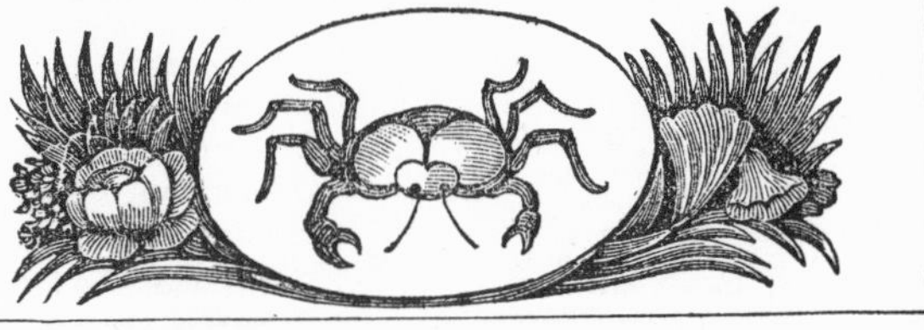

Summer smiles on all around,
And gay birds are singing;
While the zephyrs waft the sound
Of sweet anthems ringing.

D. M.	D. W.	Courts, Aspects, Holidays, Weather, &c.
1	Sa.	*Fine grow-*
2	F.	1st Sun. p. Trin. / C. C. P. Northamp. & Nant. Low
3	Mo.	tides. *ing weather.*
4	Tu.	♃ s. 6h. 12m. ev. C. C. Conc.
5	W.	N. Hampshire Legisla. meets. ♃ □ ☉.
6	Th.	Gen. Gaines d. 1849, aged 72. ♅ ☌ ☽.
7	Fr.	Wash. ap. Com. in Chief, 1775. *Rather*
8	Sa.	☿ in aph. *cooler.*
9	F.	2d Sun. p. Trin.
10	Mo.	C. C. P. Conc., Springf. and New Bedford. *Fre-*
11	Tu.	C. C. Greenf. and Northam. ☽ per. High
12	W.	N.Y. incor. 1665. tides.
13	Th.	*quent*
14	Fr.	♂ ☌ ☽. *showers.*
15	Sa.	Poet Camp. d. 1844.
16	F.	3d Sun. p. Trin. ♃ ☌ ☽.
17	Mo.	C. C. P. Ips. and Worces. / President Polk d. 1849.
18	Tu.	C. C. Worc. ♂ sets 10h. 47m.
19	W.	*More rain.*
20	Th.	J. Sparks inaug. Pres. Harv. University, 1849. *Fine*
21	Fr.	Summer solstice begins. Low
22	Sa.	tides. *growing weather.*
23	F.	4th Sun. p. Trin.
24	Mo.	C. C. P. Crim. Conc. / C. C. P. Lenox. Midsum.
25	Tu.	C. C. Spring. and Dedham. *Cooler,*
26	W.	☽ in apo. *and rather*
27	Th.	Chol. ap. in N.Y. 1832.
28	Fr.	*dull weather.*
29	Sa.	Father Mathew, the apostle of Temperance, arrives at N. York, 1849.
30	F.	5th Sun. p. Trin.

Farmer's Calendar.

Thrift, man, thrift!

Ay, neighbor Fairhill, there seems to be *thrift* ahead. Keep doing, and trust in Providence. This is, indeed, the month to make the farmer's heart elate. Earth sends up all her richness, her beauty and strength. It is a most glorious return for labor, sweat and toil. How the little Throstle jabbers out his note of approbation! Hear, hear! ye city wights that swelter in counting-rooms, come here and taste the pleasures of rational life. We have no need of double entry, and our trial balance is easily made out. But hark! "What of a drought?" says a voice. We answer, we keep doing, and trust in Providence. Yes, we keep doing. Have you preserved the Massachusetts Ploughman, of June 5th, 1847? In the first column there, we may learn what is to be done. "It is a stupid error," says the editor, "to suppose that stirring the earth around the plants will render it more dry in a dry time. Earth that is often moved, imbibes more readily moisture from the air and from the subsoil, than earth that is suffered to lie at rest. We state it as a positive fact, founded on long experience. Stir the ground, then, dry or wet."

Page 18

JULY hath 31 days. 1850.

See how Sol's first rising ray
Gilds the lofty mountain,
Chasing all the mist away
From the flowing fountain.

D. M.	D. W.	Courts, Aspects, Holidays, Weather, &c.
1	Mo.	{Wyoming Massac. 1758. Low *Very*
2	Tu.	{C. C. P. Bost., C. C. Lenox, S. J. C. Nant. tides.
3	W.	☉ furthest from the ⊕.
4	Th.	INDEPEND. DECL. 1776.
5	Fr.	{Mather Byles died, 1788. *warm.*
6	Sa.	♀ sets 9h. 28m. eve.
7	F.	6th S. p. Trin.
8	Mo.	☽ runs hi. *Changeable.*
9	Tu.	☽ in per. {C. C. Salem. Very
10	W.	Columb. b. 1447. high
11	Th.	♀ ☌ ☽. *Great heat.*
12	Fr.	♂ ☌ ☽. tides.
13	Sa.	♃ ☌ ☽.
14	F.	7th Su. p. Trin. *Good*
15	Mo.	{Now to end of Aug. best time to bud fruit trees. *hay*
16	Tu.	{Hegira, A. D. 622. *weather.*
17	W.	♂ sets 9h. 34m. eve.
18	Th.	*More*
19	Fr.	Geo. IV. crowned, 1821.
20	Sa.	7*s r. 0h. 5m. mor. *dull.*
21	F.	8th Sun. p. Trin. Mid.
22	Mo.	{Pilgrims sailed from Delfthaven, 1620. tides.
23	Tu.	{1st. Eng. newspaper published, 1588. *Grows*
24	W	☽ in apo. *much*
25	Th.	Dog days begin. *finer.*
26	Fr.	*Some signs*
27	Sa.	♃ sets 9h. 26m. eve.
28	F.	9th Sun. p. Trin. *of a*
29	Mo.	{Last plank of suspension bridge over Niag. laid, 1848. Tides
30	Tu.	decreasing. *storm.*
31	W.	♅ ☌ ☽.

Farmer's Calendar.

The Scythe.

Capt. Bluejoint is about the nicest one to handle this instrument that we have in these parts. He never brags, but keeps steady ahead, and lets his work speak for him. Some stand straddled out half their time, whetting their scythes. Others love, more than anything else, to be wetting their whistles. These are called *cheap hands*; but I would not have them in my field. To the right about face, *Thirsty*, *Crusty* and *Musty*, gin-jug and wallet. I am fond of company, but will choose for myself. Bluejoint is true blue, dyed in the wool, honest and faithful, and therefore good company for hay-time. Come on, Zaggins, there; stir up the swath; hay must be made in the air, to be sweet, and then the cattle will never turn up their noses at it. So you see that by taking pains, we have many gains. Don't forget this rhyme. The field is the place to make poetry. So Thomson said. Should it come dull weather for haying, there will be jobs enough for employment. Keep the garden clear of weeds; handle the hoe and be busy among the red-root, hearts-ease, and bitter-weed. Back ache? Your hoe-handle is too short. How excellent a good garden! Beets, carrots, turnips, cabbages, &c.

Page 19

1850. JULY, seventh Month.

Astronomical Calculations.

☉'s Declination.

Days.	d.	m.	Days.	d.	m.	Days.	d.	m.	Days.	d.	m.	Days.	d.	m.
1	23	N. 8	7	22	37	13	21	52	19	20	53	25	19	42
2	23	4	8	22	31	14	21	43	20	20	42	26	19	29
3	22	59	9	22	24	15	21	34	21	20	31	27	19	16
4	22	54	10	22	16	16	21	24	22	20	19	28	19	2
5	22	49	11	22	9	17	21	14	23	20	7	29	18	48
6	22	43	12	22	1	18	21	4	24	19	55	30	18	34

☾ Last Quarter, 2d day, 1h. 14m., evening.
● New Moon, 9th day, 9h. 43m., morning.
☽ First Quarter, 16th d. 1h. 57m., morning.
○ Full Moon, 24th day, 0h. 40m., morning.

Days of Month.	Days of the Week.	☉ Rises. h. m.	☉ Sets. h. m.	Length of days. h. m.	Day's Decre. h. m.	☉ S.	☽ A.	Full Sea, Boston. Morning h. m.	Full Sea, Boston. Evening h. m.	☽'s Place.	☽ R. S. h. m.	☽ Souths. h. m.
1	Mo.	4 26	7 40	15 14	0 3	3	21	3 25	3 47	feet	morn	5 7
2	Tu.	4 26	7 40	15 14	0 3	4	22	4 9	4 32	h'd	0 0	5 51
3	W.	4 27	7 40	15 13	0 4	4	23	4 59	5 27	h'd	0 29	6 36
4	Th.	4 27	7 39	15 12	0 5	4	24	5 59	6 35	n'k	0 58	7 23
5	Fr.	4 28	7 39	15 11	0 6	4	25	7 5	7 36	n'k	1 31	8 13
6	Sa.	4 29	7 39	15 10	0 7	4	26	8 9	8 40	arm	2 10	9 6
7	*SU.*	4 30	7 39	15 9	0 8	4	27	9 12	9 40	arm	2 54	10 3
8	Mo.	4 30	7 38	15 8	0 9	5	28	10 7	10 33	br.	3 47	11 4
9	Tu.	4 31	7 38	15 7	0 10	5	●	11 0	11 26	br.	sets	ev. 7
10	W.	4 32	7 38	15 6	0 11	5	1	11 51	——	h'rt	8 19	1 10
11	Th.	4 33	7 37	15 4	0 13	5	2	0 19	0 44	h'rt	9 6	2 11
12	Fr.	4 33	7 37	15 4	0 13	5	3	1 8	1 31	bel.	9 47	3 9
13	Sa.	4 34	7 36	15 2	0 15	5	4	1 55	2 21	bel.	10 23	4 3
14	*SU.*	4 35	7 36	15 1	0 16	5	5	2 46	3 11	bel.	10 56	4 54
15	Mo.	4 36	7 35	14 59	0 18	6	6	3 36	4 0	rei.	11 28	5 43
16	Tu.	4 37	7 34	14 57	0 20	6	7	4 25	4 52	rei.	11 59	6 31
17	W.	4 38	7 34	14 56	0 21	6	8	5 21	5 50	sec.	morn	7 18
18	Th.	4 39	7 33	14 54	0 23	6	9	6 26	6 57	sec.	0 31	8 5
19	Fr.	4 39	7 32	14 53	0 24	6	10	7 28	8 2	thi.	1 5	8 52
20	Sa.	4 40	7 32	14 52	0 25	6	11	8 36	9 11	thi.	1 42	9 40
21	*SU.*	4 41	7 31	14 50	0 27	6	12	9 39	10 6	thi.	2 24	10 28
22	Mo.	4 42	7 30	14 48	0 29	6	13	10 29	10 53	kn.	3 9	11 17
23	Tu.	4 43	7 29	14 46	0 31	6	14	11 14	11 34	kn.	3 59	morn
24	W.	4 44	7 28	14 44	0 33	6	○	11 51	——	legs	rises	0 5
25	Th.	4 45	7 27	14 42	0 35	6	16	0 11	0 28	legs	8 33	0 51
26	Fr.	4 46	7 26	14 40	0 37	6	17	0 46	1 0	legs	9 4	1 37
27	Sa.	4 47	7 25	14 38	0 39	6	18	1 16	1 33	feet	9 34	2 22
28	*SU.*	4 48	7 24	14 36	0 41	6	19	1 49	2 5	feet	10 3	3 6
29	Mo.	4 49	7 23	14 34	0 43	6	20	2 23	2 41	h'd	10 31	3 49
30	Tu.	4 50	7 22	14 32	0 45	6	21	2 58	3 17	h'd	11 0	4 33
31	W.	4 51	7 21	14 30	0 47	6	22	3 36	3 58	h'd	11 30	5 18

STINTING ON FRESH AIR

The Hon. Horace Mann, in alluding to ill-ventilated school houses, remarks as follows: "To put children on a short allowance of fresh air, is as foolish as it would have been for Noah, during the deluge, to have put his family on a short allowance of water. Since God has poured out an atmosphere fifty miles deep, it is enough to make a miser weep to see our children stinted in breath."

THE COMPLETE 1850 ALMANAC

Page 20

1850. AUGUST, eighth Month.

Astronomical Calculations.

☉'s Declination. Days.	d. m.	Days.	d. m.	Days.	d. m.	Days.	d. m.	Days.	d. m.
1	18 N. 4	7	16 29	13	14 43	19	12 50	25	10 49
2	17 49	8	16 12	14	14 25	20	12 30	26	10 28
3	17 34	9	15 55	15	14 6	21	12 10	27	10 7
4	17 18	10	15 37	16	13 48	22	11 50	28	9 46
5	17 2	11	15 20	17	13 29	23	11 30	29	9 25
6	16 45	12	15 2	18	13 9	24	11 10	30	9 3

☾ Last Quarter, 1st day, 0h. 33m., morning.
● New Moon, 7th day, 4h. 50m., evening.
☽ First Quarter, 14th day, 1h. 2m., evening.
○ Full Moon, 22d day, 4h. 28m., evening.
☾ Last Quarter, 30th day, 9h. 35m., morning.

Days of Month.	Days of the Week.	☉ Rises. h. m.	☉ Sets. h. m.	Length of Days. h. m.	Day's Decre. h. m.	☉ S.	☽ A.	Full Sea, Boston. Morning h. m.	Full Sea, Boston. Evening h. m.	☽'s Place.	☽ R. S. h. m.	☽ Souths. h. m.
1	Th.	4 52	7 20	14 28	0 49	6	23	4 22	4 45	n'k	morn	6 5
2	Fr.	4 53	7 19	14 26	0 51	6	24	5 13	5 42	n'k	0 4	6 55
3	Sa.	4 54	7 18	14 24	0 53	6	25	6 19	6 55	arm	0 45	7 49
4	*SU.*	4 55	7 16	14 21	0 56	6	26	7 31	8 7	arm	1 32	8 46
5	Mo.	4 56	7 15	14 19	0 58	6	27	8 47	9 19	br.	2 28	9 47
6	Tu.	4 57	7 14	14 17	1 0	6	28	9 53	10 22	br.	3 32	10 49
7	W.	4 58	7 13	14 15	1 2	6	29	10 50	11 17	h'rt	4 41	11 51
8	Th.	4 59	7 11	14 12	1 5	5	●	11 41	——	h'rt	sets	ev. 52
9	Fr.	5 0	7 10	14 10	1 7	5	1	0 6	0 31	bel.	8 19	1 49
10	Sa.	5 1	7 9	14 8	1 9	5	2	0 55	1 17	bel.	8 53	2 43
11	*SU.*	5 2	7 8	14 6	1 11	5	3	1 40	2 3	rei.	9 28	3 35
12	Mo.	5 3	7 7	14 4	1 13	5	4	2 23	2 45	rei.	9 59	4 25
13	Tu.	5 4	7 5	14 1	1 16	5	5	3 9	3 30	sec.	10 31	5 13
14	W.	5 5	7 4	13 59	1 18	4	6	3 52	4 16	sec.	11 5	6 1
15	Th.	5 6	7 2	13 56	1 21	4	7	4 40	5 6	thi.	11 42	6 49
16	Fr.	5 7	7 1	13 54	1 23	4	8	5 34	6 11	thi.	morn	7 37
17	Sa.	5 8	6 59	13 51	1 26	4	9	6 48	7 24	thi.	0 22	8 25
18	*SU.*	5 9	6 58	13 49	1 28	4	10	8 1	8 40	kn.	1 7	9 13
19	Mo.	5 10	6 56	13 46	1 31	3	11	9 16	9 44	kn.	1 54	10 1
20	Tu.	5 11	6 55	13 44	1 33	3	12	10 10	10 34	legs	2 47	10 48
21	W.	5 12	6 54	13 42	1 35	3	13	10 55	11 15	legs	3 42	11 35
22	Th.	5 14	6 52	13 38	1 39	3	○	11 32	11 49	legs	4 38	morn
23	Fr.	5 15	6 51	13 36	1 41	2	15	——	0 7	feet	rises	0 20
24	Sa.	5 16	6 49	13 33	1 44	2	16	0 23	0 38	feet	8 6	1 4
25	*SU.*	5 17	6 48	13 31	1 46	2	17	0 55	1 9	h'd	8 33	1 48
26	Mo.	5 18	6 46	13 28	1 49	2	18	1 24	1 40	h'd	9 4	2 32
27	Tu.	5 19	6 44	13 25	1 52	2	19	1 57	2 13	h'd	9 32	3 16
28	W.	5 20	6 42	13 22	1 55	1	20	2 30	2 48	n'k	10 4	4 2
29	Th.	5 21	6 41	13 20	1 57	1	21	3 6	3 26	n'k	10 41	4 50
30	Fr.	5 22	6 39	13 17	2 0	1	22	3 47	4 10	arm	11 25	5 41
31	Sa.	5 23	6 36	13 14	2 3	0	23	4 37	5 7	arm	morn	6 35

Page 21

AUGUST hath 31 days. 1850.

August comes with yellow grain,
Ripe, and downward leaning;
And the reapers on the plain
Are the harvest gleaning.

D. M.	D. W.	Courts, Aspects, Holidays, Weather, &c.
1	Th.	Am. Cont. discov. 1492.
2	Fr.	Arkwright died, 1792.
3	Sa.	President Taylor recom. public fast, on account of Cholera, 1849.
4	F.	10th Su. p. Trin. *Rain.*
5	Mo.	☽ runs high. ♅ station.
6	Tu.	C. C. Plym. ♀ ☌ ♃.
7	W.	Berzelius, the great Swedish chemist, died, 1848. Very
8	Th.	high
9	Fr.	Capt. Marryat died, 1848. tides. *Great*
10	Sa.	Observatory at Greenwich founded, 1675. *heat.*
11	F.	11th Sun. p. Trin.
12	Mo.	C. C. P. Greenfield and Plymouth. *Cloudy.*
13	Tu.	*Changeable.*
14	W.	Printing invented, 1437. ♂ ☌ ♃.
15	Th.	Wal. Scott b. 1771.
16	Fr.	Bat. Bennington, 1777. Low tides.
17	Sa.	Gr. Fire at Albany, 1848.
18	F.	12th Sun. p. Trin. ☽ r. l.
19	Mo.	♀ in ☋. Tides *Dry*
20	Tu.	☽ in apo. increasing.
21	W.	*More signs*
22	Th.	Wash. city taken, 1814.
23	Fr.	Sir Wm. Wallace executed, 1305.
24	Sa.	7*s rise 9h. 47m. eve.
25	F.	13th Sun. p. Trin. *of*
26	Mo.	♄ ☌ ☾. *rain.*
27	Tu.	Poet Thomson died, aged 47, 1748. ♅ ☌ ☾.
28	W.	Low *Cooler,*
29	Th.	tides. *with*
30	Fr.	♀ sets 9h. 12m. eve.
31	Sa.	*fine breezes.*

Farmer's Calendar.

The Sheaves.

"The *sheaves*, the glorious *sheaves*, how they come!" This is the merry reaper's song. What among the concerns of agriculture can give greater pleasure than to view a rich field of wheat? When *Bright* and *Broadhorn* come up the lane, slowly dragging the ponderous load, the reward of many a hard day's toil, how elate is the farmer's heart! As he urges on his team to escape the approaching shower, his wife and daughters meet him with smiles, and gratulation is heard on every side. Whip! whew! into the barn they go, and all seems safe. Now down pours the rain, the lightnings flash, and the thunder rolls! All may *not* be safe. How often do the elements prostrate the farmer's hopes! But the clouds have passed; all is bright again, and cheerfulness returns with the glorious sunbeams.

You of the city tell of the pleasures of farming! What do ye know? Some of you have attempted it; but have you put your shoulders to the wheel? To "farm it" is something more than to stand and see how others do the labor, and then take out your purse and pay their wages. Off coat, on frock, and knuckle down to the hoe-handle. That 's the way to manage.

A SCRATCH BECOMES A WOUND

Man doubles all the evils of his fate by pondering over them; a scratch becomes a wound, a slight an injury, a jest an insult, a small peril a great danger, and a light sickness often ends in death by brooding apprehensions.

1850. SEPTEMBER, ninth Month.

Astronomical Calculations.

⊙'s Declination.

Days.	d.	m.	Days.	d.	m.	Days.	d.	m.	Days.	d.	m.	Days.	d.	m.
1	8 N.20		7	6	7	13	3	51	19	1	32	25	0	49
2	7	58	8	5	45	14	3	28	20	1	8	26	1	12
3	7	36	9	5	22	15	3	4	21	0	45	27	1	36
4	7	14	10	4	59	16	2	41	22	0 N.21		28	1	59
5	6	52	11	4	36	17	2	18	23	0 S. 2		29	2	22
6	6	30	12	4	14	18	1	55	24	0	25	30	2	46

- ● New Moon, 6th day, 0h. 44m., morning.
- ☽ First Quarter, 13th day, 3h. 37m., morning.
- ○ Full Moon, 21st day, 7h. 56m., morning.
- ☾ Last Quarter, 28th day, 5h. 7m., evening.

Days of Month	Days of the Week	Rises h. m.	Sets h. m.	Length of Days h. m.	Day's Decre. h. m.	F.	A.	Full Sea, Boston Morning	Evening	☽'s Place	☽ R. S. h. m.	☽ Souths h. m.
1	SU.	5 24	6 36	13 12	2 5	0	24	5 40	6 24	br.	0 15	7 32
2	Mo.	5 26	6 35	13 9	2 8	0	25	7 5	7 46	br.	1 13	8 32
3	Tu.	5 27	6 33	13 6	2 11	1	26	8 29	9 7	h'rt	2 18	9 33
4	W.	5 28	6 31	13 3	2 14	1	27	9 39	10 11	h'rt	3 29	10 33
5	Th.	5 29	6 30	13 1	2 16	1	28	10 39	11 3	bel.	4 43	11 31
6	Fr.	5 30	6 28	12 58	2 19	2	●	11 27	11 52	bel.	sets	ev.27
7	Sa.	5 31	6 26	12 55	2 22	2	1	---	0 13	rei.	7 21	1 21
8	SU.	5 32	6 25	12 53	2 24	2	2	0 36	0 57	rei.	7 55	2 13
9	Mo.	5 33	6 23	12 50	2 27	3	3	1 17	1 38	sec.	8 28	3 3
10	Tu.	5 34	6 21	12 47	2 30	3	4	1 58	2 18	sec.	9 3	3 53
11	W.	5 35	6 19	12 44	2 33	3	5	2 36	2 56	sec.	9 39	4 42
12	Th.	5 36	6 17	12 41	2 36	4	6	3 17	3 38	thi.	10 19	5 31
13	Fr.	5 37	6 16	12 39	2 38	4	7	3 59	4 24	thi.	11 3	6 20
14	Sa.	5 38	6 14	12 36	2 41	4	8	4 51	5 21	kn.	11 49	7 9
15	SU.	5 39	6 12	12 33	2 44	5	9	6 1	6 41	kn.	morn	7 57
16	Mo.	5 40	6 11	12 31	2 46	5	10	7 22	8 4	kn.	0 41	8 44
17	Tu.	5 41	6 9	12 28	2 49	6	11	8 42	9 18	legs	1 34	9 31
18	W.	5 42	6 7	12 25	2 52	6	12	9 45	10 8	legs	2 32	10 17
19	Th.	5 43	6 5	12 22	2 55	6	13	10 29	10 49	feet	3 29	11 1
20	Fr.	5 44	6 4	12 20	2 57	7	14	11 7	11 24	feet	4 28	11 46
21	Sa.	5 45	6 2	12 17	3 0	7	○	11 38	11 55	feet	5 28	morn
22	SU.	5 46	6 0	12 14	3 3	7	16	---	0 10	h'd	rises	0 30
23	Mo.	5 47	5 58	12 11	3 6	8	17	0 25	0 44	h'd	7 35	1 14
24	Tu.	5 48	5 56	12 8	3 9	8	18	0 58	1 14	n'k	8 7	2 0
25	W.	5 49	5 54	12 5	3 12	8	19	1 30	1 46	n'k	8 42	2 48
26	Th.	5 50	5 52	12 2	3 15	9	20	2 3	2 23	arm	9 23	3 38
27	Fr.	5 51	5 50	11 59	3 18	9	21	2 42	3 1	arm	10 9	4 30
28	Sa.	5 53	5 49	11 56	3 21	9	22	3 22	3 46	arm	11 3	5 26
29	SU.	5 54	5 47	11 53	3 24	10	23	4 13	4 45	br.	morn	6 23
30	Mo.	5 55	5 45	11 50	3 27	10	24	5 22	6 6	br.	0 4	7 22

SEPTEMBER hath 30 days. 1850.

Now the Summer's fiercest heat
Seems to be retiring,
And mild Autumn takes her seat,
Meek and unaspiring.

D. M.	D. W.	Courts, Aspects, Holidays, Weather, &c.	Farmer's Calendar.
1	F.	14th S. p. Trin. *Rather*	
2	Mo.	C. C. P. Worc. and Low. New Style adopted, 1752. *wet.*	
3	Tu.	C. C. P. Barnst. C. C. Lenox, Greenfield, Northam. & Con. S.J.C.Sprinf.	
4	W.	☽ in per. ☿ in aph.	
5	Th.	Dog days end.	
6	Fr.	Pilgrims sailed from Plymouth, Eng. 1620. *Very*	
7	Sa.	♃ ☌ ☽. high tides.	
8	F.	15th Sun. p. Trin. *Dull.*	
9	Mo.	C. C. P. Taunton. State Elec., Maine. ♀ ☌ ☽.	
10	Tu.	C. C. Worcester. S. J. C. Greenf. S. J. C. L. Lenox.	
11	W.	♀ sets 9h. 36m. eve.	
12	Th.	*Much finer.*	
13	Fr.	Quebec taken, 1759.	
14	Sa.	☽ runs low. Low tides.	
15	F.	16th Sun. p. Trin.	
16	Mo.	C. C. P. Newb't and Dedham. ☽ in apo.	
17	Tu.	Federal constitution formed, 1787. *Rain.*	
18	W.	Sterne died, 1768.	
19	Th.	♂ sets 7h. 39m. eve.	
20	Fr.	*High winds.*	
21	Sa.	Walt. Scott d. 1832.	
22	F.	17th Sun. p. Trin.	
23	Mo.	C. C. P. Crim. Worc. S. J. C. L. Northamp. *High*	
24	Tu.	C. C. Taunt. and Ded. tides. *Look*	
25	W.	7*s rise 7h. 52m. eve.	
26	Th.	Days and nights nearly	
27	Fr.	equal. *out for frost.*	
28	Sa.	☽ runs high.	
29	F.	18th S. p. Trin. Mich.	
30	Mo.	C. C. P. Edgartown. *Showers.*	

The Ditch.

Alas, poor Patrick! The widow Mahooney had three sons, Jemmy, Michael and Patrick. The two former, she said, "would noo and then luse ther sanses for a time oonly; but as for Patrick, puer sowl! he would gat bastely droonk." He undertook a job of ditching for me, and though he understood it well, and performed the work to my satisfaction, from Monday to Wednesday noon, yet the afternoon of the latter day brought him all up, or rather brought him all down. I went to see how he progressed, when there lay poor *Eringobrah*, upon his beam ends, in the bottom of the ditch, with his bottle for his pillow! It was his last drink. He snored like a porker, and never survived the downfall. A plague on the baggage-wagoner, thought I, who procured him the blue ruin! Well, let him go. Paddies will be Paddies, in spite of Father Mathew. By the way, if you have ditching to do, now is the time. Good stuff comes out of an old ditch, and well pays the labor of digging. Make compost, and flinch not at the labor. But a word about highways. To dig them up and endanger the lives of travellers, is neither right nor proper.

True hope is based on energy of character. A strong mind always hopes, and has cause to hope, because it knows that mutability of human affairs, and how slight a circumstance may change the whole course of human events.

THE COMPLETE 1850 ALMANAC

1850. OCTOBER, tenth Month.

Astronomical Calculations.

☉'s Declination. Days.	d.	m.	Days.	d.	m.	Days.	d.	m.	Days.	d.	m.	Days.	d.	m.
1	3 S.	9	7	5	28	13	7	45	19	9	58	25	12	5
2	3	32	8	5	51	14	8	7	20	10	19	26	12	26
3	3	56	9	6	14	15	8	30	21	10	41	27	12	46
4	4	19	10	6	37	16	8	52	22	11	2	28	13	7
5	4	42	11	7	0	17	9	14	23	11	23	29	13	27
6	5	5	12	7	22	18	9	36	24	11	44	30	13	46

● New Moon, 5th day, 10h. 12m., morning.
☽ First Quarter, 12th day, 9h. 46m., evening.
○ Full Moon, 20th day, 10h. 27m., evening.
☾ Last Quarter, 28th day, 0h. 15m., morning.

Days of Month.	Days of the Week.	Rises. h. m.	Sets. h. m.	Length of days. h. m.	Day's Decre. h. m.	☉ F.	☽ A.	Full Sea, Boston. Morning h. m.	Evening h. m.	☽'s Place.	☽ R. h. m.	☽ S. h. m.	☽ Souths. h. m.
1	Tu.	5 56	5 43	11 47	3 30	10	25	6 51	7 36	h'rt	1 11		8 20
2	W.	5 57	5 42	11 45	3 32	11	26	8 21	8 59	h'rt	2 21		9 17
3	Th.	5 58	5 40	11 42	3 35	11	27	9 30	9 58	bel.	3 33		10 13
4	Fr.	5 59	5 39	11 40	3 37	11	28	10 22	10 47	bel.	4 45		11 7
5	Sa.	6 1	5 38	11 37	3 40	12	●	11 11	11 31	rei.	sets		11 59
6	SU.	6 2	5 36	11 34	3 43	12	1	11 52	—	rei.	6 23		ev.50
7	Mo.	6 3	5 34	11 31	3 46	12	2	0 13	0 33	sec.	6 57		1 41
8	Tu.	6 4	5 33	11 29	3 48	12	3	0 52	1 12	sec.	7 33		2 31
9	W.	6 5	5 31	11 26	3 51	13	4	1 29	1 49	thi.	8 12		3 21
10	Th.	6 6	5 29	11 23	3 54	13	5	2 8	2 25	thi.	8 54		4 11
11	Fr.	6 8	5 28	11 20	3 57	13	6	2 45	3 5	kn.	9 41		5 1
12	Sa.	6 9	5 26	11 17	4 0	13	7	3 26	3 49	kn.	10 31		5 50
13	SU.	6 10	5 24	11 14	4 3	14	8	4 12	4 41	kn.	11 25		6 38
14	Mo.	6 11	5 22	11 11	4 6	14	9	5 15	5 56	legs	morn		7 26
15	Tu.	6 12	5 20	11 8	4 9	14	10	6 40	7 21	legs	0 21		8 11
16	W.	6 13	5 19	11 6	4 11	14	11	8 0	8 36	legs	1 19		8 56
17	Th.	6 14	5 17	11 3	4 14	15	12	9 9	9 33	feet	2 17		9 41
18	Fr.	6 15	5 16	11 1	4 16	15	13	9 56	10 15	feet	3 18		10 25
19	Sa.	6 17	5 14	10 57	4 20	15	14	10 34	10 50	h'd	4 18		11 9
20	SU.	6 18	5 13	10 55	4 22	15	○	11 7	11 23	h'd	5 20		11 55
21	Mo.	6 19	5 11	10 52	4 25	15	16	11 40	11 56	n'k	6 22		morn
22	Tu.	6 21	5 10	10 49	4 28	15	17	—	0 13	n'k	rises		0 43
23	W.	6 22	5 8	10 46	4 31	16	18	0 31	0 48	n'k	7 22		1 33
24	Th.	6 23	5 7	10 44	4 33	16	19	1 5	1 23	arm	8 7		2 26
25	Fr.	6 24	5 5	10 41	4 36	16	20	1 42	2 1	arm	8 58		3 21
26	Sa.	6 25	5 4	10 39	4 38	16	21	2 20	2 41	br.	9 56		4 18
27	SU.	6 27	5 2	10 35	4 42	16	22	3 6	3 33	br.	11 1		5 17
28	Mo.	6 28	5 1	10 33	4 44	16	23	4 1	4 34	h'rt	morn		6 14
29	Tu.	6 29	5 0	10 31	4 46	16	24	5 12	5 57	h'rt	0 8		7 11
30	W.	6 31	4 58	10 27	4 50	16	25	6 40	7 25	bel.	1 19		8 5
31	Th.	6 32	4 57	10 25	4 52	16	26	8 7	8 42	bel.	2 29		8 58

OCTOBER hath 31 days. 1850.

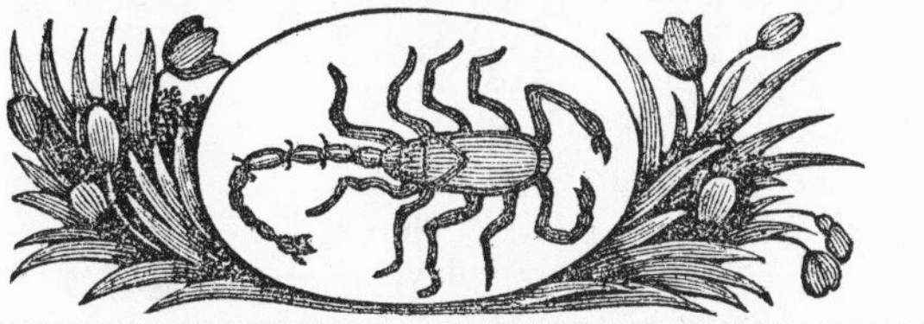

Health and plenty from the hand
Of kind Heaven descending,
Which spread blessings o'er the land,
Are our paths attending.

D. M.	D. W.	Courts, Aspects, Holidays, Weather, &c.	Farmer's Calendar.
1	Tu.	C. C. P. Boston. C. C. Springfield. S. J. C. L. Worcester.	*Butter.*
2	W.	☽ in per. Channing d. 1842. *Finer*	"Good bread and butter is good
3	Th.	4th. Selkirk left at J. F. 1704.	enough for anybody," said my
4	Fr.	7*s sou. 2h. 58m. mor.	friend Bonce, who, I believe, likes
5	Sa.	Old Parr died, aged 152, 1635. High tides.	good munching as well as any of
6	F.	19th Sun. p. Trin.	us. He at another time added to
7	Mo.	C. C. P. Springf. and Nantucket. *Cooler,*	it, sweet apples and milk, and gave
8	Tu.	C. C. Barnstable and Newbury't. *but*	us some excellent remarks on rais-
9	W.	Brainerd d. 1747. *fine.*	ing fruit. People's tastes and no-
10	Th.	Vermont Legislature meets. ♄ ☌ ☉.	tions about butter seem to differ.
11	Fr.	☽ runs low.	When I see mother Drizzle knead-
12	Sa.	*Cloudy, with some*	ing johnny-cake or patting her but-
13	F.	20th Sun. p. Trin. Very	ter with a pinch of "old Scotch"
14	Mo.	C. C. P. Ipswich. ☽ in apo. low t.	'twixt thumb and finger, I cannot
15	Tu.	S. J. C. L. Cambridge. *little*	agree, on any condition, that her
16	W.	☿ stationary. *rain.*	bread and butter are good. But
17	Th.	Burgoyne surren. 1777.	yet I have been told that it is all
18	Fr.	☿ in perihelion.	a notion. I have a notion also
19	Sa.	H. K. White died, 1806. *Cool*	that our housewives are not par-
20	F.	21st S. p. Trin. ♅ ☌ ☽	ticular enough to work out their
21	Mo.	C. C. P. Crim. Lowell. C. C. P. Northampton. *nights.*	buttermilk. The agricultural pa-
22	Tu.	S. J. C. L. Taunton. Mid. *A*	pers have said a good deal on this
23	W.	♃ rises 4h. 20m. morn.	subject. If they can make some
24	Th.	tides. *storm*	folks honest, and not sell butter-
25	Fr.	Cochituate Water introduced to Boston, 1848. *is*	milk and salt for butter, they will
26	Sa.	☽ runs high. *nigh.*	do a good service. Now, butter
27	F.	22d Sun. p. Tr. Tides	makes me think about cooking,
28	Mo.	C. C. P Lenox. R. I. Legis. meets, Newp't. *incr.*	which also brings to mind how
29	Tu.	S. J. C. L. Dedham. ☽ in per.	they cook in the western states.
30	W.	*Finer for some*	The Prairie paper says that they
31	Th.	J. Adams b. 1735. *days.*	fry all there. Bacon, pork, veal,

chicken, mutton and fish, and what not, are all fried — often cooked to the hardness of old junk. They eat warm bread, strong coffee and fried meat. Enough to give a hog the dyspepsia.

GETTING ON IN THE WORLD

Is there no general rule for "getting on" in the world? We think there is. We cannot tell what is coming; but we can hold ourselves in preparation for what may befall. A ship that goes forth upon the ocean is provided with appliances both for catching the breeze and evading the storm; and were it otherwise, she would have no chance of making a prosperous voyage.

THE COMPLETE 1850 ALMANAC

1850. NOVEMBER, eleventh Month.

Astronomical Calculations.

☉'s Declination.	Days.	d.	m.	Days.	d.	m.	Days.	d.	m.	Days.	d.	m.	Days.	d.	m.
	1	14 S.25		7	16	17	13	17	58	19	19	28	25	20	45
	2	14	45	8	16	34	14	18	14	20	19	42	26	20	57
	3	15	3	9	16	52	15	18	29	21	19	55	27	21	8
	4	15	22	10	17	9	16	18	45	22	20	8	28	21	19
	5	15	41	11	17	25	17	18	59	23	20	21	29	21	29
	6	15	59	12	17	42	18	19	14	24	20	33	30	21	39

● New Moon, 3d day, 9h. 56m., evening.
☽ First Quarter, 11th day, 6h. 31m., evening.
○ Full Moon, 19th day, 11h. 51m., morning.
☾ Last Quarter, 26th day, 7h. 48m., morning.

Days of Month.	Days of the Week.	☉ Rises. h. m.	☉ Sets. h. m.	Length of Days. h. m.	Day's Decre. m.	☉ F.	☽ A.	Full Sea, Boston. Morning h. m.	Full Sea, Boston. Evening h. m.	☽'s Place.	☽ R. h. m.	☽ S.	☽ Souths. h. m.
1	Fr.	6 33	4 55	10 22	4 55	16	27	9 12	9 41	rei.	3 38		9 49
2	Sa.	6 34	4 54	10 20	4 57	16	28	10 5	10 29	rei.	4 48		10 39
3	SU.	6 35	4 53	10 18	4 59	16	29	10 49	11 10	sec.	5 56		11 29
4	Mo.	6 36	4 51	10 15	5 2	16	●	11 30	11 50	sec.	sets		ev. 19
5	Tu.	6 38	4 50	10 12	5 5	16	1	——	0 9	thi.	6 3		1 10
6	W.	6 39	4 49	10 10	5 7	16	2	0 30	0 47	thi.	6 46		2 1
7	Th.	6 40	4 48	10 8	5 9	16	3	1 6	1 25	thi.	7 31		2 51
8	Fr.	6 42	4 46	10 4	5 13	16	4	1 41	1 59	kn.	8 20		3 42
9	Sa.	6 43	4 45	10 2	5 15	16	5	2 17	2 36	kn.	9 13		4 31
10	SU.	6 44	4 44	10 0	5 17	16	6	2 57	3 17	legs	10 8		5 19
11	Mo.	6 46	4 43	9 57	5 20	16	7	3 40	4 3	legs	11 6		6 5
12	Tu.	6 47	4 42	9 55	5 22	16	8	4 31	5 4	legs	morn		6 50
13	W.	6 48	4 41	9 53	5 24	16	9	5 44	6 25	feet	0 4		7 34
14	Th.	6 50	4 40	9 50	5 27	15	10	7 2	7 38	feet	1 3		8 18
15	Fr.	6 51	4 39	9 48	5 29	15	11	8 12	8 44	h'd	2 2		9 2
16	Sa.	6 52	4 38	9 46	5 31	15	12	9 11	9 33	h'd	3 4		9 47
17	SU.	6 53	4 37	9 44	5 33	15	13	9 53	10 14	h'd	4 7		10 34
18	Mo.	6 54	4 36	9 42	5 35	15	14	10 34	10 52	n'k	5 10		11 24
19	Tu.	6 55	4 35	9 40	5 37	14	○	11 9	11 29	n'k	6 16		morn
20	W.	6 57	4 35	9 38	5 39	14	16	11 49	——	arm	rises		0 16
21	Th.	6 58	4 34	9 36	5 41	14	17	0 6	0 27	arm	6 50		1 12
22	Fr.	6 59	4 33	9 34	5 43	14	18	0 46	1 6	br.	7 48		2 11
23	Sa.	7 0	4 32	9 32	5 45	13	19	1 27	1 48	br.	8 52		3 10
24	SU.	7 2	4 31	9 29	5 48	13	20	2 11	2 34	h'rt	10 0		4 10
25	Mo.	7 3	4 31	9 28	5 49	13	21	3 1	3 28	h'rt	11 10		5 7
26	Tu.	7 4	4 30	9 26	5 51	13	22	3 58	4 29	bel.	morn		6 2
27	W.	7 5	4 30	9 25	5 52	12	23	5 2	5 41	bel.	0 19		6 55
28	Th.	7 6	4 29	9 23	5 54	12	24	6 23	6 59	rei.	1 29		7 45
29	Fr.	7 8	4 29	9 21	5 56	12	25	7 37	8 14	rei.	2 36		8 34
30	Sa.	7 9	4 29	9 20	5 57	11	26	8 47	9 15	rei.	3 43		9 23

NOVEMBER hath 30 days. 1850.

Now the cold autumnal gale,
Through the forest raging,
Makes harsh music in the vale,
Not at all engaging.

D. M.	D. W.	Courts, Aspects, Holidays, Weather, &c.	Farmer's Calendar.
1	Fr.	♃ ⚹ ☽. *Fine*	*The Crow-bar.*
2	Sa.	*for the season.*	Dig, pry, spring, Mr. Tughard! Now for the wooden lever—chuck it under—place the fulcrum—down with it, boys—there, bounce! out comes another stone for a cellar wall. Nothing like taking right hold, and taking hold right, in these operations; and it is not every one that has the knack about using the crow-bar to the best advantage. Such a difference there is among men, that some are not much better than Hottentots—fit only for a lubber lift, or for a dead weight upon a long lever. A crow-bar is an important implement. Keep it sharp. A borrowed one comes home all battered and blunt—a job for the blacksmith. "But here, but here! neighbor," the sky begins to look growly, and if you are not prepared for a boxing-match with a northeaster, you had better be picking up your tools, that you may be ready for the encounter. *Apropos*, as to tools. The good husbandman has them in their places. The careless man knows not where to look for them. A fork may be under the snow, a shovel in the mud, an axe in the well, and the grindstone in the horse-pond! See to your underpinning, and keep out the frost.
3	F.	23d Sun. p. Trin.	
4	Mo.	♀ sets 10h. 39m. eve.	
5	Tu.	S. J. C. L. Salem. Gunpowder Plot, 1605. *Changeable.*	
6	W.	Mid.	
7	Th.	♀ ⚹ ☽. tides. *Fine*	
8	Fr.	☽ runs low. *again.*	
9	Sa.	Pilgrims in Mayflower arrive at Cape Cod, 1620.	
10	F.	24th Sun. p. Trin. *Cool*	
11	Mo.	C. C. P. Greenfield. State Elec. Mass. *winds.*	
12	Tu.	S. J. C. Bost. and New Bedford. *Much*	
13	W.	C. C. Edgartown. *finer.*	
14	Th.	♃ rises 3h. 3m. morn.	
15	Fr.	Bost. and Prov. R. Road op'd for passengers, 1834. *Tides*	
16	Sa.	*increasing. Some*	
17	F.	25th Sun. p. Tr. *snow*	
18	Mo.	7*s south at midnight.	
19	Tu.	*may be expected.*	
20	W.	High	
21	Th.	tides. *Stormy.*	
22	Fr.	☽ runs high.	
23	Sa.	☽ in peri.	
24	F.	26th S. p. Trin. *Much*	
25	Mo.	♀ stationary. *more comfortable.*	
26	Tu.	Isabella, Queen of Spain, died, 1504.	
27	W.	Tides	
28	Th.	♃ rises 2h. 15m. morn.	
29	Fr.	*decreasing. Look out*	
30	Sa.	St. Andrew. *for a storm.*	

THE STRAWBERRY CROP

No other valuable fruit can be raised so easily. An acre has produced one hundred bushels in a season. If planted early in the spring, they will bear a crop the first year. They require good corn land, a soil deep and strong, but not too rich.

1850. DECEMBER, twelfth Month.

Astronomical Calculations.

☉'s Declination. Days.	d.	m.	Days.	d.	m.	Days.	d.	m.	Days.	d.	m.	Days.	d.	m.
1	21 S.49		7	22	37	13	23	10	19	23	26	25	23	25
2	21	58	8	22	44	14	23	14	20	23	27	26	23	23
3	22	7	9	22	50	15	23	17	21	23	27	27	23	21
4	22	15	10	22	56	16	23	20	22	23	27	28	23	18
5	22	23	11	23	1	17	23	22	23	23	27	29	23	15
6	22	30	12	23	6	18	23	24	24	23	26	30	23	11

● New Moon, 3d day, 0h. 32m., evening.
☽ First Quarter, 11th day, 3h. 53m., evening.
○ Full Moon, 19th day, 0h. 19m., morning.
☾ Last Quarter, 25th day, 4h. 40m., evening.

Days of Month.	Days of the Week.	☉ Rises. h. m.	☉ Sets. h. m.	Length of Days. h. m.	Day's Decre. h. m.	☉ F.	☽ A.	Full Sea, Boston. Morning. h. m.	Full Sea, Boston. Evening. h. m.	☽'s Place.	☽ R. S. h. m.	☽ Souths. h. m.
1	SU.	7 10	4 29	9 19	5 58	11	27	9 41	10 6	sec.	4 50	10 12
2	Mo.	7 11	4 29	9 18	5 59	10	28	10 28	10 51	sec.	5 54	11 1
3	Tu.	7 12	4 29	9 17	6 0	10	●	11 13	11 31	thi.	6 58	11 51
4	W.	7 13	4 28	9 15	6 2	10	1	11 52	——	thi.	sets	ev. 42
5	Th.	7 14	4 28	9 14	6 3	9	2	0 12	0 30	kn.	6 10	1 33
6	Fr.	7 15	4 28	9 13	6 4	9	3	0 48	1 6	kn.	7 2	2 23
7	Sa.	7 16	4 28	9 12	6 5	8	4	1 24	1 42	kn.	7 57	3 12
8	SU.	7 17	4 28	9 11	6 6	8	5	2 0	2 18	legs	8 54	3 59
9	Mo.	7 18	4 28	9 10	6 7	7	6	2 35	2 55	legs	9 52	4 44
10	Tu.	7 19	4 28	9 9	6 8	7	7	3 15	3 37	feet	10 49	5 29
11	W.	7 20	4 28	9 8	6 9	7	8	4 0	4 22	feet	11 49	6 12
12	Th.	7 21	4 28	9 7	6 10	6	9	4 49	5 19	feet	morn	6 55
13	Fr.	7 21	4 28	9 7	6 10	6	10	5 56	6 31	h'd	0 48	7 38
14	Sa.	7 22	4 28	9 6	6 11	5	11	7 4	7 37	h'd	1 49	8 24
15	SU.	7 23	4 28	9 5	6 12	5	12	8 8	8 39	n'k	2 50	9 11
16	Mo.	7 24	4 29	9 5	6 12	4	13	9 8	9 32	n'k	3 57	10 2
17	Tu.	7 24	4 29	9 5	6 12	4	14	9 56	10 17	arm	5 1	10 57
18	W.	7 25	4 29	9 4	6 13	3	○	10 41	11 2	arm	6 9	11 55
19	Th.	7 25	4 29	9 4	6 13	3	16	11 24	11 49	br.	7 14	morn
20	Fr.	7 26	4 30	9 4	6 13	2	17	——	0 11	br.	rises	0 56
21	Sa.	7 26	4 30	9 4	6 13	2	18	0 33	0 56	h'rt	7 47	1 57
22	SU.	7 27	4 31	9 4	6 13	1	19	1 19	1 43	h'rt	8 58	2 58
23	Mo.	7 27	4 31	9 4	6 13	1	20	2 6	2 30	h'rt	10 9	3 56
24	Tu.	7 28	4 32	9 4	INC.	0	21	2 56	3 23	bel.	11 21	4 51
25	W.	7 28	4 32	9 4	0	S.	22	3 49	4 15	bel.	morn	5 43
26	Th.	7 29	4 33	9 4	0	1	23	4 45	5 17	rei.	0 28	6 33
27	Fr.	7 29	4 34	9 5	0	1	24	5 50	6 26	rei.	1 36	7 21
28	Sa.	7 29	4 34	9 5	0	1	25	7 0	7 35	sec.	2 42	8 9
29	SU.	7 29	4 35	9 6	0	2	26	8 10	8 45	sec.	3 45	8 57
30	Mo.	7 30	4 36	9 6	0	2	27	9 15	9 43	thi.	4 49	9 46
31	Tu.	7 30	4 37	9 7	0	3	28	10 6	10 31	thi.	5 48	10 36

DECEMBER hath 31 days. 1850.

Since the old year to the new
Must so soon surrender;
Kindest reader, our adieu
E. Camb.] With respect we tender. — J. W. D.

D. M.	D. W.	Courts, Aspects, Holidays, Weather, &c.	Farmer's Calendar.
1	F.	1st Sun. in Advent.	*Newspapers.*
2	Mo.	C. C. P. Crim. Springf. *Cold* C. C. P. Plym. & Worc.	"Hand me the print, John, and
3	Tu.	C. C. North- *High and* ampton.	light the lamp. I wish to see a little what they tell us about farm-
4	W.	tides. *blustering.*	work for this month." "Why,
5	Th.	☽ runs low. ☿ ☌ ☽.	father, Mr. Dozenbury borrowed the paper three days ago, and has
6	Fr.	*Some*	not returned it yet." "There,
7	Sa.	Mass. State Reform *snow.* School dedicated, 1848.	now, borrowed again! Now, I
8	F.	2d Sun. in Advent.	tell you all, and once for all, the
9	Mo.	C. C. P. Cambridge ☽ in apo. and New Bedford.	paper shall *not* be lent. Old Doz- enbury is well able to pay for one,
10	Tu.	C. C. Greenfield. L. Napoleon ch. Pres. of France, 1848.	and he don't have mine; again —
11	W.	7*'s south 10h. 25m. ev.	that's *flat!*" Good.
12	Th.	Low tides. *Pleasant*	Grudge not, brother farmers, a
13	Fr.	*for the season.*	few shillings for a newspaper. It
14	Sa.	WASHINGTON died, 1799.	is the medium through which you will learn what the world is about.
15	F.	3d Sun. in Adv. *Snow*	How are your sympathies? The
16	Mo.	C. C. P. Ips. or Lawr. *or* and Dedham.	begging stranger that comes with-
17	Tu.	Maria Louisa, widow of *rain.* Napoleon, died, 1847.	in your gate may deceive you; but the case of the widow over
18	W.	♄ stationary.	the heath is well known to all.
19	Th.	☽ runs high.	The Bible, yes, and the newspa-
20	Fr.	High *Very high*	per, both inculcate *charity*. Ha!
21	Sa.	Winter solstice *tides.* begins.	do you startle at that word, fear- ing a little draft upon your abun-
22	F.	Shortest d. 4th S. in Ad.	dance? Know, then, that the
23	Mo.	Washington resigned *winds.* command of army, 1783.	gatherings made here, whether by
24	Tu.	C. C. Salem, Newburyp't or Ips., as determined. C. C. Spring. & Worc.	farmer, mechanic, merchant, law-
25	W.	C. C. Christmas day. Dedh.	yer, doctor, priest or king, are not all worth the labor of a second to
26	Th.	24th. Judge Sam'l Hubbard, *Not* of Mass., died, 1847.	aid us in our final journey. A
27	Fr.	24th. Ex. Gov. Fairfield, *very* of Maine, died, 1847.	*sovereign* and a *sous* will then be of equal value, and a deed of
28	Sa.	*cold for the season.*	charity preferred to the gold of
29	F.	1st Sun. p. Christmas.	Ophir. Now for a hearty shake
30	Mo.	Adelaide, sister of *Cooler.* L. Philippe, d. 1847.	of the hand until we meet again!
31	Tu.	☉ nearest the earth.	

I presume you know that you can often bring those around you to your own standard. See that it is a high one,—never let it be low!

East Greenwich, the 2d Mond. in Feb., and 4th in Aug.

GENERAL ASSEMBLY. — There are two sessions; one at Newport, on the 1st Tues. of May, for election and other business, which adjourns to meet at Newport, in the latter part of June. The other session on the last Monday in Oct., at South Kingston, once in two years; and the intermediate years, alternately, at Bristol and E. Greenwich, and an adjournment from the Oct. session shall be held annually at Providence. (Corrected, 1849.)

COURTS IN THE STATE OF NEW HAMPSHIRE.

SUPERIOR COURTS. — At Exeter, on the 3d Tues. of July. At Dover, on the 3d Tues. of Dec. At Gilford, on the 4th Tues. of Dec. At Concord, on the 2d Tues. of July. At Amherst, on the 2d Tues. in Dec. At Newport, on the 1st Tues. of July, and at Keene, on the 1st Tues. of Dec. At Ossipee, on the 4th Tues. of July. At Plymouth, on the Tues. next after the 4th Tues. of July. At Lancaster, on the Tues. next after the term at Plymouth. At Haverhill, on the Tues. next after the 4th Tues. of Dec.

COURTS OF COMMON PLEAS. — Portsmouth, 3d Tues. of Sept. Exeter, 2d Tues. of Feb. Dover, 3d Tues. of Jan., and 1st Tues. of Aug. Gilford, 4th Tues. of Feb. and 1st Tues. of Sept. Ossipee, 3d Tues. of May and 2d Tues. of Nov. Concord, 4th Tues. of March, and 2d Tues. of Oct. Amherst, 3d Tues. of April. Keene, 3d Tues. of March, and 2d Tues. of Sept. Newport, 1st Tues. of Feb., and 3d Tues. of Aug. Haverhill, 2d Tues. of April, and 1st Tues. of Oct. Plymouth, 2d Tues. of May, and 3d Tues. of Nov. Lancaster, 1st Tues. in May and 1st in Nov. Manchester, 4th Tues. in Oct. (Corrected, 1849.)

COURTS IN THE STATE OF VERMONT.

SUPREME COURTS. — Burlington, on the 4th Tues. in Dec., and at the following places, respectively : St. Albans, 2d Tues. North Hero, 4th Thurs. Middlebury, 4th Tues. Rutland, 6th Tues. Manchester and Bennington, alternately, 8th Tues. Newfane, 9th Tues. Woodstock, 10th Tues. Chelsea, 13th Tues. Montpelier, 15th Tues. Hyde Park, 16th Tues. Irasburg, 17th Tues. Danville, 18th Tues. Guildhall, 19th Tues. All next after the 4th Tues. in Dec.

COUNTY COURTS. — Manchester, 2d Tues. of June, and Bennington, 1st Tues. of Dec. Rutland, 2d Tues. of April and Sept. Newfane, 4th Tues. of April and Sept. Woodstock, 4th Tues. of May, and last Tues. of Nov. Middlebury, 2d Tues. in June and Dec. Chelsea, 3d Tues. of June and Dec. Burlington, last Tues. but one in March, and 1st Tues. after 4th Tues. in Sept. Montpelier, 4th Tues. in May and 3d Tues. in Nov. Danville, 1st Tues. of June and Dec. St. Albans, 2d Tues. of April and Sept. Irasburg, 4th Tues. of June and Dec. Guildhall, last Tues. of May, and 3d Tues. of Dec. North Hero, 1st Tues. after 4th Tues. in April, and 4th Tues. of Sept. Hyde Park, 2d Tues. of June and Dec. (Corrected, 1849.)

COURTS IN THE STATE OF MAINE.

SUPREME JUDICIAL COURTS. — At Alfred, Tues. next but two preceding last Tues. of April, and 3d Tues. of Sept. Portland, Tues. next but one preceding last Tues. of April, and 2d Tues. of Nov. Wiscasset, 1st Tues. of May, and Wed. following the 2d Mond. in Sept. Augusta, 2d Tues. of May, and 1st Tues. of Oct. Norridgewock, 2d Tues. next after the 4th Tues. of May, and last Tues. of Sept. Ellsworth, 7th Tues. next after the 4th Tues. of May. Machias, 6th Tues. next after the 4th Tues. of May. Paris, 4th Tues. of May, and 2d Tues. of Oct. Bangor, 4th Tues. next after the 4th Tues. of May, and 4th Tues. of Oct. Belfast, 8th Tues. next after the 4th Tues. of May. Farmington, 1st Tues. after the 4th Tues. of May. Dover, 3d Tues. after the 4th Tues. of May.

DISTRICT COURTS. — Alfred, 2d Mond. of Feb., last Mond. of May, and 3d Mond. of Oct. Portland, 1st Tues. of March, 3d Tues. of June, and 1st Tues. of October. Wiscasset, 4th Tues. of October; ditto, 4th Tues. of June, and ditto, 4th Tues. of Feb. Augusta, 1st Tues. of April, Aug., and Dec. Norridgewock, 2d Tues. of Jan., 1st Tues. of May, and 2d Tues. of Oct. Ellsworth, 2d Tues. of April, and 4th Tues. of October. Machias, last Tues. of Feb., and 3d Tues. of Sept. Paris, 2d Tues. of June and Nov. Bangor, 1st Tues. of Jan., 4th Tues. of May, and 1st Tues. of Oct. Belfast, 2d Tues. of Feb., and 4th Tues. of Aug. Farmington, last Mond. of March and Sept. Dover, last Tues. of March, and 2d Tues. of Nov. Houlton, 2d Tues. of Feb., and 1st Tues. of Sept. (Corrected, 1849.)

COUNTY COMMISSIONERS' MEETINGS IN MAINE.

YORK. — At Alfred, Tues. next before last Mon. of May, and 2d Tues. of Oct. CUMBERLAND. — At Portland, 1st Tues. of June, and 3d Tues. of Dec. LINCOLN. — At Wiscasset, 2d Tues. of Jan.; ditto, 2d Tuesday of May; ditto, 1st Mond. of Sept. KENNEBEC. — At Augusta, last Tues. of April and Dec. N. B. — A recent law enacts that an additional session for this county shall be holden at Augusta, the 2d Tues. in Aug. SOMERSET. — At Norridgewock, 3d Tues. of March, and 1st Tues. of Oct. HANCOCK. — At Ellsworth, 2d Tues. of April, and 4th Tues. of Oct. WASHINGTON. — At Machias, 1st Wed. next after 1st Tues. of March, and 1st Wed. next after 3d Tues. of Sept. OXFORD. — At Paris, 3d Tues. of June, and last Tuesday of Oct. PENOBSCOT. — At Bangor, 1st Tues. of April and Aug., and 2d Tues. of Dec. WALDO. — At Belfast, 3d Tues. of April and Aug. FRANKLIN. — At Farmington, last Tues. of April and Dec. PISCATAQUIS. — At Dover, 1st Tues. of April and Dec. AROOSTOOK. — At Houlton, 3d Tues. in Jan. and 1st Tues. in July. (Corrected, 1849.)

PROBATE COURTS IN MASSACHUSETTS.

COUNTY OF SUFFOLK. — At the Probate Office, in Court Square, Boston, every Mond. in the year except the 1st and last Mond. in June, every Mond. in July, and the 1st Mond. of each of the five succeeding months.

COUNTY OF NORFOLK. — At Dedham, 1st Tues. of every month. Quincy, 2d Tues. of Feb., May, and Aug. At Roxbury, 4th Tues. of Feb., May, Aug. and Nov. At Wrentham, 3d Tues. of May, Aug. and Nov. At Medway, 3d Tues. of Feb., June and Oct. In addition to the above, courts are held, by adjournment, at the house of the Judge, in Roxbury, every Saturday, at 2 P. M.

COUNTY OF MIDDLESEX. — At Cambridge, 2d Tues. in Jan., June and Oct., and 3d Tues. in March, May, Nov. and Dec., and 1st Tues. of Sept. At Concord, 2d Tues. of Feb., April, Aug. and Nov. At Charlestown, 3d Tues. of Feb. and Aug. At Framingham, last Tues. of June and Oct. At Groton, 1st Tues. of May and Nov. At Lowell, 1st Tues. of March, June, and Dec., and 3d Tues. of Sept. At Woburn, 4th Tues. of April.

COUNTY OF WORCESTER. — At Worcester, at the Probate Office, on the 1st Tues. of every month. At West Brookfield, 2d Tues. of May and Oct. At Lancaster, 3d Tues. of May and Oct. At Fitchburg, Wed. next after the 3d Tues. in May and Oct. At Templeton, Thurs. next after the 3d Tues. in May and Oct. At Barre, Friday next after the 3d Tues. in May and Oct. At Mendon, 4th Tues. in May. At Uxbridge, 4th Tues. in Oct.

COUNTY OF ESSEX. — At the Probate Office, in Ipswich, 1st Tues. in Feb., March, May, June, Aug., Sept., Nov. and Dec. At Salem, 1st Tues. in Jan., April, July, and Oct., and 3d Tues. in Feb., May, Aug. and Nov. At Newburyport, last Tues. in March, June, Sept. and Dec. At Haverhill, 3d Tues. in April and Oct. At Gloucester, 3d Tues. in Jan. and July. At Lynn, Wed. following the 1st Tues. in Jan. and July. At Marblehead, Wed. following the 1st Tues. in April and Oct. At Andover, 2d Tues. in Feb. and Aug. At Lawrence, 2d Tues. in June and Dec.

COUNTY OF HAMPSHIRE. — At Northampton, 1st Tuesday of each month. At Amherst, 2d Tues. of Jan. and Aug. At Belchertown, 2d Tues. of May and Oct. At Chesterfield, 3d Tues. of May and Oct.

COUNTY OF FRANKLIN. — At Greenfield, 1st Tues. of Nov., 2d Tues. of Feb., March, May and Oct., 3d Tues. of Dec., and 4th Tues. of Aug. At Conway, 1st Tues. of Feb., and 3d Tues. of July. At Charlemont, 3d Tues. of May and Oct. At Wendell, last Tues. of April, and 3d Tues. of Sept. At Warwick, Wed. next after the last Tues. of April, and Wed. next after 3d Tues. of Sept.

LOW LIVING

High living is said to be where one eats and drinks inordinately, and throws away his money, and constitution, and character oftentimes, freely! Is not this *low* living? It is certainly a low way to life.

June and Nov. Bangor, 1st Tues. of Jan., 4th Tues. of May, and 1st Tues. of Oct. Belfast, 2d Tues. of Feb., and 4th Tues. of Aug. Farmington, last Mond. of March and Sept. Do-ver, last Tues. of March, and 2d Tues. of Nov. Houlton, 2d Tues. of Feb., and 1st Tues. of Sept. (Corrected, 1849.)

COUNTY COMMISSIONERS' MEETINGS IN MAINE.

YORK. — At Alfred, Tues. next before last Mon. of May, and 2d Tues. of Oct. CUMBERLAND. — At Portland, 1st Tues. of June, and 3d Tues. of Dec. LINCOLN. — At Wiscasset, 2d Tues. of Jan.; ditto, 2d Tuesday of May; ditto, 1st Mond. of Sept. KENNEBEC. — At Augusta, last Tues. of April and Dec. N. B. — A recent law enacts that an additional session for this county shall be holden at Augusta, the 2d Tues. in Aug. SOMERSET. — At Norridgewock, 3d Tues. of March, and 1st Tues. of Oct. HANCOCK. — At Ellsworth, 2d Tues. of April, and 4th Tues. of Oct. WASHINGTON. — At Machias, 1st Wed. next after 1st Tues. of March, and 1st Wed. next after 3d Tues. of Sept. OXFORD. — At Paris, 3d Tues. of June, and last Tuesday of Oct. PENOBSCOT. — At Bangor, 1st Tues. of April and Aug., and 2d Tues. of Dec. WALDO. — At Belfast, 3d Tues. of April and Aug. FRANKLIN. — At Farmington, last Tues. of April and Dec. PISCATAQUIS. — At Dover, 1st Tues. of April and Dec. AROOSTOOK. — At Houlton, 3d Tues. in Jan. and 1st Tues. in July. (Corrected, 1849.)

PROBATE COURTS IN MASSACHUSETTS.

COUNTY OF SUFFOLK. — At the Probate Office, in Court Square, Boston, every Mond. in the year except the 1st and last Mond. in June, every Mond. in July, and the 1st Mond. of each of the five succeeding months.

COUNTY OF NORFOLK. — At Dedham, 1st Tues. of every month. Quincy, 2d Tues. of Feb., May, and Aug. At Roxbury, 4th Tues. of Feb., May, Aug. and Nov. At Wrentham, 3d Tues. of May, Aug. and Nov. At Medway, 3d Tues. of Feb., June and Oct. In addition to the above, courts are held, by adjournment, at the house of the Judge, in Roxbury, every Saturday, at 2 P. M.

COUNTY OF MIDDLESEX. — At Cambridge, 2d Tues. in Jan., June and Oct., and 3d Tues. in March, May, Nov. and Dec., and 1st Tues. of Sept. At Concord, 2d Tues. of Feb., April, Aug. and Nov. At Charlestown, 3d Tues. of Feb. and Aug. At Framingham, last Tues. of June and Oct. At Groton, 1st Tues. of May and Nov. At Lowell, 1st Tues. of March, June, and Dec., and 3d Tues. of Sept. At Woburn, 4th Tues. of April.

COUNTY OF WORCESTER. — At Worcester, at the Probate Office, on the 1st Tues. of every month. At West Brookfield, 2d Tues. of May and Oct. At Lancaster, 3d Tues. of May and Oct. At Fitchburg, Wed. next after the 3d Tues. in May and Oct. At Temp' ton, Thurs. next after the 3d Tues. in May and Oct. At Barre, Friday next after the 3d Tues. in May and Oct. At Mendon, 4th Tues. in May. At Uxbridge, 4th Tues. in Oct.

COUNTY OF ESSEX. — At the Probate Office, in Ipswich, 1st Tues. in Feb., March, May, June, Aug., Sept., Nov. and Dec. At Salem, 1st Tues. in Jan., April, July, and Oct., and 3d Tues. in Feb., May, Aug. and Nov. At Newburyport, last Tues. in March, June, Sept. and Dec. At Haverhill, 3d Tues. in April and Oct. At Gloucester, 3d Tues. in Jan. and July. At Lynn, Wed. following the 1st Tues. in Jan. and July. At Marblehead, Wed. following the 1st Tues. in April and Oct. At Andover, 2d Tues. in Feb. and Aug. At Lawrence, 2d Tues. in June and Dec.

COUNTY OF HAMPSHIRE. — At Northampton, 1st Tuesday of each month. At Amherst, 2d Tues. of Jan. and Aug. At Belchertown, 2d Tues. of May and Oct. At Chesterfield, 3d Tues. of May and Oct.

COUNTY OF FRANKLIN. — At Greenfield, 1st Tues. of Nov., 2d Tues. of Feb., March, May and Oct., 3d Tues. of Dec., and 4th Tues. of Aug. At Conway, 1st Tues. of Feb., and 3d Tues. of July. At Charlemont, 3d Tues. of May and Oct. At Wendell, last Tues. of April, and 3d Tues. of Sept. At Warwick, Wed. next after the last Tues. of April, and Wed. next after 3d Tues. of Sept.

COUNTY OF HAMPDEN. — At Springfield, 1st Tues. of Jan., Feb., March, April, May, Sept., Nov. and Dec. At Westfield, 2d Tues. of March and Dec., and 1st Tues. of June and Oct. At Monson, 2d Tues. of June, and at Palmer, 2d Tues. of Sept.

COUNTY OF BARNSTABLE. — At Barnstable, 2d Tues. of Jan., March, Sept. and Dec., and 3d Tuesday of of May and June. At Sandwich, 2d Tues. of Nov. At Falmouth, Wed. next after the 2d Tues. of Nov. At Yarmouth, 2d Tues. of Aug. At Harwich, 3d Mond. of April, and last Mond. of Oct. At Brewster, Tues. next after the 3d Mond. of April, and Tues. next after the last Mond. of Oct. At Orleans, Wed. next after the 3d Mond. of April, and .Wed. next after the last Mond. of April. At Truro, Thurs. next after the 3d Mond. of April. At Wellfleet, Thurs. next after the last Mond. of Oct. At Provincetown, Frid. next after the 2d Mond. of April, and on the Frid. next after the last Mond. of Oct.

COUNTY OF PLYMOUTH. — At the Probate Office, in Plymouth, 3d Mon. of Jan., Feb. and May, 2d Mond. of April and Aug., and 1st Mond. of Dec. At Scituate, 1st Tues. of March and June, and last Tues. of Aug. and Nov. At East Bridgewater, 1st Tues. of April, July and Oct. At Middleborough, 1st Tues. of May, Aug. and Nov. At Rochester, Wed. next after the 1st Tues. of May, and Wed. next after the 1st Tues. of Nov.

COUNTY OF BRISTOL. — At Taunton, Frid. next after the 1st Tues. of January, 1st Tuesday of March and November, Friday next after the 1st. Tues. of June, and Frid. next after the 1st Tues. of Aug. At New Bedford, 1st Tues. of Feb., June, and Dec. At Freetown, 1st Tues. of Jan. At Rehoboth, 1st Tues. of April. At Pawtucket, Frid. next after 1st Tues. of April. At Dighton, Frid. next after the 1st Tues. of Oct. At Norton, 1st Tues. of July. At Westport, 1st Tues. of Aug. At Seekonk, 1st Tues. of Sept. At Fall River, 1st Tues. of Oct. At Attleboro', 1st Tues. of May.

COUNTY OF BERKSHIRE. — At Lenox, 1st Tues. and the Wed. next after the 1st Tues. of every month, except the Wed. next after 1st Tues. of Feb., May, Aug., and Nov. At G. Barrington, Wed. next after the 1st. Tues. of Feb., May, Aug. and Nov. At Lanesboro', 2d Tues. of Jan., April, July and Oct. At Adams, Wed. next after the 2d Tues. of Jan., April, July and Oct.

DUKES COUNTY. — At West Tisbury, 3d Mond. of Jan. At Holmes' Hole, 3d Mond. of April. At Edgartown, 3d Mond. of July and Oct.

COUNTY OF NANTUCKET. — At Nantucket, 1st Sat. of every month.

TIDE TABLE.

The tides given in the Calendar pages are for the Port of Boston.

The following table contains the difference between the time of high water at Boston and several other places.

When the sign — is prefixed to the hours and minutes, in the table, the time must be subtracted from the Boston time; and when the sign + is prefixed, the time must be added to the Boston time.

	h. m.		h. m.
Albany,	+ 4 12	Island, Prince Edward,	— 1 00
Bay, Buzzard's,	— 3 50	" Rhode,	— 4 45
" Narraganset,	— 3 53	Marblehead,	0 00
" St. Mary's,	— 2 00	New Bedford,	— 3 53
Bermuda Inlet,	— 4 30	Newburyport,	— 0 15
Cape Ann,	0 00	New Haven,	— 1 14
" Charles,	— 3 45	New London,	— 2 36
" Cod,	0 00	Newport,	— 3 50
" Fear,	— 3 30	Norfolk,	— 3 00
" Henry,	— 3 50	Philadelphia,	+ 2 57
" St. Mary,	— 2 30	Plymouth,	0 00
Charleston,	— 4 15	Portland,	— 0 45
Fort St. John,	— 2 30	Port Campbell,	— 2 30
Fryingpan Shoals,	— 5 00	Port Jackson,	— 3 30
Georgetown Bar,	— 4 30	Providence,	— 3 5
Harbor, Amelia,	— 3 00	St. Salvador,	+ 4 15
Island, Block,	— 3 53	Sandy Hook,	— 4 53

MOISTEN THE ROOTS

If your tree or shrub is dried too much, do not plunge it in water, but *moisten* the roots, cut away the branches severally, and bury the whole tree in the ground for three or four days.

THE COMPLETE 1850 ALMANAC

Page 34

LIST OF CITIES AND TOWNS IN MASSACHUSETTS,

With their distances from Boston, and Number of Inhabitants in 1840; also their Representation in the General Court.

N. B.—For population of many of the places named, taken since 1840, see page 45; and distances from Boston, by rail-road, see page 43.

☞The figures in the columns of towns show the number of Representatives to which each town is entitled by the amendment of the Constitution. Those towns with a dash (—) before the number are entitled to one representative that number of years in the next ten years.

Towns & Representation.		*Dist. fr. B.*	*Pop. 1840.*
SUFFOLK Co.			
Boston, (City,)	35		83979
Chelsea,	1	2	2182
North Chelsea,*			
ESSEX.			
Amesbury,	1	40	2580
Andover,	2	20	4951
Beverly,	2	17	4686
Boxford,	—5	24	908
Bradford,	1	28	2153
Danvers,	2	15	5140
Essex,	1	25	1432
Georgetown,	1	29	1553
Gloucester,	3	30	6394
Hamilton,	—5	23	823
Haverhill,	2	30	4373
Ipswich,	1	27	2958
Lawrence,†('47)		27½	5000
Lynn, (City,)	4	9	9075
Lynnfield,	—4	12	689
Manchester,	1	20	1266
Marblehead,	2	16	5539
Methuen,	1	30	2232
Middleton,	—4	19	642
Newbury,	2	31	3889
Newburyport,	3	38	7124
Rockport,	1	32	2738
Rowley,	1	28	1230
Salem, (City,)	6	14	15162
Salisbury,	1	40	2696
Saugus,	1	9	1202
Topsfield,	—6	9	1067
Wenham,	—4	21	693
W. Newbury,	1	32	1553
MIDDLESEX.			
Acton,	—7	24	1126
Ashby,	1	50	1242
Ashland,‡			1200
Bedford,	—5	14	901
Billerica,	1	20	1527
Boxborough,	—2	25	440
Brighton,	1	5	1405
Burlington,	—3	13	510
Cambridge, (C.)	3	3	8127
Carlisle,	—3	20	563
Charlest'n, (C.)	5	1	10872
Chelmsford,	1	26	1595
Concord,	1	18	1800
Dracut,	1	30	2222
Dunstable,	—3	37	587
Framingham,	1	21	2965
Groton,	1	35	2085
Holliston,	1	25	1734
Hopkinton,	1	32	2262
Lexington,	1	10	1559
Lincoln,	—4	16	711
Littleton,	—5	28	929
Lowell, (City,)	9	24	20981
Malden,	1	4	2350

Town	Rep.	Dist.	Pop.
Marlborough,	1	28	2092
Medford,	1	4	2275
Natick,	1	17	1282
Newton,	1	9	3027
Pepperell,	1	40	1541
Reading,	1	14	2187
Sherburne,	—6	21	1014
Shirley,	—6	41	966
Somerville,§('47)		2	2500
S. Reading,	1	10	1500
Stoneham,	—6	10	1007
Stow,	1	24	1205
Sudbury,	1	20	1376
Tewksbury,	—5	24	880
Townsend,	1	45	1764
Tyngsboro',	—5	30	820
Waltham,	1	11	2593
Watertown,	1	7	1896
Wayland,	—5	16	954
W. Cambridge,	1	4	1338
Westford,	1	28	1426
Weston,	—6	15	1053
Wilmington,	—5	14	831
Woburn,	1	10	2931
WORCESTER.			
Ashburnham,	1	55	1653
Athol,	1	72	1568
Auburn,	—3	50	619
Barre,	1	58	2738
Berlin,	—4	33	772
Blackstone,‖	1	35	2800
Bolton,	—7	33	1182
Boylston,	—5	45	812
Brookfield,	1	58	2306
Charlton,	1	60	2060
Dana,	—4	65	685
Douglas,	1	47	1602
Dudley,	1	55	1333
Fitchburgh,	1	42	2570
Gardner,	1	58	1238
Grafton,	1	40	2877
Hardwick,	1	70	1775
Harvard,	1	35	1571
Holden,	1	51	1880
Hubbardston,	1	53	1764
Lancaster,	1	35	2013
Leicester,	1	46	1656
Leominster,	1	46	2000
Lunenburg,	1	45	1218
Mendon,	1	32	1200
Milford,	1	30	1795
Milbury,	1	45	2129
N. Braintree,	—4	32	763
Northborough,	1	36	1221
Northbridge,	1	45	1336
N. Brookfield,	1	60	1468
Oakham,	—6	62	1030
Oxford,	1	54	1656
Paxton,	—4	55	665
Petersham,	1	66	1812
Phillipston,	—5	58	877
Princeton,	1	46	1332
Royalston,	1	70	1635

Town	Rep.	Dist.	Pop.
Rutland,	1	50	1275
Shrewsbury,	1	40	1473
Southboro',	—7	30	1134
Southbridge,	1	70	1991
Spencer,	1	51	1557
Sterling,	1	39	1653
Sturbridge,	1	70	1886
Sutton,	1	46	2330
Templeton,	1	70	1745
Upton,	1	38	1479
Uxbridge,	1	38	1948
Warren,	1	65	1280
Webster,	1	50	1346
Westborough,	1	34	1616
W.Brookfield,**			
W. Boylston,	1	45	1202
Westminster,	1	54	1660
Winchendon,	1	60	1679
Worcester, (C.)	3	40	7060
HAMPSHIRE.			
Amherst,	1	91	2415
Belchertown,	1	80	2505
Chesterfield,	1	105	1204
Cummington,	1	110	1214
Easthampton,	-4	90	724
Enfield,	—5	75	931
Goshen,	—3	105	563
Granby,	—5	93	950
Greenwich,	—5	75	850
Hadley,	1	90	1840
Hatfield,	—5	95	915
Middlefield,	1	110	1395
Northampton,	2	95	3672
Norwich,	—4	105	746
Pelham,	—6	85	1000
Plainfield,	—5	110	926
Prescott,	—4	81	781
S. Hadley,	1	90	1422
Southampton,	-7	110	1458
Ware,	1	70	1955
Westhampton,	4	100	752
Williamsburg,	1	100	1289
Worthington,	-7	110	1185
FRANKLIN.			
Ashfield,	1	105	1579
Barnardston,	—5	86	924
Buckland,	—6	105	1110
Charlemont,	—7	110	1181
Coleraine,	1	105	1930
Conway,	1	100	1394
Deerfield,	1	98	1934
Erving,	—1	108	294
Gill,	—4	90	778
Greenfield,	1	95	1754
Hawley,	—5	120	931
Heath,	—5	125	904
Leverett,	—5	85	896
Leyden,	—4	100	646
Monroe,	—1	103	260
Montague,	1	87	1288
New Salem,	1	74	1275
Northfield,	1	94	1658

* Divided off from Chelsea, in 1846, but the inhabitants voting as heretofore until next state census.
† Divided off from Methuen and Andover in 1847.
‡ Divided off from Hopkinton, Framingham and Holliston in 1846, but the inhabitants do. do.
§ Somerville divided off from Charlestown in 1842. ‖ Divided off from Mendon in 1845.
** Divided off from Brookfield in 1848; the inhabitants voting as heretofore until next state census.

MAN'S MONUMENT

There are few men whose friends will build them a monument so honorable or so durable as he builds for himself who plants an elm, maple, oak, or other good shade tree.

Page 35

Town	Rep.	Dist.	Pop.
Orange,	1	75	1492
Rowe,	—4	130	700
Shelburne,	—6	100	1034
Shutesbury,	—6	90	997
Sunderland,	—4	90	698
Warwick,	—7	80	1154
Wendell,	—6	80	844
Whately,	—6	92	1104
HAMPDEN.			
Blandford,	1	116	1512
Brimfield,	1	75	1434
Chester,	1	120	1412
Chicopee,* ('48)		98	7912
Granville,	1	120	1284
Holland,	—2	75	436
Longmeadow,	1	97	1266
Ludlow,	1	90	1365
Monson,	1	80	2102
Montgomery,	-4	110	656
Palmer,	1	82	2150
Russell,	—6	108	1000
Southwick,	1	110	1211
Springf'ld,('48)	5	97	11338
Tolland,	—3	125	587
Wales,	—4	80	718
Westfield,	2	105	3640
W. Springfield,	2	100	3707
Wilbraham,	1	89	1846
BERKSHIRE.			
Adams,	2	120	3639
Alford,	—3	125	519
Becket,	—7	110	1128
Cheshire,	—5	120	954
Clarksburg,	—2	125	403
Dalton,	—7	120	1143
Egremont,	—6	130	1036
Florida,	—2	130	435
G. Barrington,	1	125	2690
Hancock,	—5	134	958
Hinsdale,	—5	125	950
Lanesboro',	—6	125	1048
Lee,	1	120	2281
Lenox,	1	135	1323
Monterey,†		116	
Mt. Wash.,	—2	135	470
New Ashford,	1	111	229
N. Marlboro',	1	118	1619
Otis,	—7	110	1158
Peru,	—3	118	610

Town	Rep.	Dist.	Pop.
Pittsfield,	2	125	4060
Richmond,	—6	130	1052
Sandisfield,	1	112	1451
Savoy,	—5	120	913
Sheffield,	1	125	2322
Stockbridge,	1	130	1981
Tyringham,	1	116	1402
Washington,	-5	120	830
W. Stockbr.,	1	130	1330
Williamst'n,	1	130	2076
Windsor,	—5	128	872
NORFOLK.			
Bellingham,	—6	26	1045
Braintree,	1	8	2118
Brookline,	1	6	1123
Canton,	1	14	1928
Cohasset,	1	20	1411
Dedham,	1	10	3157
Dorchester,	2	4	4458
Dover,	—3	14	514
Foxborough,	1	24	1294
Franklin,	1	26	1720
Medfield,	—5	17	846
Medway,	1	20	2051
Milton,	1	7	1684
Needham,	1	12	1479
Quincy,	1	8	3309
Randolph,	1	15	3232
Roxbury, (C.)	3	2	8310
Sharon,	—6	18	1066
Stoughton,	1	17	2062
Walpole,	1	18	1465
Weymouth,	2	11	3630
Wrentham,	1	14	2902
BRISTOL.			
Attleborough,	2	28	3620
Berkley,	—5	35	951
Dartmouth,	2	62	4091
Dighton,	1	38	1417
Easton,	1	22	2076
Fairhaven,	2	48	3985
Fall River,	3	48	6451
Freetown,	1	40	1757
Mansfield,	1	26	1346
N.Bedf'd, (C.)	5	52	12585
Norton,	1	29	1554
Pawtucket,	1	38	2119
Raynham,	1	32	1319
Rehoboth,	1	37	2036

Town	Rep.	Dist.	Pop.
Seekonk,	1	38	1831
Somerset,	—6	42	1047
Swanzey,	1	47	1421
Taunton,	3	32	7524
Westport,	1	60	2644
PLYMOUTH.			
Abington,	1	17	3144
Bridgewater,	1	24	2081
Carver,	—6	38	999
Duxbury,	1	36	2741
E. Bridgew'r,	1	20	1944
Halifax,	—4	32	730
Hanover,	1	22	1478
Hanson,	—6	24	1065
Hingham,	1	14	3489
Hull,	—1	9	217
Kingston,	1	32	1395
Marshfield,	1	30	1664
Middleboro',	2	31	5006
N. Bridgew'r,	1	20	2625
Pembroke,	1	23	1239
Plymouth,	2	30	5180
Plympton,	—5	32	861
Rochester,	2	48	3986
Scituate,	2	17	3720
South Scituate,‡			
Wareham,	1	54	2002
W. Bridgew'r,	1	24	1211
BARNSTABLE.			
Barnstable,	2	66	4297
Brewster,	1	88	1471
Chatham,	1	85	2278
Dennis,	1	76	2792
Eastham,	—5	89	944
Falmouth,	1	72	2604
Harwich,	1	79	2860
Orleans,	1	85	1953
Provincetown,	1	116	2101
Sandwich,	2	54	3620
Truro,	1	107	1916
Wellfleet,	1	97	2306
Yarmouth,	1	70	2520
DUKES.			
Chilmark,	—3	92	544
Edgartown,	1	91	1803
Tisbury,	1	85	1513
NANTUCKET.			
Nantucket,	4	100	9512

* Divided off from Springfield, in 1848; the inhabitants voting for State and United States officers as before, until 1850. † Divided off from Tyringham, in 1847. ‡ Divided off from Scituate, in 1849.

Population, according to state census, in 1830, 610,408; do. in 1840, 718,592. Increase in ten years, 108,184. The next decennial census, which we hope to procure in season for the Almanac for 1851, will probably give Massachusetts one million inhabitants.

Each town not entitled to one representative each year, may have an additional representative each year in which the valuation of estates within the commonwealth may be settled. Provided, nevertheless, no such town shall be entitled to more than one representative in any one year.

The editor of the Memphis Herald, in speaking of the "Bay State," says—

A Great State.—Old Massachusetts has ever taken the lead in what is great, good, useful and profitable. She established the first school in the United States, the first academy, and the first college. She set up the first press; printed the first book, and the first newspaper. She planted the first apple-tree, and caught the first whale. She coined the first money, and hoisted the first national flag. She made the first canal and the first rail-road. She invented the first mousetrap and washing machine; and sent the first ship to discover islands and continents in the South Sea. She produced the first philosopher, and made the first pin. She fired the first gun in the revolution, and gave "John Bull" his first beating, and put her hand first to the Declaration of Independence. She invented "Yankee Doodle," and gave a name forever to the "Universal Yankee Nation." Truly a great state.

AGRICULTURE, HORTICULTURE, AND OTHER USEFUL MATTERS.

The Fruit Growers' National Convention. — This Assembly commenced its sittings in Clinton Hall, New York, on the 10th of October, 1848, and was adjourned to the first Tuesday of October, 1849, then to meet in the city of New York, under the title of the AMERICAN CONGRESS OF FRUIT GROWERS, which name it has adopted.

Between two and three hundred members, including men distinguished in the halls of our national councils, were present during its sessions; and seldom has any association been convened, comprising more practical knowledge and science. These representatives congregated from various and remote parts of the Union, and came together with the results of their experience, acquired under different latitudes, soils and locations. The deliberations, as might be anticipated, were of a highly interesting character to the man of science, and to all interested in the cultivation of fruits.

The organization of the Congress consisted of Marshall P. Wilder, Esq., of Boston, Mass., as President; a Vice-President, and a Fruit Committee of five persons from each state in the Union and the Canadas. The State Fruit Committees are to constitute a General Committee, and of which the President is *ex officio* a member, and are to report the results of their correspondence and labors at the next session.

The prudence manifested, and almost universal desire to act definitely only on subjects in regard to which there could be no doubt, was displayed throughout the debates and doings of the convention. There were, however, the following varieties of fruits recommended for general cultivation, and a few for particular localities:

PEACHES. — Varieties recommended for general cultivation — Grosse Mignonne, George 4th, Early York, (serrated,) Large Early York, Morris White, Old Mixon, (free,) Coolidge's Favorite, Bergen's Yellow, Crawford's Late. For particular localities — Heath Cling.

PLUMS. — Varieties recommended for general cultivation — Jefferson, Green Gage, Washington, Purple Favorite, Bleecker's Gage, Coe's Golden Drop, Frost Gage, Purple Gage. For particular localities — Imperial Gage.

CHERRIES. — Varieties recommended for general cultivation — May Duke, Black Tartarian, Black Eagle, Bigarreau, Knight's Early Black, Downer's Late, Elton, Downton.

APPLES. — Varieties recommended for general cultivation — Early Harvest, Large Yellow Bough, American Summer Pearmain, Summer Rose, Early Strawberry, Gravenstein, Fall Pippin, Rhode Island Greening, Baldwin, Roxbury Russet. For particular localities — Yellow Bellefleur, Esopus Spitzenburg, Newtown Pippin.

PEARS. — Varieties recommended for general cultivation — Madeleine, Dearborn's Seedling, Bloodgood, Tyson, Golden Beurrè of Bilboa, Bartlett, Williams' Bon Chrétien, Seckel, Flemish Beauty, Beurrè Bosc, Winter Nelis, Beurrè d'Aremberg. For certain localities — White Doyennè, Gray Doyennè.

The committee are also instructed to report a list of such varieties as are decidedly unworthy of cultivation.

The best feelings prevailed among the members during the session. They parted with mutual respect, and with bright anticipations of meeting each other again at the time appointed.

[We hail this movement on the part of gentlemen of knowledge and influence in these matters, and trust the "Congress of Fruit Growers" will advance and give new life and energy to the cause of fruit cultivation, in all parts of our country, enabling those interested to select the best and discard the worthless varieties. — *Ed. Farm. Alm.*]

Uncultivated Land in Massachusetts. — It is said, upon good authority, that of the "4,192,000 acres of land in this state, available for cultivation in some form, only 260,000 acres, or six and a half per cent., are under tillage; the remaining ninety-three and a half per cent. consisting of woodlands, meadows, swamps, pasturage," &c. It seems by this that it is not necessary for *all* our population to go "out west," to get "a range."

They say that we Yankees can never be satisfied to see a beautiful article without handling it—I hope your eyes are not in your fingers' ends.

Science in the Kitchen. - Professor Liebig, in a letter to Professor Silliman, says: The method of roasting is obviously the best to make flesh the most nutritious. But it does not follow that boiling is to be interdicted. If a piece of meat be put into cold water, and this heated to boiling, and boiled until it is "done," it will become harder, and have less taste, than if thrown into water already boiling. In the first case, the matters grateful to the smell and taste go into the extract — the soup; in the second, the albumen of the meat coagulates from the surface inward, and envelopes the interior with a layer which is impregnable to water.

Keeping Beef Fresh. — In preserving beef, the *ribs* will keep longest, or five or six days, in summer; the middle of the *loin* next; the *rump* next; the *round* next; and the shortest of all, the *brisket*, which will not keep longer than three days in hot weather.

Want of Fresh Air. — The Hon. Horace Mann, in alluding to ill-ventilated school-houses, remarks as follows: To put children on a short allowance of fresh air, is as foolish as it would have been for Noah, during the deluge, to have put his family on a short allowance of water. Since God has poured out an atmosphere fifty miles deep, it is enough to make a miser weep to see our children stinted in breath.

Bathing. — "As a matter of health and duty," says a medical writer, "the bath is imperative; as one of ease, and comfort, and enjoyment, and lastly, of cleanliness, incomparable; if omitted- from distrust in the first instance, folly; if from dilatoriness or indolence, or on the score of trouble or expense, unpardonable. Read what Armstrong says:

"Do not omit, ye who would health secure,
The daily fresh ablution that shall clear
The sluices of the skin; enough to keep
The body sacred from indecent soil.
Still to be pure, even did it not conduce
(As much it does) to health, were greatly worth
Your daily pains: 't is this adorns the rich;
The want of this is poverty's worst foe.
With this external virtue, age maintains
A decent grace; without it youth and charms
Are loathsome.

A Good Custom. — A Spanish peasant, when he eats a good apple, pear, peach or any other fruit, in a forest, or by the roadside, plants the seed; and hence it is, that the woods and roadsides of Spain have more fruit in and along them than those of any other country. Cannot we do the same?

"Scientific Farming" is the ascertaining of what substances the plants you wish to raise are made — which of these substances are wanting in your land — and what manures will supply them.

Strawberries. — No other valuable fruit can be raised so easily. An acre has produced one hundred bushels in a season. If planted early in the spring, they will bear a crop the first year. They require good corn land, a soil deep and strong, but not too rich.

Scions. — March is the time to cut them for use. Take care and select thrifty shoots; *not* from the lower branches, as these are apt to grow badly. Keep them for use in a dry cellar, and cover them with sand. If kept in sawdust, they mould; in damp earth, they decay; on bare boards, they dry too much.

Transplanting. — If your tree or shrub is dried too much, do not plunge it in water, but *moisten* the roots, cut away the branches severally, and bury the whole tree in the ground for three or four days.

Shade Trees. — There are few men whose friends will build them a monument so honorable or so durable as he builds for himself who plants an elm, maple, oak, or other good shade tree.

Shrub Fruits. — Your crop of currants, gooseberries and raspberries, will improve if you dig up the old plants once in three or four years, and plant young bushes, and weed and keep the ground open about them.

RAILROADS IN NEW ENGLAND.

The last year's Almanac enumerated all the Railroads which had been finished or commenced during the year previous to the 1st of August, 1848. We now give, with as much particularity as is consistent with our limits, a complete view of another year's progress of the railroad enterprise, embracing all roads completed or in actual progress, up to the 1st of August, 1849. The amount of information which the history of the year furnishes obliges us to omit the usual table of annual receipts, expenditures, dividends, &c.—our object being, not so much to present the subject in a financial point of view, as to acquaint the numerous readers of the Almanac with the actual progress, from year to year, of this important means of intercommunication. The year has been a trying one to railroads, as well as to most other mercantile and corporate interests, and both dividends and the general value of stock have been materially diminished.

MASSACHUSETTS.

The Essex R. (from Salem to Lawrence, 22 miles) is open. The Salem and Lowell R. (from the Essex R., at So. Danvers, to the Lowell and Lawrence R., at Tewksbury, 16 miles) is under contract. The Norfolk Co. R. is finished and operated to Blackstone, passing, by a branch of the Providence R., to Dedham, and thence through South Dedham, Walpole, North Wrentham, Franklin, and Bellingham, to Blackstone, 26 miles, where it intersects the Providence and Worcester R. The South Shore R. (from the Old Colony R., at Braintree, through Weymouth and Hingham, to Cohasset) is fully open. The Worcester and Nashua R. (through Lancaster, Groton, &c.) is completed and in full operation. The Vermont and Massachusetts R. is open to Brattleboro', Vt. A branch is being built from this road, at Montague, to Greenfield. The Peterboro' and Shirley R. (from the Fitchburg R., at Shirley, to the N. H. State line) is finished to Townsend, 12 miles, and is run by the Fitchburg R. It is designed to be extended to Peterboro', N. H. The Stockbridge and Pittsfield R. (passing through Lenox) will be finished this year. The Newburyport and Georgetown R. (from a point on the Eastern R., near Newburyport, to Georgetown) is under contract and in progress. The So. Reading Branch R. (from Danvers to So. Reading, 7 1-2 miles) has been commenced, with the expectation of opening it for business next spring. It will unite with the B. and Me. R. at So. Reading, and thus make a new route from Danvers and Salem to Boston, the distance being about 18 miles.

MAINE.

The Atlantic and St. Lawrence R. (designed, in connection with the St. Lawrence and Atlantic R. in Canada, to form a continuous line from Portland to Montreal) is built and in operation to Mechanics Falls, about 40 miles from Portland. It passes through N. Yarmouth, where it forms a junction with Kennebec and Portland R., and Lewiston Falls, where a junction is formed with the Androscoggin and Kennebec R. Some 30 miles of the Canada end of the route—from Montreal to Hyacinthe—is also open. The Androscoggin and Kennebec R. (to extend from the junction of the Atlantic and St Lawrence R., at Lewiston, to Waterville, on the Kennebec) is open to Winthrop, and nearly finished to Waterville. The Kennebec and Portland R. (to extend from the junction of the Atlantic and St. Lawrence R., at N. Yarmouth, to Augusta, with a branch to Bath) is completed to Bath, and in progress towards Augusta. The York and Cumberland R. (to extend ultimately from Portland through Oxford Co., and unite with the Boston and Maine R. at So. Berwick) is nearly finished as far as Gorham. When completed, this road will make a second line from Portland to So. Berwick, where the Boston and Maine R. and the Eastern R. now both unite with the Portsmouth, Saco and Portland R.; and there many thus be two distinct lines from Boston to Portland. A survey has been made for a R. from Lewiston Falls to Rumford Falls, on the Androscoggin river, 43 miles, through Turner Village, Canton and Peru.

NEW HAMPSHIRE.

The Cheshire R. (from the Vermont and Massachusetts R., at Ashburnham, to Bellows Falls) and the Sullivan R. (from Bellows Falls to Windsor, on the N. H. side of the Connecticut) are both open, completing the connection between Boston and the Vermont Central and Passumpsic roads, by way of Fitchburg. The Boston, Concord and Montreal R. is open to New Hampton, 8 miles from Plymouth; will be completed to Plymouth this season, and to Rumney early next summer. The Concord and Claremont R. is located and in progress as far as Bradford, and will be finished to Warner, 18 miles from Concord, this fall. The Contoocook Valley R. (designed ultimately to extend from the Concord and Claremont R., at Contoocookville, in Hopkinton, to Peterboro', but at present only to be built to Hillsboro' Bridge) will be finished in September as far as Henniker, 17 miles from Concord. The N. H. Central R. is under contract for a distance of 24 miles from Manchester, to Henniker, where it will intersect with the Contoocook Valley R. At Bradford, it will unite with the Concord and Claremont R. The Great Falls and Conway R. is open to Rochester. The Cocheco R. (from the Boston and Maine R., at Dover, to Lake Winnipiseogee, where it will unite with the B. C. and Montreal R.) is nearly completed to Farmington. At Rochester it intersects the Great Falls and Conway R. The Portsmouth and Concord R. will be completed as far as Epping, 15 miles from Portsmouth, this autumn. The Wilton R. is open from Nashua to Amherst.

VERMONT.

The Connecticut and Passumpsic Rivers R. is open from White River to Wells River, 40 miles. At White River it connects with the Northern R. and the Vermont Central R. It has been determined to construct the road 20 miles further north, to St. Johnsbury; and eventually it is proposed to extend it to the Canada line, to meet the St. Lawrence and Atlantic R., from Montreal. The Vermont Central R. is open from Windsor to Montpelier, and will be completed to Burlington the present year. The Vermont and Canada R. (which will connect the Vermont Central with the Ogdensburgh R. in New York) is to be immediately constructed and leased by the Vermont Central R. The Rutland and Burlington R. (from Bellows Falls to Burlington, via Rutland) is expected to be completed the present year. It is now in operation from Bellows Falls to Ludlow, 28 miles, and from Burlington to Middlebury, 33 miles. A R. from Rutland to Poultney, to connect with a contemplated R. from Troy, N. Y., is under contract.

CONNECTICUT.

The Hartford and Providence R. is in rapid progress of completion towards Willimantic, and it has been determined to extend it west of Hartford, even to the North River, so as to connect with the Erie R. It is under contract, on the western portion, as far as Bristol, 17 miles from Hartford. At Plainville, it intersects the Canal R., and will thus form a new connection between Hartford and New Haven. The Canal R. is open to Farmington, 32 miles from New Haven. This road is to extend to the Massachusetts State line, upon the route of the Farmington Canal. From the State line a few miles of road, which it is hoped ultimately to build, will connect the Canal R. with the Western R. a little west of Springfield, and thus form a distinct line between New Haven and Springfield. It is expected to complete the road to the State line the present year. The Naugatuck R. (from Bridgeport to Winstead) will be finished this autumn, being already in operation as far as Plymouth Hollow, 8 miles above Waterbury. This road connects with the N. York and New Haven R. 5 miles from Bridgeport, on the Housatonic river; follows that river to Derby; and thence passes through the Naugatuck Valley to Winstead, 57 miles.

POETRY, ANECDOTES, &C.

AGRICULTURAL SONG.

Plough deep to find the gold, my friends,
  Plough deep to find the gold!
Your farms have treasures rich and sure,
  Unmeasured and untold.

Clothe with trees New England's hills,
  Her broad fields sow with grain,
Nor search the Sacramento's rills
  For Californian gain.
Our land o'erflows with corn and bread,
  With treasures all untold,
Would we but give the ploughshare speed
  And DEPTH to find the gold.

Plough deep to find the gold, my friends,
  &c.

Earth is grateful to her sons
  For all their care and toil;
Nothing yields such large returns
  As drained and deepened soil.
Science, lend thy kindly aid,
  Her riches to unfold!
Moved by plough or moved by spade,
  Stir deep to find the gold!

Dig deep to find the gold, my friends,
  Dig deep to find the gold!
Your farms have treasures rich and sure,
  Unmeasured and untold.

HOW TO GET ON IN THE WORLD.

Is there no general rule for "getting on" in the world? We think there is. We cannot tell what is coming; but we can hold ourselves in preparation for what may befall. A ship that goes forth upon the ocean is provided with appliances both for catching the breeze and evading the storm; and were it otherwise, she would have no chance of making a prosperous voyage. Don't rush from employment to employment, but keep up to the times, and be ready for opportunities—they all occur, and the wise are those who seize them. Don't believe in getting on by chance. Think! learn! aspire! be ready! act!—*Chambers.*

THE BOOK.

The book, finally, our best festival, our most intimate friend, the expected guest of the house, the joy of the domestic hearth, the companion of wandering life, the faithful servant of regular life—the book, an angel or a demon, to which all hands are held out, to which all hearts are opened.—*Jules Janin.*

HOME.

"There is no sanctuary of virtue like home."—*Edward Everett.*

CHILDHOOD.

The scenes of childhood are the memories of future years.—*J. O. Choules.*

THE FARMER'S SONG.

"His wants are few, and well supplied
  By his productive fields;
He craves no luxuries beside,
  Save what contentment yields.

More pure enjoyment labor gives,
  Than fame or wealth can bring;
And he is happier who lives
  A farmer, than a king."

THE IRRESOLUTE, UNDECIDED, AND THEREFORE UNSUCCESSFUL MAN.

All his defects and mortifications he attributes to the outward circumstances of his life, the exigencies of his profession, the accidents of chance. But, in reality, they lay much deeper than this. They are within himself. He wants the all-controlling, all-subduing will. He wants the fixed purpose that sways and bends all circumstances to its uses, as the wind bends the reeds and rushes beneath it.—*Kavanagh, by Longfellow.*

SIMPLICITY.

In character, in manners, in style, in all things, the supreme excellence is simplicity.—*Ibid.*

WASHINGTON MONUMENT.

The foundation of the National Washington Monument, at Washington, was completed on the 23d of April, 1849, and the laying of the marble work commenced. The foundation of this mighty structure is executed in a most substantial and workmanlike manner. The corner stone was laid July 4, 1848, and in an appropriate address, delivered on the occasion, by Hon. R. C. Winthrop, of Boston, occurs this eloquent passage: "Proceed to the noble work for which you have assembled. Build the monument to the skies—you cannot overreach the loftiness of his principles; found it on the massive and eternal rock—you cannot make it more enduring than is his fame; construct it of Parian marble—you cannot make it purer and more spotless than was his life; exhaust on it the principles of ancient and modern art—you cannot make it more proportionate than was his character."

THE HOE AND THE SLATE.

I saw a lad bearing a bright new hoe, on the handle of which was suspended a slate. "Noble representative of a northern laborer!" I exclaimed. "March on, brave boy! keep thy grasp on both the hoe and the slate, and thy country will be grateful for the day that gave thee birth."

When a friend sends you fruit, flowers, or other presents, the least you can do is to return promptly whatever the gift is sent in, even if it is an old basket.

Page 40

BE WHAT YOU SEEM!

"BE WHAT YOU SEEM," and seem what
  you should be,
The child of truth, from all dishonor free;
Brave and humane, and generous, just
  and wise;
Revere what's good — the bad thou wilt
  despise.

Be what you seem — let virtue mould
  each thought,
And form the heart, with every goodness
  fraught;
Thy country's good prefer to private ends,
And taste the pleasure that high views
  attends.

Be what you seem — benevolence ope
  thine eye,
And teach thee how her objects to descry ;
Befriend the poor, dry up each briny tear,
Nor close thy bounty each revolving year.

TRYING SITUATIONS.

Trying situations bewilder and unnerve
the weak, but call forth all the strength
and energy of the strong. — *Macaulay.*

A VALENTINE.

BY FIELDS.

She that is fair, though never vain or
  proud,
More fond of home than fashion's chang-
  ing crowd;
Whose taste refined even female friends
  admire,
Dressed not for show, but robed in neat
  attire :
She who has learned, with mild, forgiving
  breast,
To pardon frailties, hidden or confessed;
True to herself, yet willing to submit;
More swayed by love than ruled by world-
  ly wit;
Though young, discreet; though ready,
  ne'er unkind;
Blessed with no pedant's but a *woman's*
  mind;
She wins our hearts; toward her our
  thoughts incline ;
So at her door go leave your Valentine.

CURIOUS SENTENCE.

Taylor, the water poet, wrote a line
that reads the same forwards and backwards, and offered a thousand pounds to
any one who would write another. Here
it is. We trust none of our readers can
say it with truth.
  "Lewd did I live & evil I did dwel."

DON'T BROOD OVER TROUBLE.

Man doubles all the evils of his fate by
pondering over them ; a scratch becomes
a wound, a slight an injury, a jest an insult, a small peril a great danger, and a
light sickness often ends in death by
brooding apprehensions.

HOPE AND COURAGE.

True hope is based on energy of character. A strong mind always hopes, and
has cause to hope, because it knows the
mutability of human affairs, and how
slight a circumstance may change the
whole course of human events. Such a
spirit, too, rests upon itself. It is not
confined to partial views, or to one particular object ; and if at least it should be
lost, it has saved itself — its own integrity
and worth.

GOOD NATURE.

Good nature is one of the sweetest gifts
of Providence. Like the pure sunshine,
it gladdens, enlivens, and cheers. In the
midst of hate, revenge, sorrow and despair, how glorious are its effects !

AN ELOQUENT SAYING.

There is much meaning in the following, which we cut from an exchange —
"No snow falls lighter than the snow of
age ; but none is heavier, for it never
melts."

EPIGRAM WRITTEN AFTER GOING
TO LAW.

This law, they say, great nature's chain
  connects;
That *causes* ever must produce *effects*.
In *me* behold *reversed* great nature's laws,
All my *effects* lost by a single *cause.*

HEROIC CONFESSION.

Mr. J. Q. Adams was once asked what
he most lamented in his life. He answered — "My impulsive temper and vi-
tuperative manner of speech, which prevent me from returning good for evil, and
induce me, in the madness of my blood, to
say things that I am afterwards ashamed
of."

ANECDOTES.

How to TELL GOOD INDIGO. — An old
lady was informing a friend how to tell
good indigo. "Put it," said she, "into
water, and if prime, it will sink or swim
— *I have forgotten which.*"

FORGOT THE BABY. — A couple, in Rochester, N. Y., who had not been made
happy by having more than one of these
"troublesome comforts," went shopping,
and while selecting their goods, put "the
baby" upon a pile of sheeting, and,
strange to say, in their hurry to get home,
left the little one at the shop. They had
not gone far before each began to ask the
other, "Why ! where's the baby !" Their
loss was soon discovered, and, upon returning, the clerks restored the little innocent, without ever expressing a wish to
retain the "precious darling," much to
the mother's joy and the father's delight.

ANSWER TO PROBLEM G.

The sides should be twice as wide as
the back, and the front as wide as sides
and back together. By A. F., N—a, N.
H.; S. E. D., M—n, Mass.

ANSWER TO PROBLEM H.

11 — 47 ✕ —. By A. F., N—a, N. H.;
H. C. C., R—d, R. I. S. H. R, of E—n,
Me.

ANSWER TO PROBLEM I.

403,291,461,126,605,635,584,000,000.
By A. F., N—a, N. H.; H. C. C., of R—d,
G. F., of W—m, Mass. C. L. W., of
E—mont, Mass.; S. E. D., M—n, Mass.;
S. H. R., of E—n, Me.; J. N. M—y, of
B—n, Mass.; E. J—n, of D—r, N. H.

ANSWER TO PROBLEM J.

Together at 10 $\frac{10}{11}$ m. past 2 ; at right
angles, 27 $\frac{3}{11}$ m. past 2 ; in opposite direc-
tions, 43 $\frac{7}{11}$ m. past 2. By A. F., N—a,
N. H.; H. C. C., of R—d; P. T., of Pl—d,
Ct.; G. F., of W—m, Mass. C. L. W.,
of E—mont, Mass.; S. E. D., M—n, Mass.;
S. H. R., of E—n, Me.; J. N. M—y, of
B—n, Mass.; H. R. W—d, of T—n, Mass.;
E. J—n, of D—r, N. H.

ANSWER TO PROBLEM K.

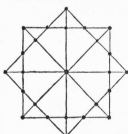

Place the trees in a square, 5 trees each
way ; count the rows each way, also
diagonally. Answered by J. O. T., of Y.
P.; J. B., mate of sch'r L—l, of B—n ;
H. C. C., of R—d, R. I.; G. F., of W—m,
Mass.; S. H. R., of E—n, Me.

ANSWER TO ENIGMA.

Wig — Tin — Waist — Ton — Gin ; —
WASHINGTON. By J. O. T., of Y. P.; W.
L. W., of F—g; A. C. N., of S. D., Cape
Cod ; H. C. C., R—d; G. F., of W—m,
Mass.; N. B., Jr., of B—n, Mass.; C. L.
W., of E—mont, Mass. S. E. D., M—n,
Mass.; S. H. R., of E—n, Me.; J. N. M—y,
of B—n, Mass.; E. J—n, of D—r, N. H.

PROBLEM L.

The year 1849 was a square year —
what is its cube ? What was the last
square year in the last century ? What
will be the next square year in the next
century ?

PROBLEM M.

Required to divide 45 in four parts, so
that the first part, with two added — the
second part, with two subtracted — the
third part, divided by two, and the fourth
part, multiplied by two, shall equal each
other. J. O. T., of Y. Port, Ms.

PROBLEM N.

How many variations will the 32 points
of the compass admit of ?
  J. C. C., Sullivan, Me.

PROBLEM O.

Required to divide 275 into four parts,
so that if you add 4 to the first, subtract
4 from the second, multiply the third by
4, and divide the 4th by 4, the result of
each operation will be the same number.
  J. N. M—y, of B—n.

ENIGMA A, (ACROSTICALLY.)

Required a word of seven letters, used
more than once upon this page, made up
of each first letter of words composed as
follows :
1, 3, 6 and 7 — a kind of writing.
2, 3, 4 and 6 — a garment.
3, 2 and 6 — an unpurified metal.
4, 3, 3 and 7 — a part of a ship.
5, 3, 2 and 6 — a word signifying learning.
6, 5 and 7 — a tree.
7, 3, 5 and 6 — an animal like a mouse.
  S. H. R., of E—n.

ENIGMA B.

Letter first is a seed oft eaten green;
  The second a measure will surely be
  found,
The third's an animal, quite useful, I
  ween ;
  Of the fourth in a cough you catch the
  sound ;
The whole is a fruit, and a treasure rare
  The rich possess, if they think they do.
The farmer's desire, the merchant's
  prayer,
  The young man's wish, and the maid-
  en's too.
Now kindly add one letter more,
  Which a thrifty and active insect is
  found,
You 'll have what a builder needs, I 'm
  sure,
  Though used the ocean's depths to
  sound.
Again for the last letter pray use instead,
  One expressed by a part of the human
  frame :
'T will make what a lady's or soldier's
  head
Will often adorn for show or for fame.

Scientific farming is the
ascertaining of what sub-
stances the plants you wish to
raise are made — which of
these substances are wanting
in your land — and what manures will supply them.

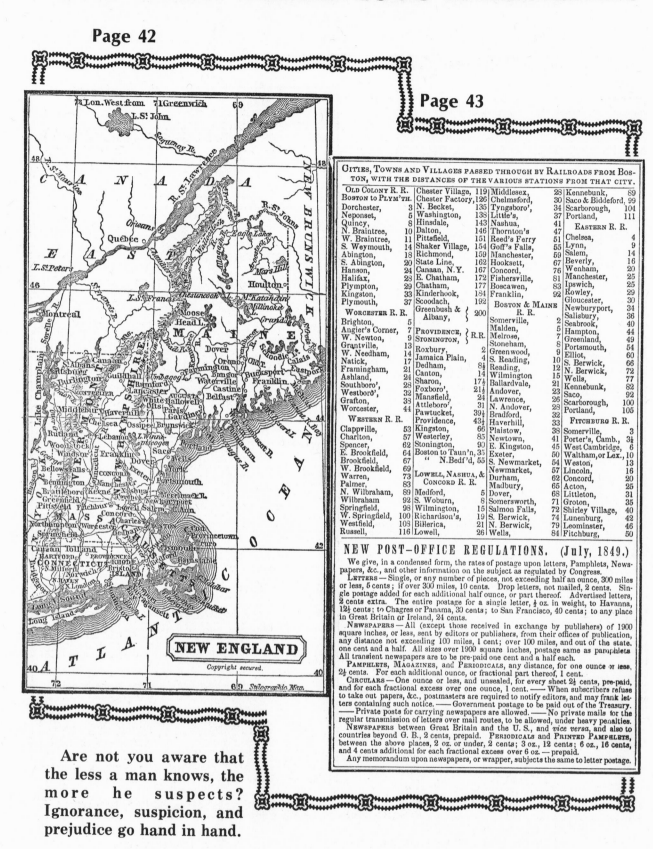

NEW ENGLAND

Copyright secured.

Stylographic Map.

CITIES, TOWNS AND VILLAGES PASSED THROUGH BY RAILROADS FROM BOSTON, WITH THE DISTANCES OF THE VARIOUS STATIONS FROM THAT CITY.

OLD COLONY R. R. BOSTON to PLYM'TH.			
Dorchester,	3	Chester Village,	119
Neponset,	5	Chester Factory,	126
Quincy,	8	N. Becket,	135
N. Braintree,	10	Washington,	138
W. Braintree,	11	Hinsdale,	143
S. Weymouth,	14	Dalton,	146
Abington,	18	Pittsfield,	151
S. Abington,	20	Shaker Village,	154
Hanson,	24	Richmond,	159
Halifax,	28	State Line,	162
Plympton,	29	Canaan, N.Y.	167
Kingston,	33	E. Chatham,	172
Plymouth,	37	Chatham,	177
		Kinderhook,	184
WORCESTER R. R.		Franklin,	92
Brighton,	5	Scoodach,	192
Angier's Corner,	7	Greenbush & Albany,	200
W. Newton,	9		
Grantville,	13	PROVIDENCE, STONINGTON, R.R.	
W. Needham,	14		
Natick,	17	Roxbury,	2
Framingham,	21	Jamaica Plain,	4
Ashland,	24	Dedham,	8¼
Southboro',	28	Canton,	14
Westboro',	32	Sharon,	17½
Grafton,	38	Foxboro',	21¼
Worcester,	44	Mansfield,	24
		Attleboro',	31
WESTERN R. R.		Pawtucket,	39¼
Clappville,	53	Providence,	43¼
Charlton,	57	Kingston,	66
Spencer,	62	Westerley,	85
E. Brookfield,	64	Stonington,	90
Brookfield,	67	Boston to Taun'n, 35	
W. Brookfield,	69	" N.Bedf'd, 55	
Warren,	73		
Palmer,	83	LOWELL, NASHUA, & CONCORD R. R.	
N. Wilbraham,	89	Medford,	5
Wilbraham,	92	S. Woburn,	8
Springfield,	98	Wilmington,	15
W. Springfield,	100	Richardson's,	19
Westfield,	108	Billerica,	21
Russell,	116	Lowell,	26

Middlesex,	28	Kennebunk,	89
Chelmsford,	30	Saco & Biddeford,	99
Tyngsboro',	34	Scarborough,	104
Little's,	37	Portland,	111
Nashua,	41		
Thornton's	47	EASTERN R. R.	
Reed's Ferry	51	Chelsea,	4
Goff's Falls,	55	Lynn,	9
Manchester,	59	Salem,	14
Hooksett,	67	Beverly,	16
Concord,	76	Wenham,	20
Fishersville,	81	Manchester,	25
Boscawen,	83	Ipswich,	25
Franklin,	92	Rowley,	30
		Gloucester,	30
BOSTON & MAINE R. R.		Newburyport,	34
Somerville,	2	Salisbury,	36
Malden,	5	Seabrook,	40
Melrose,	7	Hampton,	44
Stoneham,	8	Greenland,	49
Greenwood,	9	Portsmouth,	54
S. Reading,	10	Elliot,	60
Reading,	12	S. Berwick,	66
Wilmington,	15	N. Berwick,	72
Ballardvale,	21	Wells,	77
Andover,	23	Kennebunk,	82
Lawrence,	26	Saco,	92
N. Andover,	28	Scarborough,	100
Bradford,	32	Portland,	105
Haverhill,	33		
Plaistow,	38	FITCHBURG R. R.	
Newtown,	41	Somerville,	3
E. Kingston,	45	Porter's, Camb.,	3¼
Exeter,	50	West Cambridge,	6
S. Newmarket,	54	Waltham, or Lex.,	10
Newmarket,	57	Weston,	13
Durham,	62	Lincoln,	16
Madbury,	65	Concord,	20
Dover,	68	Acton,	25
Somersworth,	71	Littleton,	31
Salmon Falls,	72	Groton,	35
S. Berwick,	74	Shirley Village,	40
N. Berwick,	79	Lunenburg,	42
Wells,	84	Leominster,	46
		Fitchburg,	50

NEW POST-OFFICE REGULATIONS. (July, 1849.)

We give, in a condensed form, the rates of postage upon letters, Pamphlets, Newspapers, &c., and other information on the subject as regulated by Congress.

LETTERS—Single, or any number of pieces, not exceeding half an ounce, 300 miles or less, 5 cents; if over 300 miles, 10 cents. Drop letters, not mailed, 2 cents. Single postage added for each additional half ounce, or part thereof. Advertised letters, 2 cents extra. The entire postage for a single letter, ½ oz. in weight, to Havanna, 12½ cents; to Chagres or Panama, 30 cents; to San Francisco, 40 cents; to any place in Great Britain or Ireland, 24 cents.

NEWSPAPERS—All (except those received in exchange by publishers) of 1900 square inches, or less, sent by editors or publishers, from their offices of publication, any distance not exceeding 100 miles, 1 cent; over 100 miles, and out of the state. one cent and a half. All sizes over 1900 square inches, postage same as pamphlets. All transient newspapers are to be pre-paid one cent and a half each.

PAMPHLETS, MAGAZINES, and PERIODICALS, any distance, for one ounce or less, 2½ cents. For each additional ounce, or fractional part thereof, 1 cent.

CIRCULARS—One ounce or less, and unsealed, for every sheet 2½ cents, pre-paid, and for each fractional excess over one ounce, 1 cent. —— When subscribers refuse to take out papers, &c., postmasters are required to notify editors, and may frank letters containing such notice. —— Government postage to be paid out of the Treasury. —— Private posts for carrying newspapers are allowed. —— No private mails for the regular transmission of letters over mail routes, to be allowed, under heavy penalties. NEWSPAPERS between Great Britain and the U. S., and vice versa, and also to countries beyond G. B., 2 cents, prepaid. PERIODICALS and PRINTED PAMPHLETS, between these places, 2 oz. or under, 2 cents; 3 oz., 12 cents; 6 oz., 16 cents, and 4 cents additional for each fractional excess over 6 oz.—prepaid.

Any memorandum upon newspapers, or wrapper, subjects the same to letter postage.

Are not you aware that the less a man knows, the more he suspects? Ignorance, suspicion, and prejudice go hand in hand.

THE COMPLETE 1850 ALMANAC

TABLE OF SIMPLE INTEREST, AT 6 PER CENT.
So arranged that the interest on any sum may be at once ascertained.

Princi-pal.	1 Day. D. c. m.	1 Week. D. c. m.	1 Month. D. c. m.	1 Year. D. c. m.	Princi-pal.	1 Day. D. c. m.	1 Week. D. c. m.	1 Month. D. c. m.	1 Year. D. c. m.
Cts. 20	0 0 0	0 0 0	0 0 1	0 1 2	Doll.70	0 1 2	0 8 7	0 35 0	4 20
30	0 0 0	0 0 0	0 1 0	0 1 8	80	0 1 3	0 10 0	0 40 0	4 80
40	0 0 0	0 0 0	0 1 0	0 2 4	90	0 1 5	0 11 2	0 45 0	5 40
50	0 0 0	0 0 0	0 20	0 3 0	100	0 1 6	0 12 5	0 50 0	6 0
60	0 0 0	0 0 0	0 20	0 3 6	200	3 3	0 25 0	1 0	12 0
70	0 0 0	0 0 0	0 30	0 4 2	300	4 9	0 37 5	1 50 0	18 0
80	0 0 0	0 0 0	0 30	0 4 8	400	6 6	0 50 0	2 0	24 0
90	0 0 0	0 1 0	0 4 0	0 5 4	500	8 3	0 62 5	2 50 0	30 0
Dolls.1 0	0 0 0	0 1 0	0 5 0	6 0	600	10 0	0 75 0	3 0	36 0
2 0	0 0 0	0 1 0	1 00	0 12 0	700	11 5	0 87 5	3 50 0	42 0
3 0	0 0 0	0 20	1 50	0 18 0	800	13 3	1 00 0	4 0	48 0
4 0	0 1 0	0 40	2 00	0 24 0	900	14 8	1 12 5	4 50 0	54 0
5 0	0 1 0	0 50	2 50	0 30 0	10000	16 4	1 25 0	5 0	60 0
6 0	0 1 0	0 60	3 00	0 36 0	20000	32 9	2 50 0	10 0	120 0
7 0	0 1 0	0 70	3 50	0 42 0	30000	49 3	3 75 0	15 0	180 0
8 0	0 1 0	0 90	4 00	0 48 0	40000	65 8	5 00 0	20 0	240 0
9 0	0 1 0	1 00	4 50	0 54 0	50000	82 2	6 25 0	25 0	300 0
10 0	0 20	1 10	5 00	0 60 0	60000	98 7	7 50 0	30 0	360 0
20 0	0 30	2 50	10 0	1 20 0	70000	1 15 1	8 75 0	35 0	420 0
30 0	0 50	3 70	15 0	1 80 0	80000	1 31 5	10 00 0	40 0	480 0
40 0	0 70	5 00	20 0	2 40 0	90000	1 48 0	11 25 0	45 0	540 0
50 0	0 80	6 20	25 0	3 00 0	100000	1 64 4	12 50 0	50 0	600 0
60 0	1 00	7 50	30 0	3 60 0	110000	1 80 8	13 75 0	55 0	660 0
					120000	1 97 3	15 00 0	60 0	720 0

Where the interest is at the rate of seven per cent. per year, add one' sixth to the product, — of eight per cent., add two sixths, &c. Where at the rate of 5 per cent., deduct one sixth, — of four per cent., deduct two sixths, &c.

A short and easy Method of Casting Compound Interest, at 6 per cent.

RULE. — Multiply the given sum, if

For 2 years, by 1.1236	For 7 years, by 1.503630
For 3 years, by 1.191016	For 8 years, by 1.593848
For 4 years, by 1.262476	For 9 years, by 1.689478
For 5 years, by 1.338225	For 10 years, by 1.790847
For 6 years, by 1.418519	For 11 years, by 1.898298

Note. — This will give the amount of principal and compound interest for the given number of years. Subtract the principal from the amount, and it will show the compound interest. Any sum of money at compound interest will double itself in eleven years, ten months and twenty-two days.

AGRICULTURAL WEALTH OF THE UNITED STATES.

The Boston Courier furnishes the following estimate of the products of Agriculture, in the U. S., as taken from the Report of the Commissioner of Patents, Jan., 1849:

Barley,	6,222,050 bushels.	Rice,	199,199,500 pounds.	
Buck Wheat,	12,538,000 "	Potatoes,	114,475,000 bushels.	
Corn,	588,150,000 "	Hay,	15,785,000 tons.	
Oats,	135,500,000 "	Hemp,	20,380 tons.	
Rye,	32,952,500 "	Tobacco,	218,909,000 pounds.	
Wheat,	126,364,600 "	Cotton,	1,066,000,000 pounds.	

Total cereal grains, 901,727,150

The valuation of the Hay crop, at eight dollars per ton, amounts to $126,280,000. The Cotton crop, at 6 cents per pound, amounts to only $63,960,000, being but a little more than half the value of the hay.

The Hay crop in the six New England States is 4,797,000 tons, which, at eight dollars per ton, gives a value of $38,376,000, or more than half that of the whole Cotton crop.

The value of the Potato crop, at 25 cents per bushel, amounts to $28,618,750.

The products of the soil in this country, used as food for man, are unprecedented in the history of nations, for to the articles above named, are to be added, Beef, Pork, Mutton, Poultry, Eggs, Butter, Cheese, Milk, culinary vegetables, fruits, &c.

"OUR WHOLE COUNTRY." — Mr. Hilliard of Alabama, in a recent speech on the territorial bill, warmly eulogized the enterprise and the ennobling institutions of New England, and remarked that, "although he loved the South, *yet he should love it less were it not that New England, as well as the sunny South, constituted a part of the Union.*"

SPEAK THE TRUTH

POPULATION TABLES.

POPULATION OF THE UNITED STATES, ACCORDING TO FOUR ENUMERATIONS, AND THE ESTIMATED POPULATION FOR 1850;

With the square miles of each State; in round numbers; the number of Electors and Representatives for each State, and date of admission to the Union.

For the Representatives of a State, deduct two (for Senators) from the Electors.

STATES.	SQ'ARE MILES.	Elect's.	Date of admiss. to Un.	1810.	1820.	1830.	1840.	Estimated Pop. in 1850.
Maine,	32,400	9	1820	228,705	298,335	399,955	501,793	677,624
N. Hampshire,	9,500	6	Of original 13 Sts.	214,360	244,161	262,328	284,574	384,289
Massachusetts,	7,500	12		472,040	523,287	610,408	737,699	1,001,192
Rhode Island,	1,300	4		77,031	83,059	97,199	108,830	146,964
Connecticut,	4,800	6		262,042	275,208	297,675	309,978	418,595
Vermont,	10,200	6	1791	216,713	235,764	280,652	291,948	373,567
New York,	46,000	36	Original States.	959,049	1,372,812	1,918,608	2,428,921	3,279,925
New Jersey,	8,000	7		245,555	277,575	320,823	373,306	504,113
Pennsylvania,	46,200	26		810,091	1,049,458	1,348,233	1,724,033	2,328,140
Delaware,	2,100	3		72,674	72,749	76,748	78,085	105,447
Maryland,	11,000	8		380,546	407,350	447,940	469,232	633,653
Dist. of Colum.	*			24,022	33,039	39,834	43,712	50,000
Virginia,	64,000	17	Original States.	974,622	1,065,379	1,211,405	1,239,797	1,672,126
North Carolina,	48,000	11		555,500	638,829	737,987	753,419	1,017,420
South Carolina,	28,000	9		415,115	502,741	581,185	594,398	802,667
Georgia,	62,000	10		252,433	340,987	516,823	691,392	933,658
Kentucky,	40,000	12	1792	406,511	564,317	687,917	779,828	1,053,082
Tennessee,	42,000	13	1796	281,727	422,813	681,904	829,210	1,119,768
Ohio,	41,000	23	1802	230,760	581,434	937,903	1,519,467	2,051,994
Indiana,	36,000	12	1816	24,520	147,178	343,031	685,866	926,196
Mississippi,	46,000	6	1817	40,352	75,448	136,621	375,651	507,280
Illinois,	56,500	9	1818	12,288	55,214	157,445	476,183	643,040
Louisiana,	47,000	6	1812	76,556	153,407	215,739	352,411	475,897
Missouri,	70,000	7	1821	20,845	66,586	140,455	383,702	518,152
Alabama,	54,000	9	1819	—	127,901	309,527	590,756	797,759
Michigan,	61,000	5	1836	4,762	8,896	31,639	212,267	286,646
Arkansas,	55,000	3	1836	—	14,273	30,388	97,574	131,764
Florida,	56,000	3	1845	—	—	—	34,730	54,477	73,566
Wisconsin,†	92,000	4	1848	—	—	—	30,945	250,000
Iowa,‡	174,000	4	1845	—	—	—	43,112	170,000
Texas,	324,000	4	1845	—	—	—	—	215,000
Total,§				7,280,314	9,638,131	12,866,020	17,262,566	About 24,000,000
Seamen in the United States service, January 1, 1840,							6,100	
Grand Total, in 1840, (including Texas,)							17,268,666	

For the population of the United States in 1790 and 1800, and slaves in 1840, see Almanac of 1848. The slaves in 1850 are estimated at 3,354,296.

* As the Virginia side of the District has been re-ceded to that State, all estimates must be reduced accordingly, for the present actual district, and those for Virginia increased.
† Wisconsin had, by official census, December 1, 1847, 220,867 inhabitants; it has now, probably, 250,000, at least. ‡ Iowa had 120,000 inhabitants in 1848.
§ Oregon has probably about 15,000 people, as it had 12,000 in 1848. California has 50,000; New Mexico, 70,000. 500,000 Indians are subject to the United States. Add these 635,000 to the population of the United States, and it will amount, in 1850, to about 24,000,000. In 1860, the population, according to the ratio of increase heretofore, will be over 31 million; in 1870, over 41 million; in 1900, over 101 million; and in 1980, eighty years from this time, over 246 million, equaling the present population of all Europe. Moreover, if statistics may be relied on, there are 800,000 persons now living who will live to view this result.

POPULATION OF CITIES AND TOWNS IN 1840, '45, '46, '47, OR '48.

New York, ('45,)	371,102	Washington, ('45,)	30,000	Roxbury, ('45,)	13,929
Philadelphia,	205,860	Lowell, ('46,)	29,849	Hartford,	12,793
Boston, ('45,)	114,366	Rochester, N.Y., ('45,)	25,265	Cambridge, ('45,)	12,490
Baltimore,	102,313	Troy, ('45,)	21,681	Bangor, ('48,)	12,280
New Orleans,	102,193	Pittsburg,	21,115	Lynn, ('47,)	12,000
St. Louis, ('48,)	70,000	Portland, ('48,)	19,013	Manchester, N.H., ('47,)	12,000
Cincinnati, ('46,)	64,818	New Haven, ('45,)	17,674	Springfield, ('48,)	11,338
Brooklyn, N.Y., ('45,)	59,000	Chicago, ('47,)	17,000	Norfolk,	10,920
Louisville, ('45,)	38,000	Salem, ('45,)	16,697	Norwich, Ct., ('45,)	9,556
Buffalo, ('48,)	40,521	New Bedford, ('47,)	16,031	Newburyport, ('46,)	8,107
Providence, ('45,)	31,751	Worcester, ('47,)	15,643	Portsmouth, N.H.,	8,032
Newark, ('47,)	30,000	Charlestown, ('46,)	14,404	Hallowell,	5,000

I hope you always speak the truth, though never offensively.

THE COMPLETE 1850 ALMANAC

WEATHER TABLE,

For foretelling the Weather through all the lunations of each year, forever.

This table, and the accompanying remarks, are the result of many years' actual observation, the whole being constructed on a due consideration of the attraction of the sun and moon, in their several positions respecting the earth, and will, by simple inspection, show the observer what kind of weather will most probably follow the entrance of the moon into any of its quarters, and that so near the truth as to be seldom or never found to fail.

If the new, first quarter, full moon, or last quarter, happens	IN SUMMER.	IN WINTER.
Between midnight and 2 in the morning,	Fair.	Hard frost, unless the wind is S or W.
Between 2 and 4, morning,	Cold, with frequent showers.	Snowy and stormy.
—— 4 and 6, "	Rain.	Rain.
—— 6 and 8, "	Wind and rain.	Stormy.
—— 8 and 10, "	Changeable.	Cold rain, if the wind be W.; snow, if E.
—— 10 and 12, "	Frequent showers.	Cold and high wind.
At 12 M., and 2, P. M.,	Very rainy.	Snow or rain.
Between 2 and 4, "	Changeable.	Fair and mild.
—— 4 and 6, "	Fair.	Fair.
—— 6 and 8, "	Fair, if wind N. W. Rainy, if S. or S. W.	Fair and frosty, if the wind be N. or N.E. Rain or snow, if S. or S.W.
—— 8 and 10, "	Ditto.	Ditto.
—— 10 and midnight,	Fair.	Fair and frosty.

Observations. — 1. The nearer the moon's changes, first quarter, full, and last quarter are to *midnight*, the fairer will it be during the next seven days.

2. The space for this calculation occupies from ten at night till two next morning.

3. The nearer to *midday*, or *noon*, the phases of the moon happen, the more foul or wet weather may be expected during the next seven days.

4. The space for this calculation occupies from ten in the forenoon to two in the afternoon. These observations refer principally to the summer, though they affect spring and autumn nearly in the same ratio.

5. The moon's change, first quarter, full and last quarter, happening during six of the afternoon hours, i. e., from four to ten, may be followed by fair weather; but this is mostly dependent on the *wind*, as is noted in the table.

6. Though the weather, from a variety of irregular causes, is more uncertain in the latter part of autumn, the whole of winter, and the beginning of spring, yet, in the main, the above observations will apply to those periods also.

7. To prognosticate correctly, especially in those cases where the *wind* is concerned, the observer should be within sight of a *good vane*, where the four cardinal points of the heavens are correctly placed.

The above table was originally formed by Dr. Herschell, and is now published with some alterations founded on the experience of Dr. Adam Clarke.

TO THE WEATHER-WISE.

Dr. Foster, of Bruges, who is well known as a meteorologist, declares that, by journals of the weather kept by his grandfather, father, and himself, ever since 1767, to the present time, *whenever the new moon has fallen on a Saturday, the following twenty days have been wet and windy*, in nineteen cases out of twenty.

THE WINTER OF 1849.

We have, says the editor of the Springfield Republican, the authority of Dr. Robinson, the venerable Librarian of the Hartford Athenæum, for our assertion, that the winter of 1849 was the severest on record. Dr. R., as everybody knows, has made statistical and antiquarian research his "meat and drink" for these many years. He is now over eighty years old, and, we have no doubt, has kept a daily record of the weather ever since he could write. He told a gentleman of our acquaintance, that, upon reviewing his meteorological records, he found no winter there chronicled in which the aggregate of cold was so great as during the past season.

NEW ACT FOR THE PRESERVATION OF USEFUL BIRDS.

This Act, passed by the Legislature of Mass., in 1849, extends the time when it is unlawful to kill woodcocks, snipes, larks or robins, from the 4th of July to the 1st of August. The plover, curlew, cough-bird or chicken-bird, can only be killed between April 20 and July 1; and birds on salt marshes from March 1 to July 1. Half of the penalty recovered for each violation of these provisions goes to the prosecutor, and the other half to the poor of the town where the offence shall be committed.

SCHOOL BOOKS PUBLISHED BY JENKS, PALMER & CO.

School Committees, County Superintendents, and Teachers, are requested to *examine these books, before selecting* for their schools. Copies for that purpose will be supplied gratis, and satisfactory discounts made for introduction, and for permanent supply. We rely upon the merits of the books, and request for them a candid examination. The books are printed on good paper, substantially bound, and are furnished at rates as low as any other school books published. They are in extensive use in nearly all parts of the United States.

PARLEY'S FIRST BOOK OF HISTORY, or, HISTORY on the BASIS of GEOGRAPHY; comprehending the Western Hemisphere, with 60 Engravings, and 16 Maps of the different sections of the United States and countries of the Western Hemisphere, from steel plates; *revised edition, brought down to the present time.*

PARLEY'S SECOND BOOK OF HISTORY; comprehending the Modern History of Europe, Asia, Africa, &c., illustrated with 50 Engravings, and 16 Maps of the different countries, from steel plates; *revised edition, brought down to present time.*

PARLEY'S THIRD BOOK OF HISTORY; by the same author, and on the same plan; comprehending Ancient History, in connection with Ancient Geography, with Maps and new and beautiful Engravings.

In preparing this *series of Histories*, two things have been kept constantly in view, — to make it *useful* — and to make it *entertaining*. A familiar style has been adopted, and great care taken to give precise dates. Engravings have been inserted for illustration, and for fixing certain ideas in the pupil's memory; the anecdotes and incidents are designed to instruct, and train to morality and patriotism.

Each book is furnished with *Questions* on both the *History and Geography* of the countries described, and a *Chronological Table* is added, recapitulating the principal events noticed in the work.

The First Book of History has run through nearly *two hundred editions*, and acquired a most extensive circulation in schools and families. The Maps have been now redrawn, and newly engraved; the Cuts are new, and this edition, *enlarged* and adapted to the *existing* political geography of N. and S. America, embraces the leading points and events of interest not before noticed, and *brings all down to the present time.* A Pronouncing Vocabulary of Proper Names has also been added.

The Second Book has been carefully *revised* by a judicious practical teacher, *bringing the work down to the present time*, and it is believed to be the only School History of the Eastern Hemisphere brought down to so late a date.

WORCESTER'S COMPREHENSIVE PRONOUNCING AND EXPLANATORY **DICTIONARY** OF THE ENGLISH LANGUAGE; with pronouncing Vocabularies of Classical, Scripture, and Modern Geographical Names. By Joseph E. Worcester, LL. D. *Revised* and *enlarged*.

This Dictionary is recommended by the best authority. It combines, in a very condensed and *cheap* form, a greater amount of valuable matter than any other similar work. It has over 67,000 words. As a Pronouncing Dictionary, it possesses decided advantages over all others, the pronunciation of every word and of every proper name being plainly marked, not only in the *Accent*, but *also* in the *Quantity* — a most important matter. This Dictionary has noted every difference of pronunciation in our language, and the respective authorities, thus making it equivalent to ten or twelve works, and to be used with Worcester's Universal, or Johnson, or Walker, or Webster, or Richardson. Adopted in Boston Public Schools, the Free Academy of New York City, &c. &c.

WORCESTER'S ELEMENTARY DICTIONARY, FOR COMMON SCHOOLS, with Pronouncing Vocabularies of Classical, Scripture, and Modern Geographical Names. By J. E. Worcester, LL. D. With 9000 more words than any other school dictionary.

This also shows quantity and accent, and the *new edition* is revised and enlarged.

EMERSON'S ARITHMETIC. Three Parts. By Frederick Emerson.

PART I. is a *small book*, designed for children from five to eight years of age, with lessons illustrated by cuts and unit marks. It is extensively and successfully used.

PART II. is a Complete System of Mental and Written Arithmetic, sufficient for all the common purposes of business, and is a standard book for Common Schools, and most satisfactory in practically preparing pupils. It has been recently enlarged.

PART III. is designed for *advanced scholars*. It comprises a synthetic view of the science of numbers, a copious development of the higher operations, and an extensive range of commercial information. Scholars who are to be educated for the business of the counting-room, or the duties of any public office, as well as those who are to pursue a full course of liberal education, will find this book suited to their purpose. QUESTIONS on this work, and a KEY, for teachers, are published separately.

EMERSON'S WATTS ON THE MIND. THE IMPROVEMENT OF THE MIND, by ISAAC WATTS, D. D. With corrections, Questions, and Supplement, by Joseph Emerson. Improved Edition.

WHO ARE FRIENDS?

I suppose you do not count those as friends who merely come to see you when they want something?

Back cover of the
1850 Almanac

FATHER OF JEANS

Levi Strauss, a Jewish Bavarian immigrant to the U.S. during the Gold Rush, had bales  of cloth which he had intended to use for making tents and wagon coverings. But the market was too competitive, so he used the cloth to make hard-wearing work trousers. Rivets were added in 1874. Price of the trousers: $13.50 per dozen.